Arab
Detroit
9/11

GREAT LAKES BOOKS

*A complete listing of the books in this series can
be found online at wsupress.wayne.edu*

Arab Detroit 9/11

Life in the Terror Decade

Edited by
Nabeel Abraham,
Sally Howell,
and Andrew Shryock

 Wayne State University Press

DETROIT

15 14 13 12 11   5 4 3 2 1

Library of Congress Cataloging-in-Publication Data

Arab Detroit 9/11 : life in the terror decade / edited by Nabeel Abraham, Sally Howell, and Andrew Shryock.
    p.   cm.—(Great Lakes books series)
    Includes bibliographical references and index.
    ISBN 978-0-8143-3500-0 (paper : alk. paper)
    1. Arab Americans—Michigan—Detroit—Social conditions—21st century.
2. Arab Americans—Michigan—Detroit—Economic conditions—21st century.
3. Muslims—Michigan—Detroit—Social conditions—21st century.   4. Community life—Michigan—Detroit—History—21st century.   5. Detroit (Mich.)—Social conditions—21st century.   6. Detroit (Mich.)—Economic conditions—21st century.
7. Detroit (Mich.)—Ethnic relations—History—21st century.   8. September 11 Terrorist Attacks, 2001—Influence.   9. National characteristics, American—Case studies.   10. Citizenship—United States—Case studies.   I. Abraham, Nabeel.
II. Howell, Sally.   III. Shryock, Andrew.
F575.A65A73   2011
305.8927'073077434—dc23   2011016273

Designed by George Whipple

Typeset by Westchester Book Composition

Composed in Sabon, 10/12.5

Contents

Acknowledgments

This book has evolved over a period of ten years. It would be impossible to thank all the people who coaxed it into being, but we do want to acknowledge the efforts of friends, colleagues, and critics who were extremely helpful to us. First, we would like to thank our contributors, both the seasoned Detroit hands and the young authors who are publishing for the first time. It is not easy to write about traumatic events, the lives shaped by them, or the government policies built on them. Many of the essays in this book took nerve to produce. We are glad brave writers came our way.

We thank Jim West for letting us use the image that graces the cover of this book; Elena Godina for designing our map of Arab Detroit; and John Donohue for expert copyediting and production work. We are happy to repeat our thanks to Kathy Wildfong and Kristin Harpster Lawrence, our editors at Wayne State University Press, who were as deft in their handling of this volume as they were over a decade ago with *Arab Detroit: From Margin to Mainstream*. In a book about dramatic change, a healthy dose of professional continuity is a welcome gift! The two external reviewers, and the press's in-house reader, helped us improve a complex manuscript with good advice on structure and style.

Finally, we would like to acknowledge the hundreds of Arab and Chaldean Detroiters who have supported our research. The agendas that propel critical scholarship are hard to fathom even in ordinary times; but in times of crisis and vulnerability, they can seem incomprehensible. To all who understood what was important to us as scholars, and to those who were willing to share their knowledge, contacts, and time, we say: thank you for helping us create this chronicle of life in the Terror Decade.

The Terror Decade in Arab Detroit

An Introduction

ANDREW SHRYOCK, NABEEL ABRAHAM,
AND SALLY HOWELL

This volume is the latest in a rich tradition of scholarship on the Middle Eastern immigrant and ethnic communities of greater Detroit, a metropolitan area that is home to several of North America's oldest and largest Lebanese, Palestinian, Yemeni, and Iraqi populations. Ten years ago, we published *Arab Detroit: From Margin to Mainstream* (Abraham and Shryock 2000), a study that explored the history and cultural development of these communities, beginning in the late nineteenth century, when immigrants from Ottoman Syria first settled in the city's nascent industrial zones, and ending in the late twentieth century, when Arab and Chaldean Americans dominated Detroit's small business sector and were key players in multicultural politics. The communities depicted in *Arab Detroit* were growing rapidly, nearly doubling in size between 1990 and 2000. They were made up of poor and working-class people, who were disproportionately newcomers, and an energetic set of wealthy entrepreneurs, but most of the city's Arab and Arabic-speaking populations were situated comfortably in middle-class suburbs. Although they had been subjected to stereotyping and marginalization for decades, the Arab community had built powerful institutions by the year 2000, and they were flexing their muscle as a local and national political constituency.

The vibrancy of Arab Detroit in the 1990s guaranteed that our portrait of it would quickly go out of date. Like *Arabs in the New World* (Abraham and Abraham 1983), the first book to engage with the full spectrum of Detroit's Arab immigrant populations, Mary Sengstock's pioneering work on Chaldeans (1982), and Barbara Aswad's (1974) early accounts of Arab immigrants in Dearborn, Michigan, *Arab Detroit: From Margin to Mainstream* has made the inevitable passage from contemporary survey to historical

1

document. The essays we present in this volume will refresh and update information that appeared in the earlier work, but the effect we hope to create is not that of a sequel or even a series. Too much has changed in Detroit over the last decade. In countless ways—size, economic clout, levels of cultural inclusion, and continued political vulnerability—Arab Detroit as it exists today would be a shock to observers from the 1990s.

A City of Easy Targets

It is tempting to attribute this discontinuity to a single, traumatic source: the terror attacks of September 11, 2001. "Post-9/11" is now universal shorthand for the age in which we live, but what this period will mean in American history and how it should be interpreted are matters still open to dispute. Since the 9/11 attacks, the United States has introduced the world to a new kind of war—an overwhelming barrage of foreign military campaigns, domestic security crackdowns, overhauls of international monetary and banking protocols, and a radical reconfiguration of the rights of American citizens, resident aliens, and targeted communities. These projects, known collectively as the "War on Terror," were the policy centerpiece of the George W. Bush administration (2001–2009), and the Obama administration has kept most of this apparatus firmly in place. Because the principal targets of the War on Terror were commonly understood to be Arab or Muslim—all of the 9/11 hijackers fit this description, as do all of the countries the United States has invaded since 2001—it was inevitable that federal authorities would turn to Detroit in their pursuit of enemies and friends. Within hours of the 9/11 attacks, hundreds of journalists and investigators were on the ground in Detroit, looking for stories, suspects, and informants. The first terror-related arrests were made in Dearborn on September 17, 2001; by early 2002, Dearborn (not New York) was the first American city to have a local office of Homeland Security; by 2003, Federal Bureau of Investigation (FBI) headquarters in Detroit was home to the largest counterterrorism investigation in U.S. history.[1]

Against this backdrop, the term "post-9/11" holds ominous meaning for Detroit's Arab and Muslim Americans. It stands for a time/space in which they were linked to enemy Others and were expected to prove their loyalty to the nation-state in ways other Americans were not. We have decided to call the first ten years of this era "the Terror Decade." This term foregrounds the indispensible role terrorism has played in justifying key initiatives of the Bush and Obama administrations. It also describes the climate of fear that dominated the post-9/11 era, in which many Americans believed they could be attacked by terrorists at any moment; Arab and Muslim Americans believed other Americans thought they were terrorists or terrorist sympathizers; and Arabs and Muslims living outside the United States—in Iraq, Afghanistan, Sudan, Somalia, Pakistan, Syria, Lebanon, Iran, and Yemen, to name only the obvious cases—faced economic sanctions, military invasions, missile and unmanned drone attacks, covert operations, targeted killings, authorized kidnappings, travel restrictions, and other actions undertaken by the U.S. government and its allies. In short, the Terror Decade was a time in which national security was persistently defined as something Arabs and Muslims threaten, and this definition placed serious constraints on how Arab and Muslim Americans could identify as U.S. citizens.

Nolen Finley, opinion page editor of the *Detroit News*, captured the prevailing mood when, two days after the 9/11 attacks, he urged local Arab Americans to "smash the network within their own communities that provides money and shelter to terrorists. It's the least they can do for their neighbors" ("Arab-Americans Can Help Cause by Exposing Terrorist Sympathizers," *Detroit News*, September 13, 2001). In 2001, the larger society had little detailed knowledge of Arab Detroit, and Finley's indelicate advice seemed commonsensical to many observers. Yet the suspicions that led big government and the national media to scrutinize Detroit so closely were misguided. In the mind of America, Arab Detroit is a generically Muslim place, but an extensive survey conducted in 2003 by the Institute for Social Research found a more complex demographic reality.[2] The majority of greater Detroit's Arabs (58%) are Christian, and the Muslim minority is predominately Shi'a, not Sunni, a distinction that makes them doctrinal and political opponents of Al Qaeda, who consider Shi'a Muslims heretics. The 9/11 hijackers were mostly Saudi nationals, whereas most Arab Detroiters trace their ancestry to Lebanon and Iraq, with smaller groups of Palestinian and Yemeni origin. To complicate matters further, Detroit is home to large immigrant and ethnic populations that are linked to the Arab world but do not always identify as Arab or Arab American. The Chaldean community (made up of Iraqi Catholics) and the Maronites (Lebanese Catholics) come originally from Arab countries. They participate in a transnational Arabophone culture, but neither group is comfortable with the Arab label, especially in the United States, where Arabness is routinely cast in a negative light. Finally, the 9/11 hijackers were not U.S. citizens, whereas more than 80 percent of Arabs and Chaldeans in greater Detroit are naturalized or native-born U.S. citizens.

In short, the overlap between Arab Detroit and the Arab/Muslim[3] threat the Bush administration sought to confront was minimal and largely imaginary. Despite this misfit, and perhaps because of it, Arab Detroit was quickly enveloped in a war that, according to government spokespersons, would reform the Arab and Muslim world, bringing popular democracy, prosperity, and an end to religious extremism of all (but especially the Muslim) kinds.[4] None of these goals were accomplished overseas. The U.S. military found itself bogged down in Iraq and Afghanistan, terrorist and insurgent networks flourished, and popular democracy became an even greater threat to U.S. geopolitical interests in the Middle East, where anti-Americanism soared in response to wartime policies that were widely perceived as a crusade against Islamic civilization itself. In Detroit, however, the War on Terror provoked different forms of resistance. There were few "enemies" there to start with, and Arab Americans, initially a target of government and media attention, were already versed in the art of deflecting and channeling surplus media attention. Outsiders quickly found themselves in the capable hands of community spokespeople, most of whom worked for Detroit's well-established Arab American service institutions (notably, the Arab Community Center for Social and Economic Services, ACCESS), its advocacy groups (most often, the local chapter of the American-Arab Anti-Discrimination Committee, ADC), or its media-savvy mosques (foremost among them, the Islamic Center of America, the ICA, whose progressive leader, Imam Hassan Qazwini, became a "go-to" Muslim cleric for local, national, and international reporters).

This local core of Arab and Muslim leaders soon discovered ways to use the War on Terror as a mobilizing force. The larger society's desire to discipline Arab Detroit, to control and investigate it, triggered a related desire to protect and understand it. These tandem forces—all of which are rooted in popular models of multicultural democracy—led to massive educational, promotional, and advocacy efforts dedicated to creating or securing viable forms of American identity for the roughly six million U.S. citizens who, in 2001, called themselves Arab or Muslim. In Detroit, this Americanizing process was not new. The city's Arabs and Muslims had been creating civil and religious institutions that smoothed the transition from immigrant (foreign) to ethnic (American) status for nearly a century (see Terry 1999; Abraham 2000; Rignall 2000; Ahmed 2006; Howell 2009; Howell and Shryock 2010). In the aftermath of the 9/11 attacks, as this local array of mosques, business associations, village clubs, and social service agencies mobilized in defense of their reputations and their civil rights, they transformed Arab Detroit from a target, plain and simple, to a "target of opportunity." The latter term originated in military jargon, where it describes an unexpected target that suddenly presents itself to a shooter. The term's usage has broadened in recent years to describe situations in which an employer can expedite the hire of an exceptional job candidate, usually a person who belongs to an underrepresented minority group. Throughout this volume, we will argue that Arab Detroit, as both a place and an idea, has been reconfigured as a target of opportunity. Not only is it an easy domestic target that presents itself whenever Arabs and Muslims become official (and more difficult) targets overseas, but it is also a focus of concern for activists, community organizers, business investors, and political problem solvers who realize that Detroit's availability as a target has turned it into a valuable resource. Its vulnerability can be used to animate diverse agendas, some anti-Arab and Islamophobic, others strongly supportive of Arabs and Muslims in the United States and globally.

Best of Times/Worst of Times

We are aware that "target of opportunity" is a term with multiple connotations, and we intend to explore them in the pages that follow. The term pinpoints much of what is happening in Detroit, and in other American and European settings, where the larger society is attempting to incorporate and exclude Arab/Muslim populations. The target of opportunity is not the main target, and it might not be what the shooter thinks it is, hence the potential for making mistakes, for killing civilians and one's own fellow combatants. What is true on the battlefield is equally valid in Arab Detroit, where the FBI has arrested the wrong men, federal prosecutors have convicted the innocent, thousands of people have been interrogated and spied upon because of their national origin or religious affiliation, and others have been detained and deported without due process of law. Yet the target of opportunity also holds the possibility of quick gains and constructive change, hence the urgency with which corporations, universities, and other institutions compete to hire talented candidates from underrepresented groups. It is institutional racism that feeds these corrective gestures—variously described as "affirmative action" or "positive discrimination" or "selective hiring"—and the opportunities they present come mingled with a sordid past (and present) of stigma, prejudice, and false expectations. What is true in the boardroom is equally valid in Detroit, where attempts to include and recognize Arab and Muslim communities are part of a legacy of exclusion that is not eliminated—indeed, is actually given new life—by attempts to make these special populations part of the social and political mainstream.

As a result of this opportunistic targeting, Detroit has taken on an oddly Dickensian aspect. Simply put, the Terror Decade has been "the worst of times" and "the best of times" for the city's Arab and Muslim communities. The increased discrimination and harassment that followed the 9/11 attacks, the feelings of estrangement, and the persistent anxiety that things could get worse—all of these factors are central to scholarship on Arab and

Muslim American populations,[5] and they will figure prominently in this book as well. The positive side of the equation, the "best of times," is more difficult to assess, but it is no less real. Indeed, ten years into the post-9/11 era, the positive trends are the genuinely surprising ones, and they require careful explanation.[6]

Since September 11, 2001, the Arab and Chaldean community's principal social service organizations and advocacy groups have all grown in budget and membership. More than a dozen new mosques, including two of the largest in North America, have opened in Detroit since 2001, bringing the number of local mosques to about sixty. There are now twenty-five judges and elected officials of Arab ancestry in Michigan and about thirty-six Arab Americans who have been appointed to public office; the trend is decidedly upward since 2001. New cultural institutions, such as the Arab American National Museum, have opened to great fanfare; arts festivals, concert series, and street fairs are flourishing. The American Arab Chamber of Commerce, whose membership owns most of Detroit's gas stations, grocery stores, and convenience stores, now brokers international trade deals between the U.S. Department of Commerce, the city of Detroit, and the Arab Gulf states. Finally, greater Detroit's Arab and Chaldean population has grown steadily over the last decade, rising from 125,000 to more than 200,000, even as the city's non-Arab sector, and the state of Michigan as a whole, steadily loses population.

During a period of intense Islamophobia, foreign wars against Arab and Muslim countries, and a domestic war on terror that targets people of Middle Eastern descent, why is Arab Detroit doing so well? How should we interpret this dynamism, who is producing it, and how is it affecting the lives (and shaping the identities) of ordinary Arab Americans? Perhaps the most puzzling aspect of this juxtaposition of best and worst times is that developments in one sphere are clearly related to developments in the other. When good things happen to Arab Detroit, they often unfold in the company, or in the context, of more ominous trends. To show how this contradictory process works, we have selected telling examples from the middle years of the Terror Decade, several of which will be discussed in detail in subsequent chapters of this book:

> In 2003, the Michigan office of ADC participated in an American Civil Liberties Union lawsuit against the Patriot Act. It also consulted regularly with FBI and Justice Department officials, trying to maintain links between the Arab community and the agencies that monitor it. To honor the work of Imad Hamad, head of ADC offices in Dearborn, the FBI gave

him its Exceptional Public Service Award, but the award was quickly revoked when local pro-Israeli activists accused Hamad of having ties to Palestinians accused of terrorism. The FBI claimed publicly that the allegations were "accurate," but took no action against Hamad; the FBI continues to work closely with him. In 2005, ADC, still under Hamad's leadership, announced plans to build a new multimillion-dollar educational and resource center in Dearborn; one of its primary functions will be to provide sensitivity and cultural training to U.S. government agencies.

In 2004–2005, U.S. Customs pursued Operation Green Quest in Detroit, trying to locate monies sent (and received from) overseas in support of terror, shutting down Muslim charities and arresting small business owners accused of running illegal money transfer schemes. During the same period, the U.S. State Department facilitated international trade missions and fund-raising junkets in which local Arab American leaders and Detroit area politicians forged new business relations with partners in the Arab Gulf states.

In 2005, the new Arab American National Museum opened its doors in Dearborn. The facility cost $15 million to build, and most of its support came from U.S. corporate donors and charitable foundations. Meanwhile, the FBI unfurled plans for its new, $65 million headquarters in Detroit, which will house a field office that will run the largest counterterrorism investigation in U.S. history.

In 2005 and 2006, the annual Dearborn Arab International Festival, a three-day celebration of Arab American culture and community, included the Central Intelligence Agency (CIA) among its official sponsors. A U.S. Army rock-climbing wall towered over kebob and falafel stands.

On September 18, 2006, the FBI raided the offices of Detroit-based Life for Relief and Development, continuing its holiday tradition of shutting down or harassing Muslim charities just before Ramadan, hoping to cut to a trickle the amount of "green charity" headed overseas. Meanwhile, signs of localized Muslim generosity proliferate across greater Detroit. The grandest of these, the Islamic Center of America, cost more than $16 million to build and opened in 2005. It is said to be the largest mosque complex in North America. U.S. government officials and military personnel routinely visit the mosque to meet with community leaders.

These examples show how tightly national security, Islam, and Arab American identity are woven together in Detroit. One could tear this fabric apart, producing a list of only positive or only negative developments, but the result would be distorted. The ethnic festivals, new museums, public commendations, new headquarters, trade delegations, and cultural education programs evolve alongside the expanding surveillance regime, accusations of terrorism, ubiquitous military and CIA presence, and crackdowns on charitable giving. This side-by-side development is often quite literal, as in the following promotional e-mail sent to the ACCESS listserv in 2004:

Date: Tue, 20 Jan 2004 10:41:54 -0500
From: _____@accesscommunity.org
Subject: Simon Shaheen with Qantara
To: _____

Master Oud and violin player, Simon Shaheen will perform live with his fusion group, Qantara. Described by the Village Voice as "one of the world's greatest musicians", Shaheen has taken his classical and Arab music background and fused it with jazz, Latin and global sounds to create a completely new sound. Says Shaheen, "I want to create a world music exceptionally satisfying to the ear and for the soul." He will be joined by members of the Dearborn Traditional Arab Ensemble for the premier of "Waving Sands," a new composition created especially for this occasion.

ACCESS is offering a special 15% discount on tickets for all ACCESS supporters, all seats are reserved and advance purchase is recommended to insure best location. Contact _____ at Cultural Arts, _____ <mailto:> _____ for more details. The performance begins at 8:00 p.m. and will be followed by a public reception at Café Oz in Ann Arbor.

For directions, parking, and seating charts visit the UMS [University Musical Society] site at: _____.

Scrolling down in the same message, readers found information about another event sponsored by ACCESS, to be held the day after Simon Shaheen's debut of "Waving Sands."

The US Army Is Looking For Arabic Language Translators And Interpreters

The US Army Reserve is looking to enlist Arabic language natives into a special program in an effort to meet the critical need for translators and interpreters. If you are a US citizen or a legal resident (green card holder), the US Army is offering you a unique opportunity to use your language skills to serve your country and contribute to the efforts of nation rebuilding in Iraq and other locations in the world.

Applicants in the Arabic Translators/Interpreters Individual Ready Reserve program should be between 17 and 40 years of age and have either a high school diploma or a GED. They will receive up to six months of intensive English language training if necessary, in addition to 6 weeks of advanced training in translation and interpretation. At the end of the training, applicants will receive a certification as translators and interpreters from the US government. This valuable experience will prepare you! [*sic*] for many rewarding civilian careers, including jobs with government agencies, embassies and universities.

If you're interested in enlisting or for more information, the US Army is conducting the following Job Fair:

Date: Wednesday January 21st, from 3 to 7 PM.
Place: ACCESS, 6451 Schaefer, Dearborn, MI 48126, 2nd floor.

Both events were exceptional by pre-9/11 standards. The University Musical Society, an elite arts presenter based in Ann Arbor and catering to highbrow tastes, was not known for featuring self-identified Arab or Muslim artists before 2001. Likewise, ACCESS, a social service agency founded by 1960s-era radicals and led by progressive activists, was the last place one would go to attend a U.S. Army jobs fair. Yet both events were typical by the standards of the Terror Decade. The Simon Shaheen concert was part of a theme year sponsored by the University of Michigan called "Cultural Treasures of the Middle East." A seemingly endless array of talks, symposia, concerts, and special courses, this programming agenda was assembled in response to the War on Terror, doubling as a measured critique of the war and a showcase of the university's ability to create useful knowledge and sensitive representations of the Middle East. Detroit's Arab and Muslim populations were seen by university faculty and administrators as key supporters and beneficiaries of its programs; they were also seen as a new constituency to be developed for future enrollments, research partnerships, and institutional and alumni relations. The U.S. Army was similarly drawn to the Arab community, offering career opportunities in exchange for linguistic expertise, as did the FBI and CIA. Detroit's Arabic language newspapers were filled, after 9/11, with recruitment ads placed by these organizations.

Cultural production and recruitment to the security apparatus of the nation-state are not identical processes, but the Shaheen concert and the U.S. Army jobs fair were linked in ways more crucial than their appearance on a single listserv. First, it is highly unlikely that either event would have transpired apart from the War on Terror. Both events were avenues of mutual recognition and resource sharing that brought one of Arab Detroit's key institutions into contact with partners in the larger society. In both cases, Arabic and Arab cultural heritage were posed as valuable assets—as "skills" and "treasures," to be exact—that needed to be displayed, enlisted, interpreted, and understood on behalf of the nation. Arabs were, in each instance, a target of opportunity, and the targeting itself was part of an elaborate representational discourse, a way of thinking about Arabs, the Middle East, and Islam, that places all three in a larger framework of global conflict, violence, and threats to the security of U.S. citizens. Whether Arabs are targeted in order to criticize this placement (by showing that Arabs have a rich culture worth celebrating and welcoming in the United States) or reinforce it (by recruiting Arabic speakers to assist in a war against other Arabic speakers), the larger framework is never in question.

The Straitjacket of Representation

Our intention is not to upend this framework. It is too solidly in place. Moreover, much of Arab and Muslim identity has been shaped by this framework, and attempts to mobilize against it are now an indispensable aspect of community organizing and activism among Americans of Middle Eastern backgrounds. Rather, our goal is to shed light on trends the War on Terror has systematically obscured. The link between Arab/Muslim identity and themes of vulnerability and threat, we will argue, can certainly explain the intensity of the 9/11 backlash, but it cannot account for the adaptive responses of Detroit's Arab and Chaldean populations. The real gains in institutional and social incorporation made in Arab Detroit during the Terror Decade are based on historical developments and patterns of community formation that predate the 9/11 attacks by decades and are, in many ways, unique to Detroit. The city is a target of opportunity because Arabs and Muslims abroad are official targets of the U.S. military and its allies. Arab Detroit can benefit from this deadly linkage, however, only to the extent that its leaders, and their rank and file supporters, can show that they are not vulnerable (but well placed and politically effective) and are not a threat (but a vital asset). The result is a distinctive cultural politics, enabling but highly restrictive, in which suspect loyalty, incomplete belonging, and contested links to (shared) enemies define the public face of Arab/Muslim citizenship. In Arab Detroit, immense effort goes into negating the suspect, incomplete, and contested aspects of Arab/Muslim identity. Engaging willingly, and publicly, in this effort is the means by which the community protects itself from abuse and reassures the larger society that Arabs and Muslims can, in fact, be good Americans.

If a common thread runs through all scholarship on Arab Detroit, it is a concern to understand this cultural politics, which has a deep local history. What will make this volume distinctive, however, is our commitment to analyzing the effects of the Terror Decade in ways that move beyond—and allow readers to see through—a process of public identity formation that, under the heavy weight of the 9/11 backlash, has begun to crystallize, forming a cosmetic wall between the residents of Arab Detroit and the society in which they live. Each year, tens of thousands of non-Arab Americans (school kids on field trips, foreign dignitaries, interfaith groups, and professionals in search of cultural sensitivity training) glide quickly through Arab Detroit on journeys designed to inform. They visit key institutions—ACCESS, ADC, the Arab American National Museum, and the Islamic Center of America— where they are instructed in the ways of Arabs and Muslims by official spokespeople. If time permits, they visit Arab shops along Warren Avenue, buy sweets at a local bakery, or share a meal in a Middle Eastern restaurant. The experience can be valuable, even enjoyable, but the knowledge gained is formulaic and thin. It has to be; otherwise, it could not be disseminated to thousands of people who know very little about Arabs and must be taught something memorable in only a few hours of exposure. Unfolding dispro-portionately in Dearborn, these interactions take place along a contained route that functions as the "reception area" of Arab Detroit, a huge identity parlor in which Arabs and non-Arabs interact not as fellow citizens per se, but as guests and hosts, actors and observers, insiders and outsiders. Since 9/11, this semiofficial guestroom has undergone a multimillion-dollar reno-vation. The Arab American National Museum and the Islamic Center each cost about $15 million to build, and they require millions more to operate and maintain. Like any good guestroom, the double function of this collec-tive space is to welcome strangers, give them a good impression, and keep them away from parts of the house where the family actually lives. As a rule, things are more attractive in the guestroom. Pleasantries are exchanged there—indeed, interacting in this space requires Arab Americans and other Americans to recognize each other as such—but the rituals of public accep-tance work best when people do not inspect each other too intently or know each other too well.[7]

Stepping beyond this space of staged encounters is difficult, largely be-cause Arab Americans have built it themselves and members of the larger society have helped them do so. Multiculturalism requires that marked eth-noracial groups package themselves in ways that allow the larger society to acknowledge them, include them, and celebrate their accomplishments. In the case of Arabs and Muslims, however, we believe the special conditions of the Terror Decade have turned pluralist packaging into an identity strait-jacket, a set of ideas and practices that actually creates "good Arab" and "good Muslim" stereotypes as effectively as (perhaps more effectively than) it undermines stereotypes of "bad Arabs" and "bad Muslims." If the bad Arab is a sexist, a Muslim extremist, an anti-Semite, an opponent of democ-racy and modernity who hates America, and a terrorist or terrorist sympa-thizer, then the good Arab believes in equality of the sexes, is a moderate or liberal Muslim (or, better yet, a Christian), is accepting of Jews (but opposed to Israel's ongoing occupation and confiscation of Palestinian lands), believes strongly in democracy, is basically modern in lifestyle (but respects the Arab heritage and its traditions), loves America (but questions U.S. foreign policy in the Middle East), and is opposed (violently if necessary) to terrorism. Anyone familiar with Arab Americans, or Arab Detroit, knows how inconsistently these stereotypical traits, good and bad alike, map onto real people. Nonetheless, real people feel answerable to this imagery, and failure to conform to "good Arab" stereotypes can very quickly land individuals, institutions, and ideas in "bad Arab" territory, where mistreatment is all but guaranteed.

As we will demonstrate in this volume, there are vocal individuals, political groups, media outlets, and governmental agencies committed to engaging with Arabs in Detroit, and with all Arabs and Muslims, as if they were an existential threat to the United States and its allies (even when these allies are Arab and Muslim!). Outside Arab Detroit's well-kept identity guestroom is a chilling landscape filled with places and conditions that are empirically real: the most ordinary include ostracism, condescension, accusation, and outright banishment from polite society; the more extreme include places like the detention facility, the secret prison, the show trial, and, at the outer reaches of U.S. sovereignty, macabre facilities like Abu Ghraib and the Guantanamo Bay detention camp. If tens of millions of dollars have been invested in positive cultural representations of Arabs and Muslims in Detroit over the last decade, the U.S. government has invested more than $1 trillion in the enemy-monitoring, enemy-destroying, and enemy-making policies that constitute the War on Terror.

In short, the language of representation is now dangerously simple because the consequences of misrepresentation are stark. Whether positive or negative, propaganda about "Islam in America" or "America's Arabs" has acquired a shrill, distorting tone that no longer rings true. Many Arabs in Detroit insist publicly that "we are just like other Americans," whereas the city's prominent Arab haters and Islamophobes insist that "Dearbornistan" is a Hezbollah stronghold, culturally and politically isolationist. Members of both factions are challenged by a phenomenon like Rima Fakih, a Lebanese immigrant from Dearborn who was crowned Miss USA in 2010, winning the singular privilege of representing America to itself and the world. Likewise, both factions must contend with the notoriety of Sahar Dika, a resident of Dearborn Heights who, in 2010, became the first Arab/Muslim cast member on MTV's popular reality show *The Real World*, where she performs, for a titillated viewing audience, a facsimile of everyday life alongside seven other extroverted, variously appealing, and messed-up young Americans. Already, the "reality show" of identity politics in Detroit has generated predictable responses: Fakih and Dika have been accused of supporting, or being related to, Hezbollah terrorists in Lebanon, and critics in their own community have accused them of being bad Muslims (they do not cover their hair or dress modestly) who give Arab girls a bad name.[8] It would seem that many Arabs join non-Arabs in rejecting the proposition that "Arabs are just like other Americans." Ironically, good faith attempts to defend the proposition, either by countering baseless accusations of terrorism or by trying to liberalize definitions of "good character" for Arab/Muslim women, manage only to prove how difficult it is to base a viable model of Arab American citizenship on claims to cultural sameness, or even on claims to *acceptable* cultural difference. Absorption in the multicultural mainstream is a political ideal that, in practice, very few people are prepared to accept at face value.

Yet we are confronted with the obvious fact that Arab Americans are not uniformly marginalized in Detroit or anywhere else in the United States. Repeatedly, demographic surveys have shown that Arab Americans are better educated and enjoy higher incomes than members of the general population (American Community Survey 2005; Arab American Institute Foundation 2006). The Detroit Arab American Survey found that levels of national identification are very high among Arab Americans (94% said they were "proud to be American") and that confidence in key American institutions—the public schools, the local police, the legal system, the federal government—is actually higher among Arab Americans, and even higher among Arab immigrants, than it is among non-Arabs and American-born Arabs (DAAS Team 2009). Studies of Muslim Americans in Detroit (Bagby 2004) and nationally (Pew 2007) have found similar trends. Clearly, there are processes of integration and identification at work in Detroit, and nationally, that representational politics cannot fully register. Indeed, the politics of representation, with its acute sensitivity to intolerance and disloyalty, encourages us to ignore, or to look skeptically upon, evidence of Arab and Muslim incorporation into American life.

To encourage a more nuanced approach, and to create breathing room for cultural analysis and political critique, the contributors to this volume are careful to distinguish between images of Arab Detroit that are created for public consumption—images consciously designed to cast the community in a positive or negative light—and experiences that, by contrast, are oriented more toward in-group realities and personal attempts to understand or transcend these realities. It is important to draw distinctions of this kind. Over the last decade, it has become harder to see Arab Detroit as a place where people can lead normal lives that are not beholden to official models of who they are and what they are like. In a sense, Arab Detroit is now perpetually on display. It has become a place where public identities have a prominence, and a political importance, that diminishes all experiences, attitudes, people, and patterns of change that cannot be adapted to the demands of "public representation" in a hostile political climate. To work against this process, we must step out of the guestroom, with its niceties and anxious interactions, and explore alternative spaces that correspond to normal life.

Alternative Pathways through the Terror Decade

One of the appealing features of *Arab Detroit: From Margin to Mainstream* was its blend of scholarly, artistic, and lay voices. We want to reproduce that formula in the present volume. Our contributors include historians, political scientists, anthropologists, and sociologists, as well as writers of poetry and prose and memoirists who, though active in the political and social life of Arab Detroit, have never written for publication before. Many of our authors grew up in Arab Detroit; most have lived and worked there for many years; several have done extensive research in the city. We have included Palestinian, Iraqi, Yemeni, and Lebanese authors; Muslims and Christians; the American born and immigrants. This mix of perspectives will help us avoid monochrome accounts. It will also take us into parts of Arab Detroit—the most marginal and the most mainstream—that during the Terror Decade have become hard to represent as generically Arab or Muslim.

The book is divided into six sections. We begin with wide-angle views of Arab Detroit, looking first at how the community fits within greater Detroit as a whole, then presenting closer portraits of Arab Detroit's key ethnonational and religious subgroups. More personal, everyday accounts of life in the Terror Decade follow as we shift focus to practical matters such as child rearing, neighborhood interactions, going to school, and traveling domestically and to visit the home countries. Finally, we move back again, to consider the interface between Arab Detroit and the larger society, how it is maintained, how the War on Terror has distorted it, and what lessons might be drawn (about citizenship, inclusion, and exclusion) by situating Arab Detroit in broader and deeper historical contexts. Although the essays can, and ideally should, be read in order, we realize that many readers prefer to map their own itinerary through a book of this size. To help in that task, we offer the following sketch of the volume's layout and central arguments.

Part 1: The Shape of Arab Detroit

The internal social structure of Arab Detroit has features that are slow to change. The dominant role played by Lebanese immigrants, for example, dates back to the late nineteenth century. Likewise, the concentration of Muslims in Dearborn, and the tendency for Christian Arabs to live elsewhere, was firmly established by the 1930s. Other trends are demonstrably new. The arrival of Iraqi Shi'a Muslims in Dearborn dates to the early 1990s; the number of Yemeni families in Hamtramck, Detroit, and Dearborn's Southend began to grow at roughly the same time; and the departure of Palestinian Muslims from Dearborn to Cleveland and beyond, which began in the 1980s, was nearly complete by the mid-1990s.

In "Arab Detroit after 9/11: A Changing Demographic Portrait," Kim Schopmeyer looks for old and new patterns in the city's Arab and Chaldean populations. Using figures from the U.S. Census, the Detroit Arab American Study (DAAS), and other demographic surveys, Schopmeyer finds that, contrary to what many observers initially expected, Arabs did not stop coming to Detroit during the Terror Decade, nor did many leave town, as they clearly did in other American cities, like Philadelphia and New York (Salisbury 2010). Instead, the population of Arab Detroit grew from 129,000 residents in 2000 to approximately 220,000 in 2010. Greater Detroit is now the principal destination of new Arab immigrants to the United States; it absorbed more newcomers between 2002 and 2009 than New York, Los Angeles, or Chicago. Tracking variations in socioeconomic status, settlement patterns, citizenship rates, education levels, religious affiliations, and family structures, Schopmeyer puts Arab Detroit in its larger regional context, setting the stage for later chapters that focus closely on smaller niches within this overarching community.

Part 2: Aftermath Chronicles

Despite the intensity of the 9/11 backlash and its pervasive effects on Detroit, few scholars have produced systematic accounts of how the War on Terror has progressed in the city over the last ten years.[9] Caught in perpetual response mode, local Arab American and Muslim organizations have been unable to document the period, beyond the crucial work of tracking cases of discrimination and the rates at which hate crimes occur. To date, we still do not have reliable estimates of how many Arabs were detained or deported in greater Detroit. The early years of the War on Terror are now hard for people to recall, and folklore and selective memory are taking their toll on popular accounts of the period.

To compensate for the lack of solid historical accounts, we have decided to reprint material from two essays that chronicle and try to make sense of the Terror Decade and its consequence for Arab Detroit. The first, "Cracking Down on Diaspora: Arab Detroit and America's War on Terror," by Sally Howell and Andrew Shryock, deals with the early years of the Terror Decade, before the U.S. invasion of Iraq in 2003. The second, "Backlash, Part 2: The Federal Law Enforcement Agenda," is an excerpt from "The Aftermath of the 9/11 Attacks," an essay by Sally Howell and Amaney Jamal. It examines the swirl of federal investigations and show trials that have taken place in Detroit. These essays capture the mood of Arab Detroit during the Bush administration, when grand attempts were made to control the flow of people, ideas, and material resources between Detroit and key locations in the Arab/Muslim world. Howell, Shryock, and Jamal document key events during this tumultuous period, and they develop conceptual models that help explain how Arab Detroit became a target of opportunity, a status that reconfigured and reinforced the city's relationship to Arabness (as a problem) and American identity (as a solution).

Part 3: Local Refractions

Arabs of different national and religious backgrounds often have widely divergent understandings of the War on Terror. For Detroit's Iraqi Chaldeans, who can opt out of Arab identity altogether, and for Orthodox Christians, whose Arabness might not be apparent to outsiders, the Terror Decade has been an awkward period of misrecognition. Being non-Arab or non-Muslim, but linked to the larger Arab Muslim community in countless ways, these Christian communities have been pulled into the War on Terror as allies and antagonists of Muslim Americans. Chaldeans and Arab Christians feel the stigma of Muslim identity; they have suffered and benefited from this stigma. Muslim Arabs, meanwhile, have borne the full weight of the local 9/11 backlash and the federal crackdown. Their communities have received the harshest treatment, but they have also experienced the most dramatic gains in institutional growth and political influence. Less than a third of greater Detroit's Arab/Chaldean population resides in Dearborn. Yet when people call Arab Detroit "the capital of Arab America," they are almost always referring to Dearborn, Dearborn Heights, and adjacent parts of Detroit, whose Muslim communities are booming. The essays in this section move through and beyond Dearborn, showing the complexity of Detroit's Arab and Chaldean populations and their varied responses to the Terror Decade.

In "Orthodox, Arab, American: The Flexibility of Christian Arabness in Detroit," Matthew Stiffler looks at Detroit's thriving Antiochian Orthodox community. For more than a century, these Arab Christians have been immigrating to the United States from what are now Lebanon, Palestine, Syria, and Jordan. The community in Detroit has grown rapidly over the last decade. The unique "Arabness" of the Antiochians is situated between their ancient Christianity, their linguistic, familial, and cultural roots in the Middle East, and their hyphenated American ethnic identity. As Stiffler shows, Antiochian Orthodox Christians maintain a specific form of non-Muslim

Arab identity that is flexible and easily mobilized during homeland crises or community celebrations, but can be tactically downplayed in favor of being Christian only, or Orthodox, or simply American. Stiffler's essay explores this flexible Christian Arabness in post-9/11 Detroit as it is acted out in the collective life of St. Mary's Basilica, a large Antiochian Orthodox congregation located in the Detroit suburb of Livonia.

In "Fighting Our Own Battles: Iraqi Chaldeans and the War on Terror," Yasmeen Hanoosh looks at how the Terror Decade has affected one of Detroit's most distinctive ethnic and religious populations. The term "Arab Detroit" persistently obscures the fact that more than a third of the city's Middle Eastern and Arabic-speaking residents are Iraqi Chaldeans, a largely Catholic group who speak Syriac as well as Arabic and do not always identify as Arab. In fact, much of the leadership of the Chaldean community vehemently rejects Arab/Muslim identity labels. This distinctive profile has shaped the Chaldean experience of the Terror Decade in numerous ways. By situating Chaldeans in a transnational network that connects Detroit, Baghdad, London, Amman, and dozens of villages in northern Iraq, Hanoosh shows how this relatively small population has played a supportive role in the U.S. occupation of Iraq and has successfully pursued transnational political agendas designed to protect Chaldo-Assyrian minorities in Iraq even as they expedite the immigration of tens of thousands of Iraqi Christians to the United States, Jordan, and the United Kingdom.

In "Muslims as Moving Targets: External Scrutiny and Internal Critique in Detroit's Mosques," Sally Howell connects the tremendous growth and institutional advances made by Detroit's mosques and other Muslim organizations during the Terror Decade to the hostile gaze of the mainstream media, the FBI, and other enforcement arms of the departments of Homeland Security and Justice. As evidence of the FBI's use of informants and provocateurs in the city's mosques accumulates and as FBI interviews with Muslim leaders have continued unabated throughout the decade, the patience of Muslim leaders is growing thin. Howell shows how mosque leaders are responding to government treatment by shoring up their institutions, speaking out in defense of their faith, disciplining the political views and devotional practices of their congregations, and interacting directly with the federal authorities that investigate them. The result, for now, is a federal government better equipped than ever to investigate and infiltrate the community and a network of mosques and Muslim organizations better equipped than ever to aid and oppose these intrusive policies.

In "Detroit Transnational: The Interchange Experience in Lebanon and the United States," Kristine J. Ajrouch provides yet another perspective on transnational lifestyles in Arab Detroit. Using her experiences as a U.S. citizen of Lebanese descent who travels frequently between the United States and Lebanon, Ajrouch reflects on the costs and benefits of this mobility and how it has reshaped her perspectives on Lebanon, the United States, and citizenship. Recounting her family's efforts to organize a children's summer camp in Lebanon after the Israeli occupation ended in 2000, their harrowing departure from the country during the 2006 summer war with Israel, and her stint as a Fulbright scholar in Lebanon in 2008, Ajrouch shows how U.S. citizenship is a valuable resource for Arab transnationals, but one that can be seriously threatened during times of violent conflict between Arabs, the United States, and Israel. Ajrouch argues that the Terror Decade did not close down the transnational circuits that thousands of Arab Americans travel every year, but it has jeopardized the flexible forms of citizenship on which cultural interchanges between Arabs and Arab Americans so crucially depend.

Part 4: Civilian Stories

The War on Terror has placed entire communities at risk. It is a kind of collective punishment, and its generalized effects are manifest in adverse government policies and prejudice directed at Arabs and Muslims writ large. However, there are other scales on which these effects can be measured and felt. Communitywide responses to geopolitical crises do not capture the joys, aggressions, evasions, small victories, and personal losses that accumulate in the everyday lives of Arabs and Chaldeans in Detroit. The essays in this section explore the damage (and constant repair) done on individual terrain, where the War on Terror is transformed into the life stories of Arab Detroit's civilian population. We have arranged the essays in order of age. Our youngest author is a teenager; the oldest is in his sixties. These four writers have grown up in very different times and places; their shared Arab American identity is filled with unshared values and experiences.

The youngest author, Mujan Seif, made a cameo appearance in the final pages of *Arab Detroit*. She was 5 years old when that book appeared. Andrew Shryock made several predications about the world she would grow up in, and the kind of person she might be (2000, 607–609). Ten years later, Seif speaks for herself. In "My Life as a Brown Person," she describes her journey through the Terror Decade, where she has spent most of her life. Seif is a Palestinian, Chaldean, Arab American girl who confidently embraces the world around her. She is acquiring a youthful mastery over that world, which is suburban, privileged, and white. She realizes that she is both Arab and "Americanized," and she is on easy terms with both identities. Our second author, Khadigah Alasry, is a twenty-something Yemeni American and Muslim activist. Her memoir, "Subject to Change," offers a rare glimpse into a community that, even among Detroit Arabs, is considered insular and highly conservative. Alasry is deeply unsettled by the 9/11 attacks. Sensing that "her people" are now political enemies as well as cultural aliens, she must feel her way through an American society she is part of, but which her Yemeni parents consider hostile, inaccessible to them, and morally suspect. The tenets of Islam (and avid consumption of American movies) are the toolkit Alasry uses to construct pathways between her family, school, and the larger society.

Hayan Charara, whose essays and poetry appeared in *Arab Detroit*, is now a successful writer and teacher in his thirties. He lives in Texas, but he often returns to Dearborn to visit his family. The town is now partially a memoryscape for Charara. In his essay, "Going Places," he struggles to connect the city of his childhood to the imagery of Arabs that he encounters in popular media and in the relatively Arab-less places where he has lived since moving away from Detroit. It is hard to articulate these worlds. Charara is left to ponder the reality of a childhood in which being Arab was ordinary, even enviable, and a contemporary America in which those possibilities seem remote. Lawrence Joseph, our final memoirist, is a nationally renowned poet and novelist who left Detroit for New York in the 1980s. His Detroit is Arab in ways different, and much older, than those prevalent among the city's new, foreign-born majority. Joseph's grandparents came to Detroit in the early twentieth century; for decades, his relatives ran shops and small businesses, mostly in the city's black neighborhoods. In 2008, the grocery store once owned by Joseph's father and uncle was demolished. In his memoir, "And Then You Add the Arab Thing," Joseph uses this turning point to retrace his own passage through the history and now decaying neighborhoods of Detroit. The War on Terror cannot rival the magnitude of Joseph's personal stake in the city. His essay is a bittersweet tour of an Arab Detroit that is rapidly fading away. Its landmarks and lives are disappearing one by one, even as a new generation of Arab immigrants builds a community larger than the Josephs, in their store on the corner of John R and Hendrie, could ever have imagined.

Part 5: Protective Shield and Glass Ceiling

The larger society sees Arab Detroit as a single and singular community. The federal government, corporate bodies, and institutions of American civil society all tend to engage with Detroit's Arabs and Muslims as if they belonged to a unified constituency linked usefully, or threateningly, to foreign interests. This tendency has, quite predictably, provoked numerous attempts to satisfy the growing demand for a safe, accessible, recognizably American version of

Arab Detroit. Meeting this demand is a collaborative venture, shared by Arabs and non-Arabs who, during the Terror Decade, have mobilized to protect and assert the Arab community's interests. Sensitive to Arab Detroit's persistent vulnerabilities, the parties to these collaborative ventures have created an informal (but pervasive) system in which conflicts among Arabs and Muslims, and between these communities and the larger society, are tentatively contained. In this section, our authors explore how these processes have unfolded in recent years, scrutinizing some of their most intricate and elaborate creations.

In "Domestic Foreign Policy: Arab Detroit as a Special Place in the War on Terror," William Youmans studies the political actors who compete to define, represent, and use Arab Detroit for broader political purposes. He focuses on three types of actors: (1) the local anti-Arab coterie of pundits and public figures who monitor Arab Detroit and treat it as a danger to national security; (2) agencies of the federal government, which have multitiered relationships with Arab Detroit, monitoring it closely, recruiting from it for wartime agendas, "test marketing" proposed War on Terror policies there, and holding it up as a positive example of American multicultural democracy; and (3) Arab American leaders, who seek legitimacy and political influence as representatives of Arab Detroit by controlling access to the community. Each part of this triumvirate, Youmans argues, interacts with the others in vexed, counterintuitive ways, turning Arab Detroit into a site of interpretive contestation driven by larger goals and policy aims. The contest zone is filled with "frenemies" who agree that Arab Detroit is a special place, a tool in the War on Terror, and their decision to treat it as a kind of foreign "Arab Republic" on American soil, Youmans concludes, explains the paradoxical nature of Arab Detroit's post-9/11 marginality and incorporation.

In "The Arab American National Museum: Sanctioning Arabness for a Post-9/11 America," Rachel Yezbick takes us on an interpretive tour of one of Arab Detroit's newest and most influential cultural institutions. The Arab American National Museum (AANM), which opened in 2005, is a concentrated example of dominant trends in Arab American representational politics. According to Yezbick, AANM curators, exhibit designers, and tour guides attempt to reclaim a patriotic model of citizenship for Arab Americans by emphasizing socially sanctioned topics and themes: most notably, immigration history, contributions to American society, and military participation. The museum's commitment to these frameworks, Yezbick contends, silences members of the Arab American community whose experiences are not consistent with the standard ethnic/immigrant narrative favored by American multiculturalists. Yezbick asks how the AANM's mainstreaming vision operates, what messages it sends to Arab and non-Arab visitors, and why the War on

Terror is largely ignored in museum exhibits, even though a post-9/11 politics of fear was crucial to the AANM's quick construction and to the representational strategies it now favors.

In "Toward Electability: Public Office and the Arab Vote," Abdulkader H. Sinno and Eren Tatari note that the number of Arab Americans appointed to public office in greater Detroit has increased markedly in recent years. The number of Arab elected officials, however, has not kept pace, especially in areas of concentrated Arab population. Sinno and Tatari consider the extent and possible causes of this underrepresentation through interviews with politicians, party activists, community leaders, and other key players in Dearborn, Hamtramck, and Detroit. They conclude that the poor showing of Arab candidates in local elections can be explained by a mix of factors: effective representation by non-Arab incumbents, strong alliances between Arab organizations and non-Arab politicians, limited political integration among Arab American immigrants, in-group rivalries and fragmentation, the structure of the electoral jurisdictions and voting rules, anti-Arab prejudice, and possible miscalculations of the Arab community's size. Sinno and Tatari also examine the tendency, pronounced in Michigan, for elected Arabs to be Christian and appointed Arabs to be Muslim, a trend that suggests that Arab Muslims now enjoy considerable political influence, but cannot yet wield the power reserved for holders of elected public office.

In "Arabs Behaving Badly: The Limits of Containment in a Post-9/11 World," Nabeel Abraham considers the attempts Arab Americans have made to improve their image in the wider public since September 2001 and how their successes in this realm are continually undone on the individual level. Abraham argues that non-Arab business and political elites in Dearborn now realize that they can effectively govern the city and protect its reputation only if they protect the image of Dearborn's Arab residents. The result is a "Containment System" that resolves, blunts, and, whenever necessary, smothers everyday conflicts that occur between Arabs and non-Arabs. According to Abraham, the Containment System works well as a medium in which community leaders can protect their constituencies; it works poorly, or not at all, as a medium in which Arabs and non-Arabs can deal honestly with their differences. Looking at the tensions that accumulate in schools, colleges, businesses, city parks, and sporting events, Abraham paints a vivid picture of how daily exchanges between Arabs and non-Arabs can generate unflattering images on all sides. During times of heightened geopolitical conflict, these tense interactions take on exaggerated significance. They create a dark undercurrent of animosity that runs counter to public displays of goodwill. Abandoning the glib ethnic characterizations and crude cultural explanations proffered by community leaders to explain (or explain away) the phenomenon of "Arabs behaving badly," Abraham tries instead to comprehend the deeper perceptual views Arabs and non-Arabs bring to their encounters. Popular forms of multicultural tolerance give ordinary people little means to discuss or understand Arab difference. The muted resentments that result are a constant threat to the Containment System. Americanized Arabs, who are best equipped to navigate between Arab and American sensibilities, are expected to defend the Containment System by diffusing conflicts that occur in the community, tamping down unacceptable political views, and inculcating among new Arab immigrants the sense of national loyalty and American identity that the War on Terror endlessly calls into question.

Part 6: Hard Lessons

In our final section, we sift through the rich accounts assembled in this volume to find patterns that enlighten and teach. There are many such patterns—our brief tour of the book has revealed several already—and we will save further discussion for our parting essay, "The New Order and Its Forgotten Histories." Since the purpose of this volume is to remember and revise, we will end with a consideration of what has been forgotten and submerged during the Terror Decade. We will argue that local responses to the 9/11 backlash are part of larger historical trends, in Detroit and nationally. As these trends build over time, they produce local political configurations that help Arab and Muslim citizens enter the American mainstream, but not without first subjecting these citizens to a kind of cultural rehabilitation that clears them of "enemy" associations. The process is sometimes traumatic and always stressful. It works best when the details of its history are not fully remembered. We will conclude by considering the consequences, positive and negative, of this useful forgetting.

On the tenth anniversary of the 9/11 attacks, we realize that the need for integrative scholarship on Arabs and Muslims in the United States is compelling, and we hope this volume will sharpen current understandings of how citizenship and pluralism are shaped (and compromised) by the relentless merger of national security and national belonging. There are, however, more pressing reasons to assemble a book such as this. In Detroit, new realities of political marginalization and empowerment are evolving side by side. These are strange, cohesive realities. The familiar language of multiculturalism is inadequate to describe how these realities are changing Arab and Muslim communities. The essays in this volume will help readers see Arab Detroit in ways that acknowledge the impact of representational politics, national security fears, and intercommunal stereotypes and animosities while encouraging them to look beyond the constraints those frameworks impose.

Breaking free of those constraints is a constructive first step out of the Terror Decade. It is a step many of us are ready to take.

Notes

1. For an early account of post-9/11 developments in Dearborn and greater Detroit, see Shryock (2002).

2. This survey, the Detroit Arab American Study (DAAS), was designed by Wayne Baker, Ron Stockton, Sally Howell, Amaney Jamal, Ann Lin, Andrew Shryock, and Mark Tessler; it was conducted by the Institute for Social Research with funding from the Russell Sage Foundation. To date, the DAAS is the largest scientific survey undertaken among the Arab and Chaldean populations of greater Detroit. More than 1,000 face-to-face interviews were conducted using representative sampling techniques. The preliminary findings of the DAAS were published in 2004 (http://www.ur.umich.edu/0304/July19_04/img/040719_daas.pdf), and more in-depth analyses are featured in *Citizenship and Crisis: Arab Detroit after 9/11* (Detroit Arab American Study Team 2009). We will draw heavily on DAAS findings throughout this volume. The DAAS questionnaire and the full data set can be accessed online at http://www.icpsr.umich.edu/icpsrweb/ICPSR/studies/04413.

3. The term "Arab/Muslim" is meant to acknowledge the extensive but incomplete overlap of Arab and Muslim populations. Not all Arab Americans are Muslim, and not all Muslim Americans are Arab, yet the two populations face similar challenges, and they are often viewed as one and the same by members of the larger society. The backslash represents the strong links between Arab and Muslim communities even as it suggests their distinctiveness.

4. For interesting analyses of the War on Terror as official U.S. policy and as it was experienced by Arab Americans in Detroit, see Ronald K. Stockton's essays in *Citizenship and Crisis* (2009a, 2009b).

5. For some of the best and most representative examples of backlash research, see Cole (2003), Hagopian (2004), Naber (2006), Salaita (2006), Ewing (2008), Bakalian and Bozorgmehr (2009), Cainkar (2009), and Maira (2009).

6. So far, only two studies have made sustained attempts to explain the "positive" side of the Terror Decade: *Backlash 9/11* (Bakalian and Borzorgmehr 2009) and *Citizenship and Crisis* (Detroit Arab American Study Team 2009). Although the "best of times" trend is widely acknowledged by scholars and community leaders, many are reluctant to draw attention to it. Doing so might jeopardize the trend, we are often told. Scholars who endorse a strongly oppositional politics are suspicious of the "best of times" motif and prefer to explore issues of stigma and political exclusion. An excellent example of the latter approach is *Race and Arab Americans before and after 9/11*, a volume edited by Jamal and Naber (2008).

7. More detailed accounts of public cultural work in Arab Detroit, before and after 9/11, are available in essays by Shryock (2000, 2004a, 2004b) and Howell (2000).

8. The accusations of terrorism come from the network of anti-Arab, anti-Muslim blogs whose epicenter is Debbie Schlussel's site, DebbieSchlussel.com (see William Youmans's essay, "Domestic Foreign Policy," in this volume). The countervailing accusations of being "bad Muslim girls" is largely an in-group discourse among Dearborn Arabs, but its semipublic variants can be sampled in viewer comments posted on the numerous YouTube clips associated with Fakih and Dika. The latter are occasionally censored or closed down because monitors consider them sexist or personally threatening in tone.

9. The exception to the rule is *Citizenship and Crisis: Arab Detroit after 9/11* (DAAS Team 2009). At the national level, more chronicling has been done. *Backlash 9/11*(Bakalian and Bozorgmehr 2009) is arguably the most comprehensive account, and its authors make steady use of data they gathered in Detroit. Louise Cainkar's book, *Homeland Insecurity* (2009), offers the view from Chicago. It is meticulously documented, and it deals both with general analytical frameworks and with highly personal accounts of the Terror Decade. It is fair to say that Detroit-based scholars have produced nothing like it so far. This volume is an attempt to correct the trend.

References

Abraham, Nabeel. 2000. "Arab Detroit's 'American' Mosque." In *Arab Detroit: From Margin to Mainstream*, ed. Nabeel Abraham and Andrew Shryock. Detroit: Wayne State University Press.

Abraham, Nabeel, and Andrew Shryock, eds. 2000. *Arab Detroit: From Margin to Mainstream*. Detroit: Wayne State University Press.

Abraham, Sameer, and Nabeel Abraham, eds. 1983. *Arabs in the New World: Studies on Arab American Communities*. Detroit: Center for Urban Studies, Wayne State University.

Ahmed, Ismael. 2006. "Michigan Arab Americans: A Case Study of Electoral and Non-electoral Empowerment." In *American Arabs and Political Participation*, ed. Philippa Strum, 41–52. Washington, D.C.: Woodrow Wilson International Center for Scholars.

American Community Survey. 2005. "Data Profile Highlight, Dearborn, Michigan." Washington, D.C.: U.S. Census Bureau.

Arab American Institute Foundation. 2006. "Select Social and Demographic Characteristics for Arab Americans." Washington, D.C.: Arab American Institute.

Aswad, Barbara, ed. 1974. *Arabic Speaking Communities in American Cities*. New York: Center for Migration Studies.

Bagby, Ihsan. 2004. *A Portrait of Detroit Mosques: Muslim Views on Policy, Politics and Religion*. Clinton Township, Mich.: Institute for Social Policy and Understanding.

Bakalian, Anny, and Mehdi Bozorgmehr. 2009. *Backlash 9/11: Middle Eastern and Muslim Americans Respond*. Berkeley: University of California Press.

Cainkar, Louise. 2009. *Homeland Insecurity: The Arab American and Muslim American Experience after 9/11*. New York: Russell Sage Foundation.

Cole, David. 2003. *Enemy Aliens: Double Standards and Constitutional Freedoms in the War on Terrorism*. New York: New Press.

DAAS Team. 2009. *Citizenship and Crisis: Arab Detroit after 9/11*. New York: Russell Sage Foundation.

Ewing, Katherine, ed. 2008. *Being and Belonging: Muslims in the United States since 9/11*. New York: Russell Sage Foundation.

Hagopian, Elaine, ed. 2004. *Civil Rights in Peril: The Targeting of Arabs and Muslims*. Ann Arbor, Mich.: Pluto Press.

Howell, Sally. 2000. "Cultural Interventions: Arab American Aesthetics between the Transnational and the Ethnic." *Diaspora* 9(1): 59–82.

———. 2009. "Inventing the American Mosque: Early Muslims and Their Institutions in Detroit, 1910–1980." PhD diss., Rackham Graduate School, University of Michigan.

Howell, Sally, and Andrew Shryock. 2010. "Detroit, Michigan." In *Encyclopedia of Muslim-American History*. New York: Facts on File.

Jamal, Amaney, and Nadine Naber, eds. 2008. *Race and Arab Americans before and after 9/11: From Invisible Citizens to Visible Subjects*. Syracuse, N.Y.: Syracuse University Press.

Maira, Sunaima. 2009. *Missing: Youth, Citizenship, and Empire after 9/11*. Durham, N.C.: Duke University Press.

Naber, Nadine. 2006. "The Rules of Forced Engagement: Race, Gender, and the Culture of Fear among Arab Immigrants in San Francisco Post-9/11." *Cultural Dynamics* 18(3): 235–267.

Pew Forum on Religion and Public Life. 2007. *Muslim Americans: Middle Class and Mostly Mainstream*. Washington, D.C.: Pew Research Center.

Rignall, Karen. 2000. "Building the Infrastructure of Arab-American Identity in Detroit." In *Arab Detroit: From Margin to Mainstream*, ed. Nabeel Abraham and Andrew Shryock. Detroit: Wayne State University Press.

Salaita, William. 2006. *Anti-Arab Racism in the USA: Where It Comes from and What It Means for Politics*. New York: Pluto Press.

Salisbury, Stephan. 2010. *Mohamed's Ghosts: An American Story of Love and Fear in the Homeland*. New York: Nation Books.

Sengstock, Mary. 1982. *The Chaldean Americans: Changing Conceptions of Ethnic Identity*. New York: Center for Migration Studies.

Shryock, Andrew. 2000. "Family Resemblances." In *Arab Detroit: From Margin to Mainstream*, ed. Nabeel Abraham and Andrew Shryock. Detroit: Wayne State University Press.

———. 2002. "New Images of Arab Detroit: Seeing Otherness and Identity through the Lens of September 11." *American Anthropologist* 104: 917–922.

———. 2004a. "In the Double Remoteness of Arab Detroit: Reflections on Ethnography, Culture Work, and the Intimate Disciplines of Americanization." In *Off Stage/On Display: Intimacy and Ethnography in the Age of Public Culture*, ed. Andrew Shryock, 279–314. Palo Alto, Calif.: Stanford University Press.

———. 2004b. "Other Conscious/Self Aware: First Thoughts on Cultural Intimacy and Mass Mediation." In *Off Stage/On Display: Intimacy and Ethnography in the Age of Public Culture*, ed. Andrew Shryock, 3–30. Palo Alto, Calif.: Stanford University Press.

Stockton, Ronald K. 2009a. "Civil Liberties." In *Citizenship and Crisis: Arab Detroit after 9/11*, by DAAS Team. New York: Russell Sage Foundation.

———. 2009b. "Foreign Policy." In *Citizenship and Crisis: Arab Detroit after 9/11*, by DAAS Team. New York: Russell Sage Foundation.

Terry, Janice. 1999. "Community and Political Activism among Arab Americans in Detroit." In *Arabs in America: Building a New Future*, ed. Michael Suleiman, 241–254. Philadelphia: Temple University Press.

Part 1

*The Shape
of Arab Detroit*

Arab Detroit after 9/11

A Changing Demographic Portrait

KIM SCHOPMEYER

The first decade of the twenty-first century has found the city of Detroit and southeast Michigan dealing with challenges both predictable and unanticipated. In the early years of the new century, the auto industry experienced one of its periodic upswings, only to face collapse a few years later and the near-demise of two of the major companies. During the housing bubble, property values grew—especially in Detroit's suburbs. But the bursting of the bubble left southeast Michigan with one of the country's highest foreclosure rates and left the nation with a recession that pushed jobless rates into levels unseen in a generation. Although the city of Detroit experienced a few bright spots, with new construction, sporting events, and an improved nightlife appearing downtown, Detroit overall faced financial ruin and more bad publicity about its mayor and its schools.

In the midst of these dramatic shifts, Arab Detroit also underwent notable changes. Events in the Middle East have always had significant ramifications for southeast Michigan and push the region into the national spotlight. Just as the civil war in Lebanon in the 1980s sparked migration into Dearborn's and Detroit's historic Arab neighborhoods, economic and political strife in Iraq following the first Gulf War and the U.S. invasion in 2003 led to a growing Iraqi migration. The 9/11 attacks themselves brought new attention to Arab Detroit, with fears of terrorism and of Middle Eastern people in general, followed by security clampdowns and uneasiness throughout the Arab communities. This chapter will not examine these issues directly, but will focus instead on the changing demographics of Arab Detroit, which register the impact of these larger forces.

Like other large metropolitan areas, the Detroit area has historically attracted migrants from many locations, both from within the United States

29

and from regions across the globe. Although the volume of immigration from the Middle East was smaller than that from European countries, Arab migration has followed similar patterns. As with many Eastern European migrants, Arabs first entered the United States in significant numbers in the late nineteenth and early twentieth centuries, seeking economic opportunities. This early migration came largely from the area called Greater Syria—now the nations of Lebanon and Syria—and comprised predominantly single Christian men. Like many other immigrants of the time, men arrived first and later brought families over if they were able to establish themselves or after giving up their hope of returning home with newfound prosperity. It is estimated that some 200,000 Arabs were living in the United States by 1920 (Kayyali 2006, 28).

Arab migration declined in the later 1920s as the United States, seeking to reduce new entrants from areas outside Western and Northern Europe, imposed increasing restrictions on immigration. Combined with the impact of the Great Depression and World War II, these measures resulted in much slower migration from the former Ottoman Empire until the 1960s. When migration laws were changed with the Immigration Act of 1965 and non-European migrants were permitted entry in larger numbers, Arab entrants joined the new influx, along with those from Central and South America, the Caribbean nations, Africa, and Asia. Between 1965 and 1992, some 400,000 Arabs relocated to the United States, and other Arabs found entry into Canada, Australia, Europe, and South America (Kayyali 2006).

As early as the 1910s, Detroit was established as one of the major destinations for Arab immigration, along with New York and Boston. As immigration in general increased after World War II, Arab migrants continued to select Detroit as a major destination, for its economic opportunities, existing family connections, and a growing community that offered the cultural oasis that many migrants choose to aid in their transition. Most of the earlier Arab immigrants came from the less-prosperous sectors of their homelands, as farmers or merchants, but from the 1950s through the 1970s, increasing numbers of Arab entrants included urban professionals, students, and members of the political elite whose fortunes had changed with shifts in government.

In the last four decades, Arab communities across the United States—but especially in Detroit—have been reshaped by the impact of war in the Middle East. During the fifteen years of civil war in Lebanon, from about 1975 to 1990, hundreds of thousands of Christian, Muslim, and Druze Lebanese were displaced from their homes, and many left the country altogether. With its established Lebanese-Syrian communities, especially in Dearborn, the southeast Michigan region was attractive to new immigrants. Unlike the previous, predominantly Christian migrants, the newer Lebanese immigrants were more likely to be Shi'i Muslims and therefore tipped the religious composition of the region toward Islam. The next war-induced migration, in this case involving Iraqis, came from the combined impact of the Gulf War in Iraq in 1990 and 1991, the post-9/11 invasion by the United States, and the substantial political and economic turmoil in between. As Iraqis sought refuge, once again the Detroit area's established Arab communities drew migrants in search of a new homeland. Although Iraqi migrants came from both Christian and Muslim segments of the population, this second migration also contributed to the growth of Islam in Arab Detroit. Exact figures are not available, but rough estimates would suggest that Christians may have retained their majority position; however, the area may be approaching an even split between Christians and Muslims.

Thus, the earlier establishment of Arab communities in the Detroit area laid the foundation for subsequent patterns of immigration, as migrants frequently follow prior generations into cities and neighborhoods already in place. Newer migrants can take advantage of established businesses, linguistic communities, cultural and religious institutions, family networks, and, since the 1960s, immigration laws that favor family reunification. The relative prosperity of many Middle Eastern immigrants today stems in part from the foundations laid in prior decades. When war, oppression, political turmoil, ethnic competition, or economic instability occur in the Middle East, those seeking a new home tend to favor the established networks—whether in Detroit, New York, Los Angeles, or London.

Counting the Arab Community in Metro Detroit

The size of the Arab community in metropolitan Detroit has been an issue of contention for many years. The most recent estimates of the Arab population (sometimes also including the Chaldean/Assyrian communities) vary enormously, usually with figures from the U.S. Census Bureau on the low end, with intermediate estimates from various other researchers in the middle, and ending with high figures from Zogby Worldwide (2002), a major polling organization with ties to the Arab American Institute. The range between the highest and lowest estimates, depending on the year and geographic area in question, can differ by more than 300 percent. In other words, the estimates at the high end contend that the U.S. Census Bureau, due to various errors in enumeration and classification, omits or fails to properly categorize nearly 70 percent of all Arabs in metro Detroit. Zogby's estimates of Arab communities in other areas of the country are also much higher than those of the Census Bureau. For example, he maintains that the

Census Bureau failed to count two-thirds of Arabs in the United States, omitted 70 percent of all Arabs in Los Angeles and New York, and excluded 90 percent of the Arabs in Miami (Arab American Institute 2003).[1]

According to Zogby, the undercounting of Arabs by the Census Bureau results from several sources. These include the effects of sampling, mistrust of government surveys among respondents, and faulty methods for classifying Arab Americans. Zogby stresses that intermarriage between Arabs and non-Arabs over several generations results in a decline in Arab identity, such that survey respondents with a blend of national heritages may not identify themselves as Arab. This appears to be the most important factor in Zogby's claims of a 70 percent Census Bureau undercount.[2] The combination of these factors leads Zogby to use the Census Bureau numbers and adjust them roughly by a factor of three. As a result, for example, the 2000 U.S. census identified 129,296 people of Arab and Chaldean ancestry in the tri-county Detroit area, whereas Zogby cites 403,445, or 3.2 times the U.S. census figure. Similarly, for Michigan as a whole, Zogby estimates the combined Arab and Chaldean population at roughly 490,000, again 3.2 times the Census Bureau's figure of 151,493 (Arab American Institute 2003).

It is certainly true that the use of sampling—gathering information from a carefully chosen segment of a population, rather than the entire population—will inevitably generate errors in population estimates. This applies to Census Bureau figures as well. The decennial U.S. census has actually involved more than one survey instrument. Mandated by the Constitution, the U.S. census requires a count of *all* residents in the United States. This involves an effort to survey all households, using the "short form" to obtain the total population and other information, such as age, sex, and race. Meanwhile, other information has been collected from the "long form" questionnaire, which uses a sample survey of about 17 percent of households. In the 1980, 1990, and 2000 U.S. censuses, measures of the Arab population were obtained on the long form through questions about ancestry. Respondents were asked to specify one or two ancestries to indicate their national or ethnic heritage. Based on these responses in 2000, the estimate of 1.2 million Arabs, out of the total U.S. population of 283 million, involved a sampling error of about 2.4 percent, or about 30,000 people (Brittingham and de la Cruz 2005).[3] Therefore, accounting for a sampling error would increase the national estimate by no more than about 30,000. Although this estimate is accurate within an accepted error range on a national level, estimates for small geographic areas will have larger ranges of error, but not enough to triple the estimate.

Another source of error may result from the number of people who do not complete the questionnaire. Some people may be mistrustful of government surveys—a pattern found especially among immigrants from countries where mistrust is common—and this may deter them from participating in the survey. It is difficult to estimate the size of this nonresponsive population, but it is assumed that mistrust is most common among recent immigrants. Nonetheless, it is unlikely this factor could influence the overall total by very large numbers. Even assuming that all 173,000 immigrants that arrived from Arab League nations between 1990 and 2000 refused to participate in the 2000 U.S. census, this would not inflate the estimate by a factor of three (U.S. Department of Homeland Security 2003).

The remaining sources of error relate to the sociological concepts of *ethnicity* and *social identity*. In early sociological studies, ethnicity was understood as an objective category in which individuals were classified by their ancestral geographical origins and, at times, also by their participation in corresponding cultural practices. In recent decades, however, social scientists have come to view ethnicity as a social construct, emphasizing factors that shape how a group's members perceive themselves in terms of social identity (Waters 1990; Cornell and Hartmann 1998). In this sense, ethnic classification reflects the social and historical circumstances of certain populations that shape how members perceive themselves and are perceived by the larger society (Waters 1990). Where distinctive cultural practices persist—usually due to continuous immigration or the persistence of ethnic enclave communities—an ethnic social identity is more likely to be sustained. However, when immigration from the ancestral homeland slows (as during the period between the 1920s and the 1960s), when increased interaction outside the ethnic group becomes more common, and especially when intermarriage becomes more widespread, ethnic cultural practices and, therefore, ethnic identity tend to subside. This becomes especially important when surveys ask respondents to classify themselves in terms of ethnicity or ancestry (as the 2000 census long form did).

Therefore, the size of the Arab population hinges on the criteria used to classify people as Arab. The Census Bureau's classification, which relies on self-reportage of at most two ancestries, is likely to reflect the identities with which respondents most strongly associate themselves. This identification is most likely to occur when parents and grandparents share the same national origins and/or when respondents are embedded in distinct ethnic communities. By comparison, those whose parents and grandparents married outside their ancestral background or who lack strong ties to an ethnic community are less likely to adopt and report a distinct ethnic identity (Cornell and Hartmann 1998).

In the case of Zogby's estimates of Arab populations, most of the difference between his estimates and the Census Bureau results comes from those who do not classify themselves as Arabs when asked about their ancestries.

For example, if someone born in the United States has only one Arab grand-parent, does not participate in Arab cultural practices, does not speak Ara-bic, does not seek out an Arab spouse, does not belong to ethnically based religious or social organizations, and identifies with her father's Irish ancestry, she is presumably not likely to identify herself as an Arab on a census ques-tionnaire. Whether she should be counted as an Arab depends on the purpose of the research. If the goal is to count as many people as possible with any Arab ancestors, the answer might be yes. If the goal is to analyze the child-rearing practices or voting patterns of Arab Americans, the answer would quite likely be no.

As noted earlier, other researchers have generated estimates that fall be-tween the low-end figures from the Census Bureau and the high-end esti-mates discussed above. Jen'nan Ghazal Read (2007) has developed methods for improving on the U.S. census count by using additional questions from the long form questionnaire. Read's research is designed to determine how population estimates of Arabs would change if, in addition to the one or two ancestries entered on the census long form, the country in which the indi-vidual was born and languages spoken in the home were also used. In other words, if respondents did not specify an Arab national ancestry, but did in-dicate being born in one of the listed Arab countries or named Arabic as the language spoken in the home, they would be added to the count of the Arab population.

Using 2000 U.S. census data from the Public Use Microdata Sample (PUMS) file, Read analyzed a population of 1.17 million who identified themselves with one or more Arab ancestries. When adding those who did not list an Arab ancestry, but who indicated they were born in an Arab coun-try,[4] this increased the population by 15.9 percent, to 1.36 million. When adding those who indicated they spoke Arabic in the home to those with Arab ancestries, the population increased by 12.8 percent, to 1.32 million. Combining both groups, but eliminating the overlap of those who spoke Arabic *and* were born in Arab nations, the national population of Arab Americans totaled 1.46 million, or 24.9 percent higher than that based only on ancestry (Read 2007, 6).

Read's methodology has been applied to Detroit's Arab community in a recent report from the Center for Urban Studies (2007) at Wayne State Uni-versity. In this case, adding those who were born in Arab countries or who speak Arabic in the home to those who cited Arab ancestry resulted in a 36 percent increase in the measured Arab population. As a result, the Arab population was estimated to be 130,865 for 2000, compared with U.S. census results of 96,363. For 2004, using the 2005 American Community

Survey (ACS) (U.S. Census Bureau 2006)—which now replaces the long form questionnaire—the Detroit area Arab community was estimated to be 179,056, compared with the ACS count of 131,659. It is important to note that these calculations do not include those Iraqis who self-identify as Chaldean/Assyrian/Syriac (an estimated 30,000, according to the 2005 ACS) because it is impossible to distinguish these Iraqis from others using birth country and language measures. When the Chaldean population is added to the Arab total, the combined Arab and Chaldean populations by mid-decade could reasonably be estimated to have reached 210,000. Given natural growth and continued immigration from the Middle East during the century's first decade, the metro area community may have surpassed 220,000 by 2010.

Detroit's Arab Community after 9/11

As we have seen, efforts to capture a portrait of Detroit's Arab and Chaldean communities through U.S. census data encounter substantial challenges. However, data from a recent survey of the Detroit area's Middle Eastern populations allow us to obtain a degree of information previously unavailable. The Detroit Arab American Study (DAAS) (Baker et al. 2003) produced by a team of researchers from the University of Michigan, with the support and cooperation of leading members of the Arab community, has generated considerable information on the demographic, social, and cultural life of Detroit's Arab and Chaldean population. The remainder of this chapter will provide an overview of the area's Middle Eastern communities and the changes they are experiencing in the first decade of the twenty-first century.[5]

Metropolitan Detroit's Arab population is diverse in a variety of ways, and its communities are changing due to shifts in national immigration patterns, the post-9/11 environment, and their successful incorporation. One important change involves the composition of its various communities, based on their national origins. Table 1 shows several breakdowns of the various national groups using different estimates for the metropolitan Detroit area and the United States overall. The 1990, 2000, and 2005 estimates on the tri-county Detroit area come from the U.S. Census Bureau, using the 1990 and 2000 censuses, and the 2005 American Community Survey, which use ancestry data from sample surveys and include all ages of the population. The 2003 estimates come from the Detroit Arab American Study, which includes adults 18 and older only. The national origins of respondents from the DAAS survey are based on their stated nation of birth or, in the case of those born in non-Arab countries, the birth nation of one or more of their parents. The

Table 1. National Origins of Arab Detroit (in percentages)

	Metropolitan Detroit Area				
	Michigan U.S. Census, 1990	U.S. Census, 2000	Detroit Arab American Study, 2003	American Community Survey, 2005	United States, 2000
Iraqi: Arab and Chaldean	23	34	32	39	21
Lebanese	44	35	35	31	37
Yemeni	1	4	8	—a	1
Palestinian/ Jordanian	5	4	12	5	6
Egyptian	2	2	3	2	11
Syrian	8	5	5	3	11
Other	16	16	4	20	13
Total	100	100	100	100	100

a Yemeni population included in "Other" in the American Community Survey.

fifth column provides a nationwide breakdown from the 2000 census of the population, using ancestry data.

Those of Lebanese descent continue to represent the largest national Arab group in metro Detroit, at about one-third of the area's Middle Eastern population, which matches their proportion in the U.S. population. While U.S. census figures estimate the Detroit area Lebanese community to have grown by more than 30 percent between 1990 and 2005, its fraction of the overall Arab population declined from about one-half to one-third. Most of this change stems from the increase in Iraqi immigrants, from about 23 percent of the Arab population to well over 30 percent. In fact, the number of immigrants to the United States from Iraq grew from about 7,500 during the 1980s to more than 68,000 during the 1990s, compared with *decreasing* numbers of Lebanese immigrants. Between 1990 and 2000, Michigan became home to more than 35,000 new Iraqi immigrants, compared with only 17,000 from Lebanon (Camarota 2002). As economic and political conditions in Iraq deteriorated throughout the 1990s, which culminated in the invasion by the United States, massive displacement and emigration led to increased migration flows to the United States and to Detroit, home to the largest Chaldean/ Assyrian population. Iraqi immigration was not limited to the traditional Chaldean Christian communities established in the twentieth century; it also included a growing number of Muslim residents and refugees. Thus the increase in Iraqi immigration, combined with slower migration from Lebanon, resulted in a new period in Arab Detroit, where not one, but two major nationalities have come to represent the majority of the population.

Table 2. Year of Immigration in the United States, Population over Age 25, by National Ancestry (in percentages)

	Iraqi		Lebanese	Yemeni	Palestinian	Jordanian	Syrian
	Christian	Muslim					
Born in United States	16	3	28	10	27	18	43
2000 and after	5	10	5	9	7	3	2
1990–1999	21	81	23	44	12	14	17
1980–1989	18	6	23	15	9	24	19
1970–1979	28	0	15	21	20	21	14
Before 1970	12	0	6	1	25	21	5
Total	100	100	100	100	100	100	100

Source: Detroit Arab American Study 2003 (Baker et al. 2003).

Meanwhile, a sizable Yemeni community is also growing in the area, with Yemenis representing an estimated 8 to 9 percent of metro Detroit's Arab population, compared with only 1 percent of Arabs nationwide (Shryock and Lin 2009). The relatively small size of the Yemeni population makes it difficult to produce reliable estimates of its size through sampling, but the community located in southeast Dearborn and a similar enclave on the outskirts of Hamtramck have grown substantially since the 1970s. Relatively speaking, the Yemeni community is among the newer groups, with more than half migrating since the 1990s and only 10 percent of adults born in the United States.

The different rates and timing of immigration are evident when examining the different national groups, as shown in Tables 2 and 3. Overall, the adult population surveyed by the Detroit Arab American Study shows that Arab Detroit continues to be a largely immigrant community, with only 18 percent born in the United States and less than 6 percent born in the United States to U.S.-born parents. But differences among the various national groups reveal the recent history of immigration. The more long-standing national groups have substantially higher percentages of adults born in the United States. For example, among Palestinians and Jordanians, about one-fourth are U.S.-born, and nearly one-third of Lebanese and nearly half of Syrians were born in the United States. Among the foreign-born in these groups, we also see more early migrants, with 35 to 40 percent of current adults having arrived in the United States from the 1960s through the 1980s. As expected, their average age tends be older. As noted above, Yemenis are clearly new

Table 3. Average Age and Percentage of National Groups by Decade of Arrival in the United States

	All Groups	Iraqi	Lebanese	Yemeni	Palestinian	Jordanian	Syrian
Average Age	44	44	44	36	46	41	47
Born in United States	28	20	32	11	27	24	46
Arrived before 1950	1	1	1	0	2	0	4
Arrived 1950s	3	2	2	0	11	5	0
Arrived 1960s	5	7	2	1	11	12	0
Arrived 1970s	15	22	13	17	18	17	12
Arrived 1980s	17	14	22	13	8	22	17
Arrived 1990s	24	29	22	45	14	17	17
Arrived 2000s	6	5	6	12	8	2	4

Source: Detroit Arab American Study 2003 (Baker et al. 2003).

arrivals on average, with only 10 percent U.S.-born and an average age seven years younger than the Arab community overall. Iraqis include both the older and the newer segments, with an average age similar to the Lebanese, but with 57 percent arriving since 1990.

Despite the immigrant status of the majority of adult Arab Detroiters, their citizenship rates are quite high. As Table 4 shows, in every national group, with the exception of the more recently arrived Yemenis, more than half of all members born outside the United States have obtained citizenship. Among Lebanese, for example, 84 percent are citizens, with 32 percent born in the United States and another 52 percent naturalized citizens. The citizenship rates are particularly striking among the Iraqi communities. With one-third of the population having immigrated since 1990, a higher percentage than all groups except the Yemenis, about 60 percent of foreign-born Iraqis have obtained citizenship. As Shryock and Lin have noted:

> Among Arab Americans, U.S. citizenship is a highly prized status. It opens up new job and educational opportunities, provides new legal protections, enables people to bring kin to the United States, and, in many cases, makes travel within and outside the United States easier. . . . More than 90 percent of immigrants who have been in the United States since 1989 are now American citizens. Sixty-nine percent of those in the United States between eight and thirteen years have received citizenship—a very high percentage, given that five years must elapse between becoming a permanent resident and applying for citizenship. (2009, 45)

Table 4. Citizenship by National Origin (in percentages)

	Born in United States	Naturalized Citizens	Total Citizens	Noncitizens
Iraq	20	60	80	20
Lebanon	32	52	84	16
Yemen	11	43	53	46
Palestine	27	56	83	17
Jordan	24	51	75	24
Syria	46	38	84	17
Other	77	14	91	9
Total	28	52	80	20

Source: Detroit Arab American Study 2003 (Baker et al. 2003).

The Geography of Arab Detroit

Although Arabs can be found throughout metropolitan Detroit, there are two areas that contain the major concentrations of people of Middle Eastern descent. Each area contains about half of Arab Detroit's population and includes a band running from east to west. One area runs across Wayne County, and the other lies in the suburbs north of Detroit in Oakland and Macomb counties. The first area is centered in the city of Dearborn, which borders the western edge of Detroit and, with one-third of its population classified as Arab (2005 ACS), is often considered to be the largest concentration of Arabs in the United States. This is the historic home of most Lebanese Muslims and more recently includes Yemeni, Palestinian, and Iraqi Muslims. The area extends eastward from Dearborn into the west side of Detroit, includes portions of Downriver to the south, and, moves across through Dearborn Heights into Wayne County's western suburbs. This Lebanese and mixed Arab enclave extends from the outskirts of Hamtramck, into western Detroit, the Downriver area, and the western suburbs of Wayne County.

As Table 5 illustrates, the two areas differ in national composition. The Dearborn–Detroit–Western Wayne area is almost half Lebanese, with another 42 percent made up of equal-sized groups of Palestinian, Yemeni, and Iraqi. The area includes about two-thirds of those of Lebanese descent, the majority of Palestinians and Jordanians, and nearly all Yemenis in Metro Detroit.

The second area lies mostly in the suburbs north of Detroit, in Oakland and Macomb counties, and is home to the Iraqi Christian population, the

Table 5. Composition of Two Major Areas in Arab Detroit
(in percentages)

	Dearborn–Detroit–Western Wayne County	Oakland and Macomb Counties
Syrian	3	7
Iraqi	13	50
Lebanese	45	25
Yemeni	14	2
Palestinian	15	3
Other	10	13
Total	100	100

Source: Detroit Arab American Study 2003 (Baker et al. 2003).

Syrian population, the Lebanese Christian population, and a mix of other, largely professional Arab Americans. As Dearborn has historically been the entry point for Lebanese Muslims, the initial area for newly arriving Chaldeans has been a cluster of blocks surrounding Seven Mile Road in Detroit, now called Chaldean Town. The area still houses a number of Chaldean-owned businesses and a small population of Chaldean immigrants, but the vast majority of Iraqi Christians have resettled in Southfield, Oak Park, West Bloomfield, Troy, and other suburbs, especially Sterling Heights, home to the nation's largest concentration of Chaldeans.

The two areas are different in a number of ways. According to the DAAS data, about 79 percent of all Muslims reside in Dearborn and its surrounding communities (Dearborn Heights, Detroit, Downriver, and western Wayne County). Meanwhile, about 90 percent of Middle Eastern Christians reside in the northern and eastern suburbs. The Christian region is somewhat more established, with about two-thirds of the population either born in the United States or having migrated to the United States before 1980. By contrast, the area based around Dearborn, Detroit, and western Wayne County is predominantly Muslim and of more diverse national origins. The Dearborn area includes the more recent migrants from Lebanon, Yemen, and Iraq, with only about one-third born in the United States or having migrated prior to 1980. The western suburbs include the more established and more prosperous of the Lebanese Muslims and Palestinian Christians, with about two-thirds having been born in the United States or having arrived prior to 1980.

Finally, the two areas also tend to adopt rather different self-identities, despite their similar Middle Eastern origins. The Dearborn and Wayne County residents overwhelmingly possess a strong sense of being Muslim and Arab, and they expect to marry, or expect their children to marry, Muslims. The

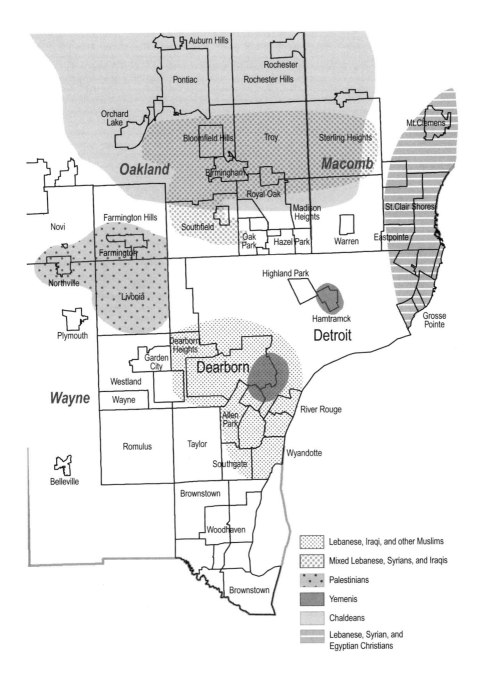

Auburn Hills
Rochester
Rochester Hills
Pontiac
Orchard
Lake
Mt. Clemens
Bloomfield Hills
Troy
Sterling Heights
Oakland
Birmingham
Macomb
Royal Oak
Madison
Heights
St. Clair Shores
Novi
Farmington Hills
Southfield
Oak
Park
Hazel Park
Warren
Eastpointe
Farmington
Northville
Highland Park
Livonia
Hamtramck
Grosse
Pointe
Plymouth
Detroit
Dearborn
Heights
Garden
City
Dearborn
Westland
Wayne
Allen
Park
River Rouge
Wayne
Romulus
Taylor
Wyandotte
Southgate
Belleville
Brownstown
Woodhaven

Lebanese, Iraqi, and other Muslims

Mixed Lebanese, Syrians, and Iraqis

Palestinians

Yemenis

Chaldeans

Lebanese, Syrian, and
Egyptian Christians

Brownstown

Iraqi Chaldeans are much less likely to identify as Arabs, frequently emphasizing their roots in Christianity and their use of the Aramaic language instead of Arabic. They also expect that marriages will occur with other Iraqi Christians. As was the case for earlier immigrant groups whose religious and ethnic identities differed sharply from the Protestant, Northern European majority, such as Irish Catholics and Italians in the eighteenth and nineteenth centuries, tensions sometimes arise between Chaldeans and Muslim and Christian Arabs, including instances of prejudice and bigotry.

Family Life and Family Structure

Among the economically advanced countries in North America and Europe, family life has been transformed in the last fifty years by changes in gender roles, the involvement of women in the workforce, and declining birth rates. The changes have led to a less patriarchal, more egalitarian family system, in which the boundaries between gender roles are more permeable. More recently, these trends have occurred in other countries experiencing economic development and among immigrants who have relocated to more technologically advanced nations. In general, migrant communities tend to move closer to the larger society in family-related behavior and expectations while retaining aspects of the culture of their ancestry. There is evidence of these trends in the immigrant communities of Arab Detroit.

In general, family life within Detroit's Arab communities reflects the traditional patterns of Middle Eastern cultures, which include strong family ties and obligations, a religiously influenced set of expectations for family life, and a patriarchal structure with distinct gender roles. Yet families in Arab Detroit are also surrounded by the dominant American culture, with its emphasis on individualism, self-expression, and weaker family obligations. The intermixing of cultural patterns, as immigrants and members of the larger society interact and comingle, leads to a blend of traditional and contemporary cultures. As Baker and Jamal note in their application of Inglehart's (1997) World Values typology to the Detroit Arab communities, the values of Arab Detroit remain similar to those of the Middle Eastern home nations. Overall, traditional values outweigh the rational-secular values of contemporary American culture, and local Arab culture is more oriented toward survival than self-expression (Baker and Jamal 2009). Nonetheless, the DAAS data show the impact of migration to the United States: in general, the values of Arab Detroit have shifted somewhat toward greater self-expression, especially among the longer-established and U.S.-born members. The degree to which Detroit's Arabs become less traditional is influenced by the length of time they have been established in the United States, their educational attainment, their income, their level of religious piety, and their proximity to the enclaves in Dearborn and Macomb County. These factors affect the structure of family life as well as attitudes about how family members should act, both within their families and in the society at large.

The DAAS results show that attitudes about family life are changing in the Arab communities of metro Detroit. Several questions were asked about family life in general, including the role of women in the workforce, premarital sex, homosexuality, and abortion. For each question, respondents were asked to rate their attitude on a 10-point scale, from "can never be justified" to "can always be justified." In Table 6, figures are shown using the 10-point scale, with those labeled "Can never be justified" including only the least tolerant viewpoint. Those labeled "Can be justified" include those giving any score between 5 and 10, the most tolerant views.

On three of the measures—premarital sex, homosexuality, and abortion—about half of Arab community members indicated no acceptance at all, and only a third placed themselves in the 5- to 10-point range of acceptance. Between 64 and 79 percent said that these practices can never be justified, and less than a fourth said these could be justified to some degree. However, respondents who were born in the United States were substantially more tolerant than immigrants, and earlier migrants were more tolerant than those arriving since 1990. For example, regardless of when they arrived, more than 70 percent of immigrants said that premarital sex can never be justified, while only 47 percent of those born in the United States held this view. Similar patterns apply to homosexuality and abortion. These patterns also appear in relation to attitudes about mothers of small children working outside the home. But Detroit's Arabs are generally more accepting of working mothers, with "only" about a fourth viewing this as completely unacceptable.

Arab families clearly reflect traditional patterns in many ways that contrast to the larger society. Table 7 provides some comparisons on two measures of family characteristics: number of household members and number of children born to adults aged 30 and over, which is a rough indicator of fertility. As the table shows, Arab households are substantially larger, with an average of 4.0 residents, compared with 2.6 residents in metropolitan Detroit overall. Household size varies among ancestry groups, from 5.3 among Iraqi Muslims and 5.0 among Yemenis, on the high end, to 3.1 among Syrians, mirroring the range from the most recent immigrants to the longest established. Compared with the U.S.-born and earlier immigrants, those arriving since 1990 are more likely to be younger and to have higher fertility rates, reflecting those of their home countries, and to include extended family

Table 6. Attitudes on Family-Related Issues, by Length of Time since Immigration (in percentages)

		Born in United States	2000 and after	1990–1999	Immigration to United States 1980–1989	1970–1979	Before 1970	Total
Premarital Sex	Can never be justified[a]	47	79	81	73	71	75	68
	Can be justified[b]	33	12	10	19	19	11	20
Homo-sexuality	Can never be justified	56	88	96	86	85	72	79
	Can be justified	29	7	2	8	10	11	13
Abortion	Can never be justified	46	75	78	70	68	57	64
	Can be justified	33	12	13	20	22	27	22
Mothers of small children working	Can never be justified	10	32	34	29	29	27	25
	Can be justified	75	49	50	54	58	58	59

[a] includes responses of 1 on 10-point scale.
[b] includes responses of 5–10 on 10-point scale.
Source: Detroit Arab American Study 2003 (Baker et al. 2003).

Table 7. Family and Household Characteristics

	Number of People in Households	Number of Children Born to Adults Aged 30 and over
Iraqi Christians	4.2	3.7
Iraqi Muslims	5.3	4.9
Lebanese	3.8	3.0
Yemeni	5.0	6.6
Palestinian	3.6	3.5
Jordanian	4.3	4.1
Syrian	3.1	2.7
Total Arab Detroit[a]	4.0	3.4
Total Metro Detroit[b]	2.6	Not Available

[a] *Source*: Detroit Arab American Study 2003 (Baker et al. 2003).
[b] *Source*: Detroit Area Study 2003 (Baker 2003).

members in their households. Similarly, the most established national groups, such as Syrians, are older, have fewer children, and are less likely to have children in the home. In fact, when adults over age 30 were asked how many children they have, whether residing with them or not, the range is substantial. On the high end, Yemenis and Iraqi Muslims reported having an average of 6.6 and 4.9 children, respectively, with Lebanese at 3.0 and Syrians at 2.7.

Detroit's Arab families display more traditional patterns regarding working mothers with children in the home, again reflecting variations among national groups and levels of education. Within the Arab communities, both Christian and Muslim, traditional patrilineal family patterns emphasize the importance of motherhood in raising children and organizing family relations. As a result, Arab mothers are less likely to be active in the workforce, especially when children are young. The DAAS survey found that 96 percent of married men of working age with children identified themselves as working or looking for work; the remaining 4 percent consisted of students or the disabled. By contrast, 51 percent of women with the same characteristics classified themselves as homemakers. Nonetheless, substantial numbers of women do blend family responsibilities with employment, as indicated by the 46 percent of married mothers with children who classified themselves as employed or seeking employment. But, as Table 8 shows, 56 percent of U.S. couples with children have both husband and wife in the workforce, compared to only 35 percent among Arab families in metropolitan Detroit. Half of Arab families rely on the husband as the sole earner, whereas only 22 percent of U.S. families do.

As Table 9 indicates, the shift toward employment among married women with children has occurred among the U.S.-born and longer-established immigrants groups. Among the most recent immigrants, Iraqi Muslims and Yemenis, rates of education and labor force participation among married women with children remain relatively low. More than 60 percent of Yemeni mothers lack a high school education, as do more than 45 percent of Iraqi Muslim mothers, and they have correspondingly low rates of employment. In both groups, less than 15 percent are working or seeking a job. But employment rates are substantially higher among married women with children from U.S.-born or earlier immigrants. Regardless of different levels of education, employment rates among Iraqi Christian, Lebanese, and Palestinian women with employed husbands reach 40 percent or more.

Table 8. Labor Force Participation of Married Couples with Children (in percentages)

	Arab Detroit Families[a]	U.S. Families[b]
Husband and Wife in Labor Force	35	56
Husband Only in Labor Force	49	22
Wife Only in Labor Force	6	6
Neither in Labor Force	10	16
Total	100	100

[a] *Source*: Detroit Arab American Study 2003 (Baker et al. 2003).
[b] *Source*: U.S. Bureau of Labor Statistics (2004).

Table 9. Working Status of Spouses of Employed Men (in percentages)

	Iraq		Lebanon	Yemen	Palestine	Jordan	Syria	Totals
	Christian	Muslim						
Working Now	48	0	46	5	43	0	10	37
Temporarily Laid Off	2	0	1	0	0	0	0	1
Unemployed	3	0	0	5	0	0	10	2
Retired	0	0	2	0	5	0	10	2
Permanently Disabled	0	0	1	0	0	0	0	0
Homemaker	45	100	48	88	52	75	50	54
Student	0	0	1	2	0	0	20	2
Other (Specify)	2	0	2	0	0	25	0	2
Total	100	100	100	100	100	100	100	100

Source: Detroit Arab American Study 2003 (Baker et al. 2003).

Learning, Working, and Earning

The economic characteristics of Arab Detroit represent the substantial diversity of a population that includes the U.S.-born, third- and fourth-generation natives, long-established immigrants, and the recently arrived in both the highly educated professional and low-skilled worker categories. Among the key economic variables, education is especially important, as it influences one's occupation and earnings. At the same time, in an immigrant community, income and education may not be as closely related as in the overall population for a number of reasons: degrees earned outside the United

Table 10. Educational Attainment of Arab Population over Age 25, by Sex (in percentages)

	Arab Population[a]			Metro Detroit[b]
	Sex of Respondent			
	Male	Female	All Sexes	
Less Than Ninth Grade	12	18	15	5
Some High School	10	11	10	13
Completed High School or GED	17	22	19	29
Some College, No Degree	16	18	17	23
Associate Degree	9	8	9	7
Bachelor's Degree	19	14	16	15
Master's Degree	8	5	7	6
Professional Degree	6	2	4	2
Doctorate Degree	3	0	2	1
Other	0	1	1	0
Total	100	100	100	100

[a] *Source*: Detroit Arab American Study 2003 (Baker et al. 2003).
[b] *Source*: U.S. Census Bureau (2003).

States are less likely to be treated the same as U.S.-earned degrees, language barriers and discrimination may reduce opportunities to be hired, and social support services are less likely to be obtained by lower-income immigrant families (Capps et al. 2005). Meanwhile, some immigrants with little education are able to succeed financially as entrepreneurs.

Education

Table 10 shows that educational attainment among adults aged 25 and older tends to be low overall in the Arab population. Twenty-five percent of Arab residents have less than a high school education, compared with 18 percent among adults in the tri-county Detroit metropolitan area. Arab adults are three times more likely to have less than a ninth-grade education than metro area adults in general, 15 percent compared with 5 percent. However, Arabs who have at least some college education are equally or more likely to finish a college degree than others across the southeast Michigan region. Within the Arab population among those aged 25 and over, educational attainment tends to be higher for men than women, especially among college graduates— 45 percent of men have completed a college degree compared with only 30 percent of women. However, this gender achievement gap may be decreasing in younger generations—among respondents aged 18 through 24, 58 percent

Table 11. Educational Attainment of Arab Population over Age 25, by National Ancestry (in percentages)

| | Iraqi | | | | | | |
	Christian	Muslim	Lebanese	Yemeni	Palestinian	Jordanian	Syrian
Less than Ninth Grade	21	48	9	35	9	15	5
Some High School	13	7	12	15	9	9	2
Completed High School or GED	20	10	18	24	25	23	21
Some College, No Degree	17	10	20	10	13	24	22
Associate Degree	10	7	9	6	12	6	10
Bachelor's Degree	12	10	18	4	18	23	14
Master's Degree	4	3	7	3	9	0	7
Professional Degree	2	3	5	0	3	0	19
Doctorate Degree	0	3	1	0	2	0	0
Other	1	0	1	3	0	0	0
Total	100	100	100	100	100	100	100
Percent Less than HS	34	55	21	50	18	24	7
Percent Bachelor's or More	18	19	34	13	32	24	40

Source: Detroit Arab American Study 2003 (Baker et al. 2003).

of men and 53 percent of women had some college education. Degree completion rates were equivalent, with 15 percent for both men and women.

Educational attainment also varies among the national ancestry groups and between religious groups among Iraqis. As Table 11 shows, among the larger ancestry groups, the Lebanese have levels of education significantly higher than the overall population in the metro area, with 24 percent having attained a bachelor's degree or higher. The Iraqi group shows substantial differences between the Christian and Muslim segments, although both groups show a majority of adults over age 25 with no more than a high school education. Among Iraqi Muslims, nearly half have no education beyond primary school, compared to one-fifth of Iraqi Christians, and Christians are twice as likely to have graduated from high school as well (20 percent of Iraqi

Christians compared to 10 percent of Iraqi Muslims) The smaller ancestry groups—Palestinians, Jordanians, and Syrians—show quite high levels of education, with the exception of Yemenis, who contrast with much of Arab Detroit. Within the Yemeni population, educational attainment is both low and sharply divided by sex, with three-fourths of adults over age 25 having completed no more than high school and the majority of women without any high school education at all. (It is important to note that the sample sizes of the smaller ancestry groups, including Iraqi Muslims, Palestinians, Jordanians, and Syrians, are relatively small, so these figures provide only rough indicators of these patterns.)

Occupations

The Arab communities in metropolitan Detroit represent an important component of the region's economy. Arabs are known to be very active as entrepreneurs in the area's small-business sector as owners and managers of a wide array of businesses, including restaurants, grocery and convenience stores, gas stations, fruit and vegetable markets, and more. Many of these are small family-owned businesses that provide employment for a considerable number of kin and other community members. Overall, according to a recent report from Wayne State University's Center for Urban Studies, using 2000 U.S. census data and classification methods, businesses owned by Arab and Chaldean entrepreneurs represented a total of 47,924 jobs in Wayne, Oakland, Macomb, and Washtenaw counties. Another estimate, based on the 2005 American Community Survey, which uses smaller sampling frames than the U.S. census, counted 68,515 jobs generated by Arab-owned businesses. Although the 2005 estimate from the ACS is less precise than the 2000 U.S. census, it does provide a more recent figure. The exact number of Arab-generated jobs is quite likely somewhere between these estimates. Either way, the economic contribution to the region is substantial (Center for Urban Studies 2007).

The employment portrait of Arab Detroit reflects a number of distinctive features of these Middle Eastern communities. First, the diversity of ancestry groups is reflected in the composition of the labor force, as shown in Table 12, with Lebanese and Iraqis representing the majority of the employed population. Second, owning a business and being self-employed are much more common among Arabs than the population overall. Whereas about 5 percent of the tri-county labor force is classified as self-employed (U.S. Census Bureau 2000), the DAAS survey indicated a rate of 31 percent among Arabs and Chaldeans. Although it varies by national ancestry, self-employment is widespread in each group, exceeding the rate for the metro Detroit area, with the exception of Yemenis. Clearly, owning one's own business is a high priority in the Arab population.

Table 12. Arab Labor Force and Rate of Self-Employment, by Ancestry Group (in percentages)

	Iraq		Lebanon	Yemen	Palestine	Jordan	Syria	Other	Total
	Christian	Muslim							
Percent of Arab Labor Force	26	2	36	8	9	4	5	9	100
Percent Self-Employed	44	20	33	4	37	9	35	18	31

Source: Detroit Arab American Study 2003 (Baker et al. 2003).

Table 13 provides a comparison of the composition of the labor force of metropolitan Detroit with the occupational distribution in Arab Detroit. Arabs are represented more highly among management occupations, 13 percent of Arabs compared with 8 percent for the metro area overall. Again, this reflects high rates of self-employment (since a "manager" may be a corporate vice president or the owner of a convenience store with two employees). Fully 40 percent of all respondents who classified themselves as managers also said they were self-employed. The high rate in sales occupations among Arabs, 25 percent compared with 11 percent regionwide, is also related to employment within family-owned retail and wholesale businesses. In most other occupational categories, Arabs are similar to the larger population, with comparable rates in professional occupations (22 and 23 percent) and service occupations (16 and 12 percent). However, jobs in semi-skilled industrial occupations are less common among Arabs than among the Detroit region overall, where industry still drives much of the economy, if less so than in the past. It is striking that in each occupational category, Arabs demonstrate significantly high levels of self-employment—even in occupations in construction, production, and transportation, from one-fourth to one-third identify as self-employed.

There are close parallels between educational attainment and occupational achievement. The composition of the labor force among the different national ancestry groups, as shown in Table 14, varies considerably, as would be expected given differences in educational attainment. Among Lebanese, Palestinians, and Syrians, more than 30 percent had completed at least a bachelor's degree, and in each group, at least 40 percent were in managerial and professional occupations. Jordanians, with only about one-fourth having achieved a bachelor's degree, were correspondingly less represented among managers and professionals, at about one-third. The nationalities with lower levels of education, from Iraq and Yemen, are much more likely to be employed in support services, sales and office occupations, and blue-collar jobs. Again,

Table 13. Occupations and Rate of Self-Employment (in percentages)

	Metro Detroit Occupations	Arab Labor Force	
		Occupations	Percent Self-Employed
Management occupations	8	13	40
Business and financial operations occupations	5	2	21
Professional and related occupations	22	23	16
Service occupations	16	12	40
Sales occupations	11	25	47
Office occupations	15	10	21
Construction, extraction, maintenance, and repair occupations	8	6	33
Production, transportation, and material moving occupations	14	9	28
Total	100	100	31

Source: Detroit Arab American Study 2003 (Baker et al. 2003).

Table 14. Occupations by National Ancestry Group (in percentages)

	Iraq		Lebanon	Yemen	Palestine	Jordan	Syria
	Christian	Muslim					
Management	11	0	16	6	23	11	7
Professional	20	33	28	3	25	22	37
Support services	15	0	8	18	15	11	19
Sales and office	46	33	30	30	30	33	30
Construction and maintenance	5	0	11	3	3	0	0
Production and transport	3	33	8	39	5	22	7
Total	100	100	100	100	100	100	100

Source: Detroit Arab American Study 2003 (Baker et al. 2003).

the estimates for these smaller groups are less precise, but the patterns appear clearly as we examine a variety of indicators of educational and occupational attainment.

Household Income

The final element of the economic circumstances of Arab Detroiters is household income. The Detroit Arab American Study provides estimates of annual household income from 2003. These can be compared to 2004 figures from

Table 15. Percent of Households in Income Groups, 2003 (in percentages)

| | Iraq | | | | | | |
	Christian	Muslim	Lebanon	Yemen	Palestine	Jordan	Syria
Less than $10,000	12	42	11	18	9	6	7
$10,000–14,999	7	24	7	16	5	6	2
$15,000–19,999	3	3	5	10	1	3	7
$20,000–29,999	11	12	10	26	9	11	12
$30,000–49,999	15	9	16	9	19	19	17
$50,000–74,999	12	3	15	9	21	25	22
$75,000–99,999	13	3	10	4	13	8	7
$100,000–149,999	10	0	14	5	12	14	10
$150,000–199,999	8	3	6	3	7	6	5
$200,000 or more	9	0	5	1	5	3	10
Total	100	100	100	100	100	100	100
Below $30,000	33	82	33	70	24	25	29
Above $75,000	40	6	36	13	36	31	32

Source: Detroit Arab American Study 2003 (Baker et al. 2003).

the American Community Survey for greater Detroit. In some ways, annual incomes are similar: about half of all Arab households and half of all greater Detroit households were below $50,000. But incomes among Arab households were more dispersed than those across the region. There were more Arab households at the lower end, with 36 percent below $30,000, compared to 31 percent for the general population. There were also more Arab households with higher incomes, with 35 percent above $75,000, compared to 30 percent for all area households. These greater extremes reflect the diversity within the Arab communities. Recently arrived immigrants typically earn lower incomes than the population as a whole, due to low skills, language barriers, or limited education. Yet the same communities include a higher than average number of family-owned businesses and others with education and occupational attainment comparable to the population overall.

Household income also varies in Arab Detroit among the different national groups in predictable ways, as shown in Table 15. The most recent arrivals report much lower incomes, with 82 percent of Iraqi Muslims and 70 percent of Yemenis living below $30,000 per year, compared to one-third or less among other national groups. Meanwhile, one-third or more of the more established groups have incomes over $75,000, while less than one out of eight Iraqi Muslim and Yemeni households attain these higher incomes.

It is interesting to compare these income patterns with those found in the 1990 U.S. census. In an earlier report on the demographics of Detroit's Arab communities, the income distribution among Arab households mirrored that of the metro area overall (Schopmeyer 2000). At the low end, 44 percent of all households and 46 percent of Arab households had an annual income below $30,000 (in 1989 dollars). Among the affluent, 13 percent of Arab households and 13 percent of all households had an annual income above $75,000. In this fourteen-year time span, an influx of new, less-educated immigrants, especially among the Yemeni and Iraqi Muslim populations, has expanded the lower end of the income distribution. Meanwhile, earlier immigrant groups have become more established, and many family-owned businesses have grown and multiplied in the last fourteen years—as any visit through east Dearborn and its surrounding areas will show.

These income differences emerge clearly among the national ancestry groups. Among Yemeni and Iraqi Muslims, low-income households are widespread, with 70 and 82 percent, respectively, living on an income below $30,000 per annum. Meanwhile, just over 30 percent of Lebanese households and about 25 percent of Palestinian, Jordanian, and Syrian homes live below $30,000 per year. This is close to the 31 percent in the metro area at this income level. Among the more affluent households, more than 30 percent of Lebanese, Palestinian, Jordanian, and Syrian households have an annual income above $75,000—exceeding the 30 percent for the metro area. Forty percent of Iraqi Christians attained this income level.

Religion in Arab Detroit

As noted, the last decade has seen a shift in the national composition of the Arab communities resulting from changing immigration patterns. Based on the 2003 data from the Detroit Arab American Study, Arab Detroit has become proportionately somewhat less Lebanese, Syrian, and Christian and somewhat more Iraqi, Yemeni, and Muslim than in the decades prior to the new century. These changes do not affect the metropolitan area uniformly, however. The region that borders southwest Detroit has witnessed a greater dispersion of the Arab population from the traditional east and south Dearborn neighborhoods. As a result, the Lebanese community, having become more established and prosperous, has spread to west Dearborn, Dearborn Heights, and nearby areas in Wayne County. Meanwhile, the Yemeni community in south Dearborn has grown significantly, and Iraqi immigrants and refugees have also joined the mix in east Dearborn and southwest Detroit. At the same time, the more recent immigration of Iraqi Christians has expanded the Chaldean communities in Oakland and Macomb counties.

As with much of the Middle Eastern population, the religious characteristics of Arab Detroit have also been influenced by more recent migration

Table 16. Religion in Groups (in percentages)

	Percent of Total	Percent of Group	Percent of Subgroup
Christian	58		
Catholic	42	73	
Chaldean	19		46
Maronite	5		12
Melkite	4		10
Roman Catholic	13		29
Other	1		3
Orthodox	14	24	
Protestant	2	3	
Total		100	100
Muslim	42		
Shi'a	23	56	
Sunni	15	34	
Other	4	10	
Total	100	100	

Source: Detroit Arab American Study 2003 (Baker et al. 2003).

patterns. Although Muslims have attracted the greatest attention in the news media, Christians continue to represent the majority in southeast Michigan, making up 58 percent of the adult population in the DAAS survey. This Christian majority in Detroit is substantially different from the Arab world at large, where only 5 percent are Christian (Howell and Jamal 2009). As noted earlier, Detroit's Middle Eastern communities were predominantly Christian in the past. Orthodox Christian and Maronite Catholic migrants from Greater Syria in the early twentieth century combined with Catholics from the Chaldean/Assyrian populations of northern Iraq, most of whom can trace their origins to a single town, Telkeif. Muslims also arrived, in much smaller numbers, from Lebanon-Syria (as well as from Turkey, Albania, and South Asia). Despite recent changes, these old historical patterns continue to shape the religious composition of Arab Detroit today.

Table 16 shows the breakdown of Arab Detroit by religious group from the 2003 data in the Detroit Arab American Study. Among the Christian population, the majority—69 percent—is Catholic. About 75 percent of the Catholics practice the rites of the Chaldean and Roman Catholic churches, and another 22 percent are connected to Maronite and Melkite churches. Twenty-five percent of Christians attend Orthodox churches, and Protestants make up a small fraction, about 4 percent. Muslims represent about 42 percent of the adult Arab community. In the DAAS survey, about 56 percent of Muslims are Shi'a, another 34 percent are Sunni, and the remaining 10 percent did not specify which branch of Islam they identify with. Again, this contrasts with Arab countries worldwide, where less than 15 percent are Shi'i Muslims (Howell and Jamal 2009).

As noted earlier, the demographic increase in Muslims in recent decades largely reflects changes in migration patterns, since a greater percentage of recent immigrants have been Muslim. The year 1990 provides a useful dividing line: 63 percent of Arab and Chaldean immigrants arriving prior to 1990 were Christian, and 37 percent were Muslim. After 1990, the proportions switch, with 65 percent Muslim and 35 percent Christian. Among migrants from Iraq, the pattern is even clearer. Prior to 1990, Iraqi immigrants were 97 percent Christian. Since 1990, newly arrived Iraqis were only two-thirds Christian and one-third Muslim. And the Yemeni population, which is nearly all Muslim, has grown more rapidly than any other group since 1990.

Based on the DAAS survey, it appears that the nature of religious life in Arab Detroit varies somewhat between the two major groups, Christians and Muslims. In one respect, members of both groups indicate that religious faith is very significant. One survey question asked, "How important is God in your life?" Responding on a 10-point scale, both religious groups indicated high levels of devotion. Among the two groups, 93 percent of Muslims and 83 percent of Christians rated God at the highest level of importance, with women in both groups showing to be more strongly devoted than men.

On two other measures, however, some differences emerge. Christians appear to be more strongly engaged in religious organizations than Muslims. As shown in Table 17, Christians were three times more likely than Muslims to say they attend services at least once a week. Less than 30 percent of Muslims reported attending services at least once a month, whereas two-thirds of Christians went to church. More than 40 percent of Muslims said they rarely attend services in a given year. By contrast, nearly 80 percent of Christians belonged to a church, and 47 percent considered themselves active members in their church. Only 18 percent of Muslims said they were active in their mosque, and more than half were not members of any mosque. Again, in every measure, women were more engaged than men in religious organizations.

Although Christians and Muslims differ in their levels of engagement, membership and participation in religious organizations may be affected by the degree to which people are integrated into established social networks. The highest levels of engagement are found among those born in the United States and those who have lived in the United States the longest. This appears in the different nationalities of Arab Detroiters. Among the longer-established groups, such as Jordanians, Palestinians, and Syrians, three-fourths or more

Table 17. Levels of Engagement in Religious
Organizations, by Religion (in percentages)

Not including weddings and funerals, how often do
you attend religious services?

	Christian	Muslim
Every week or more	29	10
Almost every week	21	8
Once or twice a month	20	11
A few times a year	23	26
Less often than that	7	44

Church, synagogue, mosque or other religious
organization. Are you active in the organization, an
inactive member, or neither?

	Christian	Muslim
Active	47	18
Inactive member	32	26
Neither	21	56

Source: Detroit Arab American Study 2003 (Baker
et al. 2003).

are members of a religious organization and nearly half are active members.
Among Lebanese and Iraqis, both of which include a mix of long-established
and recent migrants, less than two-thirds are members and only one-third
are active. Among Yemenis, the most recent migrants, only 40 percent belong
to a mosque and just 17 percent are active members. It appears that membership in religious organizations, either Muslim or Christian, tends to accompany the incorporation of immigrant groups into the larger society and
its established networks.

Incorporation and Immigration

In any immigrant community, several processes work to shape its broad
characteristics, its subgroups, and its future prospects. One process involves
its incorporation into the larger society. Depending on the financial, educational, cultural, and organizational resources immigrants bring with them
and the characteristics of the host society, new arrivals will find a place
within the new locale. Over time, this may ultimately result in a broad cultural and structural assimilation, in which the immigrant community more or
less blends in and loses a distinct social identity. This may be preceded by
varying forms of distinctiveness, marginality, or inequality—and inequality

may persist over a long time. If an immigrant population brings with it an ample stock of resources and if the larger society is not systematically hostile to it, that group is more likely to find a hospitable environment in which it can prosper. Of course, this outcome is more common in some segments of the immigrant community than in others (Portes and Rumbaut 2006).

In a hostile or passively unsupportive atmosphere, immigrant communities may pool their resources, maximize their strengths, and establish ethnic enclaves that re-create features of their home society. In addition to starting businesses that offer their home country's cuisine, clothing, and media and the religious organizations that support the community, ethnic enclaves also foster social capital through strong networks, both between and within families. The east and south sides of Dearborn are the clearest examples of enclaves in Arab Detroit, with their stunning array of shops, restaurants, fruit markets, gas stations, immigration services, religious schools (and public schools whose students are almost entirely Arab), social service agencies, doctor's offices and clinics, video and cell phone stores, village clubs, and mosques. Within the enclave, new immigrants can meet virtually all their needs in a manner quite similar to what they grew up with.

In most cases, enclaves persist through regular flows of new immigrants. Unless they face social, economic, political, or educational barriers to exit, the longer-standing and more prosperous members of the enclave tend to relocate. As we have seen, the spread of Arab communities westward from Dearborn through Dearborn Heights to more distant suburbs, and the Chaldean movement from Detroit to Southfield, Oak Park, and Sterling Heights, demonstrates this pattern. Without regular immigration to sustain them, enclaves tend to fade away (Chaldean Town in north central Detroit) or become tourist attractions (Greektown or Corktown in Detroit) or are transformed by immigrants from another country (the Italian neighborhoods in east Dearborn before the Lebanese enclave was established). On rare occasions, they may become gentrified.

Recent data indicate that the Detroit area will continue to attract new immigrants from the Middle East. Exploring the present and future of Arab Detroit, it is worth examining the patterns of immigration since 9/11. The data in Table 18 provide the numbers of Middle Eastern immigrants entering the United States as legal permanent residents and residing in the Detroit metropolitan area, based on their country of origin. It is clear that the largest influx of immigrants now arrives from Iraq, with more than 13,000 arriving since 2002 and representing 36 percent of all legal resident immigrants from the region. And although Yemenis represented only 8 percent of the 2003 DAAS survey, they made up more than 16 percent of legal residents. By comparison, Lebanese immigrants provided much smaller numbers of legal residents, with

Table 18. Legal Resident Immigrants to Metropolitan Detroit, by Country of Origin, 2002–2009

	2002	2003	2004	2005	2006	2007	2008	2009	Total
Iraq	1,547	2,450	1,295	1,420	1,476	1,309	1,268	2,489	13,254
Jordan	141	2,927	143	117	148	129	163	181	3,949
Kuwait	44	707	54	40	66	47	50	49	1,057
Lebanon	668	2,956	744	725	671	754	720	792	8,030
Oman	4	76	3	0	3	0	4	0	90
Qatar	4	72	10	5	15	5	9	6	126
Saudi Arabia	51	735	54	64	46	46	30	43	1,069
Syria	146	1,938	148	171	129	93	164	122	2,911
U.A.E.	12	17	21	23	16	31	22	24	166
Yemen	381	1,382	552	844	965	660	544	753	6,081
Total	2,998	13,260	3,024	3,409	3,535	3,074	2,974	4,459	36,733

Source: U.S. Department of Homeland Security (2009).

the exception of 2003. Thus, the trends indicate that growth in the population of Arab Detroit can be expected to continue, with an increase in the percentage of Iraqi and Yemeni residents and a decrease in the percentage of Lebanese residents (U.S. Department of Homeland Security 2009).

Moreover, the Detroit area continues to be the preferred destination for Arab immigrants. In addition to legal permanent residents, population growth is also the result of refugees arriving from Iraq. As Table 19 illustrates, between 2002 and 2009, metro Detroit consistently received more immigrants from Arab countries than the three other major metropolitan areas where Arabs tend to reside—New York, Los Angeles, and Chicago. In fact, the number of legal permanent residents arriving in the Detroit area nearly equaled the combined number of the three next-largest metro areas (U.S. Department of Homeland Security 2009). It is also evident that the more recent increase in Iraqi immigration is focused in the Detroit area. These patterns reflect the preference of immigrants to live where established enclaves provide a feeling of safe haven.

In addition to legal permanent residents, refugee populations are targeting the Detroit area in increasing numbers. As a result of changes in U.S. immigration policy, the number of Iraqis cleared for immigration as refugees nationwide jumped dramatically, to more than 32,000 in 2008 and 2009 (U.S. Department of Homeland Security 2009), representing about one-fourth of all refugees arriving in those years (Martin 2010). In that time period, approximately 3,400 Iraqi refugees were officially resettled in the Detroit area. Although the resettlement process attempts to distribute refugee families across a num-

Table 19. Number of Legal Permanent Resident Immigrants to Selected Metropolitan Areas, 2002–2009

	Detroit	New York	Los Angeles	Chicago
Iraq	13,254	532	1,240	2,648
Jordan	3,949	3,024	1,436	4,156
Kuwait	1,057	735	488	595
Lebanon	8,030	2,092	3,717	621
Oman	90	95	23	43
Qatar	126	119	34	61
Saudi Arabia	1,069	876	570	622
Syria	2,911	2,096	3,129	1,522
U.A.E.	166	578	264	342
Yemen	6,081	6,082	90	594
Total	36,733	16,229	10,991	11,204

Source: U.S. Department of Homeland Security (2009).

ber of states and cities to avoid large clusters in certain areas, many Iraqi refugees are unofficially relocating themselves to the Detroit area. According to a 2009 estimate from Lutheran Social Services in Michigan, at least 460 Iraqi refugees chose to move from their designated settlement location and relocate to Michigan (Karoub 2009). Although poor economic conditions in Michigan provide limited opportunities, refugees still choose metro Detroit, and frequently Dearborn, because of the advantages enclaves offer: stores, services, restaurants, schools, and, above all, thousands of Arab-speaking people. "All these things help to reduce the culture shock that a new immigrant may feel in America," says Imam Hassan Qazwini, who leads the Islamic Center of America, Dearborn's biggest mosque. "In Dearborn, you don't feel like a stranger" (Ghosh 2009). Given these patterns, including the fact that refugees are permitted to apply for legal permanent resident status one year after resettlement, we can anticipate continued population growth in Arab Detroit, particularly in port-of-entry areas like Dearborn, and an ongoing replenishment of new immigrants in the enclaves, alongside an increase in more established Arabs who have laid solid roots in Detroit area communities.

As noted earlier, Arab immigrants tend to achieve high rates of citizenship, which may be considered another step in the process of incorporation. Since five years of legal residency is required to apply for citizenship through naturalization, we can anticipate that upward trends in legal migration will affect naturalizations in subsequent years. Data on naturalizations of residents, shown in Table 20, indicate that between 2004 and 2009 roughly half of naturalized citizens born in Arab nations were Iraqi. In these years, Iraqi

Table 20. Naturalizations in Metropolitan Detroit, by Country of Origin, 2004–2009

	2004	2005	2006	2007	2008	2009	Total
Iraq	1,465	1,078	1,123	844	1,150	840	6,500
Jordan	143	79	101	82	77	72	554
Kuwait	43	46	44	38	33	39	243
Lebanon	762	574	533	434	597	601	3,501
Oman	0	NA	0	0	0	0	0
Qatar	0	0	3	3	0	5	11
Saudi Arabia	17	17	25	17	23	29	128
Syria	142	110	103	87	112	102	656
U.A.E.	15	16	21	3	16	10	81
Yemen	244	233	259	203	384	271	1,594
Total	2,831	2,153	2,212	1,711	2,392	1,969	13,268

Source: U.S. Department of Homeland Security (2009).

immigrants made up about 15 percent of all newly naturalized citizens in the Detroit area, surpassed only by those from India. Lebanese immigrants typically contribute about half as many new citizens as Iraqis, followed by Yemenis.

Conclusions

Throughout this discussion, it is clear that phrases like "the Arab community" and "Arab Detroit" both describe a population and conceal substantial variations within it. The differences among Arab and Chaldean subcommunities stem from key variables—the national ancestry groups that make up the population; differences among those born in the United States, the recently arrived-immigrants, and those who chose Detroit as their home thirty or forty years ago; and religious background. These characteristics, in turn, overlap or interact to produce a wide range of subgroups, each with distinctive patterns of residence, education, occupation, and household income.

This report, which follows a similar examination using 1990 U.S. census data, provides points of comparison over a decade. In some ways, Arab Detroit is more diverse, given the shifts in immigration patterns and the growth of Yemeni and both Iraqi Christian and Iraqi Muslim populations. The majority of the Arab community remains Christian, but the Muslim population is growing and the percentages were getting closer in the years preceding the Detroit Arab American Study, in 2003. The mix of religious groups is likely to have shifted again, however, given the migration patterns since that time. Although it is clear that Iraqi immigration has increased substantially, U.S. government figures classify migrants by nationality, but not religion.

As such, it is difficult to determine the current distribution of religious groups among Arab Detroiters.

Finally, the geographic patterns are changing. The Arab population in Wayne County is becoming less concentrated in the areas surrounding east Dearborn and Southfield and is relocating to the western and northern suburbs. Meanwhile, the growth of the Iraqi community in Dearborn has enhanced the mix of Lebanese and Yemenis. The influx of new migrants introduces new challenges, including the incorporation of Iraqi refugees and the increased attention, often unflattering, paid to Arabs in the post-9/11 media, as well as the shared struggle of all who live in metropolitan Detroit in an era of economic strain and uncertainty.

At the same time, Detroit's Arab and Chaldean communities are becoming more established as another passing decade has allowed earlier migrants to acquire more schooling, expand into new occupations, launch new businesses, and become more active in the political process. During this decade of crisis, several new Arab churches and mosques have opened in the area, including the largest mosque in North America. The Arab American National Museum was established in Dearborn, and roughly sixty Arab Americans now hold political appointments, elected offices, and judgeships. Through this complex array of adaptations, Arab Detroit has come increasingly to resemble the larger society, even as it grows more internally diverse.

Notes

1. The U.S. Census Bureau does acknowledge that undercounts necessarily occur and, among certain categories within the population, the undercount will vary. For example, the Census Bureau estimates that it undercounted blacks in the United States by 1 percent in 2000, which was a significant improvement compared with 1990, when the undercount was 1.8 percent. An undercount of 70 percent would be quite striking by comparison.

2. Zogby has not described his exact methodology for calculating Arab populations in his reports, but states that his estimates are based on a combination of official figures provided by the Census Bureau and "the best on-the-ground estimates compiled after years of visiting, working in, interviewing leaders in, and observations of over 100 Arab communities" (Zogby Worldwide 2002). The methodology can be obtained by purchasing Zogby's Demographic Handbook, available in hardback for $2,000 or electronically for $1,000.

3. The U.S. Census Bureau includes the following subcategories that are treated as Arab: Egyptian, Iraqi, Jordanian, Lebanese, Moroccan, Palestinian, Syrian, and Arab. An additional category of Other Arab includes various other nationalities, such as Yemeni and Algerian.

4. Countries included Algeria, Bahrain, Egypt, Iraq, Jordan, Kuwait, Lebanon, Libya, Morocco, Oman, Qatar, Saudi Arabia, Syria, Tunisia, United Arab Emirates, and Yemen.

5. The Detroit Arab American Study provides an overview of the community through the responses of 1,016 members who participated in this face-to-face survey. Although this project did not attempt to address the controversies regarding the size of the area's Arab population, the results are considered to broadly represent the diverse segments of

the adult population, omitting children under age 18. As with any sample survey, estimates of subgroups in the population include sampling error, and among small segments of the population these error ranges can be fairly large.

REFERENCES

Arab American Institute. 2003. "Arab Americans: Demographics." http://www.aaiusa .org/pages/demographics.

Baker, Wayne. 2003. "Detroit Area Study, 2003: Information and Values in Today's Society" [computer file]. ICPSR22630-v1. Ann Arbor, Mich.: Inter-university Consortium for Political and Social Research [distributor], September 26, 2008. doi:10.3886/ICPSR22630.

Baker, Wayne, and Amaney Jamal. 2009. "Values and Cultural Membership." In *Citizenship and Crisis: Arab Detroit after 9/11*, by the Detroit Arab American Study Team, 135–164. New York: Russell Sage Foundation.

Baker, Wayne, Ronald Stockton, Sally Howell, Amaney Jamal, Ann Chih Lin, Andrew Shryock, and Mark Tessler. 2003. "Detroit Arab American Study (DAAS), 2003" [computer file]. ICPSR04413-v2. Ann Arbor, Mich.: Inter-university Consortium for Political and Social Research [distributor], October 25, 2006. doi:10.3886/ ICPSR04413.

Brittingham, Angela, and C. Patricia de la Cruz. 2005. *We the People of Arab Ancestry in the United States*. Report CENSR-1. Washington, DC: U.S Census Bureau.

Camarota, Steven. 2002. "Immigrants from the Middle East: A Profile of the Foreign-Born Population from Pakistan to Morocco." Washington, D.C.: Center for Immigration Studies, www.cis.org/articles/2002/back902.pdf.

Capps, Randy, Michael Fix, Everett Henderson, and Jane Reardon-Anderson. 2005. *A Profile of Low-Income Working Immigrant Families*. Series B, No. B67. Washington, D.C.: Urban Institute, http://www.urban.org/UploadedPDF/311206_B-67.pdf.

Center for Urban Studies. 2007. *Arab American Economic Contribution Study*. Detroit: Wayne State University.

Cornell, Stephen, and Douglas Hartmann. 1998. *Ethnicity and Race*. Thousand Oaks, Calif.: Pine Forge Press.

Ghosh, Bobby. 2009. "For Iraqi Refugees, a City of Hope." *Time*, September 24, http://www.time.com/time/nation/article/0,8599,1925150,00.html.

Howell, Sally, and Amaney Jamal. 2009. "Belief and Belonging." In *Citizenship and Crisis: Arab Detroit after 9/11*, by the Detroit Arab American Study Team, 103–134. New York: Russell Sage Foundation.

Inglehart, Ronald. 1997. *Modernization and Postmodernization: Cultural, Economic, and Political Changes in 43 Societies*. Princeton, N.J.: Princeton University Press.

Karoub, Jeff. 2009. "Iraqi Refugees Move to Michigan despite Economy." Associated Press, November 22, http://www.msnbc.msn.com/id/34093325/ns/us_news-life/.

Kayyali, Randa. 2006. *The Arab Americans*. Westport, Conn.: Greenwood Press.

Martin, Daniel. 2010. "Refugees and Asylees: 2009." Annual Flow Report, April 2010. Washington, D.C.: U.S. Department of Homeland Security, Office of Immigration Statistics, http://www.dhs.gov/xlibrary/assets/statistics/publications/ois_rfa_fr_2009 .pdf.

Portes, Alejandro, and Rubén Rumbaut. 2006. *Immigrant America: A Portrait*. 3rd ed. Berkeley: University of California Press.

Read, Jen'nan Ghazal. 2007. "Alternative Definitions of Mexican and Arab Identity: Demographic and Socioeconomic Implications." Washington, D.C.: U.S. Census Bureau. http://www.sabresystems.com/whitepapers/ADMA_070207.pdf.

Schopmeyer, Kim. 2000. "A Demographic Portrait of Arab Detroit." In *Arab Detroit: From Margin to Mainstream*, ed. Nabeel Abraham and Andrew Shryock. Detroit: Wayne State University Press.

Shryock, Andrew, and Ann Chih Lin. 2009. "Arab American Identities in Question." In *Citizenship and Crisis: Arab Detroit after 9/11*, by the Detroit Arab American Study Team, 35–86. New York: Russell Sage Foundation.

U.S. Bureau of Labor Statistics. 2004. "Employment Characteristics of Families in 2003." USDL 04-719. Washington, D.C.: U.S. Department of Labor, www.//bls.gov/news.release/archives/famee_04202004.

U.S. Census Bureau. 2000. American Factfinder. http://www.factfinder.census.gov/home/saff/main.html?_lang=en.

———. 2003. American Community Survey. Detroit, MI Primary Metropolitan Statistical Area. American Factfinder, http://factfinder.census.gov/servlet/ADPTable.

———. 2006. 2005 American Community Survey. http://www.census.gov/acs/www/.

U.S. Department of Homeland Security. 2003. *2002 Yearbook of Immigration Statistics*. Washington, D.C.: Office of Immigration Statistics.

———. 2009. *2009 Yearbook of Immigration Statistics*. Washington D.C.: Office of Immigration Statistics.

Waters, Mary. 1990. *Ethnic Options*. Berkeley: University of California Press.

Zogby Worldwide. 2002. *Arab American Demographics Report: A Note about the Census and Methodology Used*. http://www.zogbyworldwide.com/news/Readnews1.cfm?ID-579.

Part 2

Aftermath Chronicles

Cracking Down on Diaspora

Arab Detroit and America's War on Terror

SALLY HOWELL AND ANDREW SHRYOCK

It is hard now to portray Arab Detroit outside the framework provided by the attacks of September 11, 2001. The idea, popular not so long ago, that the Arabs of metropolitan Detroit had finally entered the cultural mainstream, producing U.S. senators (Spencer Abraham) and union bosses (Steve Yokich, president of the UAW) and captains of industry (Jacques Nasser, CEO of Ford), is likely to be dismissed today as wishful thinking. Once hailed as "an immigrant success story," as "the capital of Arab America," the image of Arab Detroit changed within hours of the 9/11 attacks. Suddenly, it was a scene of threat, "divided loyalties," and potential backlash. In the suburb of Dearborn, home to 30,000 Arab Americans, people began, after 9/11, to describe their neighborhoods as "ghettoes" and "enclaves," a terminology of Otherness that was popular in nineteenth-century newspaper accounts of Detroit's newly arrived immigrants from Mount Lebanon. Non-Arabs, for their part, began to use terms like "you people" when talking to Arab neighbors, relatives, and friends. In the language of polite society, "you people" is replaced by unctuous, incessant references to "the Muslim American community" or "the Arab American community," a double-edged jargon that effectively subordinates individual citizens to a logic of collective responsibility even as it protects them from accusations of collective guilt. "The 9/11 attacks," Arabs in Detroit tell us, "set us back a hundred years."

Note: This essay was submitted to *Anthropological Quarterly* on March 14, 2003, before the United States invaded Iraq, deposed Saddam Hussein, and commenced its military occupation of that country. It is reprinted with permission of *AQ*. We have decided not to update our arguments, largely because the essay has been so widely cited and because later events supported our conclusions in ways we did not anticipate. We have corrected one numerical error. Otherwise, the essay is as it originally appeared in 2003.

The collapse of history is a powerful motif. It captures much of what is happening in Detroit. The Arab community has played a critical role in the development of Detroit's economy and culture throughout the twentieth century, and its influence on high politics and everyday life in the Arab homelands—which are linked to Detroit by an irregular flow of money, information, ideas, and people—is so pervasive, so taken-for-granted, that scholars of Arab immigration to the Americas are only now beginning to study it systematically (Khater 2001). As the Bush administration's War on Terror expands, however, Arab Detroit's rich history of domestic integration and transnational connection is being truncated, questioned, repoliticized, Americanized, and selectively erased. This radical transformation is rooted in anxiety about boundaries: Arabs and Muslims are clearly "in Detroit," with "us," but their hearts might still be "over there," with "them." The opposition is stark, and unrealistic, yet having it both ways, cultivating an identity that is both "here" and "there"—a sensible option that, in an era of multicultural tolerance, is still possible for many immigrant and ethnic Americans—is no longer a position Arabs in Detroit can easily embrace. The defense of boundaries, we will argue, only accentuates the centrality of the state in placing them; it also points to the moral dimension of boundary maintenance, to being on the right side of the line and the law. Rules, regulations, security protocols, and law enforcement technologies are never adequate to the task of moralizing national boundaries. Loyalty to the state (also known as "patriotism") is the affective medium in which proper identity placement is made and measured.

In the aftermath of 9/11, Arab and Muslim Americans have been compelled, time and again, to apologize for acts they did not commit, to condemn acts they never condoned, and to openly profess loyalties that, for most U.S. citizens, are merely assumed. Moreover, Arabs in Detroit have been forced to distance themselves from Arab political movements, ideologies, causes, religious organizations, and points of view that are currently at odds with U.S. policy. This coercive predicament, which thwarts scholarship as much as it curtails political activism, is the backdrop against which we write. To understand how this coercion works and what it is working on, we must reengage with the dimensions of Arab Detroit that are now being removed from the public language in which Arabs, *as Americans*, are allowed to speak of (and for) themselves. We must also acknowledge that the nation-state, once a construct to which cultural theorists attached such dismissive modifiers as "withering," "disintegrating," "eclipsed," and "vanishing," is (in its American imperial form) central to any understanding of what is happening in Detroit, where state oversight and American identification are most intense, are most openly called for, in those parts of the community that still have strong ties to Arab and Muslim worlds. The privilege of transnational identification—that is, the ability to sustain political and economic ties to sites of belonging and social reproduction that are not American and are not fully subject to U.S. sovereignty—has been, for Arabs in Detroit, the first casualty of the War on Terror.

Histories and Maps

Detroit and its suburbs are home to a large, diverse population of Arab immigrants and their descendants.[1] Population estimates, always controversial, are routinely inflated by Arab American activists—who claim numbers as high as 400,000 for the Detroit community—but even sober demographic calculations suggest a population of roughly 125,000 people. Arabs in Detroit tend to reside in the suburbs. The most visible concentration is in Dearborn, where Lebanese, Yemenis, Iraqis, and Palestinians, almost all of them Muslim, have built a vibrant terrain of mosques, ethnic business districts, social service agencies, political action committees, village clubs, and neighborhood associations. Another concentration, located along Seven Mile Road in Detroit, is home to Iraqi immigrants, almost all of them Chaldean Catholics, an Aramaic-speaking minority from northern Iraq. The Seven Mile area is much smaller than Dearborn and more transitory. Its inhabitants, as soon as they are financially able, move into the northern suburbs, where Chaldeans and other Arabic-speaking immigrants are widely recognized as an influential business and professional community. Detroit's grocery and liquor store trade is dominated by Iraqis. The Lebanese and other Dearborn-based Muslims, meanwhile, have specialized in gas stations and convenience stores. According to figures generated by the American Arab Chamber of Commerce, there are more than 5,000 Arab and Chaldean-owned businesses in greater Detroit.

In addition to newly arrived immigrant entrepreneurs, there are large numbers of assimilated second-, third-, and fourth-generation Arab Americans living throughout the metropolitan area. Immigrants from Ottoman Syria had established small enclaves in Detroit by the 1890s. Mostly Christians from what is today Lebanon, they worked as peddlers and shopkeepers. Detroit became a magnet for other Syrians in 1914, when Henry Ford began paying his factory workers five dollars a day. Political turmoil in Lebanon and economic opportunity in the United States have continued to draw new immigrants to Detroit. The most significant recent wave of immigration was precipitated by the Lebanese Civil War, which began in 1975. Between the years of 1983 and 1990, just after the war's peak, more than 30,000 immigrants came to the United States directly from Lebanon. Another 10,000 Lebanese arrived from Africa, Canada, and Europe. Nearly 4,000 of them settled in greater Detroit.

The relationship between political and economic instability in the Middle East and migration to Michigan holds for each of the nationalities that make up Arab Detroit. Although the Lebanese are the largest and most visible of Detroit's Arab communities, the city also includes America's largest Yemeni and Iraqi communities and sizable populations from Palestine, Egypt, Jordan, Syria, and other Arab countries. Each of these national groups represents an odd inversion of the demographics of their home country, giving some indication of the forces that have made migration possible and necessary. For example, Christians make up less than 5 percent of the Arab world, but in Detroit they are half the community. Detroit's Iraqi population is predominantly Catholic. Likewise, Detroit's Lebanese, who were once overwhelmingly Christian, are now at least half Muslim, with Shi'a, a minority in Lebanon, outnumbering Sunnis three to one.

This broad range of lifestyles, national backgrounds, and levels of assimilation has made the Detroit Arab community hard to represent, both intellectually and politically. It is not simply an American ethnic community. Parts of it make sense only in relation to the Yemeni highlands, the Lebanese countryside, or the ravaged "no-fly zones" of Iraq. Nor is Arab Detroit an integral part of the Arab world. The city is home, for instance, to tens of thousands of Arabs who cannot speak Arabic and have never traveled to the Middle East. Likewise, the overrepresentation in Detroit of Arab minorities and politically disenfranchised populations (Palestinians, for instance, and thousands of Iraqi Shi'a, displaced when their U.S.-inspired uprising against Saddam Hussein failed in 1991) contributes greatly to its internal fragmentation. The inhabitants of Arab Detroit often find it difficult to imagine themselves as a unified Arab American constituency, and the divide between Muslim and Christian Arabs is a stable feature of community politics.

Still, the interface between the newest Arab immigrants, the old-line Arab Americans, and the larger, non-Arab society is administered by community organizations that represent, and have struggled since the 1970s to create, an Arab American ethnic identity compatible with American multiculturalism. This model of Arab American identity is secular, progressive, and pluralist. It treats religion (whether Christian or Muslim) as one aspect of an overarching Arab identity defined in national, cultural, ethnic, and historical terms. In the aftermath of 9/11, this model of community has been put to the test, along with the more localized and globalized identities available to Arabs in Detroit. The period of testing is far from over, but its effects on

Arab Detroit are beginning to accumulate in trends that are ominous and contradictory.

Report from the War Zone

Nearly two years have passed since the 9/11 attacks. Today, the Arab and Muslim populations of Detroit have been transformed, by an elaborate array of legal and extralegal means, into a domestic front in the Bush administration's War on Terror. The suburb of Dearborn was the first American city to have its own office of Homeland Security, an honor it owes exclusively to the number of its Arab/Muslim residents. No government official has said it explicitly, but Arab Detroit is now a zone of threat, and its inhabitants have good reason to feel threatened by the mixed messages they have received from officialdom and society at large. The first months after the 9/11 attacks were a time of hate crimes and intimidation, but a simultaneous desire to understand and protect Arabs and Muslims flourished in America. The federal government quickly released statements (six coming before September 15, 2001) designed to prevent a domestic backlash. "Any threats of violence or discrimination against Arab or Muslim Americans or Americans of South Asian descent," warned the office of Attorney General John Ashcroft, "are not just wrong and un-American, but also are unlawful and will be treated as such" (U.S. Department of Justice Memorandum 01-468, September 13, 2001).

Initial attempts to reach out to anyone who might suffer from scapegoating suggested, for some, that a solid decade of pluralist conditioning had finally paid off. The "payoff" was, in some cases, quite literal. The Arab Community Center for Economic and Social Services (ACCESS), the largest social service agency of its kind in the United States, has received more than $5 million in gifts since 9/11, mostly from corporate sponsors and private charitable foundations, to fund its cultural and educational programs, which now include sensitivity training for (among others) the very law enforcement agencies that monitor the Arab community. In the days following the 9/11 attacks, mosques throughout Detroit received a barrage of death threats, by mail and phone, but they also received visits from members of local Christian churches, who offered support and friendship. Several mosques held open houses to introduce themselves to curious neighbors, and these events were well attended and generally deemed to be successful. On the economic front, Middle Eastern restaurants and other small, Arab-owned businesses weathered months of reduced sales after 9/11, but Detroit's mayor, Kwame Kilpatrick, joined Arab American business leaders in welcoming a delegation of ambassadors and trade ministers from the Arab League who, in November 2001, toured the city and discussed plans for promoting investment and trade between Detroit and the Arab world.

Gestures of support for Arabs and Muslims met with open, often vociferous assertions of patriotism by those who felt most vulnerable to hate crimes. Denunciations of the 9/11 attacks appeared on the websites of every major Arab and Muslim organization, in Detroit and nationally. Community leaders asserted publicly that Bin Laden was not a good Muslim, or was not a Muslim at all, and that "there is absolutely nothing about Arab or Muslim culture that condones or encourages violence" (ACCESS 2002). In all of these exchanges, problems of identification and doubt (about being Arab, about being American) were never far from view. The exaggerated display of American flags by Arabs in Detroit—on clothes, skin, cars, homes, storefront windows, and places of worship (Shryock 2002)—was part of a heightened desire, familiar among immigrants of manifold sorts, to belong or (failing that) to be sheltered from the brute consequences of not belonging. The singing of "The Star Spangled Banner" and "God Bless America" became, for a time, a stage on which young Arab American vocalists could shine. They vied for spots on the podium at organizational events throughout Detroit. Photogenic young singers who wore the *hijab* attracted special media coverage, and one became the subject of a brief documentary video (Mandell 2002).

Though it now seems strange, it is nonetheless true that many Arab and Muslim American observers believed, in the first months of the post-9/11 era, that their community was "being inducted into a kind of collective citizenship ceremony" (Mattawa 2002, 160). As a Muslim cleric from Dearborn told a delegation of visitors to his mosque in May of 2002: "I would say that we have seen, in this congregation, more positive developments after September 11 than negative ones. People have never been so eager to learn about Islam. We cannot meet the demand for lectures and workshops. This is a good thing that has come from a very bad situation."[2] These words came in response to a question about harassment and profiling, which the cleric acknowledged were daunting problems. His upbeat conclusion, however, is a refrain we hear often among Arabs in Detroit. It is partly a refusal to cower, but it is also testament to the adaptability with which many mosques and secular community groups have responded to the crisis.[3]

This positive take on events has been related, from the very start, to parallel trends that undermine it and, as the United States prepares for war in Iraq, threaten to overwhelm it completely. The passage of the USA Patriot Act and policy decisions made by the Department of Justice, the Immigration and Naturalization Service, and the Department of the Treasury have created a climate in which Middle Easterners and South Asians in the United States can be treated as a special population to whom certain legal protections and civil rights no longer apply. This set of policies has led to the detention of more than 1,200 people in the United States (who were never named or charged with crimes), the deportation of more than half of these detainees, the interrogation of thousands of resident aliens from Arab and Muslim countries, and the arbitrary declaration (usually based on secret evidence) that certain religious and political organizations—particularly those accused of having links to groups that oppose the illegal, but U.S.-backed Israeli occupation of the West Bank and Gaza—are providing "material support to terrorists," a status that legitimizes the freezing of their financial assets and the criminalization of their membership.[4]

The Patriot Act II, now being assembled by the Department of Justice, will increase the government's power to revoke U.S. citizenship (again, based on secret evidence), after which an accused person can be removed from the realm of civilian courts and legal protections, detained indefinitely, tried by military tribunal, deported, and even executed. Against powers of this magnitude—Hobbes himself could not have imagined a mightier Leviathan— the twentieth-century threat of internment camps seems inefficient and old-fashioned. In an age of credit cards, cell phones, and computers, Arabs and Muslims in America do not need to be rounded up *en masse* and held in detention camps, as Japanese Americans were during World War II. Instead, they can be placed under a tactically flexible "house arrest," monitored in the privacy of their homes and as they move about the country, their purchases, financial transactions, intellectual interests, and personal contacts tabulated, their bodies examined each time they board a plane or enter a federal building. When the need arises, targeted groups can be arrested and, without due legal process, be loaded onto chartered flights and discreetly shipped back to their homelands (or to third countries, where they can be subjected to "further questioning").

Not everyone, of course, is traceable in this way. The U.S. Border Patrol in Michigan is now using "unannounced, rotating checkpoints" to search automobiles for illegal aliens, drugs, and terrorists. And, lest you doubt that Arabs are being singled out, the FBI will reassure you that their Detroit office has more than doubled in size during the past year and that their agents are receiving full cooperation from "wary community leaders acting as cultural guides into the local Arab world" (*Detroit Free Press*, November 12, 2002). Mark Corallo, a U.S. Justice Department spokesman in Washington, D.C., said of the probe: "It's the largest investigation in the history of the United States" (ibid.). The result, so far, has been dozens of arrests—mostly for graft, identity forgery, cigarette smuggling, and other black market crimes— and the purported discovery of an "operational combat sleeper cell" of four "al-Qaida terrorists" (who might just be hapless immigrants who fit the profile; the evidence against them has not been made public, although federal prosecutors have characterized the evidence in a manner favorable to their case).

Appeals to common citizenship with Arabs and Muslims have been substantially degraded by this wartime regime and its rhetoric of suspicion. Historical reversions and relapses are occurring now with alarming frequency. Howard Coble, chairman of the House Committee on Homeland Security, recently defended the internment of Japanese Americans. He also said he did not support the internment of Arabs, but his wording was hardly convincing: "We were at war. They [Japanese Americans] were an endangered species. For many of the Japanese Americans, it wasn't safe to be on the street. Some probably were intent on doing harm to us, just as some of the Arab Americans are probably intent on doing harm to us" (Associated Press, February 5, 2003). The mass mediated structures of public opinion, especially those that materialize on cable news networks, in the wide circulation press, and on talk radio—Coble's remarks were made on a call-in radio talk show—have performed well as a conduit for the anti-Arab, anti-Muslim views espoused by a complex network of conservative think tanks, pro-Israeli pundits, U.S. (and other) government spokespeople, and retired military and State Department officials. It is ironic, and more than a bit depressing, to learn (from national pollsters) that Arab and Muslim Americans have a higher approval rating today than they did before the 9/11 attacks.[5] Apparently, they have never been regarded more fondly. Meanwhile, the Arabs of Detroit, despite the monetary gifts, the publicity, and the well-wishes that continue to be showered on their prominent community organizations and leaders, must find ways to interpret the growing evidence that their place in America is more vulnerable than ever.

Going out of (the Diaspora) Business

Evidence of vulnerability is abundant wherever Arab Detroit is connected to the Arab world by ties of kinship, structures of shared religious and political sentiment, and commercial relations. These linkages facilitate the flow of money, the lifeblood of Arab Muslim (and most other) diasporas, and the U.S. government—which before 9/11 was willing to "tolerate cultural pluralism, dual citizenship, and transnational activism as never before" (Werbner 2000, 6)—is now determined to regulate these material and ideological flows and, when they cannot be regulated, to cut them off entirely. Giving to international Muslim charities has declined radically as a result, but equally pervasive effects are being felt in Arab Detroit's commercial sector, a domain filled with conservative, pro-American businessmen, mostly Lebanese and Iraqi arrivistes who voted overwhelmingly for George Bush in the 2000 presidential election.

Before 9/11, the success of Arab entrepreneurs in Detroit was a major selling point for the city. The booming Arab neighborhoods of Dearborn were expanding into Detroit and Dearborn Heights, reviving local economies that were essentially moribund. Immigrant entrepreneurs, who had spent the 1980s channeling surplus income into houses, cars, financial support for relatives in the United States and abroad, and donations to churches and mosques, were finally beginning to flex their political muscle, contributing to municipal campaigns throughout the metropolitan area, backing and opposing mayors, placing their allies on school boards and town councils, and building their own political machines. By the late 1990s, these economic and political advances were attracting the attention of Arab governments and their trade representatives, who saw Detroit as a unique point of entrée. As a commercial zone, it was part of the American economy, yet it was Arabized in ways that would make transnational commerce more attractive to Middle Eastern investors.

Detroit's potential as a nexus for the flow of wealth between the Arab world and North America is now being used by federal authorities as a new managerial context in which to reward and punish Arab entrepreneurs and the diasporas they support. The American Arab Chamber of Commerce, a high-profile, Dearborn-based business association, has been working in recent months to organize a major economic forum at which dignitaries from the Arab states and Detroit's business and government officials will negotiate new trade relations and investment deals. The Chamber's partners in the project include the U.S. Departments of State and Commerce as well as the League of Arab States and the Gulf Cooperation Council. "Our goal," says Ahmed Chebbani, president of the Chamber, "is to make Detroit a hub of trade between the U.S. and the Middle East, similar to [the relationship between] Miami and Latin America" (*Detroit News*, May 7, 2002).

The American Arab Chamber of Commerce has vigorously promoted this event and has sought to keep it as apolitical as possible. Still, a glitzy "show summit" attended by Gulf royals closely aligned with the United States— worse, a forum scheduled to coincide with a U.S. invasion and occupation of Iraq—is a prospect many Arab businessmen are now reluctant to endorse (and some are unable to stomach). The optimism that once marked planning for the summit has faded even among its key organizers, who have watched the Bush administration recast Arabs and Muslims as a threat to national security. Hamoud Rizk (pseudonym), a prominent Arab American business leader, who spoke with us recently about the progress of the economic summit, feared that the old rationale for the event, which was based on a real sense of Arab American success and economic possibility, has evaporated.[6]

"People have put a freeze on all their plans," Rizk observed. "Individuals are not investing right now. Not buying homes. Not starting new businesses. If anything, they are thinking more of buying or taking care of property overseas. People are scared. They are asking, 'Are we safe?' "

This climate, Rizk continued, is disastrous for business, which depends on stability and trust. Fear of internment camps and confiscation of assets is rampant among his friends and colleagues; everyone assumes the IRS is pouring over their financial statements, looking for signs of tax evasion.

"People are beginning to think about a future in the Middle East," Rizk told us. "They're worried that Arabs won't be treated like other Americans. They've lost their faith in the U.S. legal system. It used to be that America was thought of as a place for individual freedom. America prided itself on this. But now freedom is less certain. It depends on who you are. We're no longer innocent until proven guilty. Now, in our community, you have to prove you're innocent."

Increasingly, local and national news stories feature Arab Americans who are caught up in criminal investigations—for instance, "Operation Green Quest," conducted by the U.S. Customs Office—that are clearly designed, both as propaganda and as policy, to discourage people from sending money to the Arab world. In January 2003, sixty federal and local agents raided five Yemeni American businesses in Dearborn, arresting six men for engaging in what officials called "illegal money transfers." Authorities told the media that up to $53 million is sent annually (and, it was strongly implied, illegally) from Detroit to Yemen, a claim that would seem ludicrous to anyone familiar with the small, working-class community of Yemeni immigrants (consisting of perhaps as few as 5,000 people) that was said to generate this vast sum. The charges were quickly dismissed by a local magistrate for "lack of evidence." Similar arrests have been made among Iraqis in Detroit, a much larger and wealthier community, who were said by federal authorities to be sending more than $20 million a year to relatives in Iraq—strangely, $30 million less than the amount sent by unskilled Yemeni factory workers—via indirect routes through Jordan. Since 1991, it has been illegal for Iraqis to send money home to their families, but authorities did not enforce the policy rigorously until after 9/11.

"Regardless of whether the money is going for food or clothing," said James Dinkins, special agent in charge of U.S. Customs investigations in Detroit, "ultimately some of the money makes its way back into the hands of Saddam" (*Detroit News*, January 31, 2003). Given the fact that most Iraqis in Detroit are staunch opponents of Saddam Hussein's regime, this claim seems disingenuous, but Dinkins reveals the larger agenda with his next statement: "Part of the embargo is to put pressure on people and the government to change their practices. The government only changes if the people put enough pressure on them" (ibid.). Transnational flows are acceptable only if they connect the United States to regimes it supports; otherwise, they must be blocked with the explicit goal of causing human suffering and useful political instability.

These news stories (and the disciplinary strategies behind them) are followed closely by Arabs in Detroit, who realize the numbers are grossly exaggerated; they also realize that claims that Arabs in America are providing "material support" for terrorism have become as routine as they are unsubstantiated. Increased scrutiny and suspicion, economic instability in the United States and the Arab world, and an underreported, but significant boycott of American products in the Middle East have created, according to Rizk, "a great reluctance to do business right now. Individuals are vulnerable. Where possible, they are keeping their assets liquid. Trade, commerce, shipping, these are all taking a tremendous hit. When sending $50 to a relative through Western Union provokes a federal inquiry, you question everything." The fate of the U.S.-Arab Economic Forum is now on hold. "We are waiting to hear from the State Department," Rizk told us, without a trace of eagerness in his voice. "We should know any day now. This depends on when the strikes [on Iraq] begin and on whether their projected outcomes will be as they imagine or as we imagine."

American Carrot/American Stick

The fate of the economic summit has structural parallels in every quarter of Arab Detroit. Tremendous pressures of delegitimization and criminalization are paired with levels of public and private sector support that have never been higher. In exchange for organizing and hosting the U.S.-Arab Economic Forum, for instance, the American Arab Chamber of Commerce will receive generous funding from the U.S. government, state and local authorities, and American corporations. It will also solidify its role as intermediary between the Detroit business elite and big corporate and political interests in the Arab world, especially the Gulf states. The larger goal, says Nasser Beydoun, director of the Chamber, is to increase Arab investment in the United States (which currently stands at $200 billion) and to bring more of that vast sum to Detroit, which, Beydoun claims, has so far attracted only $10 million in direct investment from the Arab world. Beydoun told reporters the summit would entice Arabs overseas to "funnel money into Detroit real estate, including the revitalization of the riverfront. Medical centers and universities could forge relationships with Arab counterparts, and General Motors Corp., Ford

Motor Co., and DaimlerChrysler Corp. could increase their share of the Arab market" (*Detroit Free Press*, September 20, 2002). Talk of reciprocal U.S. or Arab American investment in the Arab world is poorly developed in this discourse, and its lack is part of the tendency, exaggerated since 9/11, to locate Arab Muslim interests strictly within Americanizing frames of reference and control.

Attempts to regulate monetary flows between Arab Detroit and the Arab world have meant that resources once sent abroad are now flowing into U.S.-based and U.S.-focused ethnoreligious institutions. If contributions to global Islamic charities are falling, attendance and giving at local mosques is rising. "The only mosques that are suffering," a Dearborn cleric assured us, "are the ones that receive support from the Middle East. Praise God, we do not receive support from outside this country." New mosques (and Islamic schools) are being built, endowed, and enlarged in Detroit and across America, while Muslim advocacy groups in the United States—like the Council on American-Islamic Relations (CAIR) and the American Muslim Council— are awash in contributions from people who see great value in their mainstreaming agenda. "We're Americans," said a recent full-page add in the *New York Times*, placed by CAIR, "and we're Muslims. We're American Muslims." For Muslims who are self-described "modernists," or "moderates," the post-9/11 climate has opened up new possibilities for creating an Islam that is unapologetically American, and this creation, all too often, is legitimized by contrasting it to an implicitly "bad" Islam that is associated not only with fanaticism, but also, symbolically and spatially, with Arabs, the Middle East, and the cultures found there. Consider the representational window dressing in the following statement issued by CAIR: "Only about 18 percent of Muslims live in the Arabic-speaking world. The largest Muslim community is in Indonesia. Substantial parts of Asia and most of Africa have large Muslim populations, while significant minorities are to be found in the countries of the former Soviet Union, China, North and South America, and Europe" (2003).

At the household level, meanwhile, the movement of family members and liquid assets between (and around and beyond) national jurisdictions, once a highly fluid process, is being compulsively monitored and contained: the retired parents who might have come to the United States from Lebanon no longer want to; the extended family that moved regularly between Jordan and Detroit is now divided into "the ones who stay in Jordan" and "the ones who stay here"; the Yemeni whose visa is about to expire will not overstay, but will return to Sanaa with his brother's wife and children, who are all citizens, but whose relatives in Yemen are pleading with them to come home, "until it is safe again in America." Buying property in Syria, sending a wedding gift of cash to a brother in Iraq, supplementing the budgets of family members living under house arrest in the West Bank, or discreetly funneling (undeclared) income into a business in Lebanon—all these quotidian transactions, which have their equivalents in other immigrant communities, are now more difficult, sometimes even endangering, for Arabs in Detroit.

Perhaps the greatest changes, however, are occurring in realms of political and personal identification, where Arab and Muslim Americans must reimagine their communities in order to locate them securely in (national) space and represent them effectively to others. This political project is national in scope, and Arabs and Muslims are neither its principal targets nor its primary beneficiaries. PBS (the Public Broadcasting System), for instance, is now producing and promoting sympathetic, high-quality documentaries about Arabs and Islam in America; major initiatives are being devised and funded by elite U.S. research foundations, institutes, and universities, where scholars who once had no interest in Arab and Muslim communities in the United States are now dividing up the research spoils; dozens of new books and special issues about Islam in America are in print, in press, or already on shelves; and Arab American and Muslim organizations are partners in this flurry of cultural production, all of which is animated, colored, and (too often) distorted by the necessity of knowing Arabs and Muslims in relation to the events of 9/11.

It is not surprising, in this moment of redefinition, that Arabs in Detroit would be eager to assert a sense of national belonging that is demanded of them and, at the same time, is denied to them. What is unexpected, however, is the odd way in which every attempt to assert American identity must involve a simultaneous stigmatization of any sense of Arab identity that includes a strong identification with religious beliefs, political ideologies, and cultural practices that are genuinely alternative to those prevalent in America today. To reassert their status as "good" and "loyal" and worthy of respect, Arab Americans must distance themselves not only from negative stereotypes, but also from the people who are most likely to suffer from these images and their consequences. In an op-ed piece written by Jim Zogby (2001), head of the Arab American Institute, a Washington-based advocacy group, the scrutiny aimed at Arab Americans by journalists after the 9/11 attacks provides an opportunity to (re)assert the Americanness of Arabs in the United States. Note what counts here as evidence of diversity.

> Arab Americans are being discovered, or should I say being rediscovered, by the same papers and networks that have discovered us twice before in just the past decade. As I speak to those assigned to do the story, they discover yet again the diversity of my community. The fact that we are not a new ethnic group in

America (we've been here for 120 years). That most Arab Americans are not Muslims (in fact, only 20% are). That most Arab Americans are not recent immigrants (in fact, almost 80% are born in the U.S.). And that many Arab Americans have achieved prominence and acceptance in America (two proud Arab Americans, Spencer Abraham and Mitch Daniels, serve in President Bush's cabinet, and Donna Shalala served in Bill Clinton's cabinet).

The numbers, proportions, and terminology are all debatable, but Zogby's narrative is flawless in its ability to map the terrain of Otherness in which many Arab Americans, especially those in Detroit, now live. The Arab community Zogby does not speak to (and would encourage his readers not to dwell on) is new, Muslim, born overseas, unknown, unaccepted, accented, culturally peculiar, and politically untouchable. In Arab Detroit, people who belong to this zone of Otherness must keep their heads low and (just as often) their mouths shut as their own community leaders renegotiate the terms on which Arabs and Muslims will be tolerated in the American mainstream. The legal distinctions between "citizen" and "alien," between "legal alien" and "out of status," are gradually eroding, yet many Arab American spokespeople are publicly falling back on a set of binaries—an identity code spoken widely among Arabs in Detroit, but formerly as a kind of private, in-group classification system—that equates Americanness with security, loyalty, trustworthiness, and respect: "Arab Americans," "the Americanized," and "Arab Americans proper" are set apart from "Arabs," "immigrants," "temporaries," "illegals," and, in a more disparaging vein, "boaters." The fact that nearly every church, mosque, village club, and extended family in Arab Detroit is made up of people who belong on both sides of this taxonomy all but ensures that defensive labeling strategies will reinforce (and become part of) the marginalizing trends they are designed to combat.

To show the degree to which every gain in this process of remedial identification brings with it a setback, we have assembled the events of a three-day period in early November 2002, a time of national elections and the onset of Ramadan, when civic duty and religious sentiment were prominently on display in Arab Detroit and across the United States.

On November 5, 2002, George and Laura Bush extend Ramadan greetings to Muslims in America and abroad: "Islam is a peace-loving faith that is practiced by more than one billion people, including millions of American Muslims. These proud citizens contribute to the diversity that makes our country strong, and the United States is grateful for the friendship and support of many Muslim Nations that are vital partners in the global coalition to fight against terrorism" (White House Press Release).

On November 6, the American-Arab Anti-Discrimination Committee (ADC) requests that all Muslims currently held in U.S. jails and military prisons receive proper accommodation for fasting during the holy month of Ramadan. ADC and the Arab American Institute (AAI) ask the White House for guidance on holiday charitable contributions. No one wants to have their property confiscated, their accounts frozen. No one wants to face detention or deportation because they gave money to the wrong people.

On November 5, Imad Hamad, head of Detroit's ADC chapter, votes for the first time. He has spent the previous seven years fighting legal challenges, the use of secret evidence against him, and threats of deportation. His 2002 swearing-in as a U.S. citizen was attended by FBI officials, who praised Hamad for his cooperation in recent months.

On November 6, the AAI announces, on its website, that 70 percent of (forty) Arab American candidates were successful nationwide in the November 5 mid-term elections. Ismael Ahmed, Democratic candidate for regent of the University of Michigan, is not one of them. A Republican activist ran a smear campaign against Ahmed, who is director of ACCESS, a social service agency based in Dearborn. The activist claimed Ahmed was a supporter of "Islamic terror groups." A public letter of support for Ahmed signed by Jewish members of Michigan's Democratic congressional delegation came too late to kill the rumor.

On November 7, more than thirty Arab American activists from across the nation convene at ACCESS to discuss plans for a $9 million National Arab American Museum and Cultural Center. The museum, the first of its kind in the country, will be designed and built by Jack Rouse Associates, an exhibit production firm that specializes in trade shows, theme parks, and zoos. The museum's focus will be placed squarely on Arabs in America, not on ties to the Arab world, a separation that troubles some people involved in the project, even as it thrills others. "This is the great divorce," one observer told us. "They're going to replace 2,000 years of culture with Casey Kasem's Top Forty Arab Americans." "It's time for us to define who we are where we are, which is in America," said another. "This is my home. I'm not foreign. We've got over a hundred years of history in this country. People need to hear that now more than ever."

Such is life on the margins of the American body politic, where acts of inclusion and exclusion are hard to distinguish. The Arabs and Muslims of

Detroit must contend, for now—as Japanese, German, and Italian Americans have done in the past—with the dangers that accompany their status as political and cultural "dirt," what Mary Douglas so famously defined as "matter out of place."

Edward Said, in one of his recent (and more pessimistic) essays, confesses that "I don't know a single Arab or Muslim American who does not now feel that he or she belongs to the enemy camp and that being in the United States at this moment provides us with an especially unpleasant experience of alienation and widespread, quite specifically targeted hostility" (Gabriel 2002, 23). Mainstream Arab American advocacy groups repeatedly remind us that, although the conditions we explore in this essay are frightening, the majority of Arab Americans have not suffered direct abuse (though most know someone who has). Nonetheless, the alienation Said describes has forced many Arab Americans into a position reminiscent of the "double consciousness" W. E. B. Du Bois saw as a central aspect of African American life in the early 1900s. For Du Bois, this predicament brought about "a peculiar wrenching of the soul, a peculiar sense of doubt and bewilderment. Such a double life, with double thoughts, double duties, and double social classes, must give rise to double words and double ideals, and tempt the mind to pretence or to revolt, to hypocrisy or to radicalism" (Du Bois 1903, 202).

The range of options Du Bois laid out was not at all attractive, largely because it was (and still is) so effectively constrained by the defining, disdaining power of a dominant white society. The transnational and multicultural pluralism that became available to minority populations in the United States in the final decades of the twentieth century was, some would argue, an effective means by which to alleviate the most wrenching effects of double vision.[7] The benefits of multicultural citizenship have never been fully extended to Arabs and Muslims in America, however, for reasons deeply embedded in popular religious sentiment and the logic of U.S. foreign policy in the Middle East (McAlister 2001). As the United States prepares for another war—perhaps a series of wars—against Arab and Muslim people, the inhabitants of Arab Detroit are increasingly seen, and must increasingly see themselves, through a doubling lens.

Postscript: April 20, 2003

The U.S. invasion of Iraq has triggered predictable responses in Arab Detroit: protests, calls for tolerance, intensified scrutiny, political estrangement, assertions of patriotism, and widespread depression. Yet the responses, as always, have been contradictory and hard to read. During the early days of the war, crowds of Iraqis shouted "death to Saddam" at public demonstrations in Dearborn—and some kissed pictures of George Bush—while much larger crowds (mostly Lebanese, Palestinian, and Yemeni Americans) shouted "no war!" just across the street. Why, many people wondered, was the FBI interrogating 11,000 Iraqis in the United States when Iraqis seemed to be the Arabs most adamantly opposed to Saddam? Once again, patterns of inclusion and exclusion, and the political lines between "us" and "them," are overlapping in messy ways. The close cooperation between U.S. occupation forces and Iraqi expats, for instance, who are expected to predominate in Iraq's interim civilian government (whose leadership has already been culled and equipped by the United States), is yet another example of the formative relationship between the American nation-state, its geopolitical interests, and immigrant diasporas that are subject to both.

It is worth restating a point central to this essay. In the post-9/11 era, transnational ties that connect the United States to Arab and Muslim countries will be acceptable only insofar as they strengthen sites of belonging and social reproduction that are located in America (in the form of ethnic communities) or are subject to U.S. sovereignty (in the form of allied regimes). As the United States solidifies its control over Iraq, the relationship between Arab Americans and Iraq will be subordinated to the demands of military occupation. Any movements of expertise, money, technology, and information that might support opposition to the American presence will be deemed illegal, then rigorously disciplined, both "here" and "there." If accusations of developing or hiding "weapons of mass destruction" are the telltale precursor to American-imposed "regime change," then recent statements by U.S. government officials—who now claim that Syria is stockpiling chemical and biological weapons, as well as supporting terrorists and harboring Iraqi war criminals—suggest that Syrian and Lebanese Americans might soon be called upon to participate in (or keep a respectful silence concerning) the Bush administration's plans for change in their homelands. Those who openly resist U.S. policy, if they are not citizens, will be intimidated or forced to leave. If they are citizens, their resistance to U.S. policy, should it include financial transactions or political networking overseas, will land them in the newspapers, courts, and jails. As dire as these predictions sound, it is important to realize that such things are already happening in Arab Detroit.

Notes

We would like to thank Amaney Jamal, Ramez Abdelfattah, Nabeel Abraham, and Hashim Al-Tawil for helpful criticisms of our essay. The views we express are not necessarily theirs, nor are they responsible for errors in the text. The Center for Advanced Study in the Behavioral Sciences, through funding provided by the Andrew W. Mellon

Foundation (Grant #29800639), provided generous support for Andrew Shryock during the time in which this essay was written.

1. For more detailed and carefully documented treatments of this terrain, see Kim Schopmeyer's (2000) essay on the demography of Detroit's Arab communities, which is based on 1990 U.S. census figures. According to the 2000 U.S. census, there were 96,625 people in metropolitan Detroit who claimed an Arab ancestry; there were also 27,638 Chaldeans, Assyrians, and Maronites (mostly immigrants and descendants of immigrants from Arabic-speaking countries). For additional accounts of immigration history, identity politics, and transnationalism in Detroit, the reader should refer to recent essays in *Arab Detroit: From Margin to Mainstream* (Abraham and Shryock 2000) and to the earlier work of Sameer Abraham and Nabeel Abraham (1983). Larger (that is, nationally oriented) analytical frames are available in *The Development of Arab American Identity* (McCarus 1994) and *Arabs in America: ` a New Future* (Suleiman 1999).

2. We were on hand to hear this comment, having arranged the delegation's tour of Dearborn.

3. Detroit's largest, most outspoken secular Arab American organizations (ACCESS, the American-Arab Anti-Discrimination Committee [ADC], and the Arab American and Chaldean Council [ACC]) were established in the 1970s and 1980s in climates that parallel, in many ways, the current political moment. Of the three, only the ADC (a national organization with an active local chapter) attributes its establishment directly to the escalation of anti-Arab sentiment that followed the 1967 Arab-Israeli War, when Israel's occupation of the West Bank, Gaza, and Sinai set in motion a series of regional wars, embargoes, and armed Palestinian and Lebanese resistance. Still, all three organizations have struggled to address the basic needs of a community that has grown steadily as a result of the human displacements and political instability created by the Arab-Israeli wars and other Middle Eastern conflicts in which the United States plays a leading role. If ACCESS, the ACC, and the ADC are deriving temporary funding benefits in the wake of 9/11, these must be understood as aspects of a much larger, undesirable political situation. The predicament is not unique to Arab Detroit's advocacy groups. The American Civil Liberties Union, founded in 1920 in reaction to the roundups, detainments, and deportations of the anti-Communist Palmer Raids, has doubled its membership since 9/11.

4. It also functions well as a silencer. Salam al-Marayati, head of the Muslim Public Affairs Council, grappled with these issues in a November 2, 2002 lecture at Stanford University Law School. After pointing out the number of Islamic charities shut down in 2002 (three in all; more have been closed in 2003) and the number of Muslim American leaders (14; more again in 2003) whose homes and offices have been searched and their property seized by federal authorities, Marayati added the obvious: that many Muslims in America are justifiably afraid to criticize government policy. The barely concealed suspicion with which Muslims are often greeted when they do appear as "public" spokespeople, especially in mass media venues, is both offensive and politically injurious.

5. On September 11, 2002, the *San Jose Mercury News* ran a story entitled "U.S. Muslims Held in Higher Regard" (18a), announcing results of a new Knight Ridder poll in which 58 percent of Americans claimed to have "favorable feelings" toward Muslim Americans. Only 45 percent expressed such feelings in March of 2001. A similar pattern held for Arab Americans.

6. Responding to these pressures, but holding onto a semblance of optimism, the American Arab Chamber of Commerce recently announced the postponement of the Economic Forum to September 2003.

7. It is also true, but generally harder to discern, that regnant multicultural policies and the politics of representation they entail can be oppressive in their own right, stigmatizing forms of cultural difference that cannot be easily accommodated in American settings (whether these are institutional, interpersonal, juridical, political, or moral). In two recent essays on public culture in Arab Detroit (Howell 2000; Shryock 2000), we explore the complex (often counterintuitive) ways in which these stigmatizing effects are produced. For a more general take on identity politics among Arab Americans, see Naber (2000).

REFERENCES

Abraham, Nabeel, and Andrew Shryock, eds. 2000. *Arab Detroit: From Margin to Mainstream.* Detroit: Wayne State University Press.

Abraham, Sameer, and Nabeel Abraham, eds. 1983. *Arabs in the New Word.* Detroit: Center for Urban Studies, Wayne State University.

ACCESS Cultural Arts Program. 2002. *Understanding Arab Americans, the Arab World & Islam.* Dearborn, Mich.: ACCESS.

CAIR. 2003. "Islam in America National Ad Campaign," www.americanmuslims.info/ad.asp?m=02&d=16.

Du Bois, W. E. B. 1903. *The Souls of Black Folk.* Chicago: A. C. McClurg & Co.

Gabriel, Judith. 2002. "Edward Said Speaks Out before and after 9-11: Muffling the Arab Voice." *Aljadid* 8(39): 23, 26.

Howell, Sally. 2000. "Cultural Interventions: Arab American Aesthetics between the Transnational and the Ethnic." *Diaspora* 9(1): 59–82.

Khater, Fouad. 2001. *Inventing Home: Immigration, Gender, and the Middle Class in Lebanon, 1870–1920.* Berkeley: University of California Press.

Mandell, Joan. 2002. *I, Too, Sing America.* Detroit: Olive Branch Productions.

Mattawa, Khaled. 2002. "Assimilation and Resistance in Arab Detroit." *Michigan Quarterly Review* 41(1): 155–161.

McAlister, Melani. 2001. *Epic Encounters: Culture, Media, and U.S. Interests in the Middle East, 1945–2000.* Berkeley: University of California Press.

McCarus, Ernest, ed. 1994. *The Development of Arab American Identity.* Ann Arbor: University of Michigan Press.

Naber, Nadine. 2000. "Ambiguous Insiders: An Investigation of Arab American Invisibility." *Journal of Ethnic and Racial Studies* 23(1): 37–61.

Schopmeyer, Kim. 2000. "A Demographic Portrait of Arab Detroit." In *Arab Detroit: From Margin to Mainstream*, ed. Nabeel Abraham and Andrew Shryock, 61–92. Detroit: Wayne State University Press.

Shryock, Andrew. 2000. "Public Culture in Arab Detroit: Creating Arab/American Identities in a Transnational Domain." In *Mass Mediations: New Approaches to Popular Culture in the Middle East and Beyond*, ed. Walter Armbrust, 32–60. Berkeley: University of California Press Mass Mediations.

———. 2002. "New Images of Arab Detroit: Seeing Otherness and Identity through the Lens of September 11." *American Anthropologist* 104: 917–922.

Suleiman, Michael, ed. 1999. *Arabs in America: Building a New Future.* Philadelphia: Temple University Press.

Werbner, Pnina. 2000. "Introduction: The Materiality of Diaspora—Between Aesthetic and "Real" Politics." In *The Materiality of Diaspora*, a special issue of *Diaspora* 9(1): 5–20.

Zogby, James. 2001. "Rediscovering" Arab Americans. www.aaiusa.org/wwatch/111201.html.

Backlash, Part 2

The Federal Law Enforcement Agenda

SALLY HOWELL AND AMANEY JAMAL

Everybody saw George Bush go to the mosque in Washington,
D.C., and take his shoes off and enter the prayer room, the
masjid area, as a show of solidarity with the Muslims in this
country, and certainly, initially, we all thought that was a
really good thing for him to have done and we appreciated
that and really looked to him to defend our civil rights. And
then it all appeared to be a dog and pony show. As the situation
evolved a few weeks later, we started to see Muslims and
Arabs just disappearing from the country. Actually they were
being arrested, incarcerated, held without charge, without
contact, without an attorney, just kind of disappearing. . . .
And then, the infamous Patriot Act came into existence and
we could actually see in black and white that all those things
that George Bush said to us when he was running for office
prior to 9/11, about how he was going to do away with
profiling, about how he was going to do away with secret
evidence, turned out to be a lie. Not only did he not do away
with those things, he actually put his attack dog, John
Ashcroft, in a position to strengthen those violations of our
civil rights as Arab Americans, as Muslim Americans.
—Ron Amen, 2005 interview

This excerpt is drawn from "The Aftermath of the 9/11 Attacks," by Sally Howell and
Amaney Jamal. The full essay is available in *Citizenship and Crisis: Arab Detroit after
9/11* (Detroit Arab American Study Team 2009). This excerpt is reprinted with the permission of the authors and the Russell Sage Foundation, which published the original
essay and funded the research on which it was based.

When Arab Detroiters talk now about the impact of the 9/11 attacks, their greatest concern, echoing Ron Amen, is the erosion of their civil liberties and the profiling of their communities by law enforcement and the media. They speak of the silencing effect on those who want to criticize Israeli and U.S. policies in the Middle East.[1] They worry about the constriction of economic and cultural flows that connect the United States and the Arab world, and the simultaneous expansion of U.S. military campaigns in the Muslim world. It is not always easy to see, but in Washington and in U.S. national media, Arab Americans are portrayed as potential threats to American security *and* as potential assets in the Bush administration's campaign to reshape the Middle East and fight the War on Terror (Hagopian 2003). This situation has yielded a heady mix of opportunity and constraint for Arab Americans, just as it has delivered an especially violent mix of opportunity and destruction to the Arab world. Nowhere in America has the two-edged nature of increased federal attention been more apparent than in Detroit's well-established and recently arrived Arab communities. If Arab Detroit's exceptional nature sheltered it from angry, intolerant individuals bent on revenge, did it also protect Arab Americans from ill-informed federal agents who saw culprits and conspirators around every corner? Did it situate Detroit's Arab organizations to capitalize on new economic and cultural possibilities that followed (and were a part of) the backlash or did it force them to redirect their energies toward defensive educational and legal campaigns? Did it empower Arab Americans to influence policy on the national level now that many Arab ethnic associations were working closely with federal agencies? We will next explore how Detroit has responded to what Hussein Ibish, former spokesperson for the American-Arab Anti-Discrimination Committee (ADC), has described as the Bush administration's "message" to Arab Americans: "private citizens should not and cannot discriminate against Arabs and Muslims, but we [the federal government] can and will" (Ibish 2003).

The Hunt for Terrorists in Detroit Courtrooms

In the days immediately following the 9/11 attacks, the FBI, the Immigration and Naturalization Service, and local law enforcement agencies rounded up and detained without charge more than 1,100 Arab, South Asian, and Muslim men as part of Investigation PENTTBOM, which sought out individuals who were suspected, on the most speculative of evidence, of having preknowledge of the 9/11 attacks or of planning additional terror attacks (U.S. Department of Justice 2003). For the most part, these men were held without charges and in complete secrecy, often in solitary confinement. More than half were eventually deported, though none have been linked, directly or indirectly, to the 9/11 conspiracy. As the investigations widened over several months, the numbers grew to more than 5,000 detained, 155 of them in Detroit (Cole 2003). Detroit may not have been the epicenter of the public backlash against Arabs and Muslims in the United States, but it was in many ways the epicenter of the Justice Department's campaign to apprehend terror suspects and reassure the public that it was doing all it could to hunt down and prosecute those with terrorist ties. On the anniversary of the 9/11 attacks, for example, Mark Corallo, a Justice Department spokesman in Washington, announced that the FBI office in Detroit had more than doubled in size, that the agents were receiving full cooperation from "wary community leaders acting as cultural guides into the local Arab world," and that the Detroit office was at the forefront of "the largest investigation in the history of the United States" (Tamar Audi, "Secret Sweep: Detroiters Caught in Widening Investigation," *Detroit Free Press*, November 12, 2002, 1A). This vast deployment of manhours and new powers of surveillance yielded not the terrorists Bush was hoping for, but a tripling of the arrest rate of local Arab and Muslim petty criminals and visa over-stayers (Greg Krupa and John Bebow, "Immigration Crackdown Snares Arabs," *Detroit News*, November 3, 2003, 1A). As Detroit attorney Bill Swor, who has worked on several prominent terrorism-related cases, pointed out to us, these investigations had a chilling effect on the community. "When every federal investigation involving an Arab, whether a citizen or a resident alien, is vetted through the terrorism unit . . . and every illegal act treated as a federal offense . . . and each case is charged at grotesque levels, finding the most serious charges we can bring, the community remains traumatized because the community knows that it is being not only watched, but targeted" (interview, 2004).

On September 17, 2001, five days after the 9/11 attacks, the FBI raided a house in Detroit. The agents were looking for Nabil Almarabh, a noncitizen whose name had appeared on a pre-9/11 terrorism watch list. Almarabh was not in Detroit, but his four noncitizen housemates were each detained after a cache of false identity papers and other "suspicious" Arabic documents were found in their apartment. They were quickly dubbed an "operational combat sleeper cell" of "al-Qaida terrorists" by John Ashcroft, a label referenced frequently in news stories about Detroit for the next several years. Farouk Ali-Haimoud, Ahmed Hannan, Karim Koubriti, and Abdel-Ilah Elmardoudi were eventually indicted on terrorism charges when a former housemate testified, in exchange for a plea bargain, that they had attempted to recruit him for a terrorist cell. Ali-Haimoud and Hannan were acquitted of terror-related charges in 2003, but a year later, to much public fanfare, Elmardoudi and Koubriti were convicted of conspiring to provide material support and resources to terrorists. The case was not yet closed, however.

The convictions were overturned a few months later and the charges against both men were thrown out when the U.S. Attorney's office in Detroit was forced to admit that their former lead prosecutor, Richard Convertino, had withheld "impeachment and exculpatory material" from the defense (U.S. Attorney Stephen Murphy, personal communication, May 20, 2005). Convertino quickly resigned, but after three years of unprecedented investigative work and relentless international publicity, the government had failed to prove that anything remotely resembling a "sleeper cell of al-Qaida terrorists" had resided in Detroit.[2]

A former special agent in charge of the FBI in Michigan admitted that in 2001 and 2002, the Detroit FBI office strongly encouraged the public to volunteer terrorism-related tips, many of which proved to be misleading and to have been motivated by personal vendettas. "Terrorism is the hot button right now," said John Bell. "If you want to get law enforcement on someone, you accuse him of being a terrorist" (Bay Fang, "Under Scrutiny, Always," *U.S. News and World Report*, December 30, 2002, 26). Bill Swor described the resulting legal cases as both "frivolous and insidious, a waste of resources . . . a witch hunt." In its own defense, the U.S. Attorney's office in Detroit claims to "have had a number of other successful prosecutions that are aimed at disrupting terrorism that have not specifically charged crimes of terrorism, per se, but nonetheless, helped prevent terrorist attacks. These prosecutions generally fall into two categories, cases based on intelligence information, and cases that protect vulnerabilities in our homeland security" (Stephen Murphy, personal communication, 2005). When pressed for information on the number of such cases tried in Detroit, or anywhere else for that matter, local officials have been unwilling to provide further answers. The White House has been less cautious about reporting such numbers. In 2005, President Bush claimed that more than half of the 400 suspects against whom terrorism-related charges had been filed since 9/11 had been successfully convicted. His use of these numbers drew heavy criticism. On June 14, 2005, the *Washington Post* asserted that only thirty-nine people, not 200, had been convicted of crimes related to terrorism or national security, and only a few of these cases involved plots against the United States. The overwhelming majority of cases involved convictions on minor crimes, such as making false statements or violating immigration law. The median sentence meted out regardless of the charges brought to trial was eleven months, a sentence that seemed unlikely to deter people genuinely involved in campaigns against the United States or its allies (Dan Eggan and Julia Tate, "In Terror Cases, Few Convictions," *Washington Post*, A 01). To date, six Arab Americans with ties to Detroit have been found guilty on charges related to providing material support for terrorism. All had connections to Hizballah, not Al Qaeda.[3]

Although Arab Detroiters were relieved to see the "sleeper cell" convictions overturned, they are nonetheless alarmed by the prejudicial manner in which these cases (and many others like them) have been handled and by the inflammatory news coverage that accompanied each arrest and trial (Jamal 2004). The FBI's local antiterrorism unit, renamed the national security unit in 2006, continues to surface when Arab or Muslim Americans are under investigation for offenses unrelated to terrorism. In August of 2006, for example, five young men who were buying large quantities of discounted cell phones for resale in other markets were also accused of providing material support to terrorists. That all five were Arab Muslims did not go unnoticed by attorneys or the media. In one case, the men were in possession of photographs of the Mackinac Bridge. News headlines accused them of plotting to blow up the famous Michigan landmark. The other young men were found with a manual from Royal Jordanian Airlines in their car and on the basis of this "evidence" they were accused of plotting to infiltrate the airline also for terror-related purposes. The manual, like the car, belonged to an employee of the airline, the mother of one of the accused. All charges against each of the five men were eventually dropped, but not before damning headlines, such as "2 Dearborn Men Linked to Terrorism" (*Detroit Free Press*, August 10, 2006) or "3 Arraigned on Terror Charges" (*Detroit Free Press*, August 13, 2006) had done their work. Local Arab and Muslim leaders in Detroit were furious with federal authorities for how the cases were handled and very publicly bungled, accusing law enforcement agents and those who reported on the young men as being equally guilty of racial profiling.[4]

These cases, based on the flimsiest of circumstantial evidence, have done little to strengthen public trust in federal agencies that now regularly justify their investigations, prosecutions, and deportations of Arab and Muslim defendants with "intelligence reports" that are not made public. The U.S. Attorney for Eastern Michigan, Stephen Murphy, admitted that "it would not be surprising to learn that the arrest rate of Arab Americans has increased since 9/11 in light of our investigative priorities" (personal communication, 2005). And, rather than tapering off over the years as investigations in Detroit have yielded scant return on the money and man-hours invested, or as Congress and the Supreme Court have finally begun to challenge the Bush administration's interpretations of First Amendment protections, "homeland security" and "anti-terrorism" are considered among the few growth sectors in Michigan's rapidly shrinking economy. In 2006, shortly after the White House revealed its program of domestic surveillance and wiretapping operations,[5] the FBI announced another doubling—the third since 9/11—of the number of Michigan agents who are pursuing terrorism-related investigations. The agency also broke ground on a new facility in Detroit in 2007, planning to triple the square footage of its local office space and increase its security (Joe Swickard, "FBI to Have New Offices in Detroit," *Detroit Free Press,* August 29, 2006, 1A). The U.S. Attorney's office in Detroit likewise added two attorneys to its "terror unit" in 2006 (Paul Eggan, "Terror Unit to Boost Staffing," *Detroit News,* March 21, 2006, 1B), and Governor Jennifer Granholm has made attracting new homeland security jobs to the state a key anchor of the state's Twenty-first Century Jobs Fund (State of Michigan 2006). The growth of this economic niche has Arab leaders in Detroit worried that federal agents are interested in their communities only insofar as they are useful for "propaganda purposes," military recruitment, and "spying."[6]

A Damper against Discrimination?

A tally of abuses meted out by government agencies against Arabs and Muslims and legal briefs filed in response[7] would say little, however, about the larger transformations Arab institutions have undergone in reaction to the War on Terror and the new political realities it has generated. It is often difficult to determine whether these changes are driven by rewards or punishments, by a sense of belonging or exclusion. Amid the profiling and attempts to marginalize Arab Americans as a political constituency that prevails at the national level, changes taking place on the ground in Michigan have often had positive effects, strengthening an Arab community that was already confident and well connected before September 2001.

Churches and mosques in Michigan, like those across the country, have made a concerted effort to welcome outsiders, hosting film crews, open houses, and ecumenical events. They have also strengthened their support for one another. Human service organizations like the Arab Community Center for Economic and Social Services (ACCESS) and the Arab American and Chaldean Council (ACC) have provided hundreds of cultural sensitivity workshops for journalists, law enforcement agencies, corporations, lawyers, and school districts. The list is long and impressive and includes training for State Department officials and the U.S. military. ADC Michigan, the Council on American-Islamic Relations (CAIR), and the Michigan Civil Rights Commission now provide regular workshops on civil rights issues of relevance to Arabs and other citizens. Although many of these educational programs are more than a decade old, the funds available to support them have grown exponentially since the 9/11 attacks.[8] Millions of dollars have been spent on these efforts in recent years by a variety of corporate, government, and foundation sponsors. This largesse enabled the Arab American National Museum, the first of its kind in the United States, to open its doors in Dearborn in 2005.

Likewise, ADC Michigan broke ground on a new, multimillion-dollar Arab American Center for Civil and Human Rights in 2007. New funding has also been made available to scholars resulting in the Detroit Arab American Study and a plethora of edited volumes, including this one, published by presses and funded by foundations that had little interest in niche communities like Arab and Muslim Americans before September 11, 2001. Mosques, too, continue to invest in public outreach; their construction projects and educational programs have yielded equally impressive results. Since the 2001 attacks, more than a dozen mosque building projects have been completed, more than doubling the square footage of prayer space available in Dearborn and Detroit.[9] This climate of growth and success is welcomed by Arab Detroiters. They recognize that each of these developments improves their ability to assert and defend their claims to full American citizenship. Community leaders are equally aware, however, that these developments bring with them significant costs.

National and local foundations are not the only parties with a newfound interest in sponsoring research on Arab Americans or supporting events and publications that reach Arab American audiences. A motley array of individuals and organizations are lining up to benefit from these opportunities. The number of weekly and monthly newspapers and magazines published by Arabs in Detroit has doubled in recent years, for example, and most are financed, in no small part, by the full-cost, full-page recruitment ads placed in them by the U.S. Army, the FBI, the CIA, and businesses operating in and out of occupied Iraq. Likewise, the CIA has become a prominent, if unlikely, sponsor of the East Dearborn Arab International Festival since 2004, its information booth conspicuous among the falafel stands and carnival rides. Such sights have become commonplace at Arab events in the Detroit area, especially those organized by the American Arab Chamber of Commerce and ACCESS, both of which have developed close ties to the U.S. Departments of State, Homeland Security, and Commerce in recent years.

Together with the League of Arab States and the Gulf Cooperation Council, these otherwise local organizations hosted an event in 2003 called the U.S.-Arab Economic Forum. Intended to increase trade between the Arab Gulf states and Detroit, the event drew heavy criticism from local activists. "The feeling in the region that the United States is on a crusade against Arabs and against Islam is as bad as I have ever seen it," said Osama Siblani, publisher of the *Arab-American News*. "This is not the time to be having this summit. . . . Who in his right mind is going to come and invest from the Arab world when he knows if he comes here, he's going to be stripped, searched and humiliated at the airport?" (Jennifer Brooks, "Division Cloud Promise

Surrounding Arab Forum," *Detroit News*, September 26, 2003, 1A). Forum organizer Ahmed Chebanni adamantly defended the project, arguing that "peace and prosperity go hand in hand. By using Arab-Americans as a business vehicle, we will establish a real, meaningful dialogue and create a basis for long-term dialogue" (ibid.). In a political climate where actual economic ties between everyday American citizens and their relatives and communities in the Middle East were being seriously curtailed and support for Islamic charities was dwindling due to U.S. seizures and political posturing (Howell and Shryock 2003), this optimism proved difficult to sustain. Even Wayne County executive Robert Ficano could mention only another round of seven-digit contributions to the Arab American National Museum (a division of ACCESS) as a tangible, realized benefit of this partnership (Haimour 2005). "We do not wish to judge others. We do not wish to preach to others. We certainly do not wish to coerce others. We wish to help others, and by so doing, help ourselves," said Colin Powell in his address to the 2003 forum. Yet his speech also cautioned Arabs, both American and foreign, to check their criticisms of Israel and opposition to the U.S. invasion of Iraq at the door. If coercion does not account for this partnership, then the opportunism of community leaders offers little solace to those who are left on the margins of the post-9/11 boom in all things Arab American.

Just as Arab organizations have been met halfway in their educational and civil liberties campaigns by concerned foundations, corporations, public institutions, and government agencies, Arab Americans have also met federal law enforcement agencies halfway, some would say more than halfway, in their many investigations in the Arab American community. Within a week of September 11, 2001, more than 4,000 Arabs from Detroit called to volunteer their services to the FBI and CIA as translators of stockpiled communications intercepts ("Arabic Speakers Answer U.S. Need," *Detroit Free Press*, September 19, 2001, 7A).[10] Arab Americans were no less eager to catch genuine terror suspects than other Americans. They had a special interest and often specialized skills that could be of help in this regard. It was in this spirit that ADC Michigan pulled together a coalition of fifteen Arab American organizations for monthly meetings with the regional leadership of the FBI, the U.S. Attorney's office, and an additional dozen federal agencies after the 9/11 attacks. Imad Hamad, director of ADC Michigan, and John Bell, then special agent in charge of Detroit's FBI office, had already worked together through the National Conference for Community and Justice. It was through this relationship that Building Respect in Diverse Groups to Enhance Sensitivity (BRIDGES) was established as a forum for dialogue where "both sides" could communicate freely (personal communication 2005).

The first major accomplishment of this task force was the creation of a series of "best practice" guidelines the FBI in Michigan followed in November 2001 when it began questioning more than 500 of the state's Arab and Muslim noncitizens as part of a national effort that included 7,600 noncitizens nationwide. ADC was able to monitor these investigations locally, both in 2001 and on the three subsequent occasions the FBI repeated this process, making pro bono attorneys available, providing a helpline for those with questions, insuring that interviewees received advance letters to explain the program's voluntary nature, providing translators, and insisting that federal agents not confront respondents at school or in the workplace. U.S. Attorney Stephen Murphy asserts that the process also enabled law enforcement to conduct these investigations without "alienating" the Arab community and to be more efficient and effective by pairing federal agents with local law enforcement officers (personal communication 2005).[11] Although the process was inherently discriminatory—profiling informants along religious and national lines—and the best practice guidelines were reached only after extensive and heated debate, the execution of these interviews in Michigan was significantly less disruptive of individual lives and community-law enforcement relations than elsewhere. In particular, eastern Michigan was one of only four districts where letters were uniformly mailed in advance to interviewees and one of only two districts where the U.S. Department of Immigration and Naturalization was kept out of the interview process (Ramirez, O'Connell, and Zafar 2004, 24).

In 2005, several of the people we interviewed for this project were cautiously, if also strategically, optimistic about the benefits that flowed from the BRIDGES alliance, pointing to a sustained dialogue between "the state" and "the community" that enabled all parties to clarify legal, linguistic, and cultural matters in ways that improved the application of federal laws on the ground. Arab leaders argued that the process made the law enforcement community more accountable to Arab concerns, and law enforcement agreed, adding that it also brought greater trust and public support. Both sides recognized that the familiarity encouraged by an ongoing airing of principles, concerns, and grievances was able to produce better law enforcement and greater cooperation among those involved and provided a list of Arab Americans who sought and received assistance from law enforcement agencies. Several individuals, for example, had their names removed from federal "no fly" lists, several hate crimes against Arab Americans were prosecuted with speed and efficiency, and a few federal detainees who posed no threat or flight risk were freed while their cases were pending trial (personal communication 2005).

Although some are encouraged to see Arab American complaints handled in this face-to-face terrain where justice can occasionally be facilitated, BRIDGES has not yet been able to challenge the status quo in which the presumption of innocence seems to have been reversed and due process is lacking for Arab and Muslim defendants. As time passes, the volatility of the BRIDGES alliance has made it less effective and less easy to sustain. Kenwah Dabaja, then Michigan field director of the Arab American Institute, described BRIDGES as too inconsistent in its efforts, meeting less and less frequently, often in reaction to the latest crisis (personal communication 2007). Even when the group met according to schedule, outside events frequently sidetracked their discussions. In September 2006, for example, the head of the Department of Justice's Civil Rights Division, Assistant U.S. Attorney Wan Kim, was scheduled to address BRIDGES members in a public forum. After he outlined the progress his department had made prosecuting hate crimes and other forms of discrimination against Arabs and Muslims since 9/11, the meeting itself was completely overrun by comments about the cell phone cases mentioned earlier and angry complaints about a raid on Life for Relief and Development (LIFE), an Islamic charity headquartered in the Detroit area, that took place the day before the BRIDGES meeting and just before the onset of Ramadan. Daniel Roberts, special agent in charge of Detroit's FBI office, argued that the raid had been timed to take place before rather than during this month of fasting (and charitable giving) to be "sensitive to community concerns." LIFE was not closed down, nor were its assets frozen, but it took the FBI most of the month of Ramadan to issue a public statement to this effect. Dabaja summed up the FBI's participation in the BRIDGES alliance this way: "I don't get the feeling they are listening."[12]

Despite these tensions, BRIDGES is now considered an ideal model of community–law enforcement relations by observers outside Michigan, and it is being replicated in other parts of the country (Ramirez, O'Connell, and Zafar 2004), a process that is supported by Arab American activists and by the Department of Justice alike. In a study of such community–law enforcement initiatives nationwide, the Soros Foundation attributes the success of BRIDGES to the remarkable degree of institutional incorporation the Arab community in Michigan has achieved. The BRIDGES story is the latest chapter in a long history of local activism in which Arab Americans have made political gains by working with city hall, as it were, while actively fighting against it (Terry 1999; Ahmed 2006). Imad Hamad laments the fact that BRIDGES, though replicated in other locations, has met with only local success in eastern Michigan and has been able to intervene positively only on a case-by-case basis. "Of course, the dialogue needs to be with policy makers and not just those who implement policies," he argues. "In order for BRIDGES to make a difference outside Michigan, we need to communicate with those in D.C. and not only those who are in Detroit" (interview, 2005).

Conclusion

Imad Hamad's appeal was echoed by each of the Arab Americans we interviewed who suggested that the federal government, especially the law enforcement agencies managing the "state of exception" created out of our ongoing crisis, would benefit tremendously from the insight of Arab and Muslim professionals, not simply as translators, role-playing actors,[13] field agents, and civil rights watchdogs, but as intelligence officers, presidential advisors, and policy makers. Arabs in Michigan have achieved genuine political incorporation. At the state level, they shape the way social services are delivered, health data is collected, automobiles are designed and manufactured, world music is packaged, Homeland Security measures are implemented, and gasoline, milk, and other goods are distributed and sold. As in other ethnic communities, most of this work is accomplished without reference to collective identities while ethnic institutions stand by to carefully catalog and augment these efforts, ensuring that Arabs are a political constituency local governments must acknowledge and support. This process has been decades in the making, but the events that transpired on and after September 11, 2001, compelled officials to recognize that the fate of Michigan, and of Dearborn in particular, are intertwined now with the fate of their Arab citizens. This is why the public backlash in Michigan was significantly less severe than in other communities.

At the national level, Arabs have not achieved this sort of inclusion, and until they do, the exceptional privileges they have gained in Detroit will remain fragile. Arab leaders in Detroit are acutely aware of the limitations of this status, as is Imad Hamad, whose sensitivity to the difference between the local and the national is rooted in personal experience. In September 2003, the FBI in Washington sought to recognize Hamad's singular contribution to the BRIDGES effort by awarding him their highest civilian honor, the Exceptional Public Service Award. Hamad soon found himself slandered by a national media campaign that described him as "a man who supports terrorism and was himself a suspected terrorist" (Schlussel 2003). He was further humiliated when the FBI declined to award him the honor they had already announced to the media. As the public controversy around the award escalated, Arab American members of the BRIDGES alliance threatened to withdraw. Hamad was forced to defend his past, reassure the public that he is not a terrorist, and plead with BRIDGES partners to continue their collaboration with a government agency that was clearly ambivalent about Hamad and insensitive to the community he represents.[14]

Awareness of the difference between local and national politics is keen among Detroit's major Arab American institutions, each of which has found itself performing the defensive maneuvers described earlier; defending their pasts and promoting their institutional histories, investing vast resources in reassuring the public that they are not and do not support terrorists, and urging their constituents to not lose faith as they collaborate in increasingly complex ways with the FBI, the CIA, the Department of State, and other federal agencies that are interested in Arab Americans only as potential threats to U.S. security or potential allies in the U.S. War on Terror. In Arab Detroit today, local social service providers, arts presenters, civil liberties advocates, and Muslim charities find themselves working closely with, and often accepting the patronage of, federal agencies that specialize in security issues, foreign and domestic espionage, criminal investigations, and other forms of governmental discipline and control. Occasionally, Arab American groups are enlisted, mostly as window dressing, in U.S. campaigns to transform the Middle East, economically, politically, and militarily.[15] This work stands at a remove from the bread and butter efforts of Detroit's Arab ethnic associations to provide services and address community needs, activities that have garnered them strong grassroots support. When Arab organizations are included in "public diplomacy" and "community policing" efforts but are not treated as full partners with a voice in setting agendas and negotiating strategies, they risk weakening their grassroots strength and eroding Arab confidence in American public institutions and government. The new status quo suggests that, at the national level, Arab Detroit is being reconfigured as a constituency defined not by its genuine integration with a city and its society, but by its imputed associations with "foreignness" and "danger." If this odd feature of Arab Detroit's political incorporation continues to receive institutional support, it may produce tragic (and unintended) consequences for a community that has withstood the 9/11 backlash and now looks forward, longingly, to a more stable era of acceptance.

Notes

1. This silencing effect predates the 9/11 attacks, but has become more pronounced since. It was especially apparent in the Detroit area during the 2006 Israeli-Hizballah War when Arab American leaders were routinely described as "Hizballah supporters" in the media and then dismissed. This smear campaign reached its peak when gubernatorial candidate Dick DeVos cancelled his planned appearance at an Arab American Political Action Committee (AAPAC) dinner in Dearborn after the editor of the *Detroit Jewish News* argued in an editorial that "no legitimate candidate for public office should go before the Dearborn-based [PAC] . . . because its leadership has defended Hezbollah" (Robert Sklar, September 6, 2006, 7). The president of AAPAC was likewise introduced publicly,

by the head of Michigan's FBI field office, as a "supporter of Hizballah" (Osama Siblani, personal communication, 2006).

2. Hannan and Koubriti were recently indicted again, this time on a charge of insurance fraud. The new case is pending.

3. The guilty pleas include *U.S. v. Makki* and *U.S. v. Kourani*. A third man, Nemr Ali Rahal, was arrested in May 2005 for raising $600 to support the families of suicide bombers connected to Hizballah ("Dearborn Man to Be Tried in Terror Case," *Detroit News*, May 4, 2005, 3B). Finally, four men pleaded guilty in Detroit in 2006 to a variety of racketeering and counterfeiting charges related to a moneymaking scheme intended to benefit Hizballah, Youssef Bakri, Imad Hamadeh, Theodore Schenk, and Karim Nasser. For many Lebanese and other Arabs, Hizballah's status on the U.S. State Department's list of Foreign Terrorist Organizations (FTO) is problematic. Hizballah has had a violent past, but the organization's political party today plays a significant role in the Lebanese parliament and its social service arm has long aided the disenfranchised Shi'a of the south. Hizballah is credited with forcing Israel, after a grueling twenty years, to end its occupation of southern Lebanon and with defending this same territory against the full force of an Israeli air, sea, and land assault in 2006 (Deeb 2006). At a 2005 public forum in Dearborn, "Charitable Giving and Terrorism Sanctions," Chip Poncy, of the U.S. Treasury Department, warned Arab and Muslim Americans that they must regulate themselves to ensure that their charitable donations are not being rerouted to support terror. The audience objected to Hizballah's inclusion on the FTO list along with other organizations that oppose Israel but are not seen as a threat to the United States or to American citizens.

4. See *Detroit Free Press* articles from August 10 to August 16, 2006.

5. This program was challenged in court by the American Civil Liberties Union (ACLU) of Michigan, with support from several of the Arab and Muslim organizations mentioned elsewhere in this paper. It was found unconstitutional in a Detroit courtroom ("Ruling on Wiretaps Faces Fierce Challenge," *Detroit Free Press*, August 18, 2006, 1A).

6. Caroline Drees, "In Terror War, American 'Outreach' Has US Muslims Wary," *Reuters*, May 2006.

7. ADC Michigan and the Arab Community Center for Economic and Social Services, for example, joined the ACLU of Michigan in filing the first challenge to the USA Patriot Act in July of 2003 (ACLU press release, July 30, 2003) and have continued to advocate on behalf of local Arab and Muslim defendants in the years since.

8. For a careful analysis of "culture work" in the pre- and post-9/11 periods, see Shryock (2004).

9. This exponential growth in mosque construction corresponds to a precipitous drop in the funds given to international Islamic charities. Six of the largest and best-known Islamic charities operating between the United States and the Muslim world have been closed and their assets frozen since September 2001 ("Muslim Charity Sues Treasury Dept.," *New York Times*, December 12, 2006, 24).

10. The FBI does not utilize volunteer labor. Between 2001 and 2005, the Detroit office of the FBI hired fifteen Arabic translators. Hundreds applied, but the hurdles to employment are many. The agency has no tests for competency in Arabic beyond their "classical" Arabic written exam (Laura Waters, FBI recruitment officer, Detroit, personal communication, 2005). The Department of Homeland Security has also had a difficult time hiring and retaining Arab Americans in its Michigan offices, according to an anonymous former officer, although details have been impossible to track down. Independent security contractors have also sprung up in Michigan to handle work outsourced by federal agencies. They seem to have a better track record at hiring Arabic speakers. The former deputy

director of ADC Michigan, Rana Abbas, left her post in 2008 to become the co-director of one such private contractor, Global Linguistic Solutions.

11. See also Thacher (2005) for an excellent account of how the local/federal law enforcement pairings came about, how they were received by Arab activists, and the problematic role local police were able to play in this process.

12. By Ramadan 2007, six major Muslim charities in the United States had been closed and their assets frozen (three from Michigan). Several others were under investigation. Very few charges had been levied against any of these agencies or their employees, and the evidence against them had not been shared with those under investigation. Muslim community leaders now assert that the Treasury Department is among the least forthcoming of the federal agencies, indicating the significance of this financial warfare to the operation of the War on Terror (see Muslim Public Affairs Council 2007).

13. Iraqi Americans in the Detroit area are now regularly flown to U.S. military bases in several states to act the part of "Iraqi insurgents," "innocent civilians," and "government ministers" for military training exercises (see the Associated Press story by John Milburn, October 15, 2007, or the *New York Times* story by Robert Worth, December 27, 2003).

14. Hamad's alleged crime was to support Palestinian nationalist aspirations—through legal channels—when he was not yet a citizen. Like the thousands of Arab and Muslim men who have been detained and deported since 9/11, Hamad's deportation proceedings and citizenship appeal dragged on for years, and the evidence used against him was kept secret for "security" reasons.

15. This trend has been especially pronounced in relation to the U.S. invasion and occupation of Iraq. See *Detroit Free Press*, April 29, 2003, "Bush Shares Hopes for Iraqi Homeland," for example.

REFERENCES

Ahmed, Ismael. 2006. "Michigan Arab Americans: A Case Study of Electoral and Non-Electoral Empowerment." In *American Arabs and Political Participation*, ed. Philipa Strum. Washington, D.C.: Woodrow Wilson International Center.

Cole, David. 2003. *Enemy Aliens: Double Standards and Constitutional Freedoms in the War on Terrorism*. New York: The New Press.

Deeb, Lara. 2006. "Hizballah: A Primer." *Middle East Report Online*, May 31, http://www.merip.org/mero/mero073106.html.

Hagopian, Elaine. 2003. "The Interlocking of Right-Wing Politics and U.S. Middle East Policy: Solidifying Arab/Muslim Demonization." In *Civil Rights in Peril*, ed. Elaine Hagopian. Chicago: Haymarket Press.

Haimour, Muhannad. 2005. "Michigan Leaders Pave Way for Business in the Middle East." *Forum and Link* 1(16): 14–16.

Howell, Sally, and Andrew Shryock. 2003. "Cracking Down on Diaspora: Arab Detroit and America's 'War on Terror.'" *Anthropological Quarterly* 76(3): 443–462.

Ibish, Hussein. 2003. "The Civil Liberties of Arab Americans Post-9/11." Paper presented at the University of Michigan, October 17.

Jamal, Amaney. 2004. "Religious Identity, Discrimination and 9/11: The Determinants of Arab American Levels of Political Confidence in Mainstream and Ethnic Institutions." Paper presented at the American Political Science Association 2004 Annual Meeting, Chicago, September 4.

Muslim Public Affairs Council. 2007. "Ramadan and Anxiety over Charity." www
.mpac.org/article.php?id=528.

Powell, Colin. 2003. "Remarks at U.S.-Arab Economic Forum," Detroit, September
29. http://www.state.gov/secretary/former/powell/remarks/2003/24684.htm.

Ramirez, Deborah, Sasha Cohen O'Connell, and Rabia Zafar. 2004. *A Promising
Practices Guide: Developing Partnerships between Law Enforcement and American Muslim, Arab, and Sikh Communities.* New York: Open Society Institute.

Schlussel, Debbie. 2003. "The FBI's Outrageous Award." www.debbieschlussel.com/
columns/column091303.shtml.

Shryock, Andrew. 2004. "In the Double Remoteness of Arab Detroit: Reflections on
Ethnography, Culture Work, and the Intimate Disciplines of Americanization." In
Off Stage/On Display: Intimacy and Ethnography in the Age of Public Culture,
ed. Andrew Shryock. Palo Alto, Calif.: Stanford University Press.

State of Michigan. 2006. "Jobs Today, Jobs Tomorrow: Governor Granholm's Plan
to Revitalize Michigan's Economy." www.michigan.gov/documents/GFuturePlan.

Terry, Janice. 1999. "Community and Political Activism among Arab Americans in
Detroit." In *Arabs in America: Building a New Future?* ed. Michael Suleiman. Philadelphia: Temple University Press.

Thacher, David. 2005. "The Local Role in Homeland Security." *Law & Society Review*
39(3): 635–676.

U.S. Department of Justice. 2003. *The September 11 Detainees: A Review of the Treatment of Aliens Held on Immigration Charges in Connection with the Investigations
of the September 11 Attacks.* Washington, D.C.: U.S. Department of Justice.

Part 3

Local Refractions

Orthodox, Arab, American

The Flexibility of Christian Arabness in Detroit

MATTHEW W. STIFFLER

On a July weekend, the copper-domed church on Merriman Road in Livonia is filled with well-wishers as a young couple weds. Fifty yards away a thousand church members and fellow metro Detroiters eat *shawarma* and listen to Arabic music as part of a summer festival celebration of Orthodox Christian fellowship and Arab American cultural identity. On a typical Sunday, St. Mary's Antiochian Orthodox Basilica houses more than 500 parishioners for Divine Liturgy, but on religious holidays, such as Palm Sunday, nearly 2,000 people pack the church, requiring the Livonia police department's assistance with traffic.

The church building is not only the religious center for the Antiochian Orthodox faithful spread out amongst Detroit's western suburbs, but also a center of cultural and political life for the congregation of mostly Arab and Arab American parishioners. The founding priest, Fr. George Shalhoub, has served as pastor since 1972 when, recently arrived in the United States from seminary in Lebanon, he was sent to minister to the handful of Arab families in Livonia who wanted to start a parish.[1] In the thirty years between the church's founding and the opening of the new basilica in 2002, St. Mary's had grown from eleven parishioners to a thousands-strong membership of Lebanese, Syrian, Jordanian, and Palestinian parishioners. In fact, the number of children enrolled in church school, well over 400, is larger than the entire congregation of many Antiochian parishes nationwide.

St. Mary's impressive basilica was consecrated in the summer of 2002, just in time to host a gathering for the national day of prayer on September 11, 2002. The brand-new basilica has become a site of public gatherings, humanitarian efforts, and private prayers for peace in the wake of the 9/11 tragedies and the continued violence in the Middle East. The church building

St. Mary's basilica, the only church in the Antiochian Orthodox archdiocese to be designated a basilica, was completed in 2002. The church's architectural style and interior elements are modeled after ancient churches in the Middle East. Photograph by Matthew W. Stiffler.

was designated as a basilica by the spiritual leader of all Antiochian Orthodox in North America, Metropolitan Philip Saliba, because its architecture reflects the construction of an Old World church. As Fr. George wrote in a historical account of his life and his church, "Our task was to build an authentic Antiochian Orthodox church in America that would serve as a representation of churches in the Holy Land, and also as a point of reference for those who will never visit the Middle East" (2007, 207). Modeled after an ancient church in Syria—Fr. George's homeland and the current site of the Antiochian Patriarchate—it is the only basilica in an Antiochian Orthodox archdiocese of more than 250 parishes.

The Antiochian Orthodox church has always identified as the Arab branch of Orthodox Christianity. The church traces its heritage back to the city of Antioch, where the followers of Jesus were first called Christians, as the parishioners and Acts 11:26 will tell you. The Antiochian Patriarch in Damascus, Syria, is officially titled the Greek Orthodox Patriarch of Antioch, but the linguistic and cultural heritage of the Antiochian Orthodox is Arabic, not Greek. This Arab Christian heritage was transplanted to the United States by the first wave of immigrants from the Middle East in the late 1800s. Since the founding of the first official parish in Brooklyn, New York, in 1904, the archdiocese has grown to more than 250 parishes, and St. Mary's in Livonia is one of the largest and remains one of the most culturally Arab. Even though the archdiocese has long envisioned itself as an American Orthodox church, by dropping the word "Syrian" from the official archdiocesan name in the 1960s and by being the first Orthodox denomination to make English its official liturgical language,[2] the Antiochian Orthodox church remains, as this essay shows, a transnational ethnoreligion. As much as the church is invested in the building of an American Orthodoxy, the Arab cultural element remains crucial to the identity of the church and its parishioners, even the non-Arab converts.

An Arab identity is maintained through the liturgical use of Arabic alongside English (the amount of Arabic varies from congregation to congregation); the hierarchical connections to the Patriarch in Damascus; the continual immigration of new parishioners from the Middle East; the travel and communication between families and friends in the United States and "back home" in Palestine, Lebanon, Jordan, and Syria; the cultural celebrations of ethnic food and music that parishes from coast to coast have hosted for decades; and the consistent engagement with homeland political and humanitarian developments. St. Mary's parish in suburban Detroit is no exception and is, in fact, a microcosm of the archdiocese.

There are third- and fourth-generation Arab Americans who do not speak Arabic and have never been to the Middle East. There are Middle Eastern–born members who speak fluent Arabic and travel frequently between the United States and their homeland. And there is an increasing number (though still relatively small) of non-Arab converts, mostly as the result of marriage to a church member. Like other parishes, St. Mary's has to negotiate the issues of language (how much Arabic to use in services), politics (supporting social justice in the Middle East, particularly Lebanese or Palestinian causes), and culture (holding elaborate ethnic festivals). The members of St. Mary's are particularly concerned with balancing the idea of being an ancient Christian faith from the Holy Land while flourishing as an American Orthodox parish that is plugged in to the surrounding Detroit communities, both Arab and non-Arab.

This chapter will examine the flexible identity of the parishioners of the Antiochian Orthodox church in the Detroit area, focusing specifically on the members of St. Mary's Basilica in Livonia. The flexibility of being Arab, American, and Orthodox Christian manifests itself in the public interactions between members of the church (its leaders and its laity) and the larger metro Detroit community. I will first look at the politicized action and humanitarian support for a collective Arab homeland that church members have continually engaged with since the parish was founded in the early 1970s.[3] I will then look at the celebrations of Arab American cultural identity that occur at church-sponsored summer festivals. Both the politicized/humanitarian efforts and the cultural celebrations are times when the parishioners emphasize a distinct Arab cultural identity, but always within the space of the Christian church, and always as individuals with multiple intersecting loyalties to both the United States and their Middle Eastern homeland.

Post-9/11: Business as Usual

Although the members of the church were affected by the experience of 9/11 and its aftermath, in that there were worries about retaliations and concerns for fellow ethnics and Muslims, the members are adamant that nothing changed after 9/11 except that the parish kept growing. As one active member said about the last ten years, "The only difference is the size. It's amazing, the amount of people that are coming now. Every year it has just gotten bigger and bigger." After 9/11, as they have done for more than thirty years, parishioners continued to serve in public office, own and operate restaurants, doctor's offices, law firms, and retail spaces throughout southeastern Michigan. Parishioners and church-sponsored organizations have continued to collect and send money and humanitarian donations to Lebanese and Palestinian victims and refugees, St. Mary's has continued to host public, interfaith prayer services and cultural festivals, and church members have remained active in local Arab American organizations.

If anything was different after September 11, 2001, it was a new awareness, a tacit understanding that things were somehow *supposed* to be different. After all, being Arab in America has not always been the most enviable position. But Christians of Arab heritage have more flexibility in how they self-identify and how they market their cultural identity to the general public than Arab Muslims. Fr. George spoke of this difference between Muslim and Christian Arabs following 9/11: "I was asked this question by many senators and congressmen and FBI. But we [the people of St. Mary's] have never once had any problem. Don't forget at least in general public you do not distinguish an Orthodox from an Italian, but you can distinguish a Muslim by his habit." One parishioner, speaking about how they experienced the aftermath of 9/11 in ways that were different from Muslims, said that a congressperson met with the parish after 9/11, privileging them over the Muslims in the area and telling them they have nothing to worry about. The church building itself, with a large cross atop its copper dome, shelters the congregation from most anti-Arab sentiment. As one active female parishioner stated, "When [people] see St. Mary's, they think it's a Catholic church. They don't think of it as an Arabic church. We did have worries about what's going to happen, is there going to be retaliation . . . but outsiders don't see it as an Arabic church."

In the months after September 11, 2001, Fr. George and other Antiochian Orthodox who are active in the Arab American community, such as Dr. Haifa Fakhouri of the Arab American and Chaldean Council, were very vocal in their calls for peace and action to deter anti-Arab sentiment. Fr. George hosted or presided over numerous interfaith prayer services and the basilica itself became a prominent place for public prayer and reflection.[4] He has also been a visible and vocal advocate for peace and social justice in the Middle East in the metro Detroit area, giving speeches, attending rallies, and ministering to those affected by the violence in their homelands. In 2003, Fr. George received the Arab American of the Year Award from the Arab Community Center for Economic and Social Services (ACCESS) for his decades of dedication to the Arab American community, including his leadership after 9/11.

Eyes on the Homeland

Before and after 9/11, the parishioners of St. Mary's always mobilized in response to developments in their respective Arab homelands, whether it was in celebration of the Oslo Peace Accords in 1993, the mourning of the passing of King Hussein of Jordan in 1999, the vocal political support of Lebanon in 2006 and calls for a cease-fire, or the mobilizing of humanitarian relief during the 2008–2009 Israeli siege on Gaza. This activist mentality has long been a part of the parish. In a booklet that was produced for the 1991 dedication of their cultural center, a page of photographs of church members engaged in community service and politicized action is prefaced with the question, "What is St. Mary's?" The answer, written at the bottom of the page, is "A parish whose members take tremendous pride in their heritage and who believe that true Christians MUST speak out against injustices and man's inhumanity to man." This self-professed mission is evident in the fact that members of the church have consistently been leaders in the Arab Detroit community and that the parish collects thousands of dollars each year for humanitarian causes in the Middle East and across the world. Currently the children raise money to support an orphanage in Syria, and the parishioners regularly contribute to archdiocese-sponsored charities, like the International Orthodox Christian Charities (IOCC), which not only collected money for relief after the siege on Gaza, but also collected aid packages for quake victims in Haiti.[5]

It is well documented that the early Arab immigrants at the turn of the twentieth century organized into many types of associations, the most prominent and stable being religious. Antiochian Orthodox parishes, through their Ladies Aid Societies and affiliations with other Arab immigrant groups (e.g., the Syrian American Federation), were quick to mobilize in response to crises in the homeland as early as the famine in Lebanon during World War I. As the archdiocese became more organized, its charitable actions and societies became more formalized. Although parishes like St. Mary's maintain pet projects, such as orphanages, hospitals, and convents both in the United States and abroad, the archdiocese has officially sponsored a small number of international charities, the majority of which focus on aid to the peoples of the Middle East, particularly those of Lebanon, Palestine, Jordan, Syria, and, more recently, Iraq.

For example, in 1968 the Antiochian archdiocese established its Department of Near East and Arab Refugee Affairs, which was instrumental in coordinating donations from U.S. parishioners to causes in the Middle East. In the 1980s, in the midst of the violence of the Lebanese civil war, the church started the Children's Relief Fund, whereby parishes and individuals could sponsor a needy Lebanese child. Through the archdiocese, parishioners send money overseas throughout the year, but in times of crisis the amount of aid skyrockets. For example, in 2002 the archdiocese collected $70,000 for "Victims of Palestine," and in 2003, it collected $60,000 for "Iraqi War Victims." But in the wake of the 2006 war in Lebanon, the archdiocese contributed more than $570,000 to war relief.[6]

As Fr. George says, "Charity begins at home." And in the transnational Antiochian archdiocese, home is both the Middle East and the United States. Although there has always been a commitment to charity for Palestinian and Lebanese causes, money flows for domestic issues as well. Following the attacks of 9/11, the archdiocese and its parishioners collected $200,000 for the 9/11 victims relief fund. And in the same fiscal year that saw the massive 2006 donations to Lebanon, the parishioners stepped up and donated $453,000 to victims of Hurricane Katrina, demonstrating the commitment of the relatively small archdiocese to the United States as well as to the ancestral homelands of its members.

In addition to charitable work, Metropolitan Philip Saliba, as leader of the archdiocese for the last forty years, has been an outspoken critic of the Israeli occupation of Palestine and has always stood in solidarity with the Lebanese people during years of violent conflict. Saliba has met with numerous U.S. presidents, Yasser Arafat, and presidents of Lebanon and Syria, among other Middle Eastern leaders.[7] The archdiocese regularly passes "resolutions," voted on by priests, bishops, and delegates from every parish, that support the right of return for Palestinians or call for cease-fires whenever violence breaks out in the Middle East. For example, at the beginning of the Lebanese civil war, the archdiocese passed two resolutions regarding Lebanon at the yearly convention in 1976, calling for the preservation of the unity of

Lebanon. A summer 2001 resolution is vehement in its condemnation of Israel and calls on "all peace loving nations to support the Palestinian struggle against occupation."

The church in the Arab American experience has always been a space for political, social, and cultural causes, in addition to religious celebration. Fr. George believes the role of the church is to educate its people. His stance is best exemplified by something he has repeated on numerous occasions. He contends that the church does not legislate, but it lives in a political world and "is in the business of the human being," so there is certainly a place for the church's input. Parishioners in the Antiochian archdiocese have come to expect a certain level of engagement with political issues, especially those pertaining to the Middle East. Besides the resolutions that are debated and passed at biannual conventions, *The Word*, the century-old monthly publication of the archdiocese, routinely publishes editorials about conflicts in the Middle East, historical articles about Palestine, Lebanon, and Jordan, and advertisements for charitable organizations operating in the Middle East.

"Charity Begins at Home": The Siege on Gaza

The Antiochian church's official rhetoric trickles down to the parish level as the archdiocese frequently issues letters that are directed to be "read from the pulpit," detailing the stance of the archdiocese on actions or events in the homeland. One such letter from Metropolitan Philip Saliba addressed the Israeli siege on Gaza in the winter of 2008–2009 and was distributed to the parishioners of St. Mary's in liturgy on January 11, 2009. The letter reads, in part, "With each news update, we hear of more and more people, many of them women and children, whose lives have been abruptly and needlessly ended by the brutality of the ongoing invasion of a foreign army." Saliba then urges donations to be collected and sent through the IOCC, which was working to stave off the humanitarian crisis. Heading the call, the St. Mary's congregants took up collections to send to the victims of the fighting in Palestine, including a special collection from their annual Holy Land Christmas Concert, which featured Orthodox Christian choirs from across the Detroit area.

Throughout the siege, Fr. George's homilies addressed the violence and offered hopes for peace. For example, his homily on January 4, 2009, began:

> We gather on the first Sunday of the new year to pray as a community. We gather with a heaviness of heart and mind and soul that the world once again is at war. And this war is back home. Those who are powerful claim self-defense and those that are occupied claim a sense of humiliation. I do not know if the gun

can solve this conflict. It is when the world will stand up to defend what is right. A child is a child . . . whether Jew or Palestinian.

For liturgy on February 1, the IOCC sent a representative to the Livonia church to receive the donations that the parishioners had collected over the previous weeks. Fr. George said that the IOCC was the only charity left working in the West Bank and Gaza, which placed more urgency on the donations from the parishioners. After liturgy, the donations were formally handed over to the IOCC's representative, a young man named Peter dressed in a black cassock, who gave a speech about the cycle of violence in Gaza. Peter ended his speech by accepting the donations and saying, "Thank you for putting your faith into action."

Although sending money to Palestinian causes can be seen as a political act in the context of U.S. alignment with Israeli interests, the Orthodox parishioners, many of whom are Palestinian, see it mostly as a Christian, humanitarian act and as reaching out to their families, friends, and co-ethnics in the Middle East. As Fr. George says, "Charity starts at home," with home in this sense being Palestine. But the references in Fr. George's sermon to occupation and in Metropolitan Philip's letter to the Israelis as the "invading foreign army," do put the Antiochian stance at odds with most official and popular U.S. discourses about the Israel-Palestine issue.

When asked if they think that sending money to Palestinian causes is a political act, none of the parishioners saw it that way. They respond quickly with the fact that it is their homeland, and if they do not support the Arab people, who will? One second-generation male parishioner said:

> As long as whatever is being addressed from the pulpit is being done in the spirit of Christianity and the spirit of Christ I think it's okay. If the priest is saying our brothers in Gaza are dying, let's do something to help them. I think that's fine because you are helping the cause. There are thousands of causes out there. There's things going on in Rwanda and Darfur, and you can't help everybody. Obviously those people [the Palestinians] are much nearer and dearer to your heart.

A third-generation female parishioner sees the church's role as an educator and says of Fr. George's homilies and announcements about Gaza, "I appreciate it because I didn't understand what was going on. If the church had not taken that kind of role, I may not have known as much."

But as many scholars have noted, especially in the wake of 9/11, charitable contributions to the Middle East can be politicized,[8] even though Christian charities have not seen the same kind of scrutiny as Muslim ones. St. Mary's has never experienced any problems associated with gathering donations specifically for Palestinian causes, even when popular discourses in the United States equate Palestine with terror. It seems it is "safer" to stand in solidarity with the people of Gaza as Christians and to support a Christian-run charity, the IOCC, than to engage in the same activities from a Muslim stance.[9] Whereas in U.S. popular and political discourses the Muslim religion is stereotyped as having an inherently political agenda, Christian churches, even Arab Christian churches, are able to operate without the same assumptions about an a priori political motive.

In the Detroit area and across the country, the threat of Muslim charities being shut down and prosecuted is very real. But Christian charities, like the IOCC, that work within official U.S. networks have no concerns, even as their money eventually ends up in the same areas. In all of the recent post-9/11 scholarly work, there are no recorded instances of Christian-sponsored charities being investigated or shut down, even though the Antiochian Orthodox church runs, sponsors, or is involved in numerous charities that explicitly support Middle Eastern peoples in Palestine, Lebanon, and Iraq. As Howell and Shryock discuss in "Cracking Down on Diaspora" (this volume), this discrepancy has much to do with "reasons embedded in popular religious sentiment" in the United States that privilege Christianity, especially in the context of foreign policy matters. The flexibility available to Arab Christians who are less suspect than Arab Muslims is evident not only in politicized action and humanitarian aid, but also in the larger schema of cultural citizenship, which is the focus of the next section.

Cultural Identity within the Space of the Church

The majority of Antiochian Orthodox Christians in metro Detroit identify as Arab, though some would rather identify by nationality, such as Palestinian or Lebanese.[10] And those who do not self-identify as Arab typically have no problem being labeled Arab or Arab American, because they agree that they or their families come from what is generally known as the "Arab world," though there are a few who only identify as Lebanese and reject the label Arab. Finally, there are parishioners who are either part Arab or who are third- or fourth-generation Arab American, and do not typically identify as Arab on a daily basis. For these parishioners, an Arab cultural identity may be expressed only within the space of the church. In the Antiochian Orthodox church in the United States, religious identity is inherently wrapped up in cultural identity, so the line between being Antiochian Orthodox Christian and Arab or Arab American is often blurred.[11] One active second-generation female parishioner explained, "I'm like Greek Orthodox, but I'm an Arab, so I'm Antiochian." A second-generation parishioner said simply, "When I grew up, I used to think that in order to be Orthodox you had to be Arab."

When parishioners are asked to explain how they self-identify, they often give a cultural or national marker (Arab or Lebanese) followed quickly by a religious one (Christian or Orthodox). For many members of the Antiochian Orthodox faith, self-identifying to someone who may be unfamiliar with the nuances of Arab identity or the distinction between Arab Muslim and Arab Christian often involves a two- or three-step process of explanation and clarification. One parish council member, whose parents were born in the Middle East and who learned Arabic before English, describes the identity dance that he engages in when someone inquires about his ethnicity or background. He says he does not object to being labeled Arab American, but, "First and foremost I say I am Lebanese. Lebanon has a lighter connotation . . . especially after Bush. It's like, put you on that terrorist watch list and stuff. And then the second question is, 'Oh, are you Muslim?' because they assume all Lebanese are Muslim. Then I tell them, 'No, I am Orthodox.' 'Oh, so you are Catholic.' 'No, Catholicism stems from Orthodoxy.' " His experience is representative of many of the parishioners at St. Mary's. Antiochian Orthodox typically have canned answers to questions about their identity, not only because most Americans do not understand the difference between Arab Christians and Arab Muslims, but also because most people do not know much, or anything, about the Antiochian Orthodox church. Further, as exemplified by the quote about "especially after Bush," Antiochian Orthodox are fully aware of how their Arab identity is wrapped up in notions of U.S. cultural citizenship and global politics.[12]

A second-generation woman echoes how the identity dance that parishioners perform is a result of a general lack of knowledge about both Arab Christians and global politics. She used to call herself "Arabic," but since, as she says, "some people have a bad image of Muslims" and assume all Arabs are Muslim, "First, I say 'Palestinian.' " A female parishioner whose father's family emigrated from Syria in the 1920s says that she has always identified as Arab American, but that she would "say 'Syrian' first. But now people know Lebanese better, so it's easier to say Lebanese." Both of these women draw much of their identity from membership in the Antiochian faith and say that being active in the church has given them opportunities to speak or hear more Arabic and "reconnect" with their Arab roots. The third-generation woman, like most multigeneration Arab American Antiochian Orthodox, only hears the Arabic language in the context of church services. She sees the church as a place to maintain an Arab cultural identity and talks at length about her involvement with the ethnic food festivals that parishes hold.

A third-generation male parishioner similarly thinks that the church plays a crucial role in preserving heritage through the use of Arabic in church services. He explains, "I don't speak Arabic, but I still prefer more of it in Arabic than not. Thank God, 90 percent of our people are Arabic. My grandparents spoke it, my parents spoke it, I didn't pick it up. Maybe my kids will pick it up [from the church]." Especially for those members with Arab ancestry who do not speak Arabic or have never been to the Middle East, the weekly liturgies may be the only connection they have to the Arabic language, and the church social gatherings (*haflis*, ethnic festivals, banquets) may be a rare opportunity to eat homemade Middle Eastern foods (outside, of course, the fact that the metro Detroit area is home to hundreds of Middle Eastern restaurants).

My archival and ethnographic research with the Antiochian Orthodox archdiocese has shown that the space of the church becomes a main site where an Arab cultural identity is constructed and maintained for Antiochian parishioners. One of the sites within the church space most responsible for this construction is the ethnic food festival. Antiochian parishes across the United States have been holding ethnic food festivals as fund-raisers for nearly a century. Church-sponsored *mahrajans* (festivals) or *haflis* (parties) have been a yearly or twice-yearly tradition for most Antiochian parishes. For example, Antiochian Orthodox churches from Worcester, Massachusetts, Houston, Texas, and Oklahoma City, Oklahoma, were holding Syrian and Lebanese dinners and bake sales as early as the 1930s, in order to raise money. More recently, at least thirty-five parishes in fifteen different states have held a Middle Eastern–themed festival at some point in the last decade. Because the U.S. government pushed for communities and localities to celebrate their heritage by holding festivals as part of the celebration of the U.S. bicentennial in 1976, the 1970s was a particularly ripe decade for Antiochian parishes to market their cultural identity in festival form, and many parishes have carried on the tradition since then (Stiffler 2010).

St. Mary's is no exception and has held ethnic food festivals since its founding, when the church operated a booth as part of the Arab World Festival in downtown Detroit. Throughout the 1980s and 1990s, the church held occasional ethnic festivals, such as the "church fair" that was part of the 1992 Arab Culture Week celebration in metro Detroit. Recently, the parishioners of St. Mary's have undertaken the monumental task of building and sustaining a multiday festival every summer, complete with carnival rides, live Arabic music, and a wide selection of parishioner-made Middle Eastern foods. Dubbed the Sahara Fest, the church has held this festival over a four-day weekend in the summers of 2008, 2009, and 2010 in the large open field that abuts the church's cultural center and banquet hall.[13]

The Sahara Fest and Flexible Arabness

The 2009 Sahara Fest saw a steady stream of more than 2,000 visitors over a long weekend in July, despite the cool, rainy weather and the economic depression in southeastern Michigan. A huge, 180-foot-by-60-foot tent contained a selection of grilled sandwiches (*kafta*, *shawarma*, and falafel) and other Middle Eastern treats (*kibbee* and *zalabia*), a well-stocked bar, and a main stage that featured nonstop live music (mostly Arabic) each evening, as well as an array of vendors selling goods and services that catered to a mostly Arab or Arab American crowd. Adjacent to the tent was a modest carnival, contracted out from a national amusement company, complete with rides, games, and cotton candy.

The name Sahara Fest was chosen because it represented sunshine and the desert, which could be associated with summer. One deacon said the name was chosen for its "mystique," and one of the festival planning committee members said it was chosen because "it kind of implies Middle Eastern, but it doesn't." The title of the festival itself demonstrates the flexibility that Arab Christians have when marketing their cultural identity to the surrounding communities. They can be just Arab enough to sell authentic Middle Eastern foods, like *kafta*, *shawarma*, falafel, and *zalabia*, but not so Arab that it might drive the general public away from the celebration. After all, the point of the festival, besides the fellowship that it creates among the parishioners, is to make money for the church and serve as an invitation for the church's neighbors to explore the Orthodox faith and its culture, exemplified by the fact that St. Mary's, like other Antiochian Orthodox churches, offers church tours during the festival. Parishioners are happy to show off their impressive basilica, and neighbors that have driven past it for years may be intrigued and want to take a look inside.

The festival is a way for the St. Mary's community to introduce itself. Much like the identity dance that parishioners engage in when introducing themselves, the church has to craft a balanced presentation for the public through the Sahara Fest. Although the advertising for the festival marketed the Arabic music and Middle Eastern foods, it also stressed that the festival was sponsored by a church and would take place on church grounds. In a sense, the Sahara Fest was the church's way of greeting its neighbors by saying, effectively, "We are Arab American, but first and foremost we are Orthodox Christians. And if you don't know what Arabs or Orthodox are really about, come hang out and eat some *kafta*, dance the *dabkeh*, and admire our iconography in the sanctuary, which tells the story of our faith."

I was fortunate enough to have the festival planning committee allow me to sit in on the planning process for the festival (and I was even lucky enough to be put to work on numerous occasions). The discussions about the advertising and marketing of the festival were the most fascinating and revealing. Because the metro Detroit area is home to such a large Arab and Arab American population, there never seemed to be any anxieties about the local population perceiving the Antiochian parishioners as being potentially dangerous Arab "enemy others," which is a dominant discourse about Arabs in both the U.S. media and popular culture.[14] This is not to say that there were not considerations of how the festival would be perceived by non-Arab members of the surrounding localities. Even though the church was located in such close proximity to Dearborn, the heart of Arab America in the region, the church grounds were still smack dab in the middle of one of the whitest Detroit suburbs. The anxieties of self-representation stemmed from not wanting to alienate a large part of the potential customer base by being too ethnic, by offering only Arabic music and not including "American" music. The balance between appeasing "our community" and the "Americans" was a subtext for many of the decisions regarding the marketing of the festival.

The colorful festival poster that was posted and distributed throughout the surrounding suburbs contained no direct references to Middle Eastern or Arab culture, other than the ambiguously desert-sounding title. The poster listed "Food, Rides, and Live Music," and not "ethnic food" or "Arabic music." The host for the festival was simply listed at "St. Mary's Church." The poster conveyed what the committee was hoping for all along: that the Sahara Fest would be a fun, family-friendly summer event. That the festival was also a space for the celebration of an Arab cultural identity was a given to the committee and members of the Antiochian community, who did not feel the need to constantly broadcast this fact. Their hope was that "Americans" or "white people," as non-Arabs were typically referred to, would come and enjoy the festival, regardless of the ethnic component. However, discussions during pre- and post-festival meetings revealed that some committee members wanted to play up the Middle Eastern or Mediterranean (historically a popular substitute for "Middle Eastern" among Arab Americans in the marketing of their food) themes of the festival, hoping to capitalize on what has become a popular niche market in the United States. As one member proclaimed, "People love cultural festivals!"

When the first blurb was published in a local weekly newspaper, some of the anxieties about how to represent the festival became the main topic of discussion. At a meeting one month before the festival, the entire committee

Poster for the 2009 Sahara Fest.

read the blurb that had been published that day. The first reactions were that it was great to finally see some publicity. The chairperson, though, had one critique: "I wish she [referring to the woman at the paper who drafted the blurb] would have left out the Arabic names," referring to the end of article, which listed the nationalities represented at St. Mary's as Jordanian, Lebanese, Palestinian, and Syrian. An older, American-born member of the committee was also concerned and thought any publicity should "leave the Middle East out" because it might turn people off. The people he was referring to were the non-Antiochians and the non-Arabs that the committee was intent on attracting in order to have a more financially successful festival.

Between the publishing of the first blurb and the printing of the full-page color ads in numerous newspapers weeks later, the marketing became much more ethnic. Given that there are countless carnivals and festivals throughout the summer, the festival committee realized that they would have to distinguish themselves. Whereas the poster, printed in early June, announced "Food, Rides, and Live music," the July newspaper ads proclaimed "Carnival Rides, Middle Eastern Food, Music & Dancing" and boasted "a delicious assortment of Middle Eastern cuisine including: Chicken Shawarma, Beef Shawarma, Falafel, Taboulie, Hummus, Zalabieh."

Regardless of the marketing, the July festival announced to the surrounding Livonia neighborhoods that the parishioners of St. Mary's not only are largely of Arab heritage, but also are active components of the larger Arab Detroit community. This was most evident in the presence of prominent Arab and Arab American organizations as sponsors and vendors at the festival. ACCESS, the area's largest Arab American organization, handed out pamphlets and other information. Arab Detroit, an Arab American media organization that helped with the advertising of the festival, also sponsored a table to hand out a free audio CD of a local Arab American musician and to sign people up for their e-mail list. These organizations set up shop at the Sahara Fest because they knew the majority of the attendees would be Arab or Arab American. The same reasoning attracted the U.S. Census Bureau. With the slogan "Census 2010" printed in English and Arabic on their poster, U.S. census workers from the local Detroit office were hoping to spread the word about the upcoming census, particularly to Arab immigrants. The presence of leading Arab organizations and the U.S. Census Bureau at the festival shows that the church is seen as a vital part of the Detroit Arab American community.

As Fr. George will tell you, it is no accident that the members of St. Mary's decided to begin hosting a large-scale ethnic festival, even in the wake of September 11, 2001: "A hundred years ago Arab Americans were embarrassed or afraid to show who they are, so you find many of their generation could not wait until they abandoned, quote-unquote, all tradition or their language, so they would look pure American. Today it's fashionable to be different." It certainly is fashionable, and very American, to be different, especially in the context of church-sponsored ethnic festivals. Liberal multiculturalism is very accepting of an ethnic group's celebration and commodification of their culture, specifically through food and music, as long as those cultural celebrations do not assert any overtly political agenda. As cultural critic Lisa Lowe has

A typical scene under the tent at the 2010 Sahara Fest. Young men smoke *argileh* while mostly women *dabkeh* in front of the stage. Photograph by Matthew W. Stiffler.

famously claimed, multiculturalism "is concerned with 'importation,' not 'immigration,'" as the general U.S. public loves to purchase cultural artifacts (such as food and music) but only outside the social and political reality in which the peoples who generate and sell those artifacts exist (Lowe 1996, 87).

The Sahara Fest was designed to be an apolitical space. Even though the parishioners and clergy at St. Mary's continually work for social justice and humanitarian issues in the Middle East, those agendas were largely absent from the festival. There were no speeches about the continued sufferings of the Palestinian people and there were no collections taken for humanitarian relief. Further, none of the proceeds from the festival would be sent to charities working in the Middle East.[15] The church-sponsored ethnic food festival is not a space for political agendas, especially when the cultural identity being celebrated is an Arab one. With all of the negative connotations of Arabs in the media and popular culture, the Arab cultural identity presented at the Sahara Fest had to mediate those stereotypes by offering a counterrepresentation that shows Arabs and Arab Americans as having a rich heritage of food, music, and religion, that exists outside of the discourses of the War on Terror.

The Sahara Fest is a flexible space: it is Arab, but not too Arab. The festival allows church members to be simultaneously Orthodox Christian, ethnic American, and part of the Arab Detroit community. But even membership in the Arab Detroit community is mediated through Christianity. In other words, the festival, with its Arabic music, food, *argileh*, tables from ACCESS and Arab Detroit, and the flyers in Arabic and English from the U.S. Census Bureau, are all in the shadow of the Orthodox Christian basilica that dominates the landscape of the festival.[16]

As exemplified by the planning and celebration of the Sahara Fest, the parishioners of St. Mary's understand their position as (1) members of a larger Arab Detroit community, (2) participants in the U.S. multicultural industry that privileges depoliticized expressions of culture, especially within an ethnoreligious context,[17] and (3) Orthodox Christians of Arab ancestry with a political and humanitarian commitment to their Middle Eastern homeland, which is also the birthplace of their ancient Christian faith.[18] This multifaceted positionality is the same post-9/11 as it was in the 1970s when a handful of immigrant families planted the seeds for the continuously growing parish. By virtue of being Arab *and* Christian, the parishioners and leadership of St. Mary's are able to deploy a flexible identity, sometimes more Arab, sometimes mostly American, but always Orthodox Christian.

Notes

This essay is based on ethnographic fieldwork with the Antiochian Orthodox archdiocese, specifically St. Mary's Basilica in Livonia, Mich., from 2008 to 2010. A portion of the early stage of fieldwork was funded by the Institute for Signifying Scriptures at Claremont Graduate University, Claremont, California. I am indebted to my mentors Nadine Naber and Andrew Shryock for their guidance throughout my graduate studies and particularly with this project. I am grateful to the clergy and parishioners of St. Mary's, especially Fr. George Shalhoub, Fr. Jim King, Stacey Badeen, and the festival planning committee.

1. St. Mary's was founded as Antiochian Orthodox parishioners began moving and settling further from the city of Detroit. There was already a large Antiochian Orthodox church in Detroit, St. George, which is one of the oldest in the Midwest, having been founded in 1916. St. George eventually followed its membership to the suburbs as well, building a church in Troy in the 1980s.

2. The Antiochian Orthodox archdiocese is often confused with the Syrian Orthodox church (which is based in a Syriac tradition, not Greek. The Antiochian and Syrian Orthodox Churches are not in communion, though they both claim ties to biblical Antioch). Part of the confusion is because the Antiochian Orthodox archdiocese in the United States was known as the Syrian Antiochian Orthodox archdiocese until 1969, when the national label of "Syrian" was dropped in favor of emphasizing the church's roots in the biblical city of Antioch. In the United States, the Antiochian Orthodox outnumber the Syrian Orthodox, which maintains about twenty parishes.

3. The term "collective Arab homeland" reflects the ways that the parishioners and church leaders envision their relationship to the Middle East. Since the archdiocese is made up of Lebanese, Palestinian, Syrian, Jordanian, and a small number of Iraqis, whenever there is a crisis in one of these countries, the church treats it as an issue "back home." Further, because the parishioners come from multiple Arab countries, unlike the almost wholly Lebanese Maronites or the Iraqi Chaldeans, Antiochian cultural celebrations are not tied to one national identity.

4. Consider the following description of Fr. George:

> "Abouna," as Father George is called with affection by his congregants, has a world-view that extends far beyond his parish, and was asked by the White House to celebrate an ecumenical service on the year anniversary of 9/11. Nearly five thousand people, including parishioner Spencer Abraham, showed up. The service included a rousing rendition of "God Bless America."
>
> A surprising song selection for a religious ceremony? Perhaps, but, says Father George with an amused nod, "I've always been fairly non-conforming, even in the seminary."
>
> To this day, Father George displays not only a magnetic spirituality, but also fixity of purpose and confidence in his faith, his family, and his adopted country. (Famie 2007)

5. The Antiochian archdiocese was instrumental in the founding of the IOCC in 1992. An important aspect of this organization is that its "mandate is to undertake purely humanitarian activities. Thus, IOCC does not support programs of Church mission (Church reconstruction, religious education, seminary support, etc.)" (International Orthodox Christian Charities 2010). The IOCC is "registered with the U.S. Agency for International Development and is eligible to receive funds for foreign assistance from the U.S. Government. It is a member of InterAction, a coalition of U.S. based non-governmental organizations that carry out humanitarian assistance programs overseas" (ibid.).

6. As of 2009, the Department of Antiochian Charities maintained three named charities, the Children's Relief Fund, the Worldwide Relief Fund (formerly known as the Middle Eastern Relief Fund), and Food for Hungry People, all of which support people in the Middle East. All of the figures were taken from "Minutes of the General Assembly" of the archdiocese's biannual conventions, which are printed annually in the November issue of *The Word*.

7. Saliba has endured his share of criticism. In 1977, because of his efforts to get the National Council of Churches to adopt a more balanced Middle Eastern policy, a rabbi from the American Jewish Committee accused Saliba of being a "paid Arab propagandist," according to a Religious News Service article published in *The Word* in May 1977.

8. There are numerous recent works that address the politicization of humanitarian aid in the context of the War on Terror. Other than Howell and Shryock's essay in this volume, see Bellion-Jourdan (2007), Ophir (2007), Bakalian and Bozorgmehr (2009), and Cainkar (2009). All of these scholarly sources, though, focus on Muslim charities and religious organizations.

9. Although the charities of the archdiocese are born of Christian values and their missions are supported by biblical references, the aid they deliver is not intended exclusively for Christians. This does upset a few of the more nationalist Lebanese parishioners who do not want to send aid to Palestinian Muslims, but they are a vocal minority in the parish and the archdiocese.

10. I use the term "cultural identity" instead of "ethnicity," partly because ethnicity within Orthodox Christianity typically refers only to the national marker of a specific denomination (Greek Orthodox, Russian Orthodox, etc.). I also follow Appadurai (1996),

who argues that ethnicity is seen as the "naturalization of group identity," whereas cultural identity can be seen as a "conscious and imaginative construction and mobilization of difference" (13, 14). I still use the word "ethnic" in instances where it serves as an accepted compound noun, such as ethnic food or ethnic festival.

My ethnographic results reflect the findings of the Detroit Arab American Study (DAAS) (2009) and show the complexities surrounding the label "Arab" in the metro Detroit area. The DAAS reports that 84 percent of Orthodox identified as Arab American. The DAAS team found that some individuals saw themselves more as American than Arab, even if those individuals "watch Arabic satellite television and attend a church where most people speak Arabic" (Baker and Shryock 2009, 19). Some identified more with a nationality (Iraqi, Lebanese, etc.), and some did not identify as Arab at all. Additionally, and this is the case for many of the third- and fourth-generation Arab Americans, "others may know that they have a parent or grandparent of, say, Syrian descent, and are proud of this heritage, but seldom identify as Arab in their everyday lives" (Baker and Shryock 2009, 19).

11. This mirrors the findings of the DAAS, as Howell and Jamal state, "Detroit's churches and mosques are organized around beliefs and practices that lend a sacred quality to ethnic and national identities" (2009, 125).

12. Not only has the DAAS shown that in the context of the War on Terror some Christians in Arab Detroit tend to downplay the label "Arab" because of their understanding of their positionality within the War on Terror and its relation to Islam, but also a research project that I took part in among Christians from the Arab world living in metro Detroit found that identifying with or choosing not to identify with the marker "Arab" was grounded within global politics. See Naber, Stiffler, Tayyen, and Said (2010).

13. St. Mary's also produced large-scale ethnic festivals in 2004 and 2005, but they were not referred to as the Sahara Fest.

14. Nadine Naber (2008) outlines the development of the discourses of an Arab/Muslim enemy. Amaney Jamal (2008, 116–117) argues that Arabs and Muslims are characterized as "enemy Others," which helps the state justify infringements on civil liberties.

15. The proceeds for the festival support the planned construction of the Mariam Center for Family and Youth Enrichment at St. Mary's, which is envisioned as a cultural and community center for people of all ages, faiths, and cultural backgrounds.

16. See Sally Howell and Amaney Jamal (2009), who argue that "Muslim congregations . . . have fewer means by which to escape the stigma now associated with Arabness and Islam in America" (107). Jen'nan Ghazal Read (2008, 305–306) also found that Christians of Arab ancestry "may be able to use their Christian identity as a bridge to the American mainstream" and that Muslims have "fewer 'ethnic options' than their Christian peers."

17. Scholars, like Raymond Brady Williams, have long pinpointed religion as the "social category with the clearest meaning and acceptance" in the United States (Warner and Wittner 1998, 16). In the context of ethnic marketing, the Christian church in the United States had also come to serve as a main site of community and ethnic marketing and fund-raising, with community potlucks, festivals, bazaars, and the publication of ethnic cookbooks (Gabaccia 1998, 188–189). It was a very American idea for the Antiochian Orthodox parishioners to associate their ethnicity with, and base it in, their religious space.

18. Regardless of their ethnic backgrounds and their commitments to their collective homeland, the space of the church is first and foremost a space for parishioners to share a commitment to seeking spiritual engagement with the divine through worship and prayer.

REFERENCES

Appadurai, Arjun. 1996. *Modernity at Large: Cultural Dimensions of Globalization*. Minneapolis: University of Minnesota Press.

Bakalian, Anny, and Mehdi Bozorgmehr. 2009. *Backlash 9/11: Middle Eastern and Muslim Americans Respond*. Berkeley: University of California Press.

Baker, Wayne, and Andrew Shryock. 2009. "Citizenship and Crisis." In *Citizenship and Crisis: Arab Detroit after 9/11*, by the Detroit Arab American Study Team, 3–32. New York: Russell Sage Foundation.

Bellion-Jourdan, Jérôme. 2007. "Are Muslim Charities Purely Humanitarian? A Real but Misleading Question." In *Nongovernmental Politics*, ed. Michael Feher, 647–657. New York: Zone Books.

Cainkar, Louise A. 2009. *Homeland Insecurity: The Arab American and Muslim American Experience after 9/11*. New York: Russell Sage Foundation.

Detroit Arab American Study Team. 2009. *Citizenship and Crisis: Arab Detroit after 9/11*. New York: Russell Sage Foundation.

Famie, Keith. 2007. "Fr. George H. Shalhoub, St. Mary Antiochian Orthodox Church." *Our Arab American Story*, http://www.ourstoryof.com/arabic/production_18.html.

Gabaccia, Donna R. 1998. *We Are What We Eat: Ethnic Food and the Making of Americans*. Cambridge, Mass.: Harvard University Press.

Howell, Sally, and Amaney Jamal. 2009. "Belief and Belonging." In *Citizenship and Crisis: Arab Detroit after 9/11*, by the Detroit Arab American Study Team, 103–134. New York: Russell Sage Foundation.

International Orthodox Christian Charities. 2010. "Mission and Focus." http://iocc.org/aboutiocc_mission.

Jamal, Amaney. 2008. "Civil Liberties and the Otherization of Arab and Muslim Americans." In *Race and Arab Americans before and after 9/11: From Invisible Citizens to Visible Subjects*, ed. Amaney Jamal and Nadine Naber, 114–130. Syracuse, N.Y.: Syracuse University Press.

Lowe, Lisa. 1996. *Immigrant Acts: On Asian American Cultural Politics*. Durham, N.C.: Duke University Press.

Naber, Nadine. 2008. "Introduction: Arab Americans and U.S. Racial Formation." In *Race and Arab Americans before and after 9/11: From Invisible Citizens to Visible Subjects*, ed. Amaney Jamal and Nadine Naber, 1–45. Syracuse, N.Y.: Syracuse University Press.

Naber, Nadine, Matthew Stiffler, and Sana Tayyen, with Atef Said. 2010. "Christians and Muslims from the Arab Region: Between U.S. Empire, Homeland Politics, and the Pressures of Racism and Assimilation." An Ethnographic Study about Religious and Scriptural Engagements among Maronite Catholics, Orthodox Christians, and Sunni Muslims. Unpublished paper.

Ophir, Adi. 2007. "The Sovereign, the Humanitarian, and the Terrorist." In *Nongovernmental Politics*, ed. Michael Feher, 161–181. New York: Zone Books.

Read, Jen'nan Ghazal. 2008. "Discrimination and Identity Formation in a Post-9/11 Era: A Comparison of Muslim and Christian Arab Americans." In *Race and Arab Americans before and after 9/11: From Invisible Citizens to Visible Subjects*, ed. Amaney Jamal and Nadine Naber, 305–317. Syracuse, N.Y.: Syracuse University Press.

Shalhoub, George H. 2007. *Called by Grace to a Journey of Faith: The Story of a Group of Immigrant Families from the Middle East Who Placed "A Gift Upon the Lap of America."* Livonia, Mich.: Antiochian Orthodox Basilica of St. Mary.

Stiffler, Matthew. 2010. "Authentic Arabs, Authentic Christians: Antiochian Orthodox and the Mobilization of Cultural Identity." PhD diss., University of Michigan.

Warner, R. Stephen, and Judith G. Wittner. 1998. "Immigration and Religious Communities in the United States." In *Gatherings in Diaspora: Religious Communities and the New Immigration*, ed. R. Stephen Warner and Judith G. Wittner, 3–34. Philadelphia: Temple University Press.

Fighting Our Own Battles

Iraqi Chaldeans and the War on Terror

YASMEEN HANOOSH

Chaldean immigrants to the United States began to form a visible cluster in Detroit in the 1920s (Sengstock 1982). Today, members of this Catholic Iraqi minority who settle in the United States encounter multiple options for reconfiguring, consolidating, and negotiating their ethnicity. The United States is a host country where, in most cases, they have family and kin who are already well established. As recently arrived Chaldean migrants struggle to create new identities and secure their economic status, the established diasporic Chaldeans work to gain recognition in the United States and internationally, all the while maintaining links to an original homeland that must be continually reinvented, and reimagined, from afar. In this manner, Chaldean immigrants have exhibited assimilative tendencies, refurbished traditions they or their families brought from Iraq, and forged new identities that combine innovation and renovation in ways that, across several decades and generations, have come to define the hyphenated identity "Chaldean-American."

Whether they reside in Iraq, the United States, or other countries, the social lives of Chaldeans are complex; they cannot be adequately understood by looking only at what happens within the boundaries of a single nation-state. This is especially so when attempting to make sense of the political and cultural initiatives Chaldeans have undertaken during the War on Terror. Understanding how multiple locations and affiliations have intersected to shape Chaldean identities calls for a new methodology that transcends the standard focus on integration (or exclusion) in the country of settlement. This new method needs to account for the ethnic, religious, and political mobilization of Chaldeans across national boundaries. In this essay, I will interpret the U.S.-based Chaldean diaspora as a "transnational social field" in which

126

community spaces are constantly reconfigured by the transnational activities that transpire within them.

Several factors make it necessary to analyze Chaldeans as a transnational diasporic community. For one, contemporary Chaldean immigrants in the United States cannot be called "transmigrants" because most of them do not lead a daily life that "depends on multiple and constant interconnections across international borders," nor do they frequently travel back and forth between a "sending" nation-state and a "receiving" one (Schiller, Basch, and Szanton Blanc 1995). However, like the identities of transmigrants who maintain strong ties to their countries of origin, the public identities of Chaldean immigrants in Detroit are made in relation to two nation-states, Iraq and the United States, and to the many stations along their way out of Iraq, where asylum seekers, refugees, and migrants move toward preferred destinations. Moreover, in recent decades Chaldeans have been forging multifaceted cultural and economic relations between their society of origin and new settlements in the United States and elsewhere, a process that migration scholars identify as characteristic of "transnational migration." I will examine several Chaldean transnational projects in this essay. Before introducing them, however, I should first consider what makes these projects, and the people who envision and pursue them, Chaldean.

Ingredients of the Official Narrative

When U.S.-based Chaldeans explain to other Americans "who modern Chaldeans are," they offer descriptions containing some or all of the following identity tropes:

1. Modern Chaldeans are the offspring of the founders of the first civilizations, the Chaldeans and Assyrians, whose existence predates Christianity by a few thousand years.
2. They originate in the village of Telkeif, in modern-day Iraq.
3. They speak Aramaic, "the language of Jesus."
4. They are devout Catholics.
5. They are hardworking, successful entrepreneurs.
6. They are community and family oriented.

These components are stable, uniform identity benchmarks. They appear in tabloid versions on official Web sites and Internet forum discussions, in community publications, in documentary videos, and in the verbal accounts culture-makers use to instruct anyone—a non-Chaldean "outsider" or an uninformed Chaldean "insider"—who wants to learn more about Chaldeans.

When it comes to Mesopotamian antiquity, the earliest identifiable Chaldeans were Aramaeans (though nowadays some question this assumption) who settled in southern Iraq, forming the basis of the neo-Babylonian revival of the last dynasty of Babylon. The Chaldean (Babylonian) Empire fell in 539 BC, leaving no evidence of tangible racial connections that are exclusive to the ancient and modern Chaldeans. Moreover, with respect to language, the modern Chaldeans of the Nineveh Plains speak dialects of neo-Aramaic, and most cannot read or write the script. For the greater part of today's city-dwelling Chaldeans, Arabic or English is the main language, depending on their settlement locations.

The recent popularity of "Mesopotamia" in identity discourses that describe the homeland of the modern Chaldeans signals a revivalist tendency. This ancestral location—literally, the fertile land between the Tigris and Euphrates rivers—has not officially existed under a single name, as a unified political entity, for centuries. Historical Mesopotamia comprises parts of present-day Syria, Iran, Armenia, and Iraq, whereas modern Chaldeans trace their lineage to the Nineveh Plains, a region in northern Iraq, and often, among U.S.-based Chaldeans, the essential point of origin is located in a single village in that region, Telkeif.

Although the term "Chaldean" seems to have been used interchangeably with other designations, such as Syriac, Nestorian, and Assyrian, to refer to the Christians of Mesopotamia before AD 1445, the followers of the present Chaldean church were officially called the Christians of the "Church of the East." This name was given to them after a split with the Catholic Church that began to develop possibly as early as AD 325, with the first Ecumenical Council of Nicaea, a council prompted by a dispute with the Roman Catholic Church over the definition of Christ's human and divine nature. It appears that the term "Chaldean" in the Christian era was officially recognized for the first time in AD 1445 by Pope Eugenius IV. This recognition took place when a group of Mesopotamian Christians reaffiliated with the Catholic Church following a separation of more than eleven centuries (Baum and Winkler 2003).

Those referred to as "Chaldeans" continued to populate the villages of the Nineveh Plains during the rule of the Ottoman Empire. Their legal status as *dhimmis* under the millet system allowed them protective privileges from the Ottoman authorities as well as limited autonomy under the direct leadership of their Patriarchs, who were in charge of organizing the religious as well as the social life of their communities. After World War I, the Chaldeans, along with other Christian groups in the area, were granted the status of religious minorities by the newly formed Iraqi monarchy, a status they held well into the twentieth century (Joseph 2000).

By 1988, the Iraqi census revealed that approximately 5 percent of the Iraqi population was Christian, with the Chaldeans comprising the largest of the Christian minorities in the country, and arguably the only Christian body native to the land (Bazzi 1991).[1] For doctrinal reasons, Chaldeans and Assyrians separated and reunited under the same ecclesiastical orders several times over the centuries. For political reasons, the various Iraqi regimes indiscriminately lumped Chaldeans and Assyrians together as a single "religious minority" during most of the twentieth century. More recently, and mainly from their diasporic settlements, both groups have been attempting to reclaim their status as ethnic minorities in Iraq and elsewhere. In specific contexts, the two communities have come together under the hyphenated title Assyro-Chaldeans or Chaldo-Assyrians to assert that they form a homogenous and unified community; in other contexts, they have sought to assert their autonomous status as Chaldeans and Assyrians (Hanish 2008). Chaldeans and Assyrians in the American diaspora converge on many cultural and political issues, but they also diverge on issues of identity and nationalist affiliation in Iraq.

The first Chaldean immigrant to America has been identified as Zia Attalla, who reportedly arrived in the United States in 1889 (Sengstock 1983, 137; 2005, 3), but it was not until World War I and the subsequent massacres of Christian groups who lived in the southeastern region of modern Turkey and northern Iraq[2] (Hidirsah 1997, 27–30; Matar 2000, 107–117) that Chaldeans were impelled to seek asylum abroad. From the 1920s to the 1960s, political and economic turmoil—the offshoot of alternately falling out of favor with Arab, Turkish, Persian, and Kurdish powers in the region—prompted a number of Iraqi Catholic men to seek refuge in the Americas. Most of these individuals and their descendants trace their origins to the northern Iraqi village of Telkeif (Sengstock 1982, 2005; Gallagher 1999; "Chaldean Household Survey" 2007; Sarafa n.d., a, b). A majority of Chaldeans who first immigrated to multiple destinations in the United States were congregating in Detroit by the 1920s, drawn by the stable wages and low-skilled jobs available on Henry Ford's automobile assembly lines. A deteriorating political and economic scene in the homeland continued to fuel Chaldean migration from Iraq to Detroit. Added to this "push" was the "pull" of favorable modifications to U.S. immigration laws facilitating family-based chain migration, which began to reunite male immigrants with their relatives in the mid-1960s.

Since 1991, in the wake of the first Gulf War, new waves of Chaldean immigrants have entered the United States. Roughly 5,000 Chaldean immigrants are thought to have come to the United States during the early 1990s

(Betzold 1992, cited in Gallagher 1999, 5). Approximately 50,000 Chaldeans fled to Jordan as refugees during the United Nations' economic embargo on Iraq (1991–2003). The U.S. invasion of Iraq in 2003 escalated the internal displacement of Chaldeans and their search for asylum and refuge outside Iraq. Many Chaldean city dwellers returned to their ancestral villages in northern Iraq, and alarmed community reports estimate that 200,000 Christians (most of them Chaldean) left Iraq between 2003 and 2007 (Warikoo 2007). While at least half these migrants are believed to be in transit countries such as Jordan, Syria, Lebanon, and Turkey, others have relocated to refugee camps in European cities (Harris 2007). Another segment of this refugee population is making its way to the United States to join with family. By 2009, the U.S. Refugees Admission Program had admitted 19,910 Iraqi refugees to the United States, many of whom were Chaldeans (Fact Sheet 2009).

Institutional Circuits

While individual migrants create networks across state boundaries to achieve personal goals through kinship ties (e.g., transnational marriages, financial remittances, and the buildup of an ethnic economy), diasporic Chaldean institutions pursue a similarly transnational path, fostering group interest in broader collective issues. These issues include, but are not limited to, the maintenance of religious identity, the preservation of the Chaldean language, ethnic solidarity, and the provision of legal assistance in matters such as establishing a Christian settlement in Iraq and helping Chaldean refugees immigrate to America.

U.S.-based Chaldean institutional circuits are gradually becoming more intricate and wide-ranging in the ways they mobilize ideas and resources for specific community projects. Their success is evident in extremely high levels of participation, with 64 percent of Michigan-based Chaldeans belonging to some sort of community organization, a figure more than twice as high as the average participation level among non-Chaldean Americans (Henrich and Henrich 2007, 87). Organized, institutionally mobilized, and sustained connections between U.S.-based Chaldeans and the homeland require the involvement of political, economic, and cultural elites who share a commitment to transnational projects. Therefore, it is crucial to explore this emergent constituency of the U.S.-based Chaldean elites who make up the leadership of these transnational networks.

After identifying the role of this elite segment of the community, I will discuss three recent examples that effectively characterize the formal component of Chaldean transnational activity: (1) voting in the Iraqi elections, (2) the Nineveh Plains settlement project, and (3) Operation R-4, the campaign currently being waged on behalf of Chaldean refugees. All three projects involve extending the boundaries of citizenship (both U.S. and Iraqi) and reorganizing Chaldeans in the United States to act on behalf of Chaldeans in Iraq or contribute financially to improve the circumstances under which Iraqi Chaldeans are living.

Networks of Communal Elites

Questions of internal power are critical for understanding the transnational Chaldean diaspora. If, following Pnina Werbner's (2000) model, the U.S.-based Chaldeans are an example of a community of co-responsibility, wherein the advantaged are responsible for the disadvantaged, the rich and powerful for the poor and weak, then Chaldean cultural products and collective representations should be flowing from the stronger diasporic center(s) to the weaker multinational peripheries. In the case of the Chaldean community in Michigan, these centers of power are formed around diasporic elites composed of clergymen, businessmen, and wealthy philanthropists who, as Khachig Tölölyan puts it in his analogous study of the Armenian diaspora, "passionately share the conflicts that divide it" (2000, 114).

The Chaldean elites in Michigan are predominantly individuals who have relatives or acquaintances of Telkeifi descent (Sengstock 1974, 24).[3] The majority of their institutions are located in or near the city of West Bloomfield, Michigan—one of the five wealthiest suburbs in the United States. These elites and their institutions have always assumed responsibilities that are simultaneously philanthropic, cultural, and political. Over time, by virtue of the diasporic community's long-standing transnational activities through family, business, and church involvements, the issues that animate elite politics, economy, and aesthetics are shifting beyond the local to the transnational. To understand how a Chaldean ethnogeographic self-localization is emerging simultaneously with transnational political activity, one must first understand how these institutions and individuals have orchestrated their powers and channeled them into a single stream of action and publicity over recent decades.

There are 34,000 to 113,000 Chaldeans in Michigan alone (U.S. Census Bureau 2000; Sengstock 2005; "Chaldean Household Survey" 2007; "Household Demographic Survey," *Chaldean News*, May 5, 2008, 30; Sarafa n.d., a, b;); about a quarter of that estimate in other American states;[4] roughly 50,000 refugees in Syria, Jordan, and other parts of the Middle East; and a rapidly dwindling 400,000 in Iraq. A public, collective, unifying, anonymous narrative of who all these Chaldeans *are*, how they differ from the Iraqi Muslim majority, what their sociopolitical needs and demands consist of, and how they relate to the former and current political climate in Iraq and the

United States is being fostered, updated, and broadcast in American mainstream media and local community media by a local Chaldean elite and the institutions they represent in Oakland County, Michigan. Some of these institutions, their founding date, and the city in which they are headquartered (all Michigan unless otherwise specified) include:[5]

- Chaldean Americans Reaching and Encouraging (CARE) (1997, West Bloomfield)
- Chaldean American Ladies of Charity (CALC) (1961, Southfield)
- Shenandoah Country Club (2005, West Bloomfield)
- Chaldean Iraqi Association of Michigan (CIAM) (1943, Detroit)
- Chaldean Community Cultural Center (CCC) (Not yet officially established, Shenandoah Country Club, West Bloomfield)
- Chaldean Federation of America (CFA) (1982, Farmington Hills)
- Chaldean American Chamber of Commerce (2003, Farmington Hills)
- *Chaldean News* (magazine) (2004, Farmington Hills)
- Chaldean Assyrian Syriac Council of America (CASCA) (2007, no specific location)

There are numerous other Chaldean institutions in southeast Michigan that coordinate efforts with those listed above to address local needs. Churches are central among them, but what I wish to emphasize here is how these organizations operate symbiotically, and sometimes through family linkages, to mobilize transnational agendas that involve ethnicity, rather than religion in the strict sense, as their common denominator.

Founded, funded, and managed by the diasporic elites, these institutions (five of which materialized only within the last decade) have been collaboratively shoring up the functions of cultural re/production, promoting the common goal of introducing to the American mainstream, and subsequently to international audiences, one *legitimate* Chaldean culture that extends beyond state boundaries. Moreover, together these institutions labor to construct a diasporic civil society that nurtures and sustains a Chaldean public sphere of cultural production maintained by a growing constituency of Chaldean teachers, activists, journalists, investors, professionals, and performers who are associated with or dependent on these institutions. Here, briefly, is how the symbiotic circuits work.

A Symbiotic Circuit

Chaldean Americans Reaching and Encouraging was founded in 1997 by a group of young Chaldeans, both students and professionals, as a community-based organization with a commitment to "humanitarian needs" and to "strengthening and preserving our culture." Initially, CARE was sponsored by a "mother" institute, the Chaldean American Ladies of Charity, founded in 1961. As a nonprofit, church-annexed organization, the CALC works mainly through raising and distributing donations among Chaldean families in the area, with the chief objectives of "enhancing the lives of the people in our community . . . and maintaining our culture within the diverse community in which we live" (CALC Web site, http://www.calconline.org). In addition to working with Chaldeans in Oakland County's public schools and senior citizen homes, both CARE and the CALC regularly sponsor community events that are held either in St. Thomas Chaldean Catholic Church (West Bloomfield), Mother of God Church (Southfield), Southfield Manor Club (Southfield), or the neighboring Shenandoah Country Club. The CALC, which was founded through a clerical initiative, now financially backs the Chaldean Patriarch Emanuel III Delly, who in turn uses some of the funds to sponsor the Chaldean church and seminaries in Iraq (Konja 2005). And most recently, CALC members have been involved in creating the CCC in the neighboring Shenandoah Country Club.

Next on the list is the Shenandoah Country Club. It opened in 2005, but the idea of "building a community center that would unite all Chaldeans" had been in the making since the influx of Chaldeans to the Detroit area in the 1960s (Jabiro 2005). Sami Kassab, a grocer for more than thirty years and a pioneer member of the Chaldean Iraqi Association of Michigan (CIAM, later CIAAM, Chaldean Iraqi American Association of Michigan), was one of the first Chaldeans to conceptualize a project for social consolidation. Kassab and a group of twenty-five Chaldean men first formed the Chaldean Youth Club with the idea of creating a gathering place, "especially for future generations." Later in the 1970s, when the Chaldean diocese sponsored the building of the Mother of God Church, it sold the remaining lot to this group of Chaldeans, who sought to create a community center. In 1979, the plan materialized as Southfield Manor, where most of the social events (such as wedding receptions, first communions, and funerals) of the Chaldeans of Detroit's western suburbs took place for the next two decades. Through Southfield Manor's membership fees and other fund-raising drives, the CIAAM raised funds to purchase the Shenandoah property in 1989. Fifteen years later, the $25 million, 93,000-square-foot Shenandoah Club opened, featuring "one of Michigan's largest ballrooms," with the capacity to accommodate 1,300 people.

It is worth stressing the socioeconomically exclusive profile of Shenandoah. First, membership is limited to Chaldeans and their family members. Second, annual family membership fees range between $2,500 and $2,600, with a $5,000 initiation fee and a minimum monthly spending fee of $300.[6]

Clearly, less affluent Chaldeans from other parts of Michigan are unlikely to be able to afford this sum. It is also crucial to consider the massive $5 million budget of the CCC museum, which complements the high membership fees of the country club and proposes a select audience for the museum's exhibits when they become open to the public. The priorities of the members of the Chaldean community who are invested in the Shenandoah project can be discerned by a simple comparison of the space allotted to current social events at the Shenandoah Country Club and the space given to the CCC museum. While Shenandoah's Grand Ballroom totals 11,336 square-feet, the CCC has received a mere 2,500 square feet to display and narrate 6,000 years of Chaldean history. The dominating social entertainment aspect of the Shenandoah Country Club is primarily an outcome of the profit-making orientation of the club's sponsors.

Along with the CIAAM, overseeing and financing the activities of the institutions listed above is the responsibility of a nonprofit umbrella association called the Chaldean Federation of America and a business-professional partnership organization, the Chaldean American Chamber of Commerce, established in 2003. Established in 1982 through the coming together of nine major Chaldean organizations in metropolitan Detroit, the CFA claims to serve "as a catalyst for the assimilation of thousands of Chaldeans into the American culture" and to "represent" more than 150,000 Chaldeans in Michigan today.[7] It regularly hosts the annual Chaldean Student Scholarship Commencement Program, whose aim is to single out the scholarly achievements of Chaldean high school and college students. Recently, the CFA has offered its office space on weekends for the meetings of members of the Chaldean American Student Association (CASA) to encourage programs and projects organized by young Chaldean Americans across the state.

On a transnational scale, the CFA has recently dedicated considerable resources to the humanitarian relief of displaced Chaldeans in and outside Iraq. As we shall see, the organization's efforts are currently culminating in a campaign to secure support from the United States and the Office of the United Nations High Commissioner for Refugees (UNHCR) for the resettlement of Chaldean refugees through Operation R-4. The CFA has also partnered with organizations in Jordan, Lebanon, and Syria, as well as with an international Jesuit organization that was formerly involved with Chaldeans in Iraq, to launch the Adopt-A-Refugee-Family initiative, whereby diasporic Chaldeans can extend financial assistance to Chaldeans transitioning from Iraq through officially recognized channels.[8]

Ample financial resources combine with legal expertise and political connections to enhance the success of the CFA's transnational undertakings. Michael J. George, current chairman of the CFA, is the owner and operator of such business ventures as Melody Farms, Champion Wholesale Foods, Spectrum Enterprises, L.L.C., Healthtreat, Inc., Michigan Data Storage, Midwest Wholesale Foods, Port Atwater Parking, and several others. Current CFA executive director, George Kassab is the former president of the Chaldean National Congress and has co-headed numerous Chaldean American humanitarian delegations to Iraqi Christian refugees. Steven Garmo, former chairman of the CFA, employed his expertise in U.S. immigration law to assist Senator Carl Levin in drafting the Iraqi Christian Adjustment Act, whose aim is to make Chaldean immigration to the United States easier.

These individuals, along with many other active members of the CFA, participate in running the Chaldean American Chamber of Commerce, an organization that since its inception has proven itself an influential market power capable of consolidating the wealth of individually owned Chaldean businesses and creating a stronger entrepreneurial, as well as political, voice for the Chaldean collective. In addition to marshaling the cultural energies of Chaldeans in Oakland County, the Chamber offers help to Chaldean investors who wish to establish or join businesses in Michigan and Iraq. At least at the level of publicity, the Chamber is currently invested in three community projects: the Chaldean museum in Shenandoah Country Club, a survey of Michigan's Chaldeans that seeks to establish "Chaldeans' contributions to their community," and a Chaldo-Assyrian settlement project in the Nineveh Plains for the remaining Chaldo-Assyrian population in Iraq. The Chamber is sponsoring the latter project mainly through partnership with another umbrella organization, the Chaldean Assyrian Syriac Council of America.

CASCA was initiated "to educate U.S. policymakers on the plight of Iraq's Chaldean/Assyrian/Syriac Christian minorities and to advocate for policies that will support stability, security, aid, and reconstruction relief within Iraq and assistance and resettlement of the most vulnerable refugees of this fragile population outside Iraq" (CASCA 2007). CASCA, like other umbrella organizations in the U.S.-based Chaldean diaspora, was formed through the coming together of other influential organizations: the Assyrian American National Federation, the Assyrian National Council of Illinois, the Chaldean American Chamber of Commerce, and the Chaldean Federation of America. Martin Manna, who serves as the executive director of the Chaldean American Chamber of Commerce, and George Kassab, who occupies a similar position at the CFA, are the co-founders and co-directors of CASCA.

The Local Emergence of Transnational Projects

On the local level, the self-descriptions of these exclusively Chaldean institutions and their publications demonstrate how they all boast an interest in preserving and promoting "heritage," or "culture," without clearly defining the meanings of these slippery terms. Their assumption, it seems, is that members and recipients of this "heritage" or "culture" agree on a stable, communal version of Chaldeanness. This tacit agreement in turn suggests the presence of a discursive process that links these institutions in an internal, private sphere, a linkage that preexists and mediates the exposure of collective Chaldeanness to the public sphere of the American mainstream. This tacit agreement at the same time suggests strong transnational ties between the diasporic community and a larger community from which they derive distinct moral and aesthetic values. These ties extend beyond the boundaries of the United States, giving rise to a "diasporic aesthetic," that is, to material forms of culture that are expressed in the group's aesthetic activity in diaspora, in its art, literature, and myths. Diasporic attempts at *real* political mobilization occasionally materialize in "transnational moral gestures" (Werbner 2000), as we shall see in the following cases, in which Chaldean institutional circuits in the United States have begun to move politically, sometimes in opposing directions, on behalf of geographically remote Chaldean individuals and groups.

Casting the Iraqi Vote

In January 2005, under the Out-of-Country Voting Program that made voting possible for Iraqi expatriates in fourteen countries outside Iraq, U.S.-based Chaldeans were allowed to register and vote in the National Assembly elections that were to shape the government of post-Saddam Iraq.[9] Not only were Chaldeans born in Iraq eligible to cast a ballot, but also were those born abroad before 1987 to an Iraqi father (Selweski 2005). The range of Chaldean reactions to this event reveals important contrasts between "transnational action" and a "transnational imaginary."

It could be argued that the interim Iraqi government and the Bush administration sanctioned the right to vote from abroad as a way to implement policies that would reinforce Iraqi emigrants' sense of enduring membership in both the United States and Iraq and hence to draw in their economic remittances to rebuild Iraq or retain their political loyalty in both countries. The participation of expatriates in political activities, however, whether symbolic or real (i.e., whether intended mainly for expressing particular preferences or for implementing change in the sociopolitical structures of the homeland) did not depend entirely on the decisions of the Iraqi and U.S. governments. Generally speaking, institutions of diasporic civil society, including those of U.S.-based Chaldeans, tend to provide material support for a public sphere that includes a wide range of political practices. This phenomenon has driven scholars of diasporas to suggest the existence of "stateless power," a form of power that can be productive or prohibitive within a social formation ruled either by individual voluntarism or by communal compulsion (Tölölyan 2000). In the case of U.S.-based Chaldeans, the church, community organizations, and culture makers—that is, the active architects of the community's transnational social fields—expected at least half of the 113,000 U.S.-based Chaldeans to vote in the Iraqi elections. The leadership of these institutions urged individuals to vote in the elections so that Christians could maintain a foothold in Iraqi parliamentary politics. The importance of voting, according to Joseph Kassab, was twofold: one, it would prove that Chaldeans "understand and support democracy [because they live in a democratic country] for their homeland," and two, their votes for a Christian representative were necessary "to reconfirm the Chaldean presence as a religious and national minority within Iraq" (Delaney 2005).

Registration and polling stations were established in five metropolitan areas across the United States, in Michigan, Washington, D.C., Los Angeles, Chicago, and Tennessee. In Michigan, voting sites were set up in Sterling Heights, Southfield, and Dearborn. The churches and the CFA, who publicly complained about the distance of these polling stations from concentrations of Chaldean residences, organized bus trips to take groups of Chaldean voters (Delaney 2005). The all-Christian democratic slate, Al-Rafidayn, received 29 percent of all the Iraqi expatriate votes in the January elections. Disillusioned by the results and a voting process they perceived to be intentionally cumbersome, fewer Chaldeans voted in subsequent parliamentary elections the following December, bringing the figure down to 26 percent for the Rafidayn slate (Barakat 2005). Although not significant enough to have an impact on the overall results of the elections in Iraq, the victory of Al-Rafidayn, which took the top spot among U.S.-based expatriates and narrowly defeated a Shiite Muslim religious bloc with Shiite supporters in Dearborn, Michigan, demonstrates how influential diasporic Chaldean networks can be in persuading members of the community to mobilize and act politically.

There was a range of reactions to the expatriate vote among Arab and Chaldean diaspora leaders. Manna, president of the Chaldean American Chamber of Commerce, reasoned that, antagonized by media portrayals of Iraq as a country composed of Shiites, Sunnis, and Kurds, diasporic Chaldeans and Assyrians would see voting in the elections as an opportunity to show that they represent 5 percent of the Iraqi population, rather than the 1 percent suggested in the media (Selweski 2005). While Manna was himself a proud Chaldean voter, James Zogby (of Lebanese Christian descent), president of the Arab American Institute and a pollster during the Iraqi elections, was troubled by the U.S. balloting as a whole. Allowing U.S. citizens to vote in another country's elections, claimed Zogby, sends the message that Iraqi Americans are not full participants in U.S. democracy. "We send a very conflicted message about the value of U.S. citizenship," he said. "It undervalues our American citizenship" (Barakat 2005). Yet the conflict of which Zogby speaks, that between local nationalism and transnationality, is being emphasized in a growing body of scholarship on diasporic communities. As Tölölyan stressed, "Those who emerge as transnational leaders . . . always remember to speak of their local community as simultaneously *rooted* in the host society and *routing*, a node of the transnational diasporic network" (cited in Clifford 1997; emphasis in original).

The *rooted-routing* dual orientation of displaced minorities is well exemplified by the Chaldeans of Michigan who, on the one hand, fight for citizenship and equal rights in the place of settlement and, on the other, continue to live with a sense of loyalty to other places, groups, and imagined histories (Werbner 2000). The dual orientation of U.S.-based Chaldean transnational activity is complicated further by a conflicting institutional investment in helping Chaldeans leave Iraq *and* settle there at the same time. During the Terror Decade, diasporic Chaldean institutions were calling for Chaldean settlement in the ancestral land while enabling Chaldeans to *leave* Iraq as expediently as possible.

The Nineveh Plains Settlement Project

In December 2007, the U.S. Congress passed a bill authorizing $10 million in assistance to internally displaced religious minorities in the Nineveh Plains, with a particular emphasis on the "endangered" Christians of the region. The bill included the following language:

> The Appropriations Committees support the use of prior-year funds, as proposed by the House, to assist religious minorities in the Nineveh Plains region of Iraq, and direct that prior to the obligation of funds, the Department of State consult with ethnoreligious minorities and locally elected representatives to identify Iraq-based nongovernmental organizations to implement these programs.
>
> The Appropriations Committees are concerned about the threat to the existence of Iraq's most vulnerable minorities, particularly the Assyrian/Chaldean/Syriac Christians, who are confronting ethnoreligious cleansing in Iraq. The Appropriations Committees expect the Department of State and USAID to designate a point person within the department to focus, coordinate, and improve U.S. government efforts to provide for these minorities' humanitarian, security, and development needs. (CASCA 2007)

This was the first congressional bill to contain policy specifications for administering U.S. government aid to the Christians of Iraq. The language was considered by the newly formed Chaldean Assyrian Syriac Council of America to be "a tremendous victory" for its advocacy efforts.

In fact, organized co-ethnic advocacy efforts on behalf of the Chaldeans and Assyrians of the Nineveh Plains started much earlier. The first formulations of a "Christian haven" project took place at an Assyrian Democratic Movement conference in Baghdad in 2003. The conference adopted the Nineveh Plains Administrative Region program for Assyrian administrative autonomy (later recognized as Chaldo-Assyrian under the Iraqi Transitional Administrative Law of 2003).[10] In less than a year, the objectives of the program were brought into focus by transnational networks of Middle Eastern American Christians.

In 2004, the Middle Eastern American Convention for Freedom and Democracy in the Middle East convened in Washington, D.C., under the sponsorship of Maronites, Copts, Assyrians, Chaldeans, and their representative diaspora organizations, such as the American Lebanese Coalition, U.S. Copts, and the Assyrian American National Federation. During the convention, immigration attorney Robert Dekelaita, a Chicago-based, self-described Chaldo-Assyrian, delivered a keynote speech on behalf of Chaldo-Assyrians in Iraq, stressing, in consensus with the Christian groups present, the need to concentrate the convention's efforts on helping the endangered Chaldo-Assyrian community.[11] After posing the recent destruction of Babylon and Nineveh and the mass exodus of the Chaldo-Assyrians as a serious problem for the country and for its Christian population, Dekelaita proceeded to claim that the solution "lies in the Nineveh Plains," a political "unit" or "province" in Iraq's Kurdish region that would be "economically supported, secured, and administratively designated for Chaldo-Assyrians." "Iraq, without Babylon and Nineveh, is illegitimate as a nation, and Iraq without Chaldo-Assyrians is incomplete," wrote Dekelaita shortly thereafter, as a guest columnist in *The Chaldean News* (Dekelaita 2006).

Other non-Christian organizations were also invited to the convention. By refusing to acknowledge the plight of Christians in Iraq, the Kurdish Patriotic Union, the Syrian Reform Party, and a Shiite delegation from Iraq caused rancor among the Chaldo-Assyrian representatives. The antagonism surrounding this issue grew along religious lines, creating a geographical rift between diaspora nationalist organizations (composed mostly of Christian expats) and political parties headquartered in the Middle East (composed mostly of Muslims). Initially, the Nineveh Plains settlement project was to operate under Kurdish leadership. Fear of antagonizing Kurdish parties, which currently control the Nineveh Plains, created a formidable dilemma for diaspora Chaldo-Assyrians. The outcome was the religious minority's inability to reach consensus on the following issue: should Iraqi Christians cooperate with Kurdish leaders to form their autonomous area within Iraq's federal state or should they depend on external resources to create a federal state for Christian minorities alone?[12]

With the intervention of diaspora Chaldean and Assyrian organizations, the interplay of political powers, religious affiliations, and funding sources has sent the project in different directions. For example, Iraqi Kurdistan's Minister of Finance and Economy, Sarkis Aghajan, who is Christian and a member of the governing Kurdistan Democratic Party, called for a Christian region attached to Iraqi Kurdistan. His agenda gained support from many local and international Iraqi Christian political parties because Aghajan had financially sponsored several thousand Christian refugees from the south and promised to construct more than a hundred new villages and churches in their ancestral Nineveh region. Although Iraqi Kurdistan prime minister Nejervan Barzani backed Aghajan's proposal, other Iraqi Christian leaders, such as former Iraqi Minister of Displacement and Migration Pascale Warda, voiced their opposition to the project internationally, arguing that Christian and other minorities merit a separate federal state. Warda found different backers for her plan. In 2006, she visited Assyro-Christian organizations in the United States to drum up support for an autonomous federal state for Christians and other minorities. Among the diasporic networks whose favor she gained were the Assyrian Democratic Movement, the Chaldean American Chamber of Commerce, and the Chaldean Federation of America.

Although most of the Assyrian political groups in diaspora support one of the two proposals associated with the Nineveh Plains project, not all Chaldean groups, in the United States or in Iraq, were enthusiastic about the proposed settlement. One argument against the Nineveh Plains proposal popular among U.S.-based Chaldeans with relatives in Iraq is that the settlement poses a safety problem. By grouping all Christians together, a Chaldean archbishop argued, they "will become targets, sandwiched in between Kurds and Arabs"; hence, either plan would only make things worse by creating a "Christian ghetto."[13]

Reports by UN officials claim that the majority of Iraqi refugees want to return to Iraq eventually, but between 2003 and 2006 it became apparent that the Chaldean refugees are not among those wishing to return. By spring 2007, the CFA announced that 17,000 applications were received on behalf of Iraqi refugees who wished to live in the United States. Most of these applicants were Chaldo-Assyrian refugees who had received death threats from fanatic Islamist groups, operated liquor stores, or had done translation or intelligence work for U.S. troops in Iraq—experiences that made their immediate return to Iraq highly unlikely. The CFA had publicly supported Warda's Nineveh Plains campaign, but with church bombings, priest kidnappings, and other acts of religious persecution of Chaldeans in Iraq, the diaspora umbrella organization, along with its secular and religious affiliates, began to claim publicly that displaced Iraqi Christians could not return to Iraq because of the unfavorable political climate. These claims were already circulating before Congress passed its $10 million appropriation in support of Iraq's Christian minorities in December 2007.

The Nineveh Plains settlement project is one instance of the desire of Chaldean transnationals to be seriously involved in directing the political affairs of the Chaldean community in the homeland. The case demonstrates how co-ethnic transnational actors could potentially complicate political matters for Chaldeans in Iraq when pursuing goals that are prompted by symbolic ideologies, such as the "myth of return."[14] These political complications redouble when Chaldean transnational actors begin to pursue practical solutions that are in conflict with their ideological aspirations. As we shall see next, desperate to halt the mass exit of the Christian communities from Iraq, the CFA joined in a project that might seem to undermine the Nineveh Plains settlement. Operation R-4, contrary to the Nineveh Plains plan, is a transnational project that aspires to aid Chaldeans by safely removing them from their ancestral land.

Operation R-4

Launched by the CFA in May 2006, the primary goal of Operation R-4 (Research, Rescue, Relieve, and Resettle Iraqi refugees) was to "identify, locate and assist displaced Iraqi-Christian refugees throughout the world in order to reunite them with relatives already residing in the United States."[15] Phase I of the campaign, which concluded in August 2006, calculated the number of Iraqi refugees in thirty-one countries and the factors leading to their flight from Iraq. The figures were quickly revised upward from the initial projection of a few thousand potential newcomers to the United States to several tens of thousands. A dramatic transition from the local to the transnational level of activity occurred when the CFA decided to turn Operation R-4 into a worldwide movement by sharing its findings with the international humanitarian community. It began by sending reports and delegations to the Resettlement Services division of the UNHCR. Meanwhile, Chaldean Americans represented by the CFA appealed to governmental agencies and the U.S. Senate to expedite the emigration of Iraqi Christian refugees to the country of their relatives' residence.

In addition to increasing publicity regarding the plight of Iraqi Christians, the CFA aimed to implement changes in U.S. immigration policies. Since the number of Chaldeans fleeing Iraq rose steeply during Phase I of the campaign, the CFA could not depend on P1 status (athletes, artists, or entertainers) while petitioning on behalf of their displaced relatives. P1 status, the CFA asserted, was "too little, too slow, too painful, and problematic for our refugees."[16] Instead, the CFA sought to document how the refugees it identified were "persecuted religiously, ethnically and/or politically in order to fit the basic requirement for priorities P2 [persecuted group admission] and P3 [family reunification admission], i.e., to meet the refugee definition."[17]

To implement action based upon these findings, Phase II of the campaign focused on the legal procedures of admitting Iraqi refugees to the United States in mass numbers. In this phase, the CFA began appealing to U.S. legislators to secure P2 and P3 status for Iraqi Christian refugees who were kin to American citizens. The outcome (which could also be attributed to the efforts of the UNHCR and other humanitarian organizations) was the admission of 2,631 Iraqi refugees to the United States in 2007.[18] This figure rose to 12,118 and 19,910 Iraqi refugees admitted to the United States in 2008 and 2009, respectively.[19] Meanwhile, the CFA and the local Chaldean press in Michigan stressed that "85% of Iraqis who are currently residing in the United States are of the Christian faith"[20] and that the same percentage of all Iraqi refugee applicants have a family member already living in the United States (Goldblatt 2007). These figures were deliberately emphasized in order to highlight two matters critical for the American government and for public opinion: one, that by already having an established network of family support the newcomers would be less likely to become a burden to the country's economy; and, two, by virtue of being non-Muslim, these Iraqi refugees would be less likely to pose the terrorist threat much feared by political entities that had previously been reluctant to set aside state funds for the resettlement of Iraqi refugees. Accordingly, the CFA is now in the habit of concluding its reports with comments such as this one:

> The CFA strongly believes that Iraqi Christians, as past history demonstrates, can assimilate well without burdening the country of final resettlement, and will make a valuable contribution to society.[21]

"As past history demonstrates" refers simultaneously to the history of Chaldean settlement in the United States during the twentieth century and to the ancient history of Chaldean civilization, which the modern Chaldeans are quick to summon when stressing their legitimacy, authenticity, and positive collective impact on Western societies. Referring to the United States as "the country of final resettlement" puts the efforts of Operation R-4 in direct opposition to the Nineveh Plains project. Whereas the latter project calls for international aid in creating a home in Iraq for Iraq's Christians, the former project candidly admits that Iraqi Christian refugees who arrive in the United

States have no intention of returning to Iraq. What is worth noting here is that this dichotomy of goals has been minimized to the point of general invisibility. Neither local Chaldean media nor mainstream U.S. media stress this discrepancy in their reports, although both projects receive ample coverage individually.

Only in particular situations does it become efficacious for Chaldeans to admit to this discrepancy publicly, namely, when they admit their desire to both create a home for Iraqi Christians in Iraq and have them admitted as refugees in the United States. One example is the aforementioned Chicago-based attorney Assyro-Chaldean Robert Dekelaita, an enthusiastic advocate of the Nineveh Plains settlement project who also petitions on behalf of hundreds of Iraqi Christian refugees who seek asylum in the United States after entering or sojourning illegally. "My heart is wedded to the idea that they should be safe and secure in their own homeland. What I'm doing is temporary," Dekelaita said during an interview with the *Los Angeles Times* inside his law office in Skokie, Illinois (April 28, 2008). Unlike Dekelaita, however, the CFA, the majority of Chaldeans in the United States, and their displaced relatives who aspire to reunite with them do not think of the admission of the Chaldean refugees to the United States as "temporary." The thousands of dollars U.S.-based Chaldeans invest in helping their displaced kin relocate to the United States is one indication that they aspire to make their resettlement a permanent one.

That the CFA had to depend on private (mainly Chaldean American) funding for its transnational Operation R-4 campaign is a fact—the U.S. government and nongovernmental humanitarian agencies it sought out declined to supply the funding it requested.[22] The manner in which these funds were raised and allocated is a further example of how local Chaldean circuits in Michigan add a political dimension to preexisting family and church networks in order to achieve transnational goals and to implement political goals. During 2006, for instance, the CFA held several fund-raisers at the Shenandoah Country Club. Selling tickets for $250/person ensured that the gathering would include only established members of the elite clique. Less affluent contributors to the cause of Iraqi refugees could pledge their donations online. Meanwhile, the *Chaldean News* made the efforts of the CFA public and called upon the Chaldean residents in the United States to make their contributions to "authorized resettlement agencies." These were many, and they included the Chaldean American Chamber of Commerce, the Chaldean American Ladies of Charity, and Mother of God Church, among others. On Saturday afternoons the main office of the CFA welcomed individual volunteers from the Chaldean community along with groups such as CASA to carry out the task of classifying, analyzing, and storing the confidential data submitted on behalf of the refugees by their Chaldean relatives in the United States. A service to help relatives fill out the applications accurately was made available at various Chaldean churches in Michigan and at the Shenandoah Country Club.

The CFA has been successful in rallying Michigan's Chaldeans to a transnational cause that they can relate to on a personal level: virtually everyone has a relative or a friend who wants help to migrate to the United States. Because the CFA is proving to the community that its campaign is effective in helping Chaldean refugees, it can also effectively propagate the particular version of "Chaldean identity" that enhances the institution's public image. During my interview with Kassab, current executive director of the CFA, who spearheaded Operation R-4 from 2006 to 2009, he requested that I cite the following words in my publication: "We [the CFA] put all of these efforts [Operation R-4] so that we can help our people assimilate to American life . . . without forgetting their original culture" (phone interview, December 2007). Whenever there is a public opportunity, the CFA designates Chaldeans as a people with a clearly defined religion (Christianity), family values, a strong work ethic, and, most emphatically, an abiding capacity to become "American" without ceasing to be "Chaldean."

The very fact that Chaldean diasporic circuits and their leaders have reached the size and level of organization that allow them to contemplate large-scale transnational projects and to construct applicable identity narratives for them is an indication that the Chaldean diaspora in Michigan is establishing itself as a *permanent phenomenon*. As such, it is now able to generate diverse transnational social fields to meet specific social or political goals as they arise while striving to represent an image of independence from the larger networks of Arab Detroit in which it is embedded.

Closing Remarks

This discussion of transnational activity offers a new perspective on Chaldean migrant society. Instead of examining Chaldean life from the delimited context of the community's diasporic resettlement or from the religious context of the activities of the Chaldean church, it takes into account the dynamic flow of Chaldean identities, economies, and politics across territorial boundaries, a dynamism that gives the Chaldean community the public ethnic profile it now possesses and tries to project in post-9/11 America. Clearly, religion is a key component of the group's identity, and many of the transnational political projects described above involve substantial input from the Chaldean church, yet I have tried to show in this paper how Chaldean identity in the United States is not only a religious identity, but also an ethnic and political one, and at times primarily so. The power of the institutions described in this paper derives from two sources. One, they are not financially or administratively dependent on the sponsorship of the Chaldean Church; and, two, these institutions aspire to gain entry and recognition in the secular American mainstream.

U.S.-based Chaldeans are currently engaged in cross-boundary activities that are best understood by examining institutional circuits as social spaces. These spaces have the capacity to develop into overlapping transnational social fields in which diasporic Chaldeans can participate directly and indirectly in multistranded transnational activities. Currently, southeast Michigan is at the center of these social fields because the oldest and largest Chaldean community outside the Middle East resides there, giving rise to several of the critical transnational projects analyzed here. More important, southeast Michigan is home to a Chaldean elite whose powerful political and cultural influence has given shape and articulation to a modern collective Chaldean identity that resonates worldwide.

Persons living within the borders of a state as legal or potential citizens, such as the U.S.-based Chaldeans, may not make transnational claims or feel the urge to create transnational social fields until a peculiar event or crisis occurs. Operation R-4, the Nineveh Plains settlement project, and the Iraqi vote campaign are three campaigns provoked by the serious humanitarian crises that have beset Chaldeans in Iraq during the post-9/11 era. What these projects have in common is the fact that they are all diaspora-driven (i.e., local) projects aimed at making a transnational impact during the decade of the War on Terror. Indeed, the War on Terror and the U.S. occupation of Iraq have fed and facilitated these diasporic initiatives, posing existential threats to Chaldeans living in Iraq even as they bolster the institutional capacity of the Chaldean diaspora in greater Detroit.

Some Chaldeans participate in transnational networks more effectively than others. It is not easy to chart passive levels of participation in transnational life; everyone, as a member of the community, is embedded in a transnational social field and is participating in it, directly or indirectly, by contributing money to a CFA project, running a store in Detroit, marrying an acquaintance from Telkeif, or engaging in countless activities with a possible transnational effect. However, few persons and organizations have the power to become nodes that actively direct the trajectory of transnational activities. Through the symbiotic workings of community organizations, a small cohort of affluent Chaldeans presides over most of the formal transnational projects that involve multiple institutions. This small cohort also works to ensure an effective publicity of these projects within the larger public domain in order to elicit the desired level of participation from other, less involved members of the immigrant community and to obtain recognition from the broader, non-Chaldean society in which Chaldean networks are embedded.

Identifying transnational activity among U.S.-based Chaldeans brings into view the inner unity, durability, and power of the diasporic collective, but it also poses a number of questions that remain unanswered. For example, when seen as a set of multiple, interlocking networks, the diasporic social fields seem to overlap or recombine to support activities, such as well organized fund-raising campaigns to assist Chaldean refugees, that are clearly beneficial to the community and its individual families in Michigan. However, it is equally clear that some of these broad-scale transnational projects are not complementary and are, in fact, subverting each other (e.g., the simultaneous call for an enclave for Iraqi Christians in Nineveh *and* a comprehensive migration plan to help the remaining families reunite with their relatives in the United States and elsewhere).

Another important question that falls beyond the scope of current inquiry is the future of Chaldean transnational life. In light of the mass exit of Iraqi Christians from their ancestral land, aided by the relocation efforts of diaspora Chaldeans, and the rapid expansion of the size of the U.S.-based Chaldean population, it is unclear which transnational ties are likely to endure in the coming decades. We may have to rethink the contours of Chaldean communities if we cannot take their territorial sites or boundaries for granted, especially when other concentrations of Chaldean life outside the United States (in Western Europe, Syria, and Jordan) are not likely, owing to their smaller size and diminished political status, to develop influential transnational diasporas like the one now flourishing in the suburbs of Detroit.

Notes

1. After World War I, the Assyrians entered the newly formed Iraqi monarchy as refugees from Turkey and Iran. At the time, they did not consider themselves natives of Iraq, but a diasporic community striving to return to its homeland in the near future (Vine 1937; Husri 1974; Deniz 1999; Joseph 2000).

2. These groups were also known as Tiaris and Christian Kurds in reference to their regional affiliations.

3. In 1962, Sengstock established through a community census that only eight of the 305 families who participated in the census were from Iraqi villages other than Telkeif. Modern Chaldean elites, in turn, are mostly from these oldest Chaldean immigrant families or their descendants.

4. No exact figures exist. The most recent Chaldean count in Michigan revealed that 113,000 live in this state alone. However, according to the 2000 U.S. census, the category

"Assyrian/Chaldean/Syriac" was checked by 34,484 individuals in Michigan, 22,671 in California (the state's largest Assyrian communities are in San Diego and Los Angeles), and 15,685 in Illinois (with a concentration in Chicago and Niles). No other reliable figures are available.

5. In order to focus the discussion specifically on the sociopolitical activity of Chaldean Americans, I decided to leave out the influential Chaldean religious establishment, which also falls within this geographical district.

6. Compare these figures with the $50 initiation fee and $35 annual membership of the Chaldean Youth Club during the 1970s.

7. Chaldean Federation of America (n.d., b).

8. Chaldean Federation of America (n.d., a).

9. Polling sites in the United States and the other thirteen European and Middle Eastern countries were selected by the International Organization for Migration in collaboration with the Independent Electoral Commission of Iraq. Together these organizations worked with local groups from Detroit to organize the elections, using the $92 million budget allocated by the Iraqi government for the worldwide voting process.

10. Assyrian International News Agency (2004b).

11. Assyrian International News Agency (2004a).

12. Lamprecht (2006).

13. Ibid.

14. 'The myth of return" is an expression that appears frequently in immigrant and refugee studies, often in reference to symbolic transnational links to the homeland. Badr Dahya was one of the first to define the expression explicitly, in relation to his work on Pakistani immigrants in Britain: "The immigrant continues to reaffirm his adherence to the myth of return because for him to do otherwise would be tantamount to renouncing his membership of the village community and the village-kin group in Britain—for these groups together form a single whole, and for a migrant to opt out of one means opting out of the other as well. The myth of return is an expression of one's intention to continue to remain a member of both of them" (1973, 241).

15. Chaldean Federation of America (2007a).

16. Chaldean Federation of America (2007b).

17. Ibid.

18. The U.S. Department of State had initially announced its intention to admit 7,000 Iraqi refugees in 2007. See Associated Press (2007).

19. U.S. Citizenship and Immigration Services (2009).

20. Chaldean Federation of America (2007c).

21. Ibid.

22. With one exception: a $100,000 donation from the Turkish Coalition of America made to the CFA in September 2009 (Turkish Coalition of America 2009).

REFERENCES

Associated Press. 2007. "Iraqi Refugees Knocking: U.S. to Let in 7,000." *MSNBC World News*, May 30, http://www.msnbc.msn.com/id/18944557.

Assyrian International News Agency. 2004a. "Middle Eastern Christian Conference: Safeguard the Assyrians of the Nineveh Plains." www.christiansofiraq.com/Aina conference.html.

———. 2004b. "New Iraqi Census Officially Recognizes ChaldoAssyrians." http://www.aina.org/releases/2004079004216.htm.

Barakat, Matthew. 2005. "Christian Slate Wins Narrow Plurality in U.S. Expat Voting." Assyrian International News Agency, December 19, http://www.aina.org/news/20051219152044.htm.

Baum, Wilhelm, and Dietmar W. Winkler. 2003. *The Church of the East: A Concise History.* London: Routledge Curzon.

Bazzi, Mikhael. 1991. *Chaldeans Present and Past.* San Diego: St. Peter Chaldean Catholic Church.

CASCA. 2007. "CASCA Advocacy Successful in Shining Light on Plight of Chaldean/Assyrian/Syriac People and Securing U.S. Government Aid." *Zinda Magazine* 13: 19.

Chaldean Federation of America. 2007a. "CFA Begins Campaign to Secure U.S. Governmental and UN Support for Identification and Resettlement of Iraqi Refugees." News release, January 26. http://solarflareservices.com/cfa/press/pr12697.html.

———. 2007b. "CFA Progress Report." www.chaldeanfederation.org.

———. 2007c. "Statement of the CFA on the Iraqi Christian's Plight to the Senate Committee on the Judiciary." http://solarflareservices.com/cfa/news/senate.html.

———. n.d., a. "Adopt-A-Refugee-Family Program." http://chaldeanfederation.org/index.php?option=com_content&view=article&id=62:adopt-a-refugee-family-program&catid=31:general&Itemid=46. (URL no longer active.)

———. n.d., b. "Chaldean Federation of America (CFA) Organizational History." http://chaldeanfederation.org/history/index.html. (URL no longer active.)

"Chaldean Household Survey." 2007. Troy, Mich.: Chaldean American Chamber of Commerce.

Clifford, James. 1997. *Routes: Travel and Translation in the Late Twentieth Century.* Cambridge, Mass.: Harvard University Press.

Dahya, Badr. 1973. "Pakistanis in Britain: Transients or Settlers?" *Race* 13(3): 241–277.

Dekelaita, Robert. 2004. "An Ancient People's Last Stand: The Plight of the Chaldo-Assyrians in Post-Saddam Iraq." Assyrian International News Agency, http://www.aina.org/guesteds/20040614193356.htm.

———. 2006. "On the Road to Nineveh Again." *Chaldean News* 3(5): 48.

Delaney, Robert. 2005. "Local Chaldeans Urged to Vote in Iraqi Elections." *The Michigan Catholic*, January 21. Archdiocese of Detroit, http://www.aodonline.org/NR/exeres/976354C6-23BE-4488-B35C-9BB5047DADDE.htm?NRMODE=Unpublished.

Deniz, Fuat. 1999. "Maintenance and Transformation of Ethnic Identity: The Assyrian Case." Assyrians after Assyria Conference, Assyrian Education Network, http://www.atour.com/education/20000825e.html.

Dinnerstein, L., and D. Reimers. 1999. *Ethnic Americans: A History of Immigration.* New York: Columbia University Press.

Gallagher, Barbara George. 1999. "Chaldean Immigrant Women, Gender, and Family." PhD diss., Wayne State University.

Goldblatt, Jeff. 2007. "7,000 Iraqi Refugees Expected to Resettle in the United States within a Year." http://www.foxnews.com/story/0,2933,253561,00.html.

Hanish, Shak. 2008. "The Chaldean Assyrian Syriac People of Iraq: An Ethnic Identity Problem." *Digest of Middle East Studies* 17(1): 32–47.

Hanoosh, Yasmeen. 2008. "The Politics of Minority: Chaldeans between Iraq and America." PhD diss., University of Michigan. http://hdl.handle.net/2027.42/61663.

Harris, Emily. 2007. "Europe Struggles with Influx of Iraqi Refugees." NPR *Morning Edition*, March 6.

Henrich, Natalie, and Joseph Henrich. 2007. *Why Humans Cooperate: A Cultural and Evolutionary Explanation*. New York: Oxford University Press.

Hidirsah, Yakup. 1997. "Massacre of Christians in Mesopotamia and Kurds (Syriacs, Nestorians, Chaldeans, Armenians): A Documentary Study." Hannover, Germany. http://www.chaldeansonline.org/Banipal/English/massacres.html.

"Household Demographic Survey." 2008. *Chaldean News*, May 5, 30.

Husri, Khaldun. 1974. "The Assyrian Affair." *International Journal of the Middle East Studies* 5: 161–176, 344–360.

Jabiro, Crystal. 2005. "Shenandoah Opens: Long-Time Vision Finally Becomes a Reality." *Chaldean News*, January 12, 28–29.

Joseph, John. 2000. *The Modern Assyrians of the Middle East: Encounters with Western Christian Missions, Archaeologists, and Colonial Powers*. Leiden, Netherlands: Brill.

Konja, Clair. 2005. "CALC Corner." *Chaldean News* 2(6): 18.

Lamprecht, Peter. 2006. "Iraq: Christians Debate Self-Autonomy to Halt Exodus." Compass Direct News, December 22, http://www.compassdirect.org/en/display.php?page=news&lang=en&length=long&idelement=4711&backpage=archives&critere=nineveh%20plain&countryname=&rowcur=0.

Matar, Salim. 2000. *Al-Thāt al-Jarīha: Ishkālāt al-Hawiyyah fī al-ʿIrāq wa al-ʿĀlam al-ʿArabī/al-Sharqānī* (The Injured Self: Identity Challenges in Iraq and the Arab/Eastern World). Beirut: al-Muʾassasah al-ʿArabiyyah li-l-Dirāsāt wa al-Nashr.

Sarafa, Josephine, ed. n.d., a. "Chaldean Americans: Past and Present" (pamphlet). Bloomfield Hills, Mich.: Publication of St. Thomas the Apostle Chaldean Catholic Diocese of America.

——, ed. n.d., b. "Chaldean Americans of Southeast Michigan" (pamphlet). Bloomfield Hills, Mich.: Publication of St. Thomas the Apostle Chaldean Catholic Diocese of America.

Schiller, Nina Glick, Linda Basch, and Cristina Szanton Blanc. 1995. "From Immigrant to Transmigrant: Theorizing Transnational Migration." *Anthropological Quarterly* 68(1): 48–63.

Selweski, Chad. 2005. "Large Chaldean Population in Sterling Heights to Take Part in Shaping New Iraq." *Macomb Daily*, January 4, wwwchristiansofiraq.com/sterling.html.

Sengstock, Mary. 1974. "Iraqi Christians in Detroit: An Analysis of an Ethnic Occupation." In *Arabic Speaking Communities in American Cities*, ed. Barbara Aswad, 21–38. New York: Center for Migration Studies.

——. 1982. *The Chaldean Americans: Changing Conceptions of Ethnic Identity*. New York: Center for Migration Studies.

——. 1983. "Detroit's Iraqi Chaldeans: A Conflicting Conception of Identity." In *Arabs in the New World: Studies on Arab American Communities*, ed. Sameer Abraham and Nabeel Abraham, 136–146. Detroit: Center for Urban Studies, Wayne State University.

————. 2005. *Chaldeans in America*. East Lansing: Michigan State University Press.

Tölölyan, Khachig. 2000. "Elites and Institutions in the Armenian Transnation." *Diaspora* 9(1): 107–136.

Turkish Coalition of America. 2009. "Turkish Coalition of America Announces $100,000 Grant to Chaldean Federation of America." http://turkeyamericablog.blogspot.com/2009/09/turkish-coalition-of-america-announces.html.

U.S. Census Bureau. Census 2000 Summary File 3, Matrices PCT15 and PCT18. http://factfinder.census.gov/servlet/QTTable?_bm=y&-geo_id=01000US&-qr_name=DEC_2000_SF3_U_QTP13&-ds_name=DEC_2000_SF3_U.

U.S. Citizenship and Immigration Services. 2009. "Fact Sheet: Iraqi Refugees Processing." http://www.uscis.gov/portal/site/uscis/menuitem.5af9bb95919f35e66f61 4176543f6d1a/?vgnextchannel=68439c7755cb9010VgnVCM10000045f-3d6a1RCRD&vgnextoid=df4c47c9de5ba110VgnVCM1000004718190aRCRD.

Vine, Aubrey. 1937. *The Nestorian Churches: A Concise History of Nestorian Christianity in Asia from the Persian Schism to the Modern Assyrians*. London: Independent Press.

Warikoo, Niraj. 2007. "More Iraqi Refugees Permitted in Metro Detroit: Many May Settle in Area." *Knight Ridder Tribune Business News*, February 15, 1.

Werbner, Pnina. 2000. "The Materiality of Diaspora—Between Aesthetic and 'Real' Politics." *Diaspora* 9(1): 5–20.

Muslims as Moving Targets

External Scrutiny and Internal Critique in Detroit's Mosques

SALLY HOWELL

Being threatened is addictive. When those in power are
infatuated with you, you feel valued.
—Chinese artist Ai Weiwei

Political language is designed to make lies sound truthful and
murder respectable, and give the appearance of solidity to
pure wind.
—George Orwell, 1946

On April 17, 2010, the U.S. Departments of State and Justice held a Civil
Society Consultation at the Law School of Wayne State University in Detroit.
Hosted by the Civil Rights Center within the law school and the American-
Arab Anti-Discrimination Committee (ADC Michigan), this event was one
of several hosted across the country to satisfy the terms of the UN Human
Rights Council Universal Periodic Review. The Detroit event focused on
three overarching concerns—structural racism, discrimination in immigration and border crossings, and discriminatory law enforcement practices. It
featured local experts and civil rights leaders reflecting on the current state
of human rights conditions and abuses in southeastern Michigan. Well over
half the day's discussion focused on the concerns of Arab and Muslim
Americans and described policies put in place as a part of America's War on
Terror. The list of issues raised was long and the concerns serious, if now
familiar. They included the unexplained and seemingly interminable delays
"aliens" face while waiting for green cards or work visas; the detention centers
into which they can disappear if they violate their immigration status; the

trouble those with Muslim-sounding names face as they attempt to fly into or through American airspace; the use of informants and agent provocateurs in local mosques; the investigations and escalating regulations faced by Islamic charities; and the harassment of the staff, board members, and donors of local charities.[1] Arab Americans, attorney Ihsan Alkhatib told the gathering, are now concerned that the federal government "sees us as suspects rather than partners in the fight against terror."

The event's focus on Arabs and Muslims, coming late in the Terror Decade, was intentional and unremarkable to those in the audience. Home to the country's most visible Arab and Muslim populations, Detroit was an appropriate setting for this high-level engagement between officials from the Departments of Justice and State, officials from the local Arab and Muslim communities, and the civil rights establishment of southeastern Michigan. Had such hearings taken place a decade earlier, it is likely that the NAACP, rather than the ADC, would have co-hosted the session. Urban blight and structural, anti-black racism would have been more likely topics of discussion. Prior to the attacks of 9/11, a prioritization of the civil liberties crisis facing Arabs and Muslims over the traditional civil rights agenda—especially in a city like Detroit—would have drawn intense criticism from all quarters, including Arab and Muslim ones. Instead, activists who transect this seeming division drew parallels between the treatment Arabs and Muslims receive today and that imposed on civil rights and religious organizations in the black community during the era of COINTELPRO (Counter Intelligence Program), when the FBI (often illegally) targeted, infiltrated, disrupted, and undermined their work.

The Civil Society Consultation in Detroit illustrated how profoundly the status of Arab/Muslim Detroit has been reconfigured recently. Its political, institutional, and representational significance has been elevated—for better and for worse—in complex ways. Defined by the several wars of the last decade—in Iraq, Afghanistan, Lebanon, and Gaza and, of course, the War on Terror—which involved Arabs and Muslims (as both adversaries and allies of the United States), Arab/Muslim Americans have achieved a kind of sustained visibility that is highly contradictory. They are viewed as evidence of American freedoms and multicultural tolerance and as proof that Arabs and Muslims can live up to the democratic potential (and assimilate to Western values and lifestyles) world leaders envision for them. At the same time, Arabs and Muslims are taken as evidence that American freedoms cannot or should not be applied to peoples viewed (by the public and the state) as the enemy/outsider within.[2] Naber has cautioned that this new post-9/11 "visibility" of Arabs is thus a "power-laden project that has the effect of silencing critiques of state violence and the structured inequalities that produce hatred and racism" while also revealing "the objectification that often accompanies 'inclusion'" (2008, 3).

The simultaneity of being American *and* Arab/Muslim was on ample display at the Civil Society Consultation, as a long list of Arab and Muslim experts, civil rights leaders, and community representatives spoke with, to, as, for, and against the Departments of Homeland Security, Justice, and State. Some, like Abed Hammoud, an assistant prosecuting attorney for Wayne County, and Kareem Shora, a senior policy advisor with the Department of Homeland Security's Office of Civil Rights and Civil Liberties, spoke as advocates of both the government and the Arab American community.[3] Virtually every other Arab/Muslim American speaker—if not employed by the government—belonged to an advisory body tasked with closely monitoring the community/government divide.

This close working relationship between federal agencies and civil rights advocates is now pervasive in Detroit. It is especially pronounced in Arab Muslim circles. Its significance is often overlooked. As other authors in this volume (Hanoosh, Stiffler, and Youmans) have suggested, Arab Christian institutions and Arab Christian populations are not being singled out for surveillance and harassment while Arab Muslim institutions and communities are. FBI Special Agent in Charge for Detroit, Andy Arena, is a regular visitor at the monthly meetings of the Imams Committee of the Council of Islamic Organizations of Michigan (CIOM), includes a variety of imams on his Multi-Cultural Advisory Council (MCAC), and occupies an office adorned with decorative prayer beads and calligraphic passages from the Quran. His contacts in the Arab Christian community are fewer, and his office is devoid of memorabilia suggesting such ties. Similarly, it is representatives of Dearborn's (predominantly Muslim) Arab establishment who attend the meetings of groups like Advocates and Leaders for Police and Community Trust (ALPACT) and Building Respect in Diverse Groups to Enhance Sensitivity (BRIDGES), local bodies established to facilitate communication between government agencies and minority populations. It is the (Muslim) head of ADC Michigan, Imad Hamad, that the Department of Justice calls when these institutions break down, when an extraordinary incident occurs (such as a terror-related incident or arrest), or when arranging the visit of high-ranking officials to Detroit. The consequences of this intense federal focus on Detroit's Muslim populations have been profound. A similar focus is being institutionalized nationwide, but the close relationships that now exist between law enforcement officials and Arab *Muslim* leaders in Detroit are remarkable. It is precisely this high level of interconnectedness, intended on the surface at least to protect the rights of Arab and Muslim citizens, that nonetheless facilitates the mistreatment of Arab and Muslim Americans by federal authorities. The locus of this mistreatment has centered increasingly on American mosques. This chapter will explore the dialogical relations that now exist between Detroit mosques and evolving structures of public scrutiny and federal power. As the institutions linked most immediately to the practice of Islam as a religious tradition (and thus to the freedoms of religion guaranteed in the U.S. Constitution), mosques remain especially vulnerable. Many of Detroit's mosques are correspondingly proactive in seeking to redress American misconceptions by creating a (still emerging) Muslim public, a shared medium in which Muslims can discuss their legal, political, religious, and cultural concerns across the ethnic, class, and sectarian divisions that have thwarted the coalescence of such a public in the past. An unusual array of actors, Muslim and non-Muslim, have come to participate in this emerging public sphere and to represent Islam in Michigan in the effort to diminish national security threats and protect the rights of citizens. This process, which is examined below, tends to confirm the pervasive assumption that these security threats emanate from Arab and Muslim sources and not from U.S. federal policies at home and abroad, a reality that undermines the transcommunal relationships the War on Terror has produced in Detroit, jeopardizes the rights of American citizens, and leaves intact a politics of discord that singles out Muslims as a problem.

Framing Detroit's Mosques

Greater Detroit has been home to sizable Muslim communities for more than a century (Howell 2009) and has a population of roughly 185,000 Muslims today.[4] This population has been diverse in terms of race, class, sect, and ethnicity from the very beginning, and this diversity is reflected in its fifty-seven mosques. Several of these congregations are among the nation's largest, oldest, and most influential; others are small and unstable. Southeast Michigan is also home to a burgeoning Muslim public sphere that includes a growing number of parochial schools (and charters that cater to Muslim families), three Islamic charities (and the administrative offices of several others), newspapers and other media producers, a food and clothing infrastructure catering to Muslim dietary and sartorial needs, civil rights organizations, representative councils of imams and other community leaders, an Islamic seminary, a Muslim chaplaincy program, and even a Muslim American think tank (the Institute for Social Policy and Understanding). The infrastructure that supports Muslim daily life is thriving in Detroit, despite—and in many ways because of—the War on Terror.

Fourteen new mosques have opened their doors since 2001, and even more mosques have completed impressive renovation and construction projects, more than doubling their square footage, expanding the space available for prayer, education, youth programs, social activities, and management. Much of this growth is a result of demographic change. Muslims in greater Detroit are a larger, better educated, more American-born, more immigrant, and more upwardly mobile community than they were in the 1980s (Pew 2007; Detroit Arab American Study Team 2009). Yet some of this growth has been fueled by the War on Terror. As Muslim charities were raided in 2001 and years following, their assets frozen and their CEOs prosecuted, many Muslims decided to keep their almsgiving closer to home, spending money on mosques and education programs, rather than on (or in addition to) relief and development projects overseas (Turner 2009; Howell forthcoming). Similarly, as the Muslim community came increasingly under attack, it began to develop an improved, better organized, increasingly differentiated, and more articulate civil liberties and representational infrastructure. The Council on American-Islamic Relations–Michigan (CAIR-MI) has led and been the primary beneficiary of this new support, largely because its staff has been both articulate and effective at navigating the demands of multiple constituencies. The organization's new prominence has come at a price, however. Its national affiliate has been included by federal prosecutors (with many other prominent Muslim American organizations) on a list of "un-indicted co-conspirators and/or Joint Venturers" with "ties" to Hamas. Although CAIR has never been charged with a crime, and the courts have ruled that the list in question should not have been made public,[5] the right-wing media have seized on this list to paint CAIR and other Muslim American organizations as "supporters of terrorism" and thus as illegitimate and unfit participants in American civil discourse (Salisbury 2010a; Youmans, "Domestic Foreign Policy," this volume).

The Imams Coordinating Committee (ICC) is a new body, pulled together initially by CAIR in 2006 to address the Danish cartoon scandal and respond to negative portrayals of the prophet Muhammad. The group was reconvened when several Shi'i mosques in the area were vandalized in the wake of Saddam Hussein's execution in Iraq. The group issued a Muslim Code of Honor in 2007, primarily a pledge to promote civility between Shi'i and Sunni segments of the community. Its last point reads, "Finally, we encourage all Muslims living in the United States to emphasize their commonality in accordance with God's statement, 'Hold fast, all together, to the rope of God and be not divided among yourselves" (CIOM 2007). Today, the IC is managed under the umbrella of the CIOM. It meets monthly, enabling the imams to speak with one voice when crises arise, as they frequently have in the Terror Decade, and addressing general concerns that arise within the Muslim community and between it and the larger society.

These advocacy groups are newly influential in post-9/11 Detroit, often acting as a go-between for the city's mosques and the local FBI. In the Terror Decade, all but a handful of Detroit's mosques have been questioned by FBI agents about their presumed ties to suspect Muslim movements overseas (Salafis from Saudi Arabia and Yemen, the Muslim Brotherhood, Hizballah, Hamas, Al Qaeda, a variety of Iraqi groups in and outside the government, and Pakistani militant organizations). In more than a dozen mosques, federal agents have tried to pressure congregants into informing on their leaders and fellow worshipers; several mosques report troubling encounters with newcomers who have tried to incite violence or illegality among young congregants (presumed to be the work of agent provocateurs).[6] One mosque was subjected to a two-year covert investigation by the FBI that uncovered a petty crime ring, not a network of terrorist plotters; in a dramatic sting operation, the group's imam, Luqman Abdullah, was killed by federal agents in 2009 (see below). The case studies that follow will trace the development of mosque/government relations in institutions that have been targeted by the FBI in Detroit. Old and new institutions; Arab, African American, and multiethnic; urban and suburban; large and small—these mosques had little in common prior to their run-ins with the FBI other than the faith their members practice. Today, like other mosques in Detroit, they share a feeling of intense vulnerability.

Targeted mosques have responded to federal and public pressure by disciplining their members' behavior, recording and preserving the speeches of their preachers, instituting new structures of governance and transparency, lobbying Congress for changed policies, walling out strangers, opening their doors to visitors, and cooperating, warily, with law enforcement. [7] Working together with the leadership of the Arab/Muslim community, the FBI is also closely involved in the political and representational politics of Muslim Detroit today. FBI press releases, affidavits and press conferences influence how Muslim institutions are represented in the media and to other governmental bodies. FBI campaigns to survey and surveil Muslim institutions are ongoing and are frequently made public. In 2003, for example, the FBI announced that specially equipped radiation detection devices had been driven past each of the city's mosques.[8] In the years that have followed, the public reputation of Detroit Muslims is increasingly dependent on the changing state of mosque/government relations.

Mosques and the Spies Who Love Them

Case 1: Making over the American Moslem Society

In May 2009, the American Moslem Society (AMS) hosted a large banquet to celebrate its seventieth anniversary. In doing so, it sought to illustrate not just its deep roots in Dearborn, but also the extent to which its board of directors, young, mostly professional, and new to mosque governance, had managed to reinvent the institution in recent years. The grand banquet they hosted at Greenfield Manor in Dearborn was the first event of this kind that the mosque had held in over a generation. Although it is the oldest mosque in the Detroit area, the AMS—also known simply as Masjid Dearborn[9]—is today a congregation composed largely of Yemeni immigrants who have been in the United States fewer than twenty years.[10] The Muslims who built the AMS in the 1930s, and developed and sustained it during its first forty years, were largely of Syrian and Lebanese origin. Voted out of office in an ideological coup in 1977, the founding congregation is not, for the most part, on friendly terms with the current AMS leadership, and the remnants of this earlier congregation worship at new and breakaway mosques across town. This disconnect between past and present congregations compelled the banquet organizers to focus more on the institution's recent past than on its early history, but even this recent past presented them with something of a challenge.

In the immediate aftermath of the 9/11 attacks, as Muslim institutions across the United States attracted the attention of law enforcement officers, government officials, journalists, scholars, and interfaith activists, the AMS underwent a crisis of identity that resulted in a second ideological coup. Much softer than the first coup, this transition managed to keep most of the congregation intact.[11] After firing their spiritual leader of more than 25 years—after he had clashed with the board over the 1990 Gulf War, over a recent mayoral campaign, over the management of mosque renovations, and over the priority given to foreign policy over spiritual concerns among certain congregants—who was considered "too pro-American" by some, the mosque found itself rudderless and straining to mend fences with a hostile city administration.[12] These stresses were compounded by external problems: namely, several rounds of FBI questioning of its congregants, National Security Entry-Exit Registration System registration (and for those who were in the United States on expired visas, detainment and eventual deportation), a clampdown on the transfer of money between Yemen and the United States, and the voluntary exodus of a few of the mosque's prominent members.

It was in this climate of heightened tension and self-awareness that the mosque elected a new board in 2003 consisting mostly of younger Yemeni American men with college degrees, U.S. citizenship, professional jobs, and young, American-born families.[13] After a period of sustained institutional soul-searching, this new board overhauled the mosque's corporate structure to allow greater participation in mosque governance and activities by members. The idea was to make the institution more democratic and transparent, to open it up to greater participation by women, young people, and non-Yemenis, and to actively reengage with the American society in which it was located. Although the mosque's leaders do not describe the transition in this way, their goal seems to have been to modernize and Americanize the AMS. They did this by drastically slowing down the growth of their voting membership, redefining the pool of potential board members, and requiring greater service commitments from anyone hoping to have a say in the institution's governance.

When I interviewed the outgoing president of the mosque, Mahdi Ali, in February 2010, he emphasized continuity with the mosque's past leaders rather than the sort of ideological or social break I describe here. He also downplayed my suggestion, based on conversations with other AMS members and observers, that outside pressures had been responsible for the changes Ali helped encourage during his years on the board: "I haven't seen in our organization any pressure for the old board to leave and give a chance to the new generation. It just happened by itself. Those people did a good job in the time that they were in charge. They focused mostly on the construction that started in 2000."[14] He mentioned as well that the mosque's major renovation project—a doubling of its square footage, the building of a new entrance for women, the expansion of its library and classrooms, the addition of a large new social hall—was a response to the natural growth the congregation experienced in the 1990s. The new board, he argued, was an extension of this growth, especially after the new facilities opened in 2003. With a larger facility, there was now more room for both men and women to circulate comfortably (and still separately) in the facility. And with construction and fundraising behind them, the board could turn its attention to providing new services—social, educational, recreational—for the community. The board sought to include more people in the life of the congregation and created new committees that focused on education, seniors, youth, mosque finances, charitable activities, and *dawa* (outreach and religious witness).

I asked if these changes were not in some way a response to external scrutiny of the congregation after 9/11.

Ali: One of the most important factors I want to say is that the Muslims, the scholars, now especially after September 11—they want Muslims to spread the message of Islam, and in order for you to spread the message, you cannot do it while you are isolated. And Islam you know—the religion—if you read the Quran it asks everyone to present *dawa* to all non-Muslims—just to present it to them. . . . You give them the message. So how would you do that unless you get out of isolation? Maybe the old generation also wanted to do this, but they didn't have the capability. . . . My father, when he came to the U.S. in the 1970s, he wanted to present Islam to the non-Muslims, but he didn't have enough confidence. I probably can do this better, and my kids will do this better than me. So I do anticipate that the Muslim community will become more open with the new generation.

Ali's point, then, was that the new anti-isolationist and self-disciplining agenda of the AMS was not based on any particular pressures applied to the AMS, but were part of a broader, national response made by American Muslims to their collective crisis. Mosque open houses and "get to know your neighbor" campaigns are now common across the country (Bakalian and Bozorgmehr 2009).[15] In Detroit, these campaigns predate 9/11. The AMS began educating non-Muslims about Islam as early as the 1940s (Howell 2009). By the late 1980s, the AMS was a regular stop for groups visiting "Arab Town," for K–12 groups visiting the Museum of Arab Cultures at ACCESS, and for university classes studying religious and ethnic diversity. Yet neighbors, interfaith activists, and college students are not the only people curious about the AMS; the institution was indeed under tremendous pressure from outsiders to represent itself in post-9/11 Detroit.

Ali: Unfortunately, in the last eight years under the Bush administration we saw a lot happen that was unjust against the Muslims, and they used the War on Terror like a cover to close a lot of charities, to wiretap Muslims communities, sending spies to mosques, etc. We are trying to work in our mosque, you know. We are frustrated about this because we have been unjustly targeted. We are good people, you know. If you take the Southend, our *masjid*, you know, it has been here for seventy years. Give me one instance where people from this *masjid*, from this community, did something bad to the United States: seventy years.

They came and they worked in factories. They work very hard. They were like any other American peoples in building this country, paying taxes, raising their kids, like normal. . . . The American country is a great country. I strongly believe in that, and I feel a lot of respect. I owe this country a lot because I came in the 1990s from Yemen and I got my education here. I got help from the government—and this is from the American people—so how would I harm a community that hosted me and gave me the ability to go to school and helped me achieve my degrees? But one of the things that I don't like in the American community (and I am one of them) is generalizations. . . . They take examples of bad action from one person and they generalize it over the whole community.

Ali is not the only person I spoke to about the recent history of the AMS. I also discussed the mosque with Andy Arena in his office at the FBI. Although

Ali did not volunteer stories about his congregation's recent encounters with the FBI, Arena was quick to tell me about one of these instances:

> *Arena:* I was down there last fall. We had a white convert on the west side of the state, and he wakes up one day and he has got the call to jihad. I think it was voices in his head. He went off his medication. So he talks to his buddy, and he says, "You got to take me over to the mosque—the Dix Street mosque—and I am going to get my weapons or something there, and then I'm going to go out and . . ." He talked about going to Chicago and blowing up some facility there. So the family gets—they are afraid—so they call. So we are looking for this guy, 'cause we don't know where he is going.
>
> We finally [tracked him down to Dearborn].
>
> So we go over there [to the AMS], and we are kind of standing around, and the agents are uncomfortable, so I went out there. And we just went in the mosque, and I said what I was there for: "We know a guy was here earlier and this is what he looked like, and he is crazy." So initially they were kind of like very standoffish, and then one person, the president of the mosque, started talking to us. The maintenance guy came up and said, "Oh yeah. That guy was here." And [they] showed us their, they have wonderful outdoor video. And we were able to actually identify the guy in the car he left in, and [we] found him. Actually he was committed.
>
> And I went back like two weeks later just to thank them, and they were so nervous. They were very helpful. It's funny; when I went back the second time, I went in and talked and thanked them. I said, "I want to formally thank you." And I wanted to tell them what happened; we found the guy later that night, over in Hamtramck. We got him help. And the family came and they actually committed him for a while, so . . . and when I was leaving, Melanie Elturk [a lawyer], who was with CAIR at the time, was coming in. They had called CAIR and said, "Hey, the FBI is here. Will you come over?" I heard them saying to her, "No. Really, they just wanted to say thank you." [He laughs.] And she is going, "No, no. Really, what do they want?" And they said, "No. They just wanted to thank us." That is all we did.[16]

It is no coincidence that both Arena's agents and the mosque's congregation are awkward and wary around one another. Arena's agents did not want to enter the mosque without him present, and the mosque leadership was equally unwilling to visit with Arena without a representative from CAIR on hand (standard operating procedure now for Detroit's mosques). This wariness is a result of several years' worth of sustained interaction between the two parties, interaction that usually involves questioning rather than expressions of gratitude. In the case of this "white convert," however, the "threat advisory level" was apparently low enough for the media not to have been called in, for no arrests to have been made, and for no accusations of "providing material support" for terrorism (or worse) to have been levied against the mosque, or even the individual involved.[17] I asked Ali about this incident, and he was surprised to hear Arena had shared it with me.

Ali acknowledged that he feels his institution, and the Muslim community as a whole, are being targeted, harassed even, by the FBI.[18] He has sat through several meetings with local agents, always in the offices of CAIR and usually with a lawyer present, responding to their questions about his congregation and, as in the following example, asking a few questions of his own.

> *Ali:* We like them to do their job, because that brings safety and security to all. We can't live without law enforcement. But what bothers me and others in the community is that sometimes the FBI, they have informants, and these informants, in order for them to continue their jobs, they have to make up stories and sometimes this leads them into wrong acts. So they are trying to get youth 14-, 15-year-olds in trouble by talking to these kids about violence. And these youth, because they are still young, they will say, "Oh yeah, we need to do this. We need to bomb . . ." And sometimes these agents and FBI—it can go up to leaders. They are trying to keep their job by getting others in trouble, not [trying] to keep the whole country safe. We want them to focus and do their job—to use their energy to keep the country safe and to get those people who are making trouble, but not to use . . . tactics that are not [ethical], like talking to the youth about the Gaza war and trying to get statements from them. And, you see, [the youth] talk like [this] because they are young and they do not know what they say sometimes, and that is a real concern. I am sure you follow CAIR and you know that sometimes those informants put wrong statements about someone, "this person said this and this and this." And to be honest, when someone came to talk to our youth about violence, we thought of them as informants.

The AMS has contacted the FBI twice about such instances, and neither contact has been reported in the news media.

> *Ali:* We had in our mind that this person was FBI—because, you know, we have in mind these tactics. They are trying to get other people into troubles, you know. Any good, reasoned person would not talk to youth about something like that.

Similarly, Arena did not mention these exchanges to me. At the AMS, at CAIR, and at the other mosques in Detroit where I spoke to people about the FBI, the consensus was clear: these instigators are FBI informants making trouble on behalf of the government rather than in opposition to it. In this context of fear, suspicion, and growth, the AMS's celebration of its long history can be read not simply as a tale of its survival and success over seven decades, but rather as a celebration of its survival and success quite specifically in this decade, the decade of the War on Terror.

The use of informants in mosques is troubling to Muslim leaders nationwide, a concern that escalated after the U.S. Justice Department produced the Domestic Intelligence and Operations Guide in 2008, increasing the FBI's power to use undercover sources.[19] In 2009, the American Muslim Task Force, a coalition of six Muslim groups, accused the FBI of targeting Muslim houses of worship and inhibiting the free speech and religious freedom of Muslims. In response, they announced that they were considering suspending relations with the FBI entirely (*Detroit Free Press*, March 18, 2009). Dawud Walid points out, however, that such a boycott would be difficult for both populations—law enforcement and Muslim organizations—to finesse. The FBI is simply too involved with Muslim American institutions at the moment, frequently investigating charges of hate crimes, religious discrimination, and physical threats made against Muslims, and just as frequently, investigating Muslim institutions. Throughout 2009, news stories broke on a regular basis announcing the arrest of would-be terrorists at a variety of American mosques, from California to New Jersey to Florida to Michigan.[20] The thread that seemed to tie these stories together was not a network of extremists plotting against targets within the United States, but rather a network of FBI operatives and informant provocateurs targeting American mosques. As Stephan Salisbury (2010b) has argued:

> Informers . . . regularly do the dirty work—suggesting and encouraging the plots, laboring as bag men to move the money, fashioning the bombs, and eliciting the flamboyant dialogue, even while following the scripts of their handlers to the letter. They have attended to all the little details that make for the successful and now familiar arrests, criminal complaints, trials, and (for the most part) convictions in the ever-distracting war [on terror].[21]

The government's informers were frequently desperate men: the homeless, the terminally ill, the addicted, the siblings and kin of those with extensive medical bills, aliens about to be deported. Caught up in schemes to save themselves from jail time, deportation, or financial duress or offered quick and easy money (sometimes in the hundreds of thousands of dollars), they were willing not only to inform on their fellow Muslims, but also to entrap them.[22] News of terror plots began to escalate significantly in 2009, making it appear as though American mosques were indeed centers of "homegrown terrorist" organizing. CAIR-MI, like other CAIR affiliates across the country, began offering Know Your Rights sessions for local mosques, providing advice on how to handle potential problems, especially those involving suspected informants/provocateurs. Audience members were reminded that spying and informing on fellow Muslims is explicitly forbidden in the Quran.[23] And yet Muslims were also reminded to obey the laws of the lands in which they reside, to seek justice always, and to live according to the teachings of the Quran, which forbids violence against the innocent. As Mahdi Ali told me, "This is our obligation, for sure. If we see any person trying to do something bad, any act of crimes or terrorism, we will talk to the FBI right away about it. Because if that person commits something, it is against us all, including Muslims and Islam." For most of Detroit's Muslims, the first step to be taken in the face of suspicious activity is to call CAIR. The second step is for CAIR to call Andy Arena, the Special Agent in Charge of Detroit's FBI office. Resolving such problems internally is no longer an option for Detroit Muslims. The stakes are simply too high.

This relationship between the Muslim American community and the FBI is volatile and saturated by oppressive power differentials. Nonetheless, it binds Arab and Muslim Americans to the governmental agencies charged simultaneously with defending their rights *and* waging the War on Terror. Arena has been a special guest at several Imams Committee meetings. He has been invited to address the new guidelines put in place by the Department of Justice and then to defend his agents' actions in carrying out these and other directives. He also addresses complaints of vandalism at local mosques, alleged hate crimes against Muslims, and other instances of actionable discrimination. At many Arab/Muslim public meetings he also shows up with a team of minority recruitment officers in tow and encourages young Arab and Muslim Americans to consider careers in the FBI. In this context of familiarity, co-dependence, discipline, and mutual suspicion, the problem of FBI reliance on informants and agent-provocateurs is sheer poison. Virtually every mosque leader I have spoken to in recent years assumes informants, and often undercover agents as well, have been active in their institutions.[24] Arena readily admits that this fear of informants is rampant in Dearborn and that Arab Americans have frequently used this fear to settle scores among themselves, blackmail one another, and otherwise police one another's thoughts and activities. But given the high level of cooperation the FBI receives from the Muslim population, and the regularity with which local mosques are asked to submit to new investigations and surveys (the relevance of which are sometimes difficult to fathom),[25] it is especially galling to leaders who

work closely with Arena to find their own institutions subjected to undercover prying and worse.

*Case 2: Mainstreaming the Islamic Organization of
North America*

Imam Mustapha "Steve" Elturk, is a publically engaged Muslim leader
who has come to believe that the FBI tried to turn a young convert from his
congregation into an informant charged with collecting information on
Elturk, his mosque, and the national organization he represents, the Islamic
Organization of North America (IONA). Elturk, a Lebanese immigrant and
longtime citizen of the United States, was more introverted with his career in
the 1990s, focusing on dynamics internal to the Muslim community. In the
Terror Decade, he found himself playing a much more public role, representing the faith as an agent of change and public outreach and also acting as a
defender of Islam and of his rights as an American citizen. Elturk is a leading
interfaith activist in Detroit, co-chair of the Imams Coordinating Committee
(ICC), head of IONA (both a mosque and the American home of an international Muslim spiritual movement), and a member of the FBI's Multi-
Cultural Advisory Council. He is also clearly being monitored by the federal
government, has a difficult time crossing back and forth between the United
States and Canada, and now finds himself the target of a botched investigation by the same agency he thought himself to be working with (if not for)
in a constructive manner.

IONA is a new congregation that opened in the northern suburb of
Warren, Michigan, in 2007. The city's first mosque, IONA was not warmly
welcomed. Warren's population is largely a product of white flight from
Detroit in the 1960s and 1970s. The municipality shares a mile-long border
with Detroit, and it has a reputation for policing this boundary between blackness and whiteness vigilantly. The city's police department is often accused of
racial profiling. But Warren is also home to large corporate, research, and
engineering facilities owned by General Motors, and thus to many Muslim
workers and, increasingly, to Muslim residents as well. IONA provides both
workers and residents with a nearby home for congregational prayers, holiday celebrations, and religious education. It is also the American offspring of
the Tanzeem-e-Islami movement, a Pakistan-based *dawa* movement that encourages Muslims to live a Quran-centered life.[26] As Elturk describes the
movement, it is a bit to the right of the Tablighi Jumaat, who encourage Muslim believers to return to the mosque and to the everyday practice of Islam.
Elturk's group wants Muslims also to be compliant with Islamic traditions
in regard to their mortgages and other finances and to be revitalized in their
iman (faith and conviction). Practicing complete transparency, Elturk's group

provides an extensive history of their organization on the Web, including a rundown of their ideological and spiritual connections to men such as Abul Kalam Azad, Sayyid Abul A'la Maududi, and Israr Ahmad, intellectuals associated with the Islamic revivals of the early twentieth century who are sometimes linked with the Muslim Brotherhood and Jama'at-e-Islami, both frequent targets of the right-wing media's Islamophobic scaremongers.

Elturk and his congregation were shocked when a neighborhood association adjacent to their lot tried to block IONA's renovation project (and thus prevent the establishment of the mosque in Warren). In April 2006, the association, along with several anti-Muslim activists in the city, brought a complaint before the city's Planning Commission that the mosque was in violation of the city's zoning regulations. They had been coached on how to subtly and politely prevent Muslims from setting up shop in their community (by a local mailman who lives in Hamtramck, a much smaller nearby community with close to ten mosques and a high concentration of Muslim families).[27] Other attendees were less concerned with appearances. Some complained about parking and traffic congestion on Fridays and holidays, argued that the call to prayer would violate the city's noise ordinances, and asserted that a "storefront" mosque would transgress city aesthetic standards,[28] and others simply shouted at the congregation to go back where they had come from— "hell"—asked how they would be able to distinguish worshippers from members of Al Qaeda or other terrorists, and suggested human sacrifices might be practiced at this mosque. A wide array of interfaith activists, especially Christian clergy from Warren and Jewish activists from neighboring communities, were articulate spokespeople on behalf of the mosque, but the Planning Commission initially voted against IONA's renovations and sought to block its move to the city. Only after a city attorney stepped in and made clear to the commission that they could not defend their decision legally—that they would cost the city hundreds of thousands of dollars in legal fees to defend a decision based on straightforward religious discrimination—and only after IONA voluntarily agreed to forgo broadcasting the call to prayer did the head of the planning commission, Gus Ghanam (a Lebanese American Christian), reverse his vote, giving IONA the 5–3 majority it needed. After this evening of high drama, Elturk announced, "We see the outcome of this meeting as favorable, but it underscores the need for deeper understanding between Muslims and the community. It is natural for people to be apprehensive when someone new moves in. We will treat our neighbors with the utmost respect. . . . Good relations with neighbors is a requirement of Islamic belief."

True to his word, Elturk began hosting open houses and went out of his way to include both the interfaith crowd who had been outspoken in supporting the mosque and the neighborhood association who had been outspoken in resisting them. No *adhan* (call to prayer) is heard from IONA's rooftop. These experiences, both negative and positive, helped convince Elturk that he needed to focus more of his energy on interacting with the larger American society. As in the AMS example, it was not the 9/11 attacks themselves that encouraged this focus, but a heightened American awareness of Islam (and, in this case, fear of Muslims) that nudged Elturk in new directions. His ecumenical work and outreach on behalf of Islam has been impressive over the past few years. He heads the new Muslim chaplaincy program at the Detroit Ecumenical Theological Seminary. He is a leading and reliable participant in the InterFaith Leadership Council of Metropolitan Detroit, and he is president of the Interfaith Center for Racial Justice and co-author of their curriculum on Islam and Muslims with Imam Aly Lela (see www.icjr.org). He regularly attends, and speaks out in protest at, events at the Thomas More Law Center (the site of an organized campaign to misrepresent Islam and thwart Muslim incorporation in the media and courts).

Despite Elturk's energetic and cooperative nature, despite his already close interaction with local FBI leadership, and despite his role as a respected religious leader, he still finds himself on the receiving end of FBI investigative agendas. At the national level, IONA's leaders have been questioned in great detail about their connections to al-Tanzeen in Pakistan. Elturk, for example, was interviewed in Chicago, where IONA's attorneys are located. The FBI's investigation focused on the group's finances, the background of its leaders, its ideology, and the strength of its ties to Pakistan. Closer to home, Elturk is concerned that his congregation—which has not been subjected to direct questioning—has been the target of an FBI "fishing expedition" and worse. When Arena claims, as he often does, that the FBI does not "have the resources to put informants everywhere," Elturk greets such statements with extreme skepticism.[29]

In March 2010, Elturk outlined his congregation's recent skirmish with the FBI:

> *Elturk:* They cannot have an agent directly come and spy, because this is against federal laws. But what they do is they get somebody, like in one case, Abdullah, a young man who converted, right. His name is Lawrence. He gets in trouble because he was at TACOM [U.S. Army Tank-automotive and Armaments Command], you know, this defense facility, the tank facility [a weapon systems research, development, and sustainment organization linked to General Motors] on Mound [Road] and 12 [Mile Road]. He gets arrested there because he was standing, well actually, he had this garb on. I told him, "Don't wear this." You know, checkered kuffiyyeh, and this dishdash and all that. He is a young man . . .
>
> *Howell:* So what was he doing there?

Elturk: He lives near there and he goes to Burger King, which is right by the gas station, and he was cutting across the lawn and somebody inside saw him. And what I heard from one of the officers was—because I went and visited him in the jail—they told me that somebody, I think he had just come from Iraq, and he sees this and he says, "These are the people who come and bomb us and kill us over there. What the hell is going on?" So they arrested him for trespassing. They give him to the Warren police. They take him to jail.

Then the FBI go and investigate him for a couple of hours. Then he tells them, "I am from IONA."

"IONA, oh. We know Iona. I know Steve. He is a nice guy," etc., etc.

Things like that. No problem. Anyway, then we take his case. I got a lawyer, I got my daughter. Then I got another lawyer. Then we got him out of this whole thing. They dropped the charges because it was all baloney. He was not trespassing. The lawyer challenged this and said, "Show me this is trespassing. There were no signs saying 'No Trespassing' or anything like that." So they had to drop the case altogether.

[Before the case was dropped, however,] he gets approached by FBI agents on the phone, saying, "Oh, Lawrence, how are you doing? Everything is okay? We can help you out with your case." . . . And, you know, "We can give you a cell phone and some money, all you need to do is find out who comes and goes inside IONA—give us some names and things of that sort."

You help us out and we'll get you a cell phone. . . . They will help reduce the charges and all that. So this is . . . what they do. They find people who are in trouble with the law and they are very vulnerable and ask them to help them, and those people want out of, in most cases, people who have actually committed a crime or have an immigration issue. I know of some cases among our members nationwide who this has happened to. "Either you work with us or we are going to deport you."

Andy Arena denies that Lawrence/Abdullah was asked to inform on Elturk or the IONA congregation. He says it was only natural that the FBI would interview someone found with a compass (in his version of the narrative) and dressed in "Islamic apparel" on the grounds of the TACOM facility and that his agents found that Lawrence had simply been lost. He says that he has read through the notes of their interview with Lawrence and found nothing suspicious there, that the questioning focused mostly on Lawrence's roommates and associates, not on the mosque or its leaders. It would be illegal, he asserts, for his agents to try to turn Lawrence into an informant for them. Yet Lawrence claims this request to blackmail him into informing on the mosque came over the phone, not during his face-to-face interview with Arena's agents. Lawrence received this call in the presence of a witness who has also backed up his version of events, not just with Elturk, but also with Arena's assistant, Brian Young, when he met with and questioned Lawrence about the incident. Elturk and other Muslim leaders in Detroit are convinced the

FBI tried to create an informant out of Lawrence, whereas Arena insists that "we never asked him to inform on Steve Elturk." The matter continues to resurface in Arena's face-to-face meetings with Muslim leaders.

Elturk has also found that his name appears on government no-fly and other watch lists. The last two times he has returned from Canada with his family, he found himself at the center of a swarm of armed officers with their weapons drawn. He was handcuffed, his car searched, his family questioned about their contacts in Canada, Pakistan, Lebanon, Saudi Arabia, and the United States, and detained for hours. He has complained to Senator Carl Levin, Homeland Security Secretary Tom Ridge, U.S. Customs Commissioner Robert Bonner, and many others. He has been told that he seems to be suffering, as are thousands of Muslim American citizens, from a case of "mistaken identity." After trying repeatedly to have his name cleared, Elturk and others familiar with his case have come to the conclusion that his identity has not been mistaken, but that he himself is being watched.

Being the subject of this intense scrutiny is something Elturk, like other Muslim leaders in Detroit, is learning to live with. He has no choice in the matter. Like many other Detroit mosques, IONA has video security monitoring the entrances to its building, and it has begun video-taping all their public events. The security cameras, like those at the AMS, can be used to identify precisely who enters and exits the building on any given occasion. They have already been used to apprehend mosque vandals. And the documentation of lectures and sermons can be used to provide the full content of Elturk's and other lecturers' speeches, should an informant ever attempt to misquote them. Elturk posts most of his sermons and lectures online. For Elturk, this self-documentation and self-discipline have become increasingly important as the term "sharia" (Islamic law) has come under attack in recent years. Right-wing pundits, politicians, and FBI case officers have begun to problematize the term and argue that when Muslims seek to live by the tenets of the Quran and *sunna* (example of the Prophet), they are also seeking to impose these rules and obligations (in their most conservative and literalist interpretations) on other Americans.[30]

This issue surfaced in the criminal complaint the FBI filed against several members of Masjid al-Haqq, the Detroit mosque headed by slain imam Luqman Abdullah, characterizing the group's efforts to create a sharia-oriented space around their mosque as a sinister and violent secessionist plot (text cited below). As Elturk read the al-Haqq affidavit, he became seriously concerned. He has no problem advising young Muslims to curb their sartorial enthusiasms or to deliver the call to prayer inside the mosque, but when it comes to the basic tenets of Islam, he is unwilling to compromise.

Elturk: Is that going to hinder our preaching? Because we are Muslims and we believe in Islamic sharia. Islamic sharia is part of our way of life. So now if I go ahead and preach Islam is a way of life, you know, preach Islam is this and that, are they going to intervene? This could have repercussions for me or for any imam. . . . This is very disturbing. . . . I believe in what I believe in, and if I am living in a country that I cherish and love because of its freedoms, I am going to continue to speak what I think is correct.

I am not going to be silenced, but I have got to be careful. Really, we cannot ignore this case. We have to find out what is going to happen after that. Is the government going to issue some laws based on this case saying that anybody who preaches Islamic sharia will be arrested?

Lest it appear that Elturk sounds paranoid, it should be noted that Arena makes repeated public statements about Islam that seem to imply that he has the right to arbitrate what is both "true Islam" and "acceptable" Islamic speech. On January 28, 2010, Arena spoke at a Know Your Rights session sponsored by the Muslim Student Association at the University of Michigan–Dearborn, where he asserted that "if you are preaching the true Islam in your mosques, you have nothing to fear. You are not going to be investigated." When asked if the FBI claims the authority to determine what is and is not "true Islam," he said, "Of course not," but went on to speak vaguely of his Muslim staff members and to affirm that "the vast majority of the Muslim community are good, decent people." Such reassurances provide small comfort to men like Elturk, who will continue to preach Islam and to seek to bridge the political and social gaps that have come to define Muslim-American relations during the Terror Decade. In February 2010, Elturk participated in an in-depth training workshop about Islam for local judges and federal prosecutors. "They were so happy that they now understand," he said, "they have repeated this session twice." As Elturk sees things, "the sharia is the greatest thing since sliced bread, and I confidently say that because I know what it is."

Case Three: Provoking Masjid al-Haqq

The worst nightmares of Elturk and other Muslim leaders in Detroit came true on October 28, 2009, when news broke that a local imam had been shot and killed in an FBI raid in Dearborn. The AP headline read "Luqman Ameen Abdullah, Leader of Radical Islam Group, Killed in Raid."[31] Word quickly spread that Imam Luqman Abdullah of Masjid al-Haqq, one of the city's smallest, poorest, and otherwise most marginal congregations, had been shot to death in an FBI sting operation. It seemed highly unlikely that Masjid al-Haqq was the center of a radical Islamic movement. The mosque had recently been shuttered due to unpaid taxes and financial collapse.[32] It also seemed unlikely that Imam Luqman, an affable, somewhat shy man who seemed content with his place on the margins of Detroit's Muslim community, was plotting "offensive jihad" against the United States, threatening to spread Islam through the use of violence, and seeking to set up a "separate, sovereign Islamic state ('The Ummah') within the borders of the United States, governed by Shariah law . . . to be ruled over by Jamil Abdullah Al-Amin, formerly known as H. Rap Brown" (Criminal Compliant Case: 2:09-mj-30436, filed October 27, 2009, 4).

Luqman had a criminal past; he was convicted of felonious assault in 1981, but as a convert to Islam, he had devoted his life to issues of social justice and moral reform. He taught Quran classes at the Muslim Community of the Western Suburbs Mosque (the "Canton mosque") for many years, and was especially appreciated in the suburban, South Asian, professional community as a thoughtful teacher and scholar. Masjid al-Haqq, located in the Petosky-Otsego neighborhood of Detroit, a community plagued by high unemployment, low home ownership, and a general lack of law and order, was a local landmark where the homeless could come in from the cold, the hungry could count on a hot meal, and drug dealers and prostitutes knew their trade was unwelcome. The mosque had reopened in a new neighborhood shortly before the FBI raid, quickly reinstating its soup kitchen and other service activities. The text of the FBI's criminal complaint against Luqman, which portrayed the imam as a tough-talking, gun-toting, cop-hating, dangerous felon, came as a second shock to Muslim Detroit, although he had refused to attend IC meetings when Arena was scheduled to speak because he did not like the way the city's other imams seemed to "kiss up" to the FBI (Dawud Walid, personal communication). Rather than dwell on the circumstances of the shooting, which drew condemnation from the national civil rights establishment, my concern here is over the legal grounds the FBI used to justify their infiltration of the mosque in the first place, over the use of informant/provocateurs in the investigation, and over the consequences of this investigation and its tragic outcome for the Muslim communities of Detroit writ large.

In my conversation with Arena, he did not explain what first drew his unit's attention to Masjid al-Haqq. Instead his comments provide insight into his overall approach to community law enforcement.

Howell: What are your policies in terms of approaching religious associations for any sort of investigation?

Arena: For investigative purposes, you have got to have predication.[33] We don't target buildings. We don't target religions. We focus on groups or individuals involved in criminal activity or threats to the United States—to national security. So you have got to have, basically, predication—that something is going on in that religious facility such as an imam recruiting people to go and fight in Afghanistan or to go to train.

Howell: And how would you hear about that?

Arena: It would be basically—the other part of it is, when I approach a mosque or whatever—as the head of the FBI outreach program, I meet with the Imams Committee probably quarterly. I also meet with them at the BRIDGES meeting, at ALPACT, at all these different community meetings that I go to, and I also meet with them individually. I have a Multi-Cultural Advisory Council. I have two imams that sit on that. . . .

Howell: And how often does that group meet?

Arena: My group meets—probably three or four times a year. So what we will find is twofold. It may be that people from the community come to us. It may be through another investigation that will lead us to that place, or it may be these people coming to us. I have had . . . I have people from the community coming to us and saying, "Hey, you had better look at these people over here. We think they are up to no good. They are preaching an extremist view. They are recruiting." You have to have that predication. If you don't, then it is unconstitutional. It is illegal. I can't just say, "Boy, I would like to know what is going on in the Dix Street mosque."

This is an explicit acknowledgment that the bureau's partnerships with the Arab/Muslim community are undertaken as a means of data gathering. The BRIDGES and ALPACT partnerships are not usually described as conduits for government surveillance. Yet Arab and Muslim leaders in the city also understand that this function is an important part of the relationship. They are eager to help the government do a better job of identifying and prosecuting transgressions, although they are quick to argue that racial, ethnic, and religious profiling is counterproductive. The agencies waste critical resources (and, in fact, manufacture crimes) rather than rely on time-honored intelligence-gathering methods that profile behaviors rather than communities. An Arab American civil rights advocate in Detroit, speaking off the record, told me that everyone knows the BRIDGES and ALPACT alliances are, at heart, intelligence-gathering vehicles for Immigration and Customs Enforcement, the FBI, Homeland Security, the Department of Commerce, and the other governmental participants. "Who would you rather the FBI get their information about the Arab community from," he asked, "ADC or a couple of gas station owners?" Andy Arena reinforced this idea when he announced in an Imams Committee meeting, held the morning after Luqman's death, that "two of you mentioned to me that we should look into Luqman Abdullah's activities" (interview with Dawud Walid, March 2, 2010; interviews with Mustapha (Steve) Elturk, Warren, Michigan, March 3 and April 17, 2010).

The FBI and other federal agencies also use these community-government alliances as recruitment networks. Several well-placed community advocates have switched sides, as it were, moving from positions within the ADC to those within government. Kareem Shora is one such example. Rana Abbas, former deputy director of ADC Michigan, has made a similar leap. She currently serves as senior manager of Corporate Communications for Global Linguistic Services, a contractor for the Department of Defense. Not all community advocacy groups work closely with the FBI, however. The American Civil Liberties Union, CAIR, and several Muslim legal defense funds have been more effective at challenging the new laws and regulations passed during the Terror Decade by filing lawsuits against the Bush and Obama administrations than through face-to-face meetings with federal officials.[34]

In the black community, people are less likely to blame Imam Luqman's incrimination by the FBI on the War on Terror. The imam was a loyal associate of Jamil al-Amin, a Muslim cleric from Atlanta who was convicted of killing a police officer in 2000 and is now serving a life sentence in a maximum-security facility in Utah for this crime. Formerly known as H. Rap Brown, the chairman of the Student Nonviolent Coordinating Committee and later the Justice Minister of the Black Panther Party in the 1960s, Brown became a Muslim while serving a sentence for robbery in the 1970s and changed his name to Jamil al-Amin. Al-Amin studied Islam seriously while in prison and upon his release, and became a respected religious leader among African American Muslims in the 1980s. Many of his supporters within the Dar ul-Islam movement and the Muslim Alliance of North America (MANA) feel that al-Amin was framed for the murder and point out that his case fits a long-standing pattern of FBI and other law enforcement harassment of black religious and civil rights activists, most famously documented during the period of COINTELPRO (1956–1970). As Sohail Daulatzai describes al-Amin's situation, "During his trial, he was constructed by the state as the embodiment of the 'homegrown terrorist,' but [he better resembles] the revolutionary who is imprisoned by the state" (2009, 219). Those who were close to Imam Luqman assume his association with al-Amin accounts for the FBI's interest in him, not the suspicious whispers of Detroit's Muslim clerics.

Arena's comments also suggest this possibility, as he references "other investigations" as a source for inquiries into local mosques. The official affidavit supports this theory as well, characterizing the "Ummah" community Luqman was supposedly leading as a radical, separatist association, a caricature that drew rapid criticism from MANA, which issued a statement in support of the imam, a member of their national shura council.

The National Community or "Ummah" was established by Imam Jamil Al-Amin (formerly known as H. Rap Brown). It is an association of mosques in several cities in the US that coordinate religious and social services primarily in the Black community and to refer to the "Ummah" as a "nationwide radical fundamentalist Sunni group consisting primarily of African Americans" is an offensive mischaracterization. (Muslim Alliance of North America 2009)

MANA also reminded readers that the complaints listed by the FBI against the imam alleged he was involved in criminal and "not terrorist activity." This is a point that Arena also emphasized, somewhat confusedly in our conversation, when I objected to the way the FBI affidavit spends so much energy painting Imam Luqman and his followers as would-be revolutionaries or violent terrorists, when the actual case brought against them was for fencing stolen property and illegally carrying firearms. The FBI's informant/provocateurs tried to entice Luqman into supporting an attack on the 2006 Super Bowl in Detroit by offering $5,000 that could be used to hire a third party to carry out the attack, but the imam refused on religious grounds. Under these circumstances, it seems inappropriate that Gary Leone, from the FBI's Counter-Terrorism Squad, was responsible for the al-Haqq investigation. When I pointed this out to Arena and asked for clarification about the (ab)use of anti-terrorism labels and resources in this investigation, Arena admitted only that the Patriot Act had given his office new "techniques" to be used only in cases involving "suspected terrorists." He suggested that it is often the media, as in recent cases involving Islamic charities, who draw the association between Arab/Muslim suspects and terrorism, not federal authorities. Yet the federal agents involved in high-profile raids are uniformly photographed wearing boldly emblazoned Joint Terrorism Task Force jackets, and the media is uniformly on hand to capture their investigations in Arab/Muslim communities.[35]

Akil Fahd, the current treasurer of Masjid al-Haqq, and a close friend of Imam Luqman's, sees the case from a very different perspective.

Fahd: The reality of it is that this is something the government has always done. This is not anything new to any of the nontraditional religious institutions in the black community. The FBI went and infiltrated and did spying with the Marcus Garvey movement, the Moorish Science Temple, with the Nation of Islam, with other groups too. This has nothing to do with the Patriot Act. I know other people say that, but when you look historically, it has always been done . . . there has never been a time when black people congregated that the government did not infiltrate the group . . . [He provides several additional examples]. Any time there is a congregation of black people that express any type of opposition to the government, whatever type of government it is, you are going to have infiltrators, you are going to have conspirators, you are going to have provocateurs. (Interview, Detroit, March 3, 2010)

When I pressed him further about why the federal government would be interested in Masjid al-Haqq, and not some other congregation, he returned to the issue of the public space Luqman and his followers were trying to produce around their mosque. The Ummah community, in Fahd's understanding, is about trying to create drug- and alcohol-free zones around their mosques and communities, and "Muslims who live Islamically," he argued, "are bad for business."

> *Fahd:* Meaning if a person's business is selling alcohol to impoverished persons, then Islam is going to be bad for business, because Islam forbids alcohol. And Muslims who live according to [the sharia] are going to want to see their environment reflect that. Similarly, if a person's objective is to exploit people with lotteries and gambling, primarily the poor . . . Islam is opposed to that, and Muslims who subscribe to that and believe that and try to have that shown and reflected in their neighborhoods, well, then that makes Islam bad for the lottery business.

The use of informants and provocateurs in the al-Haqq case was disturbing to Muslim leaders because it validated so clearly their ongoing fears about the federal government's willingness to go beyond its efforts to survey and discipline the community and to cross the line into framing and entrapment. The primary informant used in the al-Haqq case was apparently a long-standing member of the congregation. His testimony, as presented in the affidavit, combines the literal and documentable facts of the case with a great deal of spin and speculation, building a narrative that suggests the imam supported "violent jihad" without ever providing such evidence on tape.[36] Two additional informants surreptitiously recorded conversations with the imam and other members of al-Haqq and sought to involve them in petty money-making schemes and eventually the "warehouse scheme" (involving the resale of stolen goods) in which the group was entrapped. Yet much of the recorded conversations that are presented in the affidavit are filled with bravado and vivid anti–law enforcement rhetoric, of "selling wolf tickets" in the language of the streets. The FBI had ample cause and opportunity to arrest the imam at any time because he illegally carried a firearm. Ensnaring the al-Haqq members as they did in the warehouse sting strikes leaders of the Muslim establishment as extreme and unnecessary and has greatly exacerbated their sense that they are under siege.

Arena: I think it was a two-year investigation. When we do a big investigation, we don't pick people off one, two people at a time. To have the optimum—you take as many people in the organization, you basically—you take out the cancerous tumor. You don't just do radiation; you take the whole thing out. That's the way you stop a criminal enterprise. (Interview, March 4, 2010)

Fahd agrees that after spending millions of dollars on the investigation, the FBI needed to show a big payoff. It needed headlines. Fahd also pointed out that the late summer and fall of 2009 was a busy period for raiding mosques and apprehending would-be terrorists nationwide.

Fahd: Could it have been because the Patriot Act was about to sunset? . . . [The Luqman raid was] designed to keep the money flowing. I don't have to target people just because they are activists, but if I can pull one person out of each group—out of thousands of people, and I can get that individual to either say something that is controversial, or I can compromise them into doing something that is radical by enticing them, then this gives me the justification to spend these billions of dollars on other things. So if I pull off this one instance, then I have justified these massive, massive amounts of money. So a lot of people get paid for that. . . . How can you shut off the spigot when everybody is used to going to the trough? You can't. The Detroit Police Department, the FBI, the county, all of them get massive dollars if they can tie things to terrorism. (Interview, March 3, 2010)

Arena puts things a bit differently. "Our position on Luqman Abdullah is— and I can't say a lot because there are ten other people awaiting trial—all I tell people is that over the next couple of months there is going to be a lot of evidence that is released, hundreds of hours of audio tape. The crux of the case is his own words. Over the next two months it will all come out. Then you make up your own mind." And yet on the day after the imam's slaying, even Arena was trying to both milk and distance himself from the al-Haqq investigation's links to terrorism. In a press conference held just after his meeting with the IC, Arena said his agents were still trying to figure out whether Abdullah and his followers were "homegrown jihadists" or "a bunch of thugs with bluster" (Associated Press, October 30, 2009).

The disproportionate use of force the FBI exhibited in killing Luqman Abdullah has provided the Muslim community with a powerful tool of resistance. In a less publicized follow-up to the raid, Detroit police officers also raided Masjid al-Haqq during an evening prayer on the same day the imam was killed. With congregants already in a state of shock and grief, their prayers were disrupted when more than a dozen officers stormed and entered the mosque with their weapons drawn.[37] There is simply no parallel for this sort of assault in other American houses of worship.

Imam Luqman was not an Arab American; he was a black American, and the law enforcement community in America has a long history of punishing and disciplining black bodies with an excessive use of force. Although many immigrants take away the important lesson from the slaying that they need to toe the line of legality and nonconfrontational speech with precision, many nonimmigrant Muslims have begun to come together around the tragedy of Luqman's death and what it means to the multiple communities in which they live. For the first time since 9/11, the Detroit NAACP and CAIR have found they have much in common. The NAACP, ADC, and the American Arab Chamber of Commerce have also joined forces on this case, and Dawud Walid has established relations between CAIR and the Council of Baptist Pastors of Detroit, the largest association of African American clergy in the area. Jesse Jackson agreed to keynote CAIR's banquet in 2010. Ron Scott from the Coalition against Police Brutality has taken the Luqman case under his wing, railing against the FBI on radio, in the editorial offices of the *Detroit Free Press*, before Michigan's congressional delegation, and in front of large public audiences. The *Detroit Free Press* has published several editorials on the case, and Congressman John Conyers, head of the House Judiciary Committee, insisted that the Department of Justice investigate the shooting fully.[38] This flurry of protest is also a tool of discipline and instruction that might not have been so actively engaged had the imam been Arab American.

Those who were inclined to feel safe, to feel on good terms with their partners in ALPACT and BRIDGES, are now more aware of the double jeopardy involved in their relationships with the law. The seriousness of the situation has edged black and Arab leaders closer together as well as black and Muslim leaders. This turn of events did not immediately follow the killing. As Khadigah Alasry mentions in her memoir "Subject to Change" in this volume, very few Arab or other non-black Muslims attended Abdullah's funeral at the Muslim Center of Detroit, and like Khadigah, I heard many Arab Muslims asking what Luqman's death had to do with them. "He was just reverting to what he knew best," I was told by the board member of a prominent Dearborn mosque, "a life of crime. If he wanted to go out guns blazing, he should have taken off his Muslim clothes and put on a hoodie." This sentiment, tainted with references to the class and race of Imam Luqman and suggesting that the imam's faith could easily be discarded, hints at some of the real challenges that face Muslim leaders in Detroit as they attempt to work across emotionally and politically charged cultural differences.

Yet for those members of the Muslim public sphere engaged in this work already, Imam Luqman's death has galvanized their efforts, cast a spotlight on the needs of low-income congregations, and reminded congregations that regardless of their political and social interests, in the imagination of the state, they are Muslims first. Imam Mustapha Elturk, now more aware of the conditions in which some of the city's poorer Muslims are living, is researching ways his congregation can support their neighbors in Detroit. Life for Relief and Development, an Islamic charity headquartered in Southfield, Michigan, is seeking similar opportunities to direct some of its dollars toward local development efforts. Many suburban mosques are doing the same. This crisis has put them in touch with a group of black professionals who want to realize the vision of Imam Luqman—to develop a neighborhood with good, safe housing, good schools, and one that is, in the words of Akil Fahd, "bad for business." And when Thomas Perez, the new leader of the Department of Justice's Civil Rights Division, met with Arab community leaders on September 15, 2010, concern about the FBI's use of agent provocateurs and informants, about the targeting of mosques for investigation, about the profiling of Arab and Muslim Americans, about the selective questioning of Yemeni Americans, and about the killing of Imam Luqman were the primary issues raised. Perez was in town to announce the opening of a new Department of Justice Civil Rights Unit in Detroit. One Arab leader expressed concern that conditions seem to have worsened under President Obama rather than improved and suggested to Perez that it was time for the president to make a public speech showing leadership and clarity on the topic of Islamophobia, as he has done of the topic of race.[39]

Conclusion

Detroit's Muslims are moving targets. The vibrant, competitive market of institutions, communities, ideologies, and individuals who make up Arab/Muslim Detroit is evidence of how very American this religious minority has become. Yet their recent entanglements with law enforcement are evidence of how far they must go before other Americans can accept them as fellow citizens. Alliances like BRIDGES and ALPACT are not simply about building trust and respect, as their names imply, but about creating the means to communicate when trust and respect are no longer assumed or possible. In this sense, they are very useful bodies. They are tools of discipline and control. The Imams Committee, an organization more concerned with internal Muslim politics and with redressing stereotypes than with monitoring the federal government's efforts to monitor Muslims, has nonetheless also found itself working with the FBI, an agency most of the imams are learning to fear, regardless of their politics.

On the day after Imam Luqman's death, Andy Arena met with the IC to discuss the situation. He may have tried their patience when he played three very effective, long-established law enforcement cards:

1. "Divide and Conquer." He suggested during his meeting with the IC that two of the imams present in the room had ratted out Luqman to his agents, thus setting off speculation and concern among those who remained.

2. "Keep the Pressure On." He gave the following speech to "reassure" the gathered clerics that his agents are/were not operating in their mosques.

> And I said to them, "How many of you here carry weapons right now? How many of you are running a shooting range in the basement of your mosque? How many of you have owned stolen property? How many of you are involved in narcotics trafficking? How many of you are preaching support of Al Qaeda? How many of you are telling your people to go over and train and fight the Americans? How many of you are sending money to support Al Qaeda?"
>
> Nobody raised their hand.
>
> Then I am not in your mosque. I am not investigating you. If you are doing that, then I guarantee you that I am investigating you.[40]

3. "Publicly Co-opt." He arranged a press conference just outside the meeting so the very presence of the calmly departing imams would give the appearance of their support for the agency and their acquiescence in the killing of one of their own.

This is a dangerous strategy for the government to deploy. As Arena's confidence in local mosques increased in 2009, he turned his attention to the problematic of radicalized Muslim youth. This specter has raised its head in several ways in recent years. A blip in the findings of the Pew study on Muslim Americans suggested young Muslims are ever so slightly more likely to sympathize with Al Qaeda than others (Pew 2007). In 2009, five young Pakistani Americans traveled to Pakistan and attempted to join the Afghan resistance, and several Somali Americans joined up with Al-Shabab, an Al Qaeda affiliate in Somalia. Young Muslim Americans, each of my informants told me, are not radicalized in mosques. And even Arena agrees that mosques are the most effective tool in fighting such extremism. Concern over the radicalization of youth was the subject of the last IC meeting to which Arena was invited before Imam Luqman was killed. Detroit's Muslim leaders and the FBI recognize that they are going to need to work together in the future. It would help if the two sides had qualities now in short supply: trust, respect, and a realistic knowledge of each other's key beliefs and agendas.

Ironically, it is in its close working relationships with Muslim organizations that the U.S. government reveals its most phobic assumptions about its Arab/Muslim citizens. Distrust and a desire to control permeate and direct the power of the state vis-à-vis Arab/Muslim Detroit. The disciplinary agenda of the FBI and other federal agencies is producing its intended effect. Detroit's mosques are more transparent and better organized than ever before. They are also less trusting. Their members feel a greater sense of exclusion. And the government has produced effective routes for an ongoing supply of money to increase its powers of surveillance. The city's mosques are resisting this power in the only ways available to them: by thriving, by disciplining themselves, by creating a powerful and effective Muslim establishment, by building schools and seminaries, and by encouraging their imams to speak English and to speak out. They are resisting the powers that surround and suffuse their communities by responding from the only space left to them: from within.

Notes

Source for first epigraph: Evan Osnos, "It's Not Beautiful," *The New Yorker*, May 24, 2010, 59.

1. For a more detailed examination of the problems faced by Islamic charities in Michigan and beyond, see Turner (2009) and Howell (forthcoming).

2. In the 2010 election cycle, Dearborn has attracted the attention of Tea Party candidates like Sharron Angle of Nevada, who suggested the city is living under "sharia" and is subject to some sort of "militant terrorist situation" (see Scott Wong, "Dearborn Mayor to Sharron Angle: No 'Sharia Law' Here," *Politico*, October 12, 2010, http://www.politico.com/news/stories/1010/43451.html#ixzz12eS4VwxC).

3. Shora was appointed by the Obama administration to this post after several years as the national executive director of ADC. Hammoud has been a county prosecutor since 1996. He has also served on the board of the Arab American Political Action Committee, ADC-Michigan, and the Islamic Institute of Knowledge.

4. The U.S. Census Bureau does not collect data on religious identification, so this number is cobbled together from several sources. Based on the size and number of the city's mosques and the ethnic composition of each, I suggest that the area's Muslim population is roughly 50 percent Arab, 30 percent South Asian, 10 percent African American, and 10 percent European (Bosnian, Albanian), African (Nigerian, Senegalese), and white American converts. The Arab American population is roughly 220,000 (see Schopmeyer, "Arab Detroit after 9/11," this volume), 42 percent of whom identify as Muslim (Detroit Arab American Study Team 2009). Thus the Arab Muslim population stands roughly at 92,500, and, by extension, the Muslim community as a whole at 185,000. Bagby's 2004 study, using a different methodology, produced a similar finding of 125,000 to 200,000.

His ethnic breakdown was 53 percent Arab, 34 percent South Asian, 7 percent African American, and 6 percent other (2004, 10–11).

5. *United States of America v. Holy Land Foundation for Relief and Development et al. and North American Islamic Trust* (no. 09-1085), United States of America Court of Appeal for the Fifth Circuit.

6. Most mosque leaders report their contact with the FBI to CAIR-MI, frequently requesting that Executive Director Dawud Walid or a CAIR attorney attend their FBI interviews. The only mosques not to have been questioned by the FBI, to Walid's knowledge, are associated with the ministry of the late Imam Warith Deen Muhammed and a few Bangladeshi congregations.

7. For evidence that these practices are not unique to Detroit, see Schanzer, Kurzman, and Moosa (2010).

8. Niraj Warikoo, "Nuclear Search Targets Muslims," *Detroit Free Press*, December 24, 2005. See also Howell and Jamal ("Backlash, Part 2," this volume) for a more comprehensive list of the FBI's press releases, raids, and other activities pertaining to the city's mosques and other Muslim institutions.

9. The mosque is also called the "Dix Mosque" by people who live in Dearborn's Southend neighborhood. The Dix Mosque appellation appears frequently in the literature about Muslim communities in the Detroit area (Wigle 1974; Abraham 1978, 2000; Terry 1999; Howell 2000a, 2009).

10. Fifty-eight percent of Yemeni Americans in the Detroit area arrived in the United States after 1990 (Detroit Arab American Study Team 2009, 43).

11. The AMS and the ideological transitions it has experienced have received attention from both scholars and journalists. See Abraham (2000) for an excellent discussion of the gender dynamics that underlay much of the 1978 transition, Howell (2009) for a comprehensive look at the earlier history of this institution and the aftermath of the 1978 transition, and Abdo (2006) for a journalistic and somewhat more sensational look at the recent transition.

12. The mosque's former imam, Mohammad Musa, who now works at a prosperous suburban mosque, asserted in 2004 that the mosque's leaders needed to have their "hands held over the fire," meaning that the inflammatory and sometimes anti-American rhetoric he heard at the mosque was just that, rhetoric, but nonetheless dangerous in post-9/11 America (interview with Mohammed Musa, West Bloomfield, Michigan, September 22, 2004).

13. The older board was composed mostly of working-class immigrants with little formal education, often weak English language skills, and from an earlier period of migration when men often came to the United States as sojourners while their families remained in Yemen (see Swanson 1988).

14. Interview with Mahdi Ali, Dearborn, Michigan, February 2010.

15. Mosque open houses and public service announcements also followed the controversy over the construction of the Park 51 Mosque in New York City, the so-called Ground Zero mosque that was the target of much election-year hysteria in 2010.

16. Interview with Andy Arena, March 4, 2010. This story provides a good illustration of the "containment structure" Abraham discusses in "Arabs Behaving Badly" (this volume), although here we see a non-Arab Muslim being protected.

17. It is unclear if it was the media or the FBI who did not find the story newsworthy. Had the suspect been African American, Arab, or South Asian, it is difficult to imagine a similar outcome of events. In 2010, for example, a pair of Yemeni Americans became the focus of an international media frenzy when they were found with "suspicious" items in their luggage. For a discussion of the racialization process and how it is being applied to

Muslims in the Terror Decade, see Naber (2006), Salaita (2006), Jamal and Naber (2008), Bakalian and Bozorgmehr (2009), Cainkar (2009), Maira (2009).

18. Shortly after I spoke with Ali and with Arena, the FBI began a special outreach campaign in the Yemeni American community arising from concern that the radical cleric Anwar al-Awlaki, an American citizen of Yemeni origins who has been tied to several recent attacks and attempted attacks on American soil and is now hiding in Yemen, might attract followers in Dearborn and Hamtramck. The local Yemeni community initially cooperated with the FBI, but trust was severely frayed when the *Detroit Free Press* quoted Arena as reassuring members of the local Jewish community that his office was actively interviewing and investigating Yemeni Americans and their mosques (*Detroit Free Press*, September 1, 2010). Arab Americans found it particularly galling that Arena's concerns were about the frequency and motives for travel between Yemen and the United States. Such questions would be offensive if asked of American Jews about their travel between Israel and the United States. Similarly, when two American citizens of Yemeni origins were pulled off a plane in the Netherlands after the Department of Homeland Security alerted Dutch authorities about their "suspicious" travel profile and irregularities in their luggage, Yemeni Americans were distressed to see their community subjected to an international media frenzy and rush to judgment of the travelers (see "ADC Requests Clarification on Detention of U.S. Resident Travelers," September 1, 2010, available at http://aams .blogspot.com/2010/09/adc-requests-clarification-on-detention.html). Al-Awlaki is the first American citizen to have been placed on the CIA's "targeted assassination" list, a decision approved by President Barack Obama in April 2010 (see Greg Miller, "Muslim Cleric Aulaqi Is 1st U.S. Citizen on List of Those CIA Is Allowed to Kill," *Washington Post*, April 7, 2010, http://www.washingtonpost.com/wp-dyn/content/article/2010/04/ 06/AR2010040604121.html).

19. The American Civil Liberties Union, CAIR, Muslim Advocates and several other organizations petitioned the FBI in July 2010 for records pertaining to their investigative priorities in Michigan because the FBI's ability to profile based on race, ethnicity, behaviors, and lifestyle "raises alarm" (see http://aclumich.org/issues/post-9-11-activity/2010 -07/1458).

20. See "FBI Tries to Deport Muslim Man for Refusing to Be an Informant," *Miami New Times*, October 7, 2009; "Probes Test Trust That Authorities Strove to Win from U.S. Muslims," *Washington Post*, October 5, 2009; "Feds Raid Sacramento-area Mosque," *ABC News* (KGO), November 13, 2009; "Jordanian Man Gets 24 Years in Dallas Bomb Plot," *Dallas/Fort Worth News on CBS11*, October 19, 2010.

21. Convictions, yes, but seldom on charges related to terrorism. Detroit's would-be terrorist supporters and suspects are routinely brought up on and occasionally found guilty of a variety of non-terrorism-related charges, such as visa violations and tax fraud and other financial infringements.

22. See Council on American-Islamic Relations (2009); "Muslims Describe FBI Offers to Act as Informants," *Detroit News*, June 18, 2009; Salisbury (2010a).

23. I attended two of these sessions, one in June 2009 at the Islamic Center of Detroit and one in January 2010 at the University of Michigan at Dearborn. "O you who have believed, avoid much [negative] assumption. Indeed, some assumption is sin. And do not spy or backbite each other. Would one of you like to eat the flesh of his brother when dead? You would detest it. And fear Allah; indeed, Allah is Accepting of repentance and Merciful" Surah 49:12, Al-Quran.

24. In the immediate aftermath of 9/11, the Arab American community seemed to be the locus of much informant-based spying. Dearborn, Arena admits, was home to much "score settling," with neighbors, ex-spouses, in-laws, former business partners, and the

like frequently accusing one another of visa violations, smuggling, supporting Hizballah, or some such act in order to pursue personal vendettas.

25. Often, these fact-finding missions are tied to national or international events. African mosques were questioned after Umar Farouk Abdulmutallab tried to detonate explosives in his underwear on a Detroit-bound flight in 2009. African American Muslim leaders have been questioned with regard to the "Ummah organization" in the aftermath of Imam Luqman Abdullah's death in 2009. South Asian leaders were questioned after Pakistani Americans from Virginia were arrested in Pakistan in 2010. Shi'i clerics were interviewed before and after the U.S. invasion of Iraq and when cigarette smugglers with ties to Detroit were charged with providing support to Hizballah in 2003. The list is extensive and reaches into almost every ethnic and sectarian pocket of Muslim Detroit. Sometimes these visits are conducted professionally, by appointment and at the convenience of the clerics. In other cases, they entail late-night home visits and surprise visits at the day jobs of Muslim leaders (engineering firms, university faculty offices, hospital chaplaincy suites, assembly lines) and seem as intent on intimidation as on collegial information gathering (interview with Dawud Walid).

26. IONA became independent from Tanzeem-e-Islami in 2003 and changed its name from Tanzeem-e-Islami North America to the Islamic Organization of North America.

27. While waiting outside for the April 2006 Planning Commission meeting to begin, I was mistaken for a concerned Warren resident. I am a middle-aged white woman, middle class in appearance. Thus, I was filled in on much of the planning strategy before seeing it carried out inside the auditorium. I also recorded the public meeting itself.

28. The reference to storefront mosques was made by several speakers, each referring to storefront churches in Detroit and associating such institutions with blackness, urban poverty, and blight, insinuating that a storefront mosque in Warren would disrupt the city's image as a haven for whites.

29. Interviews with Mustapha (Steve) Elturk.

30. See the Act for America Web site (http://www.actforamerica.org/) for an example of this well-organized, well-funded campaign.

31. October 28, 2009, story accessed at http://www.huffingtonpost.com/2009/10/28/luqman-ameen-abdullah-lea_n_337763.html.

32. My understanding of the mosque's closure provides a small glimpse into Luqman's nature. In early 2009, he visited a dinner at the Canton mosque, where he mentioned the financial duress his mosque was suffering. Supporters at the Canton mosque gave the imam the roughly $10,000 he needed to resolve his back taxes. Upon reflection, however, the imam decided that this $10,000 could be better used in Gaza, which Israel had recently devastated in the Gaza War. Rationalizing his decision by saying his South Asian supporters were also sympathetic to the plight of those in Gaza but feared donating money to charities working in Palestine, he signed over the $10,000 to the Islamic Relief Fund rather than bail out his own institution (interview with Joe Abdullah [pseudonym], June 22, 2009).

33. Note his use of the phrase "for investigative purposes," implying that much of the agency's intelligence gathering is done for other purposes, where restrictions are not so clearly spelled out.

34. The American Civil Liberties Union has the greatest resources and does the best job of keeping track of its accomplishments. See http://aclumich.org/issues/post-9-11-activity for a full list of its post-9/11 activities.

35. Similarly, the agency pushing the charity investigations, the Department of Commerce, is acting on guidelines set in place specifically as components of the War on Terror (Turner 2009).

36. For example, the report details that the mosque had a self-defense team that trained in martial arts, kickboxing, boxing, and swordplay and implies this "armed" group was training to take on the police rather than defending worshippers, if need be, from local street gangs and drug dealers.

37. See the affidavit submitted by Jihad El-Jihad to Wayne County, Michigan, available at http://www.cairmichigan.org/news/affidavit_of_jihad_abdul_el_jihad.

38. The Department of Justice issued the results of its inquiry on October 13, 2010, exonerating the officers involved (Federal Bureau of Investigation Press Release, Washington, D.C., http://www.fbi.gov/news/pressrel/press-releases/abdullah_101310).

39. Dawud Walid, personal communication, September 15, 2010.

40. Interview with Andy Arena.

REFERENCES

Abdo, Geneive. 2006. *Mecca and Main Street: Muslim Life in America after 9/11.* New York: Oxford University Press.

Abraham, Nabeel. 1978. "National and Local Politics: A Study of Political Conflict in the Yemeni Immigrant Community of Detroit, Michigan." PhD diss., University of Michigan.

———. 2000. "Arab Detroit's 'American' Mosque." In *Arab Detroit: From Margin to Mainstream,* ed. Nabeel Abraham and Andrew Shryock. Detroit: Wayne State University Press.

Abraham, Sameer, and Nabeel Abraham, eds. 1983. *Arabs in the New World: Studies on Arab American Communities.* Detroit: Center for Urban Studies, Wayne State University.

Al-Khatib, Ihsan. 2010. "Law Enforcement: The People and the State." Testimony at the UN Human Rights Council Universal Periodic Review Civil Society Consultation, Wayne State University Law School, April 7.

Aswad, Barbara, ed. 1974. *Arabic Speaking Communities in American Cities.* New York: Center for Migration Studies.

Bagby, Ihsan. 2004. *A Portrait of Detroit Mosques: Muslim Views on Policy, Politics, and Religion.* Clinton Township, Mich.: Institute for Social Policy and Understanding.

Bakalian, Anny, and Mehdi Bozorgmehr. 2009. *Backlash 9/11: Middle Eastern and Muslim Americans Respond.* Berkeley: University of California Press.

Cainkar, Louise. 2009. *Homeland Insecurity: The Arab American and Muslim American Experience after 9/11.* New York: Russell Sage Foundation.

Cole, David. 2003. *Enemy Aliens: Double Standards and Constitutional Freedoms in the War on Terrorism.* New York: The New Press.

Council of Islamic Organizations in Michigan. 2007. Muslim Code of Honor. Detroit: CIOM.

Council on American-Islamic Relations. 2009. "The FBI's Use of Informants, Recruitment, and Intimidation within Muslim Communities." Rev. June 23. Los Angeles: CAIR.

Daulatzai, Sohail. 2009. "Protect Ya Neck (Remix): Muslims and the Carceral Imagination in the Age of Guantanamo." In *Black Routes to Islam,* ed. Manning Marable and Hishaam Aidi, 207–226. New York: Palgrave Macmillan.

Detroit Arab American Study Team. 2009. *Citizenship and Crisis: Arab Detroit after 9/11*. New York: Russell Sage Foundation.

Howell, Sally. 2000a. "Cultural Interventions: Arab American Aesthetics between the Transnational and the Ethnic." *Diaspora* 9(1): 59–82.

———. 2000b. "Finding the Straight Path: A Conversation with Mohsen and Lila Amen about Faith, Life, and Family in Dearborn." In *Arab Detroit: From Margin to Mainstream*, ed. Nabeel Abraham and Andrew Shryock. Detroit: Wayne State University Press.

———. 2009. "Inventing the American Mosque: Early Muslims and Their Institutions in Detroit, 1910–1980." PhD diss., Rackham Graduate School, University of Michigan.

Howell, Sally, and Andrew Shryock. 2003. "Cracking Down on Diaspora: Arab Detroit and America's 'War on Terror.'" *Anthropological Quarterly* 76(3): 443–462.

Jamal, Amaney, and Nadine Naber, eds. 2008. *Race and Arab Americans before and after 9/11: From Invisible Citizens to Visible Subjects*. Syracuse, N.Y.: Syracuse University Press.

Maira, Sunaima. 2009. *Missing: Youth, Citizenship, and Empire after 9/11*. Durham, N.C.: Duke University Press.

Muslim Alliance of North America. 2009. "The FBI Raid and Shooting Death of Imam Luqman." http://www.mujahideenryder.net/2009/10/31/mana-the-fbi-raid-and-shooting-death-of-imam-luqman/.

Naber, Nadine. 2006. "The Rules of Forced Engagement: Race, Gender, and the Culture of Fear among Arab Immigrants in San Francisco Post-9/11." *Cultural Dynamics* 18(3): 235–267.

———. 2008. "'Look, Mohammed the Terrorist Is Coming!' Cultural Racism, Nation-Based Racism, and the Intersectionality of Oppressions after 9/11." In *Race and Arab Americans before and after 9/11: From Invisible Citizens to Visible Subjects*, ed. Amaney Jamal and Nadine Naber. Syracuse, N.Y.: Syracuse University Press.

Orwell, George. 1946. *Politics and the English Language*. London: Horizon.

Pew Forum on Religion and Public Life. 2007. *Muslim Americans: Middle Class and Mostly Mainstream*. Washington, D.C.: Pew Research Center.

Salaita, William. 2006. *Anti-Arab Racism in the USA: Where It Comes from and What It Means for Politics*. New York: Pluto Press.

Salisbury, Stephan. 2010a. *Mohamed's Ghosts: An American Story of Love and Fear in the Homeland*. New York: Nation Books.

———. 2010b. "Stage-Managing the War on Terror: Ensnaring Terrorists Demands Creativity." *Tomsdispatch*, http://www.tomdispatch.com/blog/175270/tomgram%3A_stephan_salisbury,_plotting_terrorism__/.

Schanzer, David, Charles Kurzman, and Ebrahim Moosa. 2010. *Anti-Terror Lessons of Muslim-Americans*. Washington, D.C.: National Institute of Justice.

Swanson, Jon. 1988. "Sojourners and Settlers in Yemen and America." In *Sojourners and Settlers: The Yemeni Immigrant Experience*, ed. Jonathan Friedlander. Provo: University of Utah Press.

Terry, Janice. 1999. "Community and Political Activism among Arab Americans in Detroit." In *Arabs in America: Building a New Future*, ed. Michael Suleiman, 241–254. Philadelphia: Temple University Press.

Turner, Jennifer. 2009. *Blocking Faith, Freezing Charity: Chilling Islamic Charitable Giving in the "War on Terrorism Financing."* New York: American Civil Liberties Union.

Weiner, Isaac. 2009. "Religion Out Loud: Religious Sound, Public Space, and American Pluralism." PhD diss., University of North Carolina.

Wigle, Laura. 1974. "An Arab Muslim Community in Michigan." In *Arabic Speaking Communities in American Cities*, ed. Barbara Aswad. New York: Center for Migration Studies.

Detroit Transnational

The Interchange Experience in Lebanon and the United States

KRISTINE J. AJROUCH

The transnational paradigm has emerged in recent years as a way of better understanding how the links between immigrants, their descendants, and their various homelands influence incorporation into American society (Basch, Glick Schiller, and Szanton Blanc 1994; Levitt and Waters 2002; Levitt and Glick Schiller 2004). The life experiences of migrants and their descendants are shaped not only by their country of origin, but also by their class position and by the political relationships between sending and host societies (Ong 1996). These factors greatly influence how migrant populations are received and perceived and how transnational they are allowed to become.[1] Transnational experiences are not homogenous. My personal experience as a Lebanese transnational is privileged by human capital and economic resources, yet limited by political circumstances. It is different in many ways from the experiences of Yemenis, Guatemalans, or Filipinos living in the United States. The advantages and limitations of transnationalism, which provide the focus of this essay, are not evenly distributed among immigrant populations.

Living a transnational life involves commitment to crossing the physical and legal boundaries of two (or more) nation-states. It also requires openness to bridging the sociocultural divides that exist between separate national communities. By implication, becoming transnational involves forging discrepant cosmopolitan identities that draw from the cultural landscapes of multiple countries (Clifford 1997). This status frequently entails economic mobility and the ability to make political claims in jurisdictions that are legally distinct. Of particular significance to my research is uncovering the meaning of U.S. citizenship in a transnational context. This essay illustrates

186

the experience of U.S. citizenship via transnational activities by elaborating my personal and family experiences of becoming part of two worlds, that of the United States and that of Lebanon.

Immigration Background

I was born in the United States, the daughter of an Iranian immigrant father and a second-generation Lebanese American mother. My personal transnational experiences began, however, after I married my Lebanese immigrant husband, Abraham. The Lebanese have been migrating to the United States since the late 1800s, and today the United States is home to almost 1 million Americans of Lebanese ancestry (U.S. Census Bureau 2000). The migration experiences of my maternal grandparents, who came at the dawn of the twentieth century, differed markedly from the experience of my husband, who immigrated in the early 1970s. First, mode of transportation differed, with my grandparents traveling by ship for one month, and my husband by plane for twelve hours. The effort, time, and experience of traveling between Lebanon and the United States differed enormously for my maternal grandparents and my husband. The political and economic climate varied as well. When my maternal grandfather returned to Lebanon to marry and subsequently bring my maternal grandmother to the United States in 1925, laws were changing to significantly curtail immigration, and the country was about to enter one of the worst economic eras in history, the Great Depression. Syrians (Lebanese) had just won a series of legal cases that granted them "white" racial status, thus securing for them the privilege of U.S. citizenship, a status they had held, despite occasional legal contests, since the late nineteenth century (Gualtieri 2001).

My husband, who was 13 years old when he left Lebanon in 1970, was able to migrate because of the change in immigration law that occurred in 1965, which allowed for increased family reunification and lifted the restrictions on immigration from Asian countries. His mother's sister, who emigrated to the United States more than forty years earlier, filed for his mother to come to America with her family. The United States was quite different by this time in history, with the passage of the Civil Rights Act and a new focus on celebrating ethnic culture and difference. As various scholarly works demonstrate, migration from Syria and Lebanon has been influenced historically by a variety of push and pull factors, including economic opportunity, family reunification, and political instability (Hourani and Shehadi 1992). These factors produced unique ties between the host country and the homeland, leading both to integration and to ethnic differentiation (Humphrey 2004).

My maternal grandparents' experiences upon arrival differed from those of my husband not only because American society was different, but also because of the ages at which they entered the United States (my maternal grandparents as young adults and my husband as an adolescent) and the conditions prompting migration. Though all sought economic opportunity, my grandfather was the only one to migrate specifically for this reason. My grandmother arrived through marriage (though also seeking economic opportunity, and hence the allure of my grandfather), and my husband because he was the child of parents seeking economic opportunity. The transnational activities that followed their arrival in the new world emerged differentially, based on the resources available to facilitate such connections.

Visits to the homeland are a key element of transnational participation. My maternal grandmother returned to Lebanon four times. She made her first return in 1947, along with four of her seven children, my mother being one of them (at age 14). They traveled by ship and stayed for one year. Her second trip was with my grandfather, in the 1960s. Her last two visits were with me, once in 1991 and the second time in 1996. My mother also visited a second time, alone, in the early 1950s, traveling by ship. She longed to experience Lebanon without my grandmother's watchful eye. She stayed for one month. My husband, on the other hand, visits Lebanon annually. He first returned when he was 21 and had begun working. Thereafter, he has visited every year, staying for at least one month each visit. Increases in this pattern of transnational activity stem in part from technological advances that have made global connections affordable for increasing numbers of people (i.e., air travel, long distance telephone, and Internet communications), but that nonetheless remain differently accessible based on economic and other resources.

The historical backdrop provided by the experiences of my grandparents, my mother, and my husband helps contextualize my own transnational activities. I have visited Lebanon at least annually since 1987 because my husband encouraged such travel. In the ensuing years, I benefited from many opportunities to participate in and witness interchanges between citizens residing in the United States and Lebanon. These myriad and sometimes life-changing exchanges have made me increasingly aware of my own status as a transnational citizen living at the intersection of Lebanese and American possibilities. I will elaborate on three recent events that illustrate how American cultural and legal citizenship have shaped my experiences as a third-generation, transnational Lebanese American.[2] Specifically, I will discuss my involvement with the Emigrant-Resident Camp organized initially by my husband in 2000, living through the July 2006 war, and, finally, my experience as a Fulbright scholar in 2008, when I taught and conducted research in Lebanon for six months.

Emigrant-Resident Camp

We (my husband, Abraham, and our children) were in Lebanon in the summer of 2000, the year the Israeli occupation of south Lebanon finally ended.[3] Relief, joy, and optimism emerged as Israel withdrew its forces, especially in Kfarhouna, a village in the Jezzine district and the birthplace of both my grandparents and my husband. Kfarhouna is composed of two religious communities: Catholics and Shi'a Muslims. This religious diversity in some ways resembles a microcosm of Lebanese society. When the occupation ended, resentment lingered between Christians and Muslims owing to the perception by Muslims that some Christians had sided with the occupiers. This perception was rooted in Israeli discrimination against Lebanese citizens based in part on their religious identities. During the occupation, Muslims found it difficult to remain in their homes or to visit their hometown on weekends. Similarly, the Lebanese civil war had sharply divided inhabitants of the region along lines of religious affiliation. After two decades of war and occupation, a new generation of Christians and Muslims from Kfarhouna did not know one another. Additionally, a new generation of Lebanese living in America, both Christian and Muslim, did not know the land of their parents.

Envisioned as a means to reconnect Christians and Muslims in Kfarhouna, and to instill local belonging among children of emigrants, my husband developed and organized the Emigrant-Resident Camp of Kfarhouna for youth between the ages of 14 and 18. Camp activities were organized so that all participants experienced hardships together (sleeping on mats and eating "camp" food), worked with one another on collective goals (planting trees in the village and cleaning the small river that runs through the village), visited Lebanese tourist sites (the Cedars, Baalbek), and collaborated to create nightly entertainment for themselves and the entire village. Young people from both religious communities and both countries of residence (the United States and Lebanon) interacted with one another to create a united community and provide a model of tolerance and cooperation. The camp also afforded opportunities for young people, both males and females, to assume leadership roles among their peers. Taking place over a seven-day period at the end of July and beginning of August, the camp has hosted 75 to 100 residents every summer since it opened in 2000.

The Emigrant-Resident Camp of Kfarhouna began as an attempt to heal the deep local divisions that had opened up during fifteen years of civil war and almost twenty years of occupation, but it also represented a transnational project whereby children of immigrants would come to know the homeland of their parents and grandparents. The transnational character of the project eventually drew the attention of both the Lebanese and the U.S. governments. In the post–civil war period, both governments have been interested in promoting constructive economic and political ties between their citizens. In Lebanon, for example, an entire ministry (the Ministry of Foreign Affairs and Emigrants) is charged with establishing and strengthening links to Lebanese living abroad, and many other ministries seek to benefit from the resources of expatriate nationals. A main impetus for this investment is the importance of diasporic remittances to the Lebanese economy. For example, in 2007 Lebanon received $5.5 billion in remittances,[4] a number that is thought to be small in comparison to the actual amount, much of which is not officially documented (Schimmelpfennig and Gardner 2008).

Indeed, Abraham was able to secure funding for the camp initially through donations received from expatriates living in greater Detroit who, like himself, saw value in organizing a camp that would allow their U.S.-born children to experience the homeland. In subsequent years, funding was also obtained from the Ministry of Youth, almost annually. The idea was considered so innovative that the U.S. ambassador to Lebanon, Vincent Battle, visited with the campers during the 2004 and 2005 sessions.

The role U.S. citizenship played in this effort can be discerned on many levels. First, Abraham's U.S. citizenship, coupled with his long absence from Lebanon, uniquely positioned him to succeed as organizer of the camp. Not having lived through the civil war in Lebanon, he was able to escape accusations of complicity in the family and religious conflicts of the period. Family and religious ties shape access to resources in Lebanon. Because he did not live in Lebanon, he did not need the resources of a particular family or a religious group to make his way in the world. Additionally, his U.S. citizenship in a sense trumped his religious identity as a Shi'a Muslim. Though religious affiliation in large part determines status and belonging in Lebanon, U.S. citizenship does much to minimize such facets of identity, whether they are announced by emigrants or perceived by others (see Ajrouch and Kusow 2007). As a result, Abraham was able to gain the trust of families in both religious communities.

Furthermore, Abraham's U.S. citizenship and leadership in the Lebanese American community of Detroit provided the impetus for Ambassador Battle's official visit to the Emigrant-Resident Camp in 2004. Abraham had been named a leader within the Lebanese community in Michigan by the General Consulate of Lebanon in recognition of his founding the Kfarhouna Club of America in 1996. Indeed, it was members of this club who initially played a key role in financing the camp and in sending their U.S.-born children to participate.[5] Abraham met Ambassador Battle when the ambassador toured various Lebanese communities in the United States in 2004. It was on the occasion of this meeting in Dearborn that Battle first learned of the camp and requested to visit. This request was not uniformly popular in Kfarhouna, where many dislike U.S. foreign policy and hence objected to a U.S. government representative visiting the area. Abraham was able to overcome these reservations and persuade the people of Kfarhouna to accept Ambassador Battle's visit by reminding them that 400 families from Kfarhouna live in the United States. He made clear that denying the request would be a disservice not only to the emigrants, but also to the south of Lebanon, which, he suggested, needed more positive support from the United States.

In addition to these minor diplomatic skirmishes, activities within the Emigrant-Resident Camp engendered occasional conflicts between the American and Lebanese participants, illustrating the extent to which the cultural values of each placed them at odds with one another. An idea I proposed at the camp was to institute "mock elections," where campers would be nominated for various awards, such as best personality, nicest hair, nicest smile, most likely to succeed, and so on. This idea was well liked by both the emigrant and the resident camp counselors. Accordingly, ballots were created in both Arabic and English and distributed to the campers. But when the ballots were collected and the counselors met to tally the results, an interesting situation arose. Resident counselors felt that because they occupied positions of authority in the camp, it was their right, and indeed their duty, to decide who should be named in each category. In other words, the number of votes was to be disregarded, and instead the counselors would name the winners based on their assessment of who deserved the award.

The emigrant counselors were outraged, and they came to Abraham and me to voice their concern. The entire process of engaging in an election was about to be undermined. Abraham called a meeting with all counselors and explained the process of elections, the importance of counting votes, and the necessity of letting votes determine winners. In other words, a major building block of U.S. citizenship, votes representing the will of the people, was being taught. He and I then proceeded to participate in the vote tallies so that we could ensure that the mock election results identified winners according to those with the most votes. Lebanese residents were influenced by American values only after they were confronted.

The U.S.-born also learned important cultural and social values dominant in Lebanon. In particular, developing close relationships with others is expected so that social groups can be cohesive and unified. Accordingly, the Lebanese residents displayed a high level of friendliness and were exceedingly interested in meeting new people. The willingness of the Lebanese resident youth, both males and females, to initiate communication with the Americans (Lebanese emigrants) and fold them into their social circles, introduced a more hospitable, less cliquish approach to social relationships. For instance, on the eve of the camp's grand opening, people used music to encourage mingling among the campers. The popular line dance known as the *dabkeh* was the perfect pretext for Lebanese resident campers to invite the American (Lebanese emigrant) campers to join in. As the Lebanese resident campers took the initiative to introduce themselves, welcoming the emigrants with open arms to their activities, the American campers experienced a new level of inclusiveness that many said they had never experienced as newcomers in similar situations in the United States. As a result, many emigrants were eager to incorporate this more open approach to social relationships upon their return to the United States.

In sum, the Emigrant-Resident Camp is a context in which both U.S. and Lebanese citizenship create and enhance opportunities for cultural interchange between Lebanese living in the United States and those living in Lebanon. It builds bridges between Christians and Muslims in Lebanon and ties the second generation to their ancestral homeland, encouraging future encounters. Although the camp experience highlights cultural differences that have emerged between Lebanese living in the Middle East and those who live in the United States, it also shows that these differences are surmountable when people can interact on familiar terms and hence gain experience navigating both cultural spaces. Perhaps most promising in this transnational experience is the implication that the values of American cultural and political citizenship and the commitment to social inclusiveness exhibited by Lebanese youth can, when consciously combined, serve as a progressive resource for civil society building in Lebanon and in the United States.

The July 2006 War

The benefits of American citizenship have not always been available to my family in south Lebanon. This became disturbingly clear to us with the events that transpired during what is known in Lebanon as the July 2006 war. We arrived in Lebanon at the end of June in 2006 to prepare for camp activities, planning to spend the summer between Beirut and Kfarhouna. On July 12, 2006, members of the Hizballah militia crossed the border into Israel and took two Israeli soldiers prisoner.[6] This event constituted one more chapter in Hizballah's long-standing resistance to Israeli intimidation and occupation (Lowenstein 2000; Mowles 1986). In response, Israel launched a "strategic attack" on Lebanon. Within hours they bombed all runways at Beirut International Airport and destroyed all major roads linking Beirut and the rest of Lebanon to the south. Israel continued to bomb the south of Lebanon as well as the southern suburbs of Beirut for the next thirty days.

On the morning of July 13, I woke up in our apartment just outside Beirut to the news that all the city's airport runways and all the major roads leaving Lebanon had been destroyed. We decided to leave Beirut and make our way to Kfarhouna. We found the main road to Jezzine bombed, so we detoured through the Chouf Mountains. What was normally a one-hour drive became a two-and-a-half-hour journey. Our decision to travel to Kfarhouna was based on the knowledge that Israel was targeting primarily Shi'i Muslim areas. Kfarhouna, in the predominantly Christian Jezzine district, is itself half Christian. The overriding sentiment within the country was that in the company of Christians, we would be safe because Israel would not bomb predominantly non-Shi'i areas.

It also occurred to me that we had no way to leave Lebanon. As a U.S. citizen, I became quite concerned. I called the U.S. Embassy for some indication of what to expect. The cultural attaché told me that U.S. citizens should not be in Lebanon in the first place, since a travel advisory had been put in place in May. Second, the attaché assured me that the conflict would end shortly because the Arab League was about to condemn the acts of Hizballah. Finally, I was told that the U.S. Embassy was monitoring the situation. The following day, July 14, news spread that most European and Asian countries were evacuating their citizens. Convoys were heading out of Lebanon via Syria. U.S. citizens, however, were not being evacuated.[7] Indeed, they would not be evacuated en masse until one week later.

The reasons the United States did not immediately evacuate its citizens remain unclear. It could have been because of the sheer number of Americans present (an estimated 25,000 or more). Indeed, the State Department had to work with the Department of Defense (DOD) to address the challenges of evacuating U.S. citizens in a war zone where air, sea, and ground transportation options either were not available or were dangerous (Kouri 2007). Jim Kouri's presentation of the unraveling of events provides insight into why the American evacuation plan was significantly slower to materialize compared with that of European and Asian governments. Kouri suggests three key areas in which the State Department and the DOD faced challenges in evacuating U.S. citizens: (1) the magnitude of the Lebanon crisis challenged the State Department's capacity to respond; (2) effective communication with Americans in Lebanon and their family and friends in the United States was not possible; and (3) miscommunication between the State Department and the DOD, resulting from divergent cultures and operation practices, led to delays in chartering ships and planes for the evacuation.

In addition to these factors, an alternative perception surfaced among those trapped. Most Americans in Lebanon had Lebanese ancestry. Did the U.S. government consider us not quite American? Did we not deserve access to the same protection and rights as Americans without Lebanese ancestry? Though this assessment may not reflect the official U.S. government stance, it nevertheless arose as a distinct possibility.[8] It was the first time in my life that I felt personally marginalized, as if I were something less than a valuable and important part of American society. These questions about our inclusion as valued U.S. citizens are particularly pertinent when official reports suggest that Americans began to be evacuated on July 16. A press release posted on July 20, with the headline "Every American Who Wants to Depart Will Be Helped: 'Helping Americans Depart Safely Is Our First Priority,'" reported the following:

> The U.S. Government is using all resources possible to facilitate the speedy and safe departure of American citizens currently in Lebanon using every means available. The departure of every single American citizen who wishes to leave Lebanon is the first priority for the U.S. Government. The Secretary of State and the Secretary of Defense are ensuring that all available military, civilian, and private sector resources in the region are being directed to accomplish this goal. The U.S. Embassy in Beirut has made possible the departure of over 1,500 American citizens via helicopter and cruise ship in the past four days. Urgent medical need cases are still the first priority.

This statement reached us on July 20, after we had already left Lebanon on our own. While we were in Lebanon searching desperately for a way out, we never received confirmation from the U.S. Embassy that a plan was in place for evacuation.

To better illustrate our experience as American citizens in Lebanon during the July 2006 war, I will present a summary of our encounters with the U.S. Embassy. As citizens from countries around the world were being immediately evacuated, a message to American citizens in Lebanon was sent to me via e-mail on July 14:

> The Department of State continues to closely monitor the situation in Lebanon and make plans for every contingency.
> The Consular Section at the U.S. Embassy in Beirut will be open from 8 a.m.–5 p.m. (local time) on Saturday, July 15.
> The Department of State and Embassy Beirut are working on options to facilitate the departure of private Americans who wish to depart and would require assistance in doing so, but these plans are not yet finalized. We will provide further information as it becomes available. Here are some reports issued at 1:00 p.m. on July 14, 2006.

Both Beirut international airport, which is heavily damaged by bombings, and the Port of Beirut remain closed.

Road conditions vary greatly and are subject to change. For example, the road from Beirut to Syria at Masna was bombed and not passable. However, people located close to the border may be able to get to the border and cross into Syria.

If people encounter difficulty at crossing into Syria, they should contact the American Embassy in Damascus at 963-11-333-1342.

American citizens in Lebanon should avoid any areas where demonstrations are possible and exercise caution if within the vicinity of any demonstrations. They should maintain a high level of vigilance and take appropriate steps to increase their security awareness.[9]

The following day (July 15), as we watched television to get a sense of what was happening, we listened to a CNN report. CNN stated that more than 25,000 Americans were in Lebanon and that in general U.S. citizens did not want to leave. The same day we received the following message via e-mail from the U.S. government:

Message to Americans in Lebanon

The Department of State continues to work with the Department of Defense on a plan to help American citizens depart Lebanon. As of the morning of July 15, we are looking at how we might transport Americans to Cyprus. Once in Cyprus, Americans can then board commercial aircraft for onward travel. Commercial airlines provide the safest and most efficient repatriation options to final destinations.

The Department of State reminds American citizens that the U.S. government does not provide no-cost transportation but does have the authority to provide repatriation loans to those in financial need. For the portion of your trip directly handled by the U.S. Government we will ask you to sign a promissory note and we will bill you at a later date. In a subsequent message, when we have specific details about the transportation arrangements, we will inform you about the costs you will incur. We will also work with commercial aircraft to ensure that they have adequate flights to help you depart Cyprus and connect to your final destination.

The Department of State continues to work around the clock and will continue to send updates to you as appropriate.[10]

That day, at 5:00 p.m., I e-mailed the public affairs officer to inquire about the message that a way out via Cyprus was a possibility. Addressing the public affairs officer, I wrote in the subject line, "Cyprus?" then proceeded with:

I received an email message this morning that the US govt. is working to get Americans out of Lebanon via Cyprus. Is there any news on this front? A woman just came to my door to tell me that LBC [Lebanese Broadcasting Company] reported Americans will be departing via Cyprus. Has this now been finalized?

Thanks for your help.

Warm wishes,

Kristine

The response I received, six minutes later, was as follows: "Not finalized. Stay tuned. No date yet but sometime in the next week. Watch the website. You'll have our latest info."

The following day, Saturday, July 16, we had a second contact with the U.S. Embassy. Alarmed by CNN news reports that U.S. citizens did not want to leave Lebanon, I telephoned the embassy again to inform them that we wanted to leave and that dozens of others I knew also wished to leave. We received assurance that they continued to monitor the situation. Yet the tone was distant, and we, along with many others, felt vulnerable. At the same time, the Arab American Institute (AAI) in Washington, D.C., was actively soliciting information from those trapped in Lebanon. Feeling helpless and abandoned, I registered with the AAI in the hope that it could do something to help us get out of Lebanon. That same day we received the following e-mail from the U.S. government:

> *A message to American citizens in Lebanon:*
>
> The US Department of State and the US Department of Defense continue working on a plan to help American citizens who wish to depart Lebanon to leave in a secure and orderly manner. To assist in the development of that operation, the U.S. Government is sending an assessment team to Beirut to facilitate the safe departure of Americans who wish to leave.

On Sunday, July 17, five days after the conflict began, there was still no clear plan from the U.S. government for protection and escape from an increasingly dire situation. My sisters-in-law and father-in-law decided to travel on their own to Syria. On this day, we received the following message from the U.S. government via e-mail:

> This Warden Message is to update Americans to the ongoing security concerns in Lebanon. The Embassy is monitoring the situation in Lebanon closely and is reviewing all options for assisting Americans who wish to depart Lebanon. The U.S. Department of State continues to work with the U.S. Department of Defense on a plan to help American citizens safely depart Lebanon. Additional information on departure plans, as it becomes available, will be

released via the media, Embassy warden announcements, and on the Embassy website. The Department of State continues to work around the clock to ensure the safety and well-being of its citizens.

Throughout this period, I continued to contact the U.S. Embassy via e-mail. I never received any concrete information about what the U.S. government would do to help its citizens leave. Furthermore, the public affairs officer at the embassy threatened that we would be on our own after I asked why it was taking so long for a plan to be implemented that would evacuate American citizens from what was essentially a war zone. The exchange presented below illustrates the tentativeness of the U.S. plan and provides a glimpse into the experience of how U.S. citizenship can be threatened and sometimes limited, especially with regard to the provision of rights and privileges.

On the morning of July 17, I wrote in the subject line "Evacuation plans" and, addressing the public affairs officer, conveyed the following:

> We are very frightened, and still no word on how to get out. What is more disturbing is that CNN is reporting that the US govt. claims Americans in Lebanon are not requesting help. I know of dozens who are looking for a way out. Now the word we receive is that it will be sometime this week. Believe me, we all prefer to leave on our own, but see no safe way out. We are waiting in anticipation. Your support is greatly appreciated.
>
> Best wishes,
>
> Kristine Ajrouch

An hour and a half later the public affairs officer responded by asking me to provide her with our local telephone numbers. She called, and we had a conversation in which she asked whether we were all U.S. citizens. I confirmed that we were and reminded her that we had all registered on the State Department Web site providing our passport information. She then asked that I send her an e-mail with the names, ages, and relationship to me of all those traveling with me.

A little after noon, I sent the following message:

> Thanks for the phone call, and comforting words. As per your request, the following individuals—all U.S. Citizens—are traveling with me: Abraham Ajrouch, Husband, 48 years old; Ali Ajrouch, Son, 18 years old; Rachelle Ajrouch, Daughter, 14 years old; Campbell Eastman, Uncle, 65 years old; Omar Soubra, Nephew, 13 years old.
>
> My uncle (Campbell Eastman) is on his way to Beirut to retrieve his ticket, which he left in Beirut—he flew in on Emirate Air via Dubai. We expect him

to return to Kfarhouna this afternoon. My nephew (Omar Soubra) is currently in Zahle, visiting his father who lives in Lebanon.

We just received word from Middle East Airlines (the carrier on which my husband, children and nephew arrived into Lebanon) that they have us confirmed to depart out of Damascus to Frankfurt on Thursday. We then were going to try to find a spot on Lufthansa to return to Detroit. Our current plan is to drive to Damascus, via Zahle so that we can pickup my 13-year-old nephew, and then continue on to Damascus, so that we may make it to our confirmed flight on Thursday.

As per your direction, we will pack one bag each (that does mean suitcase, right?). Thanks again for your support. I know this is not easy for you as well as for us.

Best wishes,

Kristine

I received a response ten minutes later:

You are giving me very confusing information. It sounds as if you have a plan to drive to Syria with your group. If you want to depart with our DOD-organized departure then it would be sometime this week. It sounds as if it will take a while to get your group together and get to Beirut. We will not be taking you to Damascus.

What do you want to do: Leave with our DOD organization? Or go to Syria with your group? How far are you from Beirut? Timewise.

I responded with the following:

We are trying to figure out the best plan. What is the DOD plan? Is it only to get us out, or is it to get us home? We would prefer the plan that would get us home in the quickest and safest manner.

My nephew is in Zahle, but I can ask his father to bring him to us in Kfarhouna today, if there is a plan for us to leave for home with the DOD-operation. It would take us approximately 2-hours to get to Beirut under the current circumstances.

We thank you again for the work you are doing on our behalf. We wait in anticipation.

Best wishes,

Kristine

We received directions to gather together and wait for more information:

Ok given what you have told me, I suggest you all gather in one place and be on standby. Check with me in the a.m. tomorrow and I may be able to give you instructions. I suggest that you all go the DOD assisted way which will be in the next couple of days. That's safest. And please get closer to Beirut because if I have some way of getting you out sooner it may be at the very last moment.

The tentativeness of the plan was unsettling. We had no idea when we would be able to leave, nor how we would ultimately get home. We had stayed in Kfarhouna, as opposed to returning to our apartment in the predominantly Muslim area of Doha-Khalde,[11] because we believed we would be safer in a predominantly Christian area. Nevertheless, we were situated at the beginning of the south. The following day, on July 18, Israeli bombing edged closer to Kfarhouna. At 7:00 a.m. the entire house shook after a loud sound indicated bombing was occurring in the vicinity. Local news reported the escalating offense, with detailed accounts of targeted bombings in the south. It was clear the situation was getting worse and not likely to end any time soon. We still had received no word from the U.S. Embassy on the plan for evacuation. Though later I learned from news reports that the embassy began evacuating U.S. citizens on July 18 by ship, we never received confirmation that evacuation began. Indeed, because the plan was still communicated to us as tentative, we decided the following morning, July 19, to take our chances and leave for Damascus on our own.

The trip to Damascus was frightful because we knew Israeli forces were using airstrikes to bomb roads and isolate the south from the rest of Lebanon. We traveled from the south, and indeed, fifteen minutes after we arrived at the Syrian border, we received word that the road we had been on was bombed again. Nevertheless, we made our way to Damascus safely, stayed there for two nights, and then left for home via Frankfurt. We arrived in the United States on July 22.

The experience of being caught in the cross fire between Israel and Hizballah during the July 2006 war as an American of Lebanese descent introduced a new level of complexity to my understanding of my American citizenship. The U.S. government officially supported the 2006 Israeli aggression.[12] Yet having spent almost twenty years traveling back and forth between Lebanon and the United States, living through part of the civil war, enduring the Israeli occupation of south Lebanon, and witnessing the near-constant Israeli violation of Lebanese airspace, all of which has been experienced by most Lebanese as acts of terror, my perceptions of Israel, and of the U.S. government, were at odds with those of other Americans. The United States saw (and sees) itself as Israel's strongest ally, at the expense of Lebanese lives. During the July 2006 war, these included my life and the lives of my family as well as countless other U.S. citizens in Lebanon. Though Israel was presented to U.S. citizens as the victim in this conflict, a majority of Lebanese, including myself, experienced Israel as an extremely violent aggressor and oppressor.[13]

More poignant, responses from the U.S. government to its citizens in Lebanon after the July 2006 war began, and as it escalated daily, conveyed abandonment. I found myself relying more on, and having deeper faith in, an ethnic organization (AAI) to hear our case and find a solution to our predicament. As an American citizen, I had expected that the U.S. government would address our safety needs directly, not via an ethnic organization.[14] The U.S. government's position on the July 2006 war, and the mainstream media's support of Israel, made it difficult for the United States to offer full and immediate protection to Lebanese Americans in Lebanon. The official U.S. stance, which justified Israeli aggression, marginalized our experience. Finding a way to legitimate and give voice to an alternative perspective became the challenge for transnational people like us.

On Being a Fulbright Scholar

I received the news just before we successfully escaped the July 2006 war that I had been awarded a Fulbright to go to Lebanon during the 2006–2007 academic year. Our experiences had, however, made me hesitant to return to Lebanon that fall. Though a cease-fire had been negotiated, I felt that if another conflict were to break out, I could not assume that the U.S. government would help me should I find myself in a life-threatening situation. As a result, I declined the opportunity for that academic year. The following year I was told my Fulbright award had been carried over in recognition of the war and political events of 2006. A year had passed in relative calm, so I decided that, yes, I did want to go. Carrying out a research project in Lebanon along with teaching sociology provided me with one more genuine transnational, emigrant-resident interchange.

I spent six months in Lebanon during 2008. My Fulbright project involved teaching an undergraduate course at Haigazian University and collecting data on social relations and health from older adults. My Fulbright experience in Lebanon played a transformative role in my life, enriching my understanding of social relations, both practically and theoretically. This effect extends into my personal life, particularly how I interact with others, and into my research on social relations in the United States. In Lebanon, I came to recognize the importance of an overlapping sense of self. The ties that bind Lebanese people together extend beyond family and are achieved through interactional norms that cut across religion, gender, class, and age (Khuri 1990; Joseph 1993).

Learning this fact, and living it, provided insight into how Lebanese social relations vary and are similar across national contexts. Most centrally, I came to realize the extent to which social status in Lebanon is a negotiated fact, not a guaranteed ranking. It is redefined in almost every social interaction one has with others. Though this assessment is hardly a dramatic revelation—it is consistent with the tenets of the analytical approach sociologists call "symbolic interactionism" (Blumer 1986)—the negotiated aspects of daily life in Lebanon are more numerous, and occur with more intensity, than would seem normal in a country like the United States. This heightened level of negotiation (which is perceptible to Americans but taken for granted by Lebanese) fosters an outlook in which no situation may be defined or assumed a priori. To illustrate, I will present a case in which my students felt they had the right, indeed the duty, to constantly negotiate assignments, due dates, attendance, and workload with me, their professor, an experience I found especially illuminating.

There were five students enrolled in my course; four were social work majors in their senior year, the fifth was an education major in her sophomore year. The course, taught in English, was designed to introduce students to theories about the study of aging and to teach them social science research methods as a means to better understand their own society. Having students carry out the research activities on their own leads, I have found, to an unparalleled internalization of the social science method and direct application of course material. I also hoped the course would allow me to overcome the language barrier (I am not fluent in Arabic). The students would learn social science methods and, at the same time, collect data for my research project. After the students engaged in translation activities and ethics and interview training, I accompanied each on their first interview. They all performed beautifully.

The students in my course were bright and diverse. I learned much about Lebanese culture from them, and I hope they learned something of American culture from me. The most striking aspect of Lebanese culture I observed concerned the importance of persistent negotiation for a desired outcome, regardless of status position. This lesson occurred within the context of a period of political instability in Lebanon that had threatened the students' education by interrupting their classes and progress over several years. Even in 2008, our classes canceled twice during the semester, once because of a general anti-government rally, and a second time when the university closed for ten days due to armed conflict between two political factions: those siding with the opposition in support of a unity government (made up of political constituencies that support Tayyar, Amal, Hizballah) and those siding with the current government, led by Prime Minister Saad Hariri. The conflict occurred when the government threatened to dismantle an elaborate communication system developed by Hizballah to defend against possible Israeli invasion.

Most alarming for me was the attitude such instabilities cultivate in the youth, faculty, and administration. Not feeling secure in one's personal life breeds a kind of distance from higher education. After all, if there is no official government, bombs are dropping, gunfire is occurring in the streets, and there is no guarantee of social order or any evidence that tomorrow will bring anything better, how can one dedicate attention, energy, and effort toward learning (students), teaching (faculty), or even working (administrators)?

In my classroom, this situation generated a series of confusing cross-cultural exchanges. One obstacle I encountered in fulfilling the goals of my research project was student attitudes toward their own education. My class was considered an "elective," an optional course students can take to supplement their program of study. In the minds of my students, an elective is supposed to involve less time, effort, and work than a required course. This sentiment was expressed to me on the first day of class and repeated over the course of the semester as students attempted to negotiate assigned tasks. I later learned from colleagues at surrounding institutions—Balamand, the American University of Beirut, the University of St. Joseph—that this sentiment was not unique to Haigazian University.

The repercussions of this attitude surfaced when *not one* student came to class the day their first assignment was due. This shocked me. I had never experienced a situation where every single student was absent. Moreover, their assignment was meant to facilitate the course project. If the time line for the assignment changed, then so did the rest of the course. Not one student contacted me to let me know they would miss class, nor did any attempt to explain why their assignment was not turned in. In response, I had a discussion with the students during the next class period, expressing my concern. I explained that late assignments were not acceptable, and though I would very much like to spend an undefined period of time with them, the reality was that we only had fifteen weeks together. I then devised a rule, after consulting with colleagues at Haigazian University, that for future assignments, I would deduct 10 percent from their grade for each day they submitted it late.

In addition, attendance was not consistent. I learned at the end of the semester from my colleagues at the university that I could/should have required attendance, something that would have set a completely different tone. At my university in the United States, we are not permitted to grade based on attendance, so the thought never crossed my mind. At Haigazian University, however, the situation requires that attendance be counted, and indeed instructors may drop a student from the course if they do not come to class.

These challenges culminated in a confrontation I had with my students three weeks before the semester was scheduled to end. For two consecutive class periods, students did not attend class. It was a critical week to miss, as I had planned to instruct them on qualitative data analysis, which was a requirement for their final project. When only one student showed up on the second day of that week, I decided I would e-mail the class the information I had intended to convey to them in class, detailing the final project expectations. This communication prompted every single student to attend class the following week. Their goal, however, was to try to convince me to reduce my expectations for the course.

The exchange that ensued highlighted a variety of assumptions. It started when Nadia,[15] the student who attended class the least, arrived early and said she had something to "nag" about. She informed me I was expecting too much in terms of the assignments due at the end of the course (a final paper and presentation based on their field work and a final exam based on the course material). I responded that assignments were nonnegotiable and that everything would stand as originally planned. Shortly afterward, the rest of the students filed in, and a second student, Yasmeen,[16] raised her hand to complain that my course was an elective and I was expecting too much from them. She then explained that she would have to spend the next weekend working only to complete the requirements for this course, yet she had other assignments in her "required" course. Naturally, the students were feeling squeezed because they had missed key lectures that would have helped them complete their final projects. After some further attempts to sway me to reduce the amount of required work, Yasmeen announced that I needed to understand that "this is Lebanon."

The phrase "this is Lebanon" was one I heard throughout my stay. It was a disclaimer, and an apology of sorts, offered whenever expectations could not be met. I heard it when business transactions somehow did not materialize as originally planned. I heard it when people tried to explain why something did not happen as expected or why people were not accountable for their word. Although "this is Lebanon" is an all-purpose justification for low standards, I had seen many Lebanese overcome this excuse to achieve great success and become reliable, dependable, and well-respected members of U.S. and Lebanese society. It was this event in my classroom, however, that made me realize how such an outlook could potentially hurt my students. I took this opportunity to inform the students that saying "this is Lebanon" was not acceptable in a university classroom. In my view, university studies should be an escape from everyday problems, an opportunity to stretch one's mind and learn to think about things in a different way, from a new perspective. To convey this sentiment, I shared with them a perspective that I hoped would inspire them to make better use of their own educational opportunities:

> If you choose not to come to class, or not read assigned materials, or not study or complete the course assignments, the only person you hurt is yourself. It does not hurt me. I have my education, and I am working in a job that I love. I do not ever want to hear you tell me that you cannot do the assigned work because "this is Lebanon." Now, you may choose to spend the rest of our hour here today "nagging,"[17] telling me that you cannot do the work assigned, and then you can leave, still being held accountable to me, however, for today's material. Or you can choose to stop the "nagging," and we can spend the hour with me teaching you the planned topic. It is up to you.

They chose to stop "nagging." After that day, all except Nadia (four of the five) attended each of the three remaining classes for the semester. Despite my regular summer visits to Lebanon, I had been completely unprepared for this negotiating strategy. It was an interchange based on different worldviews. I entered the situation with an obviously American perspective on university class expectations, and this perspective was tested by Lebanese expectations that demanded firmness and flexibility simultaneously. My role as a transnational Lebanese American taught me something not just about Lebanon, but about my own position as a bicultural citizen, which had not equipped me to deal with certain kinds of cultural difference. This experience illustrates that U.S. citizenship is a valuable resource for transnationals, but also one that can be limiting, especially when it carries assumptions that make Lebanese values and behaviors hard to understand. Though my U.S. citizenship was not directly threatened by my teaching experience in Lebanon, I came to appreciate how transnational encounters could lead me, and my Lebanese students, to question the rights and mutual obligations that guided our interactions. This process of renegotiation was a helpful challenge to our shared sense of cultural belonging as Lebanese.

Concluding Thoughts

The present-day experiences of Lebanese in their homeland and in the United States are shaped by the forces of globalization, not the least of which include satellite television, Internet communication, relatively affordable travel, and increasing contact between those who have immigrated to the United States and their friends and family who remain in Lebanon. Frequent visits to Lebanon by U.S. emigrants and to the United States by Lebanese nationals have contributed significantly to the development of civil society in Lebanon after the civil war. This is especially noteworthy when interactions occur among and between youth, that is, U.S.-born children of Lebanese immigrants and their counterparts in Lebanon. The exchange of American and Lebanese culture during these encounters has the potential to mend the damaging effects of sectarianism; challenging sectarianism is one of the most critical social issues on which the emergence of civil society in Lebanon depends.

The descendants of those who migrated from Lebanon and now live in the United States are uniquely positioned to influence Lebanese society. On the one hand, they have an intimate connection to Lebanon through their parents and grandparents. Often, visions of their ancestral land are ones of warmth, respect, and understanding. At the same time, in this sociopolitical era of unrest within the Middle East and between the Middle East and the United States, a period in which Arab violence or resistance to hegemonic political structures is often labeled "terrorism," the ethnic differentiation of Arabs in the West is of paramount concern (to Arabs, Americans, and Arab Americans), contributing to "discrepant localisms" (Howell 2000), identities that are not easily accommodated within existing models of American multiculturalism or Lebanese sectarianism. Lebanon remains a distinct source of identity for Lebanese who were born and raised in the United States, who have learned and adopted American values that emphasize freedom, democracy, and equality. These values often pit Lebanese Americans against U.S. policy in the Middle East, which has allowed Israel to devastate Lebanon and expose Lebanese Americans and their relatives to lethal violence. Likewise, Lebanese Americans routinely find themselves at odds with key aspects of Lebanese political culture, largely because Americans place such a high value on individual rights, which contrasts with the Lebanese emphasis on rights derived through family and religious ties and through steady renegotiation of the status quo. Despite these complexities, Lebanese emigrants are viewed as legitimate messengers in their homeland, having an understanding of Lebanese culture on the one hand while being intimately tied to American culture on the other. Encounters between emigrants and residents provide opportunities for unique intercultural exchanges.

The transnational interchanges detailed above all took place within the Terror Decade. Despite U.S. foreign policy in the Middle East region (including armed conflict between the United States and various countries in the

Middle East), despite the U.S. government's labeling Hizballah a terrorist organization even though it is widely perceived as a resistance movement within Lebanon, despite the U.S. government's unflinching support for Israel during a war in which American citizens (of Lebanese descent) were targeted by the Israeli military, these exchanges have been ongoing and continue unabated. One could argue that transnational ties actually become more vital to both countries during these times of crisis.

My transnational interchanges have been affected by my privileged socioeconomic position, which has given me the opportunity to travel frequently and to experience and potentially bridge different cultural worlds (American and Lebanese). Such activities, undertaken by hundreds of thousands of emigrant and ethnic Lebanese, contribute to the development of civil society in Lebanon and promote cultural understanding in the United States about Lebanon specifically, and the Middle East generally. My discrepant cosmopolitan identity places me in a unique position, as a global citizen, to comment on my rights and power (or lack thereof) as an American. Parts of my identity—as American, Lebanese, and Muslim—at times put me in a vulnerable, powerless position. Able to contribute, but not quite fully as an American and not quite fully as Lebanese, I have lived out the double bind of the Terror Decade, a period in which I gained access to rights and resources from the same state (the United States) that was willing to sacrifice or abandon me in my hour of greatest need.

The interchange experiences I explore in this essay include new issues for transnational living among American citizens of Lebanese descent. The political instabilities that inform Lebanon's past and present make emigrant involvement in Lebanese society imperative, yet this instability is potentially a threat to Americans in Lebanon and Lebanese in the United States. By chronicling the transnational activities of organizing an annual summer youth camp in south Lebanon, living through the 2006 war between Lebanon and Israel, and teaching and doing research as a Fulbright scholar, I have tried to show the value, and the challenges, of interchange experiences. These experiences generate unique opportunities to build bridges between countries, but an acknowledgment of when and how U.S. citizenship is a resource and when it is a liability allows for a more nuanced understanding of what transnational ties between Lebanon and the United States can ultimately accomplish.

Notes

1. Americans wishing to support Arab and Muslim homelands financially are quite restricted in their ability to do so. The Treasury Department has closed numerous Muslim charities in the United States (see http://www.mathaba.net/0_index.shtml?x=622182),

and many American Muslims fear being targeted by federal investigators if they donate to the charities still allowed to operate (see http://www.wrmea.com/archives/sept-oct02/0209082.html). By contrast, American citizens may donate to the American Jewish Joint Distribution Committee to support "overseas Jewish communities, and help Israel" with tax-deductible benefits (see https://www.jdc.org/donation/donate.aspx).

2. Though I self-identify as half Iranian and half Lebanese, I use the term "Lebanese American" to signify my identity here because my transnational activities have been almost exclusively concerned with Lebanon.

3. The occupation of south Lebanon lasted eighteen years, from 1982 to 2000. The withdrawal in 2000, however, was not complete. Israel continues to occupy the water-rich area known as Shebaa Farms (Harik 2005). Hizballah is universally credited as the Lebanese party most responsible for Israel's withdrawal (see Norton 2000).

4. World Bank (2008).

5. The first camp cost approximately $18,000 to operate, all of which was donated by emigrants. Though the Emigrant-Resident Camp continued to operate annually, emigrant financial support waned as the U.S. economy weakened. To compensate for the dip in emigrant financial support, the Lebanese government (Ministry of Youth and Ministry of Emigrants) provided financial support. The most recent iteration includes support from a Lebanese nongovernmental organization funded by the United States Agency for International Development called Relief International.

6. See Tur (2007) for an analysis of what precipitated the July 2006 war.

7. Nonessential embassy personnel and their dependents began to be evacuated by helicopter on July 14 (Sean McCormack, Department of State Press Briefing, July 14, 2006, http://2001-2009.state.gov/r/pa/prs/dpb/2006/69007.htm).

8. Secretary of State Condoleezza Rice likened the human suffering in Lebanon to birth pangs as she predicted the creation of a new Middle East would result from the war.

9. What was not stated was the fact that Americans in Lebanon were more wary of Israeli bombings and aggression than they were of any imminent danger from contact with Hizballah.

10. The Department of Defense was important to this effort because they needed to negotiate with Israel to ensure evacuation missions would not be attacked by the Israeli military. See http://www.gao.gov/new.items/d07893r.pdf for a report on the challenges and success of the evacuation mission.

11. Doha-Khalde is a religiously diverse area, though predominantly Muslim. It is situated within five miles of Beirut International Airport, which had been bombed the first night.

12. Secretary of State Condoleezza Rice said that a cease-fire should be put off until "conditions are conducive" (see http://www.newyorker.com/archive/2006/08/21/060821fa_fact#ixzz0n9jvhhXA).

13. See http://www.hrw.org/en/reports/2007/09/05/why-they-died-0 for a detailed presentation of human rights violations committed by Israel during the July 2006 war.

14. The U.S. Embassy announced initially that evacuation would incur a cost to American citizens. The first messages explicitly stated: "The Department of State reminds American citizens that the U.S. government does not provide no-cost transportation but does have the authority to provide repatriation loans to those in financial need. For the portion of your trip directly handled by the U.S. Government we will ask you to sign a promissory note and we will bill you at a later date." The Arab American Institute was instrumental in protesting this charge and having it waived.

15. A pseudonym.

16. A pseudonym.

17. "Nagging" is the term the students used to describe their own behavior.

REFERENCES

Ajrouch, Kristine J., and Abdi Kusow. 2007. "Racial and Religious Contexts: Situational Identities among Lebanese and Somali Muslim Immigrants." *Ethnic and Racial Studies* 30(1): 72–94.

Basch, Linda, Nina Glick Schiller, and Cristina Szanton Blanc. 1994. *Nations Unbound: Transnational Projects, Postcolonial Predicaments, and Deterritorialized Nation-States.* London: Gordon and Breach Science Publishers.

Blumer, Herbert. 1986. *Symbolic Interactionism: Perspective and Method.* Berkeley: University of California Press.

Clifford, James. 1997. *Routes: Travel and Translation in the Late Twentieth Century.* Cambridge, Mass.: Harvard University Press.

Gualtieri, Sarah. 2001. "Becoming 'White': Race, Religion, and the Foundations of Syrian/Lebanese Ethnicity in the United States." *Journal of American Ethnic History* 20(4): 29–58.

Harik, Judith P. 2005. *Hezbollah: The Changing Face of Terrorism.* New York: I. B. Tauris & Co.

Hourani, Albert, and Nadim Shehadi, eds. 1992. *The Lebanese in the World: A Century of Emigration.* London: Centre for Lebanese Studies.

Howell, Sally. 2000. "Cultural Interventions: Arab American Aesthetics between the Transnational and the Ethnic." *Diaspora* 9(1): 59–82.

Humphrey, Michael. 2004. "Lebanese Identities: Between Cities, Nations, and Transnations." *Arab Studies Quarterly* 26(1): 31–51.

Joseph, Suad. 1993. "Gender and Relationality among Arab Families in Lebanon." *Feminist Studies* 19(3): 465–486.

Khuri, Fuad I. (1990). *Tents and Pyramids: Games and Ideology in Arab Culture from Backgammon to Autocratic Rule.* London: Saqi Books.

Kouri, Jim. 2007. "State Department Reviews 2006 Evacuation of Americans from Lebanon." http://www.renewamerica.com/columns/kouri/070610.

Levitt, Peggy, and Nina Glick Schiller. 2004. "Conceptualizing Simultaneity: A Transnational Social Field Perspective on Society." *International Migration Review* 38(145): 595–629.

Levitt, Peggy, and Mary Waters, eds. 2002. *The Changing Face of Home: The Transnational Lives of the Second Generation.* New York: Russell Sage Foundation.

Lowenstein, Jennifer. 2000. "News Not 'Fit to Print.' Fighting the Lebanon War: Hizbullah and the Press." *Middle East Report Online*, http://www.merip.org/mero/mero022300.html.

Mowles, C. 1986. "The Israeli Occupation of South Lebanon." *Third World Quarterly* 8(4): 1351–1366.

Norton, A. R. 2000. "Hizballah and the Israeli Withdrawal from Southern Lebanon." *Journal of Palestine Studies* 30(1): 22–35.

Ong, A. 1996. "Cultural Citizenship as Subject-Making: Immigrants Negotiate Racial and Cultural Boundaries in the U.S." *Current Anthropology* 37(5): 737–762.

Schimmelpfennig, A., and E. H. Gardner. 2008. "Lebanon—Weathering the Perfect Storms." Working paper, International Monetary Fund.

Tur, O. 2007. "The Lebanese War of 2006: Reasons and Consequences." *Perceptions* (Spring): 109–122.

U.S. Census Bureau. 2000. *Current Population Reports.* Washington, D.C.: U.S. Department of Commerce.

World Bank. 2008. "Middle East and North Africa: Migration and Remittance." http://go.worldbank.org/V8AQP1ATF0.

Part 4

Civilian Stories

My Life as a Brown Person

MUJAN SEIF

I grew up hearing stories about racism and attending leadership conferences where videos illustrated a world in which Arabs were constantly called
terrorists or A-rabs and harassed endlessly. However, I have to say I was in
disbelief. At Bloomfield Hills schools, I have never been discriminated against
or personally harassed for being Arab in the post-9/11 decade. This will not
be some story of persecution or tears. This will be the story of a teenager
who grew up happily in this decade, surrounded by close white friends and
Arab acquaintances. These acquaintances have experienced a few isolated
incidences, but nothing serious, nothing violent, and nothing coming from
people of authority. Keep in mind, I am not speaking for anyone other than
myself. I am writing my own experiences. This is my recollection of my life
in the post-9/11 decade.

I am Mujan Seif, the daughter of Wejdan Azzou and Nader Seif. I was
born on August 11, 1994, in Dearborn, Michigan, the home of tens of thousands of Arabs. My mother emigrated from Baghdad when she was in high
school. My mother's side of the family is Chaldean. This facet of my ancestry has been discussed numerous times among my friends. As I have had to
point out, not all denizens of the Middle East are Muslim; rather, the Chaldeans are essentially Christian Arabs. In the words of a friend, "[Chaldeans]
come from over . . . in the Middle East-ish area. Dark skinned, dark hair, all
that. Usually Chaldean Catholic. They think they own the world. They are
usually rich. Oh, and they rent party buses for school dances." Although I
am friends with young Chaldeans who do not fit this description, the majority of Chaldeans at my school—also referred to by the teenage population
as Chaldos, Boaters, and Grease Monkeys—display these attributes fully. In

213

fact, the stereotype rings so true for teenage Chaldeans that I, the daughter of a Chaldean, often forget that this stereotype does not extend to Chaldean adults. I must be reminded that adult Chaldeans worked hard to grind out a living and that the kids do not provide an accurate representation of Chaldean values.

My father is a Sunni Muslim from Jordan. His family is originally from Palestine and fled to Jordan during a conflict between Palestinians and Israelis. I was brought up Muslim. This eventually became common knowledge among my peers and teachers when I started fasting as a second grader. I enjoyed speaking about my religion, never forcing it on people. I have given two presentations on Islam. The first, in 2004, was an in-depth description of the religion to a group of educators from Ferndale schools. I was a fifth grader; I actually enjoyed it, and it sparked my interest in public speaking. The second, in 2008, was as part of a group of Muslims giving a presentation to my freshman World Studies class at International Academy, the high school I attended for the first semester of my high school career. Interestingly enough, when my teacher asked me to help out, I made it clear that I was now an agnostic. He just liked that I was a pretty enthusiastic kid who obviously still knew all about the religion and could help out. I am Arab, but now I am an agnostic. My belief in God ends with: I admit that I just do not know. I have no problem with people who show great faith; I even enjoy a good discussion on our different views. I do not like extremism in any form. I know that suicide bombers are not Muslims. They are extremists. Suicide is forbidden in Islam. Muslims do not kill in the name of Allah. Those who kill are extremists. Muslims are people who believe in one God, Allah, and believe that Muhammad is His prophet. As an agnostic, I am open to the concept. I do not hate atheists either. They are just another group of people with their own beliefs.

Cupcakes were on the counter, I remember. Wrappers were strewn all over the classroom. My good friend, Alex, had just had his classroom birthday party. He was choosing who would get to accompany him as he toured the school, distributing extra cupcakes to other teachers. We had already decided I would be one of his companions because my birthday is in August, meaning I never got to celebrate it at school. We continued joking and laughing, trying our best to stall the return to education. Just then, our teacher received a telephone call. Upon answering, his calm face went to one of total shock and disbelief. Because the average seven-year-old is carefree and joyful, I did not think much about it. Immediately after he placed the telephone on the receiver, he motioned for us all to sit down quietly. He strode to the television, looked at us, and said, "The [school] district doesn't want

Mujan Seif and her adoring parents, Nader Seif and Wejdan Azzou, 1995.
Photograph by Millard Berry.

me to show you this, but I think you need to see." Nervous looks were exchanged throughout the room, and the anxiety built up. And then I saw the Twin Towers fall to the ground, saw the red and orange flames, saw people jumping to their deaths, saw level after level collapse, and saw New York's Bravest sprinting into the tumbling structure. I knew what I had just seen was a big deal, something that would never be forgotten. My then barely developed mind did not understand its magnitude or its instigation of fear, chaos, and hatred.

That was almost ten years ago. I am not the same little kid transfixed by that television. I am a teenager now, trapped in the limbo that is adolescence.

When I was 3, Andrew Shryock and my father each predicted how I would change as I grew up, and Andrew wrote about it in one of his books. My father believed I would never be Americanized, whereas Andrew felt that road was inevitable. I became Americanized. However, my rebellion was not fought consciously. I did not sing "The Itsy Bitsy Spider" in English at 3 years old because I thought it would be fun to totally shock my parents; I probably sang it to impress Andrew and Sally. I never had the intention of becoming Americanized, but it is clear that I am. I will always be Arab, but I am more American.

There are photographs of me singing along with Abdel Halim Hafez,[1] my father's favorite singer, in my grandmother's living room. I was smiling and dancing around, donning a red cast on my right arm. Hafez was always playing in my house, and my father was always singing. As a teenager, I do not hate that music. I do listen to it occasionally and still know the lyrics, though to be perfectly honest, there was not a single point in my life where I actually knew the definition of any words I was singing. After Arab music, there came rap and hip-hop music. I hated that music when I first heard it and I hate it now. Now, I love indie rock and alternative. However, I listen to a wide range of groups, varying from MGMT to indie techno to Tool to alternative metal; hell, I blasted Sinatra in the car today. Anyway, the point is that no, I do not listen to Arabic music anymore, but I do not shun it or trash it. It was just a part of my childhood that I grew out of.

I love sports. I love the thrill, the energy, the competition, the power. My father was a soccer player in his youth. He told me stories about how he used to kick ass in his youth back in the home country. I am sure he was that good, considering how he still dominates today. He occasionally talks of his time, commenting that when he played, if the kid who brought the ball had to go home, the game was over. That remark always made me laugh for some reason. I played soccer until I was 13 and then switched to softball, a very American game. This was not an easy switch, as I was a naturally gifted soccer player and I had not picked up a softball bat until I was a sixth grader. Although it seems innocuous, that switch was, in my eyes, a pretty significant event in my cultural metamorphosis. I had stopped playing a sport that was practically in my blood and switched to a game I just picked up a few years ago. I do not know exactly why I quit soccer, but I do know that it was no conscious effort to rebel. Once again, American culture just crept up on me.

Ever since I had an excellent history teacher in eighth grade, I have loved learning American history. It just captivates me; I think there's beauty in seeing a tiny seed growing into a majestic tree. I loved every minute of my Advanced Placement U.S. history class. I put more effort into the coursework than any other class. I read articles about Mark Twain, Theodore Roosevelt, and Thomas Jefferson. Then I wrote articles on a range of issues, like Reconstruction, Jewish immigration, World Wars I and II, and the Middle Passage. I learned about the exaggeration of Paul Revere's famous ride, about the serious, almost understandable, reasons behind Benedict Arnold's act of treason, and even about the hypocrisy of Thomas Jefferson. I loved every review I wrote, loved the sleepless nights spent making them perfect while my friends were fast asleep on their warm, cozy, maybe Tempur-Pedic mattresses. I am really not interested in the history of the Middle East. I know the history of its religions and its history with the United States, but I know

Mujan Seif (right) and her sister, Maysam, 2010. Photograph by Wegdan Azzou.

nothing of its esoteric history. I do not know its greatest leaders or any of its social and economic history. I am enthralled by the history of the United States and will continue with my exploration of it; I am mildly interested in the history of the land of my ancestors.

I speak, read, and write English. That was not the case in the first years of my life. My first language was Arabic. I spoke Arabic to everyone, even if they were white and could not speak it. My parents actually had to write basic translations for the nice ladies watching me at day care. I cannot pinpoint the exact time my primary language changed from Arabic to English; I just know that I entered pre-school speaking English, when I was approximately 5. That said, I still know Arabic; I have not locked it away with the intention of never letting it see the light of day again. I cannot speak in proper grammar and I cannot speak formally. I can speak in the informal. I do not know a plethora of nouns, but I can name basic objects and respond to commands. In other words, if someone gave me instructions, I could understand and follow the instructions. If someone asked me to speak in Arabic about Arab poets or give my opinion on historical events, I would be at a total loss. With regards to writing, I can write out the alphabet and, on a good day, write out simple phrases. I cannot, by any stretch of the imagination, read or write calligraphy. All the calligraphy in my house is mostly art to me, and I do not even attempt to read it. English is now my language. I love writing and I love reading. My favorite authors are Edgar Allen Poe,

Ernest Hemingway, and F. Scott Fitzgerald. I do not think I know any Arabic authors. I do wish I could be fluent again, but it does not faze me that I am not. Since my enrollment in public school, I have been surrounded by all authors and texts American. I know my father tried to keep Arabic in my life, but one man cannot stop his daughter from being inundated with English books and other English speakers. My elementary, middle, and high school are some of the most academically revered in the nation; my father did not stand a chance.

As I said at the very beginning of this essay, I have never been discriminated against or personally harassed for being Arab in the post-9/11 decade. I do not get any threats, have never been told to "go back to my own country," or anything of that nature. However, there have been some instances where the situation would have been different if I were white and not Arab. None of these anger or offend me, and I find none of them serious. First and most harmless, my friends tease me for never having seen *The Wizard of Oz*. I did not watch that when I was a kid and now that I am older I really have no desire to see this movie. It was never a part of my childhood, but, quite honestly, I do not care. Another small, rather humorous situation arose when all my friends read Dan Brown's *Angels and Demons*. Because the story explains the role of cannabis in Arab history, they all asked whether I had any great weed. Lastly, one recurring issue is that of being misrepresented by standardized tests. When filling out the general information, one has to choose a race. I did not know what to pick, as Middle Eastern or Arab is not a choice. When I was filling out my Advanced Placement information card for my U.S. history exam, I asked my teacher what race I should mark. He said just to choose "Other." I was agitated that there was not some choice for people like me. As I said, none of these situations offend me and certainly none of them have traumatized me.

Although I have never been teased, some friends of mine have. Because nothing has happened to me, I needed to gather data from other Arab kids at my school. They shared their ideas on the treatment of Arabs at Andover High School. My closest friend of those interviewed is Dalia Alhusein. She is Syrian and Muslim. She does not wear a *hijab* and when I asked why years ago, she replied honestly: "I just don't feel ready." One of Dalia's main problems is that she believes that too many Americans cannot differentiate the many countries of the Arab world. She does not like how all Arabs are thrown into one group, despite the significant differences amongst them. Unlike me, Dalia has had an angry encounter with someone because of her being Arab. Her freshman year she was given an assignment to make a presentation on her heritage for a social studies class. According to Dalia: "[A student] raised his hand and, wanting to make the class laugh, rudely asked if I was related to Saddam Hussein, if I was related to any terrorists, and if I had any information on the weapons they used." When I asked how she responded, she said, "I was really hurt by what he said, so I calmly informed him that I am an American, I was born here, and just because I am Arab doesn't mean that I have connections to terrorists or that I am a terrorist. He grouped all Arabs together and labeled them as terrorists."

Although I am appalled by this story, I am not surprised. That kid is known for being obnoxious and an attention seeker. The teacher supposedly in charge of this classroom did not do anything to end the commotion or punish the kid. However, before you begin to think that all teachers would have done that, let me clarify. Any teacher the students at my school actually like would not have sat back and let this ensue. This teacher is one who is generally despised and ridiculed amongst her students. Dalia believes that the problem is actually quite serious, going as far as calling me "one of the lucky few." She says she has been called "terrorist" multiple times and has been teased because of her last name ever since she moved to West Bloomfield when she was in the fourth grade, back in 2003. Sarah, another Arab and Muslim friend, faces even more racism because she wears the *hijab*. Along with the "terrorist" and "towel head" jabs, she also experienced a more memorable instance of racism. She was picking cherries with some other Muslim friends. Some of the cherries were not that great, so they thought it would not be so rude to ask the farmers to knock a few dollars off the price. She continues: "We went to go pay for the cherries, and all we did was ask the guy if he could take off a couple bucks from the total because half the cherries weren't good. So the guy goes off on us and yells at us, saying that we shouldn't have picked them up in the first place, and we're just ungrateful Arabs. Then he says, 'How 'bout you go kneel on the dirt and pray to your damn Allah, asking him for some perfect cherries.' All of us thought, 'What the hell?' My cousin told him to stop being so offensive and there was no need to act like that. His wife apologized for him, but he just walked off." Although some ignorant person could easily pass off a student's rude behavior as harmless, this is the type of shit that cannot be ignored. Sarah concluded that "most of these things happened like a year or so ago, you learn to ignore it later on. I'm not going to change the way anybody thinks of Muslims just by telling them they're wrong and being mean." Sarah is a tough girl, and I commend her for wearing a *hijab* every day. I know that other Arab kids are teased, or blatantly insulted, but I maintain that I never have been.

Some teenagers are racists and bigoted. I know that the majority of high school kids are stupid. There are good reasons we are not allowed to vote or run for public office. If teenagers ran the world, it would be chaotic. Society as we know it today would be razed and replaced by one ruled by hormones and jocks. However, I will bravely defend the rest of us, the teenagers who befriend or avoid people based on their actions and values, not their race. We do not dislike other teenagers because they are Jewish or Asian or black. We have problems with people who are fake, people who lie, and people who hurt our friends. If I cannot stand a girl who broke my friend's heart, I cannot stand her because she broke his heart, not because she is Catholic. We do not stereotype, even when it is so tempting. Hell, we do not stereotype even when the stereotype is actually being exhibited. As my good friend Felix puts it, "I'm not racist, but I can't ignore when stereotypes just play into themselves. Like I have good friends who are Jewish, but then I walk down the hall at my school and see five Jewish girls who look the same, wearing Sugarlips[2] and texting on their Blackberries." In a high school like Andover, where every other girl looks the same and some guys like to believe that they're thugs, people think and say nasty things about each other all the time. I believe those morons who insulted Dalia and Sarah will see the absurdity of their actions when they are adults. They will feel ashamed. I am sure.

But for me, growing up Arab in the post-9/11 decade was happy and safe. I know some people will find that hard to believe. But it's true, and I'm glad.

Notes

1. An Egyptian singer who was hugely popular in the 1960s and 1970s.
2. A fashionable line of tight, seamless tank tops.

Subject to Change

KHADIGAH ALASRY

That day remains a crystal clear memory in my mind, as it does for most Americans. A sophomore in high school at the time, I knew it was a big deal because normal television ceased for two or three days. That had never happened before. At the time, I did not get it, and I did not feel the grief that other Americans felt. I am not sure if that was because I was just 15 years old and too young to understand, if I was emotionally inept, thus preventing me from having such feelings, or if I was fulfilling unsaid expectations by not feeling grief. After all, "my people" were the ones responsible for the grief felt by millions of others. I remember some friends and I actually chuckled during the moment of silence at school on the following day. But then again, I always had problems containing my laughter during moments of seriousness. This personality flaw was cause for much discipline at home and at school for most of my childhood and adolescence, before and after the fateful day that is 9/11.

Childhood was fun and confusing. That's how I would describe it. My neighborhood was a Yemeni neighborhood. We were very tight-knit, like the *Cheers* theme song describes, "Where everybody knows your name." Summertime was freedom. I played all day with my friends and never had a worry. We rode our bikes, played "throw the tennis balls over passing cars," and other games we made up, which had very long titles. Nights ended with doo-wop improv, which was inspired by our favorite movie, *A Bronx Tale*. Things made sense during the summertime.

School, on the other hand . . .

At an early age, I questioned why Santa Claus came to school every year and gave all of my peers and me Christmas presents. I enjoyed the dolls, the

Walkman sets, and the fruit and candy. But it didn't add up. My school was predominantly Muslim, and my older siblings made it clear to me that we, Muslims, do not celebrate Christmas. I knew what Christmas was, as defined by *Family Matters* and *Full House*. It seemed like a really pleasant idea, but I was not accustomed to feeling good about doing anything that my family stood against, especially when I sensed it was connected to religion.

I could tell by my father's interactions that he was a highly respected figure in our community. He was connected to a lot of the influential figures and families in my neighborhood, many of whom were authorities at the local *masjid* (mosque). We were invited to all of the weddings in our neighborhood, and I interpreted that as being connected. He was not around much during my upbringing, though, as he worked for most of the day. He was there when my seven siblings or I needed him outright, but much of his time was spent providing for his family. Although he was rarely present physically, his expectations and moral standards were very clear to our whole family: no stealing, no lying, no swearing, and no Christmas or Valentine's Day. I understood all of his conditions, without explanation, and respected my father's no-fuss attitude. Still, walking into school and seeing all of the Christmas decorations and witnessing my peers handing out Valentine's Day cards were still uncomfortable experiences.

April 19, 1995—Oklahoma City Bombing

I am in the third grade. There is a lot of watching of the news and a moment of silence. No explanation of it, and life goes on.

September 1997—Not Exactly the Little Rock Nine

The annual Christmas episode was one point of confusion for me in grade school, but the confusion would only increase.

Middle school would be even more confusing.

Bus rides nauseate me. The luxury of walking in the fresh air to school is a thing of the past. I would now be bussed, every day, to the other side of the city for middle school. Middle school is in the West End, a side of Dearborn I rarely go to. The school is huge and brighter. There are more windows and so many white people. I am not prepared for this. My friends and I try and remain close, but we are sprinkled throughout the school. During first-hour class, I have no one from my neighborhood in my class, nobody who looks like me. I get by on my smarts and sense of humor. Some of the other kids from my neighborhood have one or the other, or both, so they make out okay. Many of them do not have smarts or a sense of humor, and they do not make out okay.

Weekend School Is a Bust (1993–2004)

I have learned that I can sleep in for two hours on Saturdays and skip the first half of weekend school. Since my father has been working overtime, he gets home at 10:30 a.m. If I leave at 10:00 a.m., he does not catch me. I walk in during brunch-time and nobody notices that I was missing. None of the students dare say anything. That's breaking the code. It is the smartest idea I have had in a long time. Instead of being forced to memorize scripture, which I have no idea what it means, and being yelled at by a teacher in a dialect of Arabic that I completely do not understand, I sleep for two additional hours. Nice.

"Ouchhhhh!" I wake up to a burning ear and my father's angry face very close to mine. He is still dressed in his work clothes. "Why aren't you in school?" he asks me.

"Umm. I had an earache so I stayed home . . . ?" He gives me a look and I jump out of bed, get dressed, and am out of the door very quickly. Back to attempting to memorize scripture that I do not understand and getting yelled at in a dialect of Arabic that I do not understand.

I start attending a Sunday study circle after morning weekend school. This is not bad at all. A group of girls and women come together to learn about Islam. Some woman gives a lecture on topics like the signs of the Day of Judgment, the lives of different prophets, and proper Islamic dress. I often leave the lecture scared. "I am going to be so straight this week. I promise, God." That lasts me until about Wednesday, and then the fear is forgotten. I love when we learn about the interpretation of our dreams. This is my favorite Sunday lecture.

"Are we learning about dreams today, *ma'alamah*?" I ask the lecturer.

"No. You and the girls will do an activity, and the rest of the older girls will hear a lecture on a very mature topic."

"What is it? What are they learning about that you can't teach to us, too?"

"We will be discussing marriage," she replies. I inwardly roll my eyes. Whatever. I am old enough to learn about marriage. I am more mature than half of those high school girls anyway. I walk, in defeat, to the circle of kids gluing macaroni onto pop bottles on the other side of the room. I glue the word "Kids" in macaroni onto the bottle. It is my sarcasm manifesting in an art form. I never was very creative.

April 20, 1999—Columbine High School Shooting

I am in the eighth grade. There is a lot of watching of the news and a moment of silence.

I cannot believe this. Did it really happen? Did those two boys *really* do what everyone is saying they did? Why would anyone do that? My sister says her high school principal banned everyone from wearing trench coats. This is the same year *The Matrix* is released on DVD and I finally get to watch it. In one scene, Neo and Trinity enter a very large skyscraper with maximum security. They gun down nearly every single security guard, snap the necks of the others. In silence, Trinity and Neo slide into the building elevator, and I cannot help but admire how great they look in their black trench coats. "Is that what it looked like at Columbine on April 20?" I wonder. But I think, "No. It could not have looked so cool." Trinity and Neo take their trench coats off and hurry up the elevator to save Morpheus, and I am thrown back into the action of the movie.

We are far outnumbered in high school. There are tons of white people from many different middle schools. I am lucky to have one of my neighborhood friends in my first-hour class, so I am not alone. It is during fourth hour that I feel lonely. Many of the white friends I made in middle school reinvented themselves over the summer break, and I have to re-friend them all over again. Talk about identity crisis.

September 11, 2001—Two Airliners Crash into the Twin Towers of the World Trade Center

I am in the tenth grade and am hanging out in the girls' locker room. We just finished a game of soccer in Phys. Ed. Ms. Smith walks in and calls for our attention. She looks so somber. "Girls, I have some very sad news." The details of what she says are not clear and they do not resonate with me. I go to my locker, pack my stuff, and load onto the bus. There is an undercurrent in the school, but I do not get what the big deal is.

"The Twin Towers were bombed!" my friend Fizah tells me as I sit next to her.

"I know. I heard! Why didn't we feel the shaking though?"

"Because the Twin Towers are in New York, not here," Fizah replies. I am not sure if it is my ego or the fact that I had not traveled outside Michigan to know better, but I do not believe her.

"No, stupid. The Twin Towers in Dearborn were bombed. You know the place that everyone goes to take their pictures when it's a wedding? The two twin buildings with the pretty water fountain behind them? I think it's on

Ford Road. This is what was bombed." We argue for a while and then move on to the next topic.

I walk into my home. The eyes of my parents and older siblings are glued to the television screen. I see the explosion of a building—a real one. I am reminded of another scene from *The Matrix*, the one where Trinity is holding onto a rope and she smacks into the side of a huge glass skyscraper. The building does this weird thing where it collapses in, then explodes. This is very real, though.

There are three days of watching news and then a moment of silence in Phys. Ed., during which my friends and I can't contain our laughter. We did this once at a funeral, too. Just busted out laughing. I don't know why we can't handle being serious. Ms. Smith's eyes dart at us to say, "SHUT your mouths, girls." She is typically really nice and smiley, so her darting eyes work and we shut up and feign sadness.

It is near the end of sophomore year. I am sitting in my least favorite class: English Humanities. Because the new student who sits in front of me is quite entertaining, I drift off for only 80 percent of the hour.

"You know, I used to be totally against war. But now I'm not so sure." I look up and focus on the speaker, my teacher, Ms. Henson. She is standing in front of the chalkboard with a look of such concern on her face. "Seventy-eight days." She has been counting the days after the September 11 attacks and keeps track on the chalkboard. I don't understand why she can't just let things go. It's been months since that happened, and your stupid countdown isn't going to change anything. Plus, this is English class, not political science, or math for that matter, so get rid of your annoying countdown. I knew she was weird when she had all of my classmates and I sit in a big circle and look at images of Hiroshima. She had music playing and the lights turned down low while we gazed at the photographs.

Often, when there is a Yemeni person mentioned in the news under the very common headlines, "Suspected Terrorist" or "Ties to Al Qaeda," Ms. Henson asks a few of her Yemeni students, "Is he your cousin or a relative?" This is a deal-breaker for me, and I learn that a title like "teacher" doesn't bar one from being wrong or crazy.

"Are you kidding me? We are *so* not hanging that up in our locker." I am arguing with my friend. She has a small picture of Osama Bin Laden taped in the back of our locker, concealed from most people but visible to her, when she chooses to look at it.

"Yeah, we are. He's awesome." Vomit! "My favorite feature on his face is his bone structure. It's really cute." More vomit. I look at the picture of this man, who is famous for all of the wrong reasons, and I am reminded of my father. They both have similar skin tone, gray hair and beards, and wear a *mashadah*. Who is this man, though, really? My father is a very kind and giving person who always looks very serious. This man, Osama, I know nothing about. I have seen him over and over on television and have heard the hum of his voice under the voices of the translators. He speaks calmly and is living in hiding. I don't really know what he is saying in the poor-quality video footage that CNN plays ad nauseum because I don't trust the translators of American news. "Whatever. We can keep him up." The picture soon found its way down into a space created by a dent in our locker. At the end of the year, we would find the picture and laugh at the argument. "What was I *thinking?*" my friend would say.

A twisted ankle is the worst pain any person may feel. I am sure of it. Due to poor body awareness and overconfidence during a basketball game in gym, I spent one week of my junior year on crutches. I generally dress up for school, but I dressed down during that week in jogging pants, T-shirts, and hoodies. One day, during journalism class, I was leaning against a table in my "lounge-wear" when my teacher walked up to me. "How could you wear that?" he asked.

"Wear what?" I was embarrassed by the question. Do I have a stain on my shirt? Oh. "Since I twisted my ankle, I decided to dress down so I can be comfortable. After my ankle heals, I'll be back in my normal clothes."

"No. That's not what I meant. I meant *that.* How could you wear that?" I looked down at what my teacher was pointing at: my T-shirt. Specifically, he was pointing at the design of the New York City skyline, with the Empire State Building, the Chrysler building, and the World Trade Center as they looked before September 11, 2001. A knot finds its home in my stomach. I don't know what he is suggesting exactly, but a familiar feeling of guilt by association begins to fill my chest. It is the same feeling that I get when I watch the news and see images of Muslim men with their faces covered, holding fiery American flags in their grip. It is the feeling I will get years later when watching my favorite actors die cruel deaths in movies, like *Syriana* and *Munich*. My teacher smirks in a way I have become very familiar with. He is being sarcastic. I laugh nervously.

Bowling for Columbine (2003)

It is my senior year. The past few years have been full of Muslim teenage girl angst. Cliquishness, tests, Sweet Sixteens—oh my! I have found that my greatest teachers are Steven Spielberg, James Cameron, and Martin Scorsese. I do well in school, but it is through movies that I learn about the real world.

"Hey, Kay, did you hear about this movie?" My sister flashes the DVD cover of *Bowling for Columbine*.

"That's with that guy Michael Moore, right?" I ask.

"Yep, that's the one. He made *Roger and Me*, too." I do not know what she is referring to.

"The documentary about Flint, Michigan?"

"So, are you watching that now? I want to watch it with you."

Disgust, fear, anger, and true sorrow fill every fiber of my being. I watch the shrieking and running. One person flies across my TV screen after the sound of bullets parading out of a gun. My sister's and my eyes fill with tears at the sight of terror. I turn to her, "How could they let him put this in a movie? What are the families of these people saying about that?"

"Michael Moore isn't exploiting the Columbine 13. He's trying to get at the root issue that enabled the two boys who killed all of those students, and that's the lack of gun control laws," my sister replied to me, without moving her eyes from the TV screen. I would remember this very conversation while watching John Cusack and Rachel Weisz battle lenient gun control in *Runaway Jury* a few years later.

I was so impressed with Michael Moore in *Bowling for Columbine*. He asked very powerful people very tough questions. Charlton Heston, the president of the NRA, nearly kicked Moore out of his home because he could not handle his interrogation. Moore does not wear a suit, and he is very loud. He breaks all of the rules and offends. But he makes a ton of great points.

This experience, and many more like it, help me build the critical consciousness that would empower me to become an activist and advocate for truth and justice. It is not anything I learned in weekend school, in English class from my teacher and her stupid countdown, or from my journalism teacher and his sarcastic questions.

Graduation comes and goes. I did not prepare much for college until the end of my senior year. I managed to rake in a few scholarships, and my sister pressured me into starting college only weeks after graduating. I was the only one of my friends who was taking classes during the second summer semester. I wait for hours between my two classes. During these hours, I spend time flipping through the headlines of American news.

Saddam Hussein Is "Captured" (December 14, 2003)

"Wake up, guys! Wake up! Saddam Hussein was captured by the United States military!" I shake my brother awake.

"Are you serious?" he asks.

"Yes! It's on CNN." We all gather around the television and watch the news. I don't really know what to make of it, but I know it is big news.

Abu Ghraib Prison Pictures Exposed (2004)

Things I thought I knew, that I was sure of, are blown out of the water. How could they let this happen? A flash of the pictures was all I needed to cause radiating heat in my face and to get my veins pumping. This was not a rebel guerrilla force in Rwanda depicted so savagely by CNN; these were members of the U.S. military who committed such atrocities. These were people my tax money supported, who received twenty-one-gun salutes after graceful and selfless deaths befall them in honor of their country. Where is the honor in this? An unfamiliar feeling finds its way into my chest—contempt.

Detox (Late 2004)

I do not know what to believe. I sense God, but I am not sure how to approach Him. I drop old habits and am far less social than I used to be. I am very focused on finding truth. I attend my first Muslim American Society (MAS) Youth Detroit event. Honor and honesty are in the people there. It is a workshop on the Fiqh of Priorities, during which I engage in serious discussion and am treated very equitably, although I am far younger than the group moderators. It is a discussion grounded in Islamic texts, but it is very relevant to me. This is an unfamiliar experience. I do not temper my personality at all, and I talk and talk until the moderator stops me.

Participating in MAS activities, in addition to watching a lot of movies, now contributes to my developing a new life perspective. I bear witness that there is no God but one and that Muhammad was His final messenger to all of mankind! I have duties to carry out in this world; duties to the Lord, my family, my local communities, my country, and the entire world. These responsibilities do not contradict one another. Pursuing justice is what my Lord asks of me. Civic engagement within the country's existing framework and processes is a great thing. This is all new to me.

George W. Bush Jr. Is Reelected President of the United States of America (2004)

My first time voting: what a doozy.

I am taking Introduction to Political Science this semester. We analyze the presidential election as it is happening. I begin to see a different side of politics—an ugly side. I watch as a crowd of thousands of people chants mean things against both candidates. "Flip-flop! Flip-flop!" many scream at Senator John Kerry as he begins to debate foreign policy.

"Media has many different roles in the American society, one being the role of watchdog. An example of when the media played the watchdog role is during the Watergate scandal of the 1970s," Professor Jackson lectures us, as we take notes vigorously, with highlighters and all the works. I do not write anything down yet and look puzzled.

"Question?" he asks me.

"Hmm? No. No questions." I am taken back to sophomore year in government class when we watched *All the President's Men*. Deep Throat was some guy who worked for the Nixon administration and put the administration's illegal activities on blast to a couple of reporters named Bob Woodward and Carl Bernstein. They were being watchdogs.

Watergate, Hiroshima, Abu Ghraib, Guantanamo Bay, slavery, the Rodney King beating, Little Rock Nine. Sensory images of all of these events from government class, English class, movies, and episodes of *The Fresh Prince of Bel Air* are stored in my mind. I can't make sense of them. The assassination of Malcolm X, the assassination of Martin Luther King Jr., *To Kill a Mockingbird*. More images flash through my mind. The United States of America is the home of the free. We have freedoms in this country that people can only dream of in other countries. How is it that all of these horrible things have happened by our own doing? Under our radar? Where was the watchdog media when President Bush invaded Iraq to find "weapons of mass destruction"? Why is every elected president in our country a white man? Why is it that I learned very narrow tales about all of the horrible things the U.S. government and people were responsible for in courses like American History or World Civilizations? Why is it that the history of my people, the Muslim societies of the past several centuries, barely makes it into our social studies textbooks? Why did Deep Throat maintain his anonymity throughout his life when he should have been celebrated for committing a courageous act in service to our country? Where is his medal of honor? How many other shady scandals are past and current presidential administrations responsible for, where a Deep Throat did not step up to be our watchdog? If one of them had no problem dropping an atomic bomb on a city of more than 200,000, killing more than 60,000 people, I am sure they had no problem doing illegal things every now and again.

Multiculturalism in the School and Society (2006)

"Close the door behind you, please," Dr. Anderson says with an eye roll to a girl who walks in tardy on the first day of class with little remorse in her face. Bimbo. "OK. Eyes on the board. You see this?" Dr. Anderson asks, pointing to a small figure he has drawn on the board. "This is a cave. This is you and you and you in the cave." He signals to random people in the class. "During this class, I will give you a ticket out of this cave. It will be your choice in the future whether you want to return to this cave or stay out of it."

This all sounds very familiar. "You take the blue pill, the story ends. You wake up in your bed and believe whatever you want to believe. You take the red pill, you stay in wonderland and I show you how deep the rabbit hole goes." We have all watched the movie, Doc Anderson. Nice try. But you have caught my attention.

"Just an FYI, people. Most of you will return to the cave. I am sure of it. Here are your syllabi. Learn your syllabus well."

Racism, patriarchy, and artificial democracy are the topics of this class. We study, in depth, how these concepts are wired into our systems, as individuals and as a country. As much as we Americans seem to have achieved as a society, as individual citizens, and as human beings, we have transgressed our limits over and over again. We have oppressed the weakest people in our society and although we are a very glitzy nation, little progress has actually been made toward the protection of the oppressed.

"Indeed Allah does not change the condition of a people until they change the condition of themselves" (Quran, 3:11). I totally get it now.

Loose Change—Final Cut (2007)

As I learn to be critical of my government and other governments, a whole world of media opens up to me. Not only are many activists critical of their governments, but also they accuse our government of some heinous acts. As I watched the documentary *Loose Change*, I did not mind the low-quality sound and constant pauses for buffering on YouTube. My father sat next to me and we watched it together. We had little to say during the film, even during the long pauses.

"Professor, *Loose Change* was *insane*! It accuses President Bush's administration of orchestrating the September 11 attacks, and it points to all of this crazy evidence that support this theory," I tell my professor before class starts.

"Why are you so shocked? The theory they present is widely supported."

"I knew this guy was a bit nutty," I thought.

"If it is a popular theory, then why isn't it being presented on the news? This would make huge headlines if it had any legitimacy to it," I replied. "The United States media is not about playing legitimate news. Think about it. We are the only country with two major political parties who are both part of the same team. The news caters to these people, not to what is true." I nod my head so as not to offend. What a paranoid, conspiracy theorist!

Dr. Sami Al-Arian Begins His Hunger Strike during His Incarceration (January 22, 2007)

I hear of Dr. Al-Arian's story through newsletters from alternative news sources, not CNN, MSNBC, or Fox. He is a man accused of supporting a "specially designated terrorist organization." He suffered a long trial and, after several acquittals, took a plea bargain in hopes of being deported from the United States and being allowed to reestablish his life in another country. During his months of prison, Al-Arian claims he suffered severe beatings and maltreatment. He went on a hunger strike, and this brought him to the attention of many. Very Gandhi-esque.

MAS Youth Hosts Leadership Retreats for More Than 200 Youth Countrywide! (August 2007)

"Road trip! I wonder which chapters are going to be there?" Mariam asks me. We pile into the rental car and get ready to travel to Chicago for my first national MAS Youth gathering.

"Time for the hot seat," says Hazem, president of MAS Youth. What the heck is that? It's been one day of intense sessions, unpacking the history of MAS and how it has evolved into the organization we are a part of today. "Who's up first?" Hazem pulls a name from a bowl. "Tanya, from New York."

"Ohhhh!" The other girls were all pointing to Tanya and giggling. "You're in trouble," one girl says. Tanya sat in front of the group and people began to ask her questions.

"What is a strength that you see within yourself?"
"Describe your weakest moment in life."
"What is your favorite thing about MAS New York?"
"What social justice cause are you most passionate about?"

I walked into that weekend doe-eyed and left realizing just how "big" this was. We weren't just a group of people getting together to organize a few fun activities for our local communities. We were seeking depth and purpose in

Muslim American Society Youth work on a mural on the east side of Detroit, 2009. Photograph by Leslie Wade.

this life and in the Hereafter. We were about true change, and that would lead to many headaches. Soon. I saw this concept of "change" come alive, the following year, in another movement: Barack Obama's "Yes, we can."

Turntable Dhikr Makes an Impression at MAS-ICNA Convention in Chicago (December 2007)

The entertainment session of the conference has just concluded. All of us remain in our seats in the near dark. There are about 200 people. A bunch of us twenty-somethings, some kids, and a ton of teenagers. My eyes are darting back and forth from the stage to the crowd. It is near silent and tension slices the air. One of the performers, a member of the band Turntable Dhikr, sits on the stage with his head bowed in front of him. His dreads pour over his face and his eyes are closed. His arms are hanging straight in front of him.

"Is he dead?"

"Is he sleeping?"

"Dude! What is *up* with him?"

"I think they're trying to act like he is in some sort of spiritual trance. They are a Sufi band. You get it?"

I don't get any of it. As far as I know, music is a touchy subject. Some religious leaders have said that it is prohibited. My father made it clear to me growing up that he didn't approve, and others thought it was a very important and prescribed part of life. Always had been and always will be. All I know at this moment is that whatever just happened was *not* normal. This band started performing using words from Islamic supplications as their lyrics. All the while, a PowerPoint presentation was playing on a huge screen, with these wacky images flashing slowly and then quickly. Images of monks, tae kwon do artists, and even Flava Flave! Next, one of the singers slips into a spiritual trance and passes out *right* on stage. I've never seen *anything* like this before! Wait. Allow me to rephrase: I have seen plenty of artists perform art like this. It isn't really my thing, though. I prefer my art on the walls, not mixed in with my music. Where was my sense of shock and, worse, tension originating from? Ah. Aha. It makes sense. This band's display of art wasn't foreign to us, nor were the break-dancers who were up there before Turntable Dhikr tore it up. But, they *were* foreign to the parents in the room. This wasn't the first time any of us had seen this, but it *was* the first time any of us had seen *Muslims* perform stuff like this at a "Muslim" conference. The entertainment sessions I'd been to at Muslim-organized events always included an Arab dude drumming some percussion instrument and singing the Muslim equivalent of gospel music.

Everyone is frozen on the stage. Maybe they are all in a spiritual trance. There's Omar, the MAS Youth Chicago director, shuffling down the aisle in the dim light and silent air. He looks disheveled and completely out of place. His dress shirt is still tucked into his suit pants, but his tie is hanging loosely around his neck, and his sleeves are rolled up. He runs up to the stage and grabs the microphone. He speaks. In Arabic.

"What we just witnessed was not only something beautiful, but it was also a means to bring us closer to our Lord." Omar's passion poured through his words that night like nothing I had ever witnessed. He was defending the performers, but without an ounce of defensiveness. That night, his words spoke directly to the hearts of many and alerted the caution in others. "Do we know the story of our beloved Prophet, may the peace and blessings of our Lord be upon him? The day he witnessed the dance of the Abyssinians and made sure that his wife, Aisha, was sitting in a position where she could see them well and appreciate their art fully? The art he welcomed was *not* usual to him or his people. They were Arabs. But still he embraced it. Why? Our faith does not endorse any culture, not the Arab culture or any other, but our beloved Prophet understood, appreciated, and embraced the beauty in the threads of individuality that bind the human family. These young boys and girls and men and women who sit before us, your sons and daughters, and the millions more who are just like them, have their own art, which looks very different from what you may be accustomed to. In fact, their art may shake you, like it has tonight."

Omar continued on, but at that moment, at 11:30 p.m., I had one important phone call to make to help me figure this experience out. I walked out of the ballroom and dialed quickly.

Lots of questions would be raised in the MAS national forums soon after: "Who? What? Where? Why? Why? Why?" We had just entered a world of gray haze. It was uncharted territory for us, a territory that other Muslim organizations, like the Inner-city Muslim Action Network, had explored long ago and a space where Islamic jurisprudence would be applied and examined. Then, decisions would be made and people would be moved, some toward embrace and others toward rejection.

MAS Youth Voices for Change Six-City Concert Tour featuring Outlandish (June 2008)

"Outlandish![1] Oh my God! I'm so excited! I love their song, "I'm callin' you, when all my goals, my very soul ain't fallin' through . . ." my sister hums along.

"Yup. We will be hosting them for a six-city concert tour and the tickets are going fast, so you'd better get yours now," I told my sister. This was going to be the highlight of the summer. I knew it. All the MAS Youth Detroiters had changed our e-mail signature lines to read: "Voices for Change . . . ((it's time for a NEW Tone !!!)) rockin the nation & commin to Detroit 6.14.08."

It was such a noble project, one definitely worth my attention, which is why I accepted the role of tour director for the Detroit concert. We wanted to promote Outlandish's art as a positive alternative to the unhealthy art we are bombarded with on a nano-second basis. For five months, a band of very driven individuals from across the United States worked relentlessly on this project. We faced off against many forces, took a few major blows, and celebrated a few sweet victories:

1. "Oh man, guys, it's six months away!" Five, four, three, two, one . . .
   "It's tomorrow, and I forgot my phone charger at Tanya's house! Crap! I'm the tour director and I *need* my phone!"

Alasry speaks about Muslim American Society youth programs at an Expressions concert in Detroit, 2010. Photograph by Leslie Wade.

2. "*Assalamu alaikum*, Sister Khadigah. I noticed in your signature line mention of this project 'Voices for Change.' I have heard that this is a concert. Do you know that music is prohibited, Islamically? Why are you involved in this?"

3. "Awesome. A project for us, by us. It's like FUBU, the clothes brand, ha-ha. Kidding!"

4. "To whom it may concern: MAS Youth as a movement has taken a firm position on the permissibility of music and singing in Islam. This decision is based on solid research and the opinions of highly respected, mainstream scholars. MAS Youth's position on music is not one of weakness or compromise. It is a position of confidence, grounded in strong evidence and exemplifying the amazing flexibility and inclusiveness of Islam." (widely distributed document via Web and mail)

5. "What? Only 450 tickets sold at the Tampa concert? How is that possible when they attract thousands to their annual MYathalon?"

6. Several meetings at Starbucks with potential Voices for Change volunteers: "This is *exactly* what I am looking for. I am so glad you guys are doing this project! Count me in."

7. "*Back* up. I mean it." The concert venue's booking coordinator stands two inches away from my face. We are backstage and Outlandish's acoustics fill the room. I look at her dead in the eyes. "If you are going to speak to me with such reproach, then you can consider this business over with. That includes the rest of the payment you are expecting." She steps back and smiles. Business carries on, as usual.

8. We did not meet our ticket sales goal. Sad face. This is a blast, though! "I'm callin' you, when all my goals, my very soul ain't fallin' through . . ." I hum along in my seat on June 14, the night MAS Youth finally hosted Outlandish in Detroit.

Detroit Mosque Leader Killed in FBI Raids
(October 30, 2009)

What? Who? Why? Why? Why? It is 10:30 p.m. and I lie in bed staring at my computer, not realizing that my jaw has found a home on my chest. "I have heard of him," I say aloud, to no one. Blink. It's still there. "To God we belong and to Him is our return," I whisper to myself as I rock myself to sleep. Sleep is difficult that night and attentiveness to the questions my co-workers ask me the next day is faked.

"We have to do something about this. How could this *actually* happen, in my backyard?" I am sitting across from Dawud Walid, the executive director of the Michigan branch of the Council on American-Islamic Relations (CAIR) at their headquarters in Southfield. The CAIR staff and interns are at a loss for words and look toward Dawud.

"They said . . . that he shot . . . at a *dog*." Emotion has overcome Dawud's face and his eyes look glossy. His phone rings and he glances at the Blackberry screen. "Reporters," he says with an eyebrow lift. He answers and gives a few comments on the tragedy.

Dawud filled me in on the few events that took place that morning in response to the death of Imam Luqman, including a meeting on the matter hosted by the Council of Islamic Organizations of Michigan. I wonder, how many women were at the meeting? Hmph. I silence my thoughts. It's not time for that issue. Focus.

"What are people's reactions like in Dearborn?" Dawud asks me.

"Anyone I speak with is completely shocked. The news hasn't spread as quickly as I had expected, though, which is odd. I mean, come on. An imam was shot nineteen times within miles of our homes in our city by the FBI. That's not exactly typical news," I reply.

Imam Luqman's burial took place that week, and I made sure to e-mail all of my Muslim contacts. They would definitely want to be able to show their support for his family and community. I went to the Muslim Community Center early that day to help with the preparation of the food and was very busy as hundreds of people filled the mosque. When I heard the imam announce the prayer, I finally came out of the kitchen. I was shocked at the enormous turnout. After prayer, I scanned the crowd. There was Amal, talking; my father was giving *salaams* to Imam Luqman's son; Ayman was putting his shoes back on. Where were the others? I was appalled. Only a handful of Muslims who were not African American had shown up. Resentment was back and it filled my chest.

"Ms. Alasry, Ms. Alasry!" I turn around at the sound of my name. A parent of one of my former students is calling my name, with tear-filled eyes. I reach over a few women and we embrace. "Fatimah wants to see you. You know it is her *abu* [father]." A surge of emotion overtakes me, and my knees are weak. I had only worked with Fatimah a few times and had never met her father. One degree of separation that I never would have guessed.

"May God magnify your reward," I say with strength and squeeze Fatimah's mother close. Fatimah walks up to me and I look down into her eyes. It's been two years, but she hasn't changed much. She always had a look of hopefulness in her eyes. Somehow, it is still there. I crouch down.

"*Assalamu alaikum*," I say joyfully as I bump her nose with mine. She half-smiles. "You know that it'll be okay?" I whisper into her ear. "The trick is to take all the good that your *abu* has taught you and pass it on. It's the best thing you can do for him. There are a lot of us who love you so much and are here for whenever, *whenever* you need us." Her head falls onto my shoulder and we stand there for a minute in the crowd, arms wrapped around each other tightly.

As I sit in my car in the parking lot across from the Muslim Community Center, I slide open my phone and skim through my e-mails. One from a friend catches my attention:

Re: Janazah/Burial for Imam Luqman

So, what about the weapons they found with this guy? Where are they gonna bury those? Imma pass on this one, K.

Peace,

Signee

Perception and Reality

There are a few absolute truths I have to work with in life. I grew up in a unique environment. But don't we all? I am a daughter of immigrant parents, raised in a community filled with Arab minorities. I am a seeker of truth who learned about the world through movies and about faith through people.

Eventually, I realized that my relationship with God is a truth I can absolutely depend on. Everything else takes figuring out. Everything else is subject to change.

Note

1. Outlandish is a hip-hop trio from Denmark, whose members have family ties to Mexico, Morocco, and Pakistan. Two of the group's members are Muslim and much of their music explores the contemporary challenges of Muslim youth.

Going Places

HAYAN CHARARA

On the morning of September 11, 2001, from the shoreline of the Jersey City neighborhood I lived in, I watched the World Trade Center buildings collapse, engulfing the streets below with billowing clouds of debris.

I was scheduled to teach my first class that day as a full-time faculty member at a college in Queens. I'd been living in New York City for seven years, and I had visited the World Trade Center only once, and only the ground floor, to buy discounted tickets to a Broadway show. I never made it to the observation deck of what was once the world's tallest man-made structure. A few weeks after the start of the semester I admitted this to my students, most of whom were lifelong New Yorkers. To my astonishment, I discovered that nearly all of them hadn't been to the now-gone skyscraper either. Or the Statue of Liberty, or Ellis Island. Only a handful had taken the subway to the Bronx to watch a Yankee game. Even fewer had spent any time in Grand Central Station, except to transfer between trains. I asked if they'd been to the Met, or MoMA, or the Guggenheim, or the American Museum of Natural History. What about the 42nd Street Library? Almost to a student, they answered no.

"Okay," I said. "Visit a landmark."

The course I was teaching was an introduction to creative writing. In addition to visiting a site, I required they write something related to their visit—a poem, a story, or a scene. One of my students, Mohammed, who was shy and quiet, asked me to suggest a place to go.

"Have you gone up to the Empire State Building?"

He shook his head.

"Go there."

The destruction of the World Trade Center returned to the Empire State Building its status as the city's tallest skyscraper. Mohammed went there, paid the admission fee, and rode the elevator to the eighty-sixth-floor observatory, which offers visitors 360-degree panoramic views of Manhattan and the surrounding landscape. On a clear day, a person can see as far as eighty miles out. After a short while, Mohammed sat down and began collecting his thoughts in a notebook. Within minutes, two men approached him. One talked while the other stood watch.

"What are you doing?"

Mohammed looked up but didn't answer.

"What are you doing?"

"Excuse me?"

The man repeated himself, this time deliberately stopping between each word. "What . . . are . . . you . . . doing?"

"I'm writing."

"What are you writing?"

"Notes."

"Notes?"

The two men looked at each other, and then back at Mohammed.

"What are your *notes* for?"

Across the country, numerous acts of violence had been committed against Arabs and Muslims and against people who "looked" Arab or Muslim. The number of attacks on business owners and employees alone were astounding. I took note of these over the others because my father used to run a grocery store in Detroit.

On September 11, a man in Palos Heights, Illinois, attacked a Moroccan gas station attendant with the blunt end of a machete.

On September 12, in Gary, Indiana, a man wearing a ski mask fired a high-powered assault rifle at Hassan Awdah, who survived because of the bulletproof glass behind which he worked. That same day, on Long Island, New York, a man with a pellet gun made threats to a gas station attendant who he believed was of Middle Eastern descent.

Nearby in Brooklyn, less than twenty-four hours later, on September 13, an Arab grocer was threatened with violence by one of his grocery suppliers. That same day, in Salt Lake City, a man tried to set fire to a Pakistani family business.

On September 15, in San Gabriel, California, Adel Karas, 48 years old, of Egyptian descent, was shot and killed. The FBI investigated his murder as a hate crime. That same day, in Mesa, Arizona, Frank Silva Roque gunned down a gas station owner, Balbir Singh Sodhi, because he mistook him for an Arab. After killing him, Roque shot at another man who was Lebanese, and then he fired at the home of an Afghan family. Also on that day, in Dallas, Waqar Hasan was found shot to death in his grocery store.

Nearly a week after the attacks, on September 17, an Afghan restaurant in Encino, California, was set on fire at 1:40 a.m. South of San Francisco, in Fremont, an Afghan restaurant was pelted with bottles and rocks. Further south, on a Los Angeles freeway, someone displayed a sign that read "Kill All Arabs."

West of Los Angeles, in Oxnard, which is home to two large U.S. Navy bases, four men threw a turbaned Sikh grocer to the ground and beat him. Shots were fired into another convenience store in Palmdale, and in Quartz Hill a store was shot at for the second time in three days.

On September 29, a Yemeni grocer was killed at his convenience store in Reedley, California, after having received a death threat. The grocer's name was Abdo Ali Ahmed.

Mohammed, my student, noticed that people were staring at him. The two men moved closer. They told him to get up, to go with them. When he refused, they flashed badges. They were FBI agents. They found his note taking suspicious, and they did not immediately believe his college assignment excuse. They interrogated him for a few hours. At our next class meeting, Mohammed told me what had happened. "They might call you," he said, after which he dropped the course. I never saw him again.

A month later the FBI contacted my father, who lived in Dearborn, a suburb of Detroit. Two agents went to his house. The inquiry took place early in the morning. Normally a loud and irate man, my father was nice to them. He welcomed them into his house and he asked them if they wanted something to drink. They didn't. They wanted to ask him questions—about me.

"Where does he live?"

"New York."

"Did he contact you on September 11?"

"He called."

"What did he say?"

"He was okay."

"What do you mean?"

"He was okay—nothing happened to him."

"Did he say anything about the attacks?"

"What do you *mean*?"

"Did he say anything about the attacks?"

"No."

"Are you positive?"

"Yes."

The FBI's visit, and questions, unnerved my father. He was troubled most by what might happen next—to me. I hadn't done anything wrong. He knew that, but he also believed that *they* could do whatever they wanted. So he gave me advice on how to deal with them when they showed up. "Be polite. Offer them coffee. If they stay long, ask them to sit. Don't give them any reason to screw you."

I told him, "Don't worry, I'll be good," but I was indignant at the FBI for suspecting that I might know more about what took place on 9/11 than the next guy, simply because of my ethnicity. To let off steam, and to let people know what had happened, I shot off an e-mail to friends, family, and colleagues, and in it I went on about how being Arab made others believe I had an intimate relationship to treachery and violence. I also sent a letter to the *New York Times* and several other newspapers, and I talked about the incident with my students and with colleagues and fellow poets and writers. The presumption under which the FBI had operated made me feel negated as a person. No longer a man, or a teacher, or a writer, I was turned into a suspect, a profile, into something less than human.

Eventually, I received a phone call from the Department of Justice. They wanted to know if I would speak with them. I said yes, but only under the following conditions: the agents would come to me, and not to my house but to the college where I taught, and I would have with me my colleagues, and we would record the conversation. The college president had in fact suggested this, and faculty I hadn't yet met volunteered to be at my side.

I never heard back from the FBI.

A few months later, for the first time since 9/11, I boarded a plane. I was with Rachel, my wife. We were going to the Midwest, to attend two weddings on the same weekend. The itinerary was to fly from New York to Chicago for the first marriage and the next day take a short flight to Detroit for the second, after which we'd spend another day in Detroit and then head back to New York.

We purchased our airline tickets at the same time. We requested side-by-side seats. At the airport, we arrived together, and we checked a single piece of luggage. My carry-on was a suit. Rachel brought along knitting materials to keep herself occupied while in flight. Her knitting bag contained a set of sharp metal needles, each more than a foot in length. At the time, security regulations prohibited the carrying-on of such items as nail clippers and small scissors. When she first took up knitting, I used to make wisecracks about using the needles as weapons. "I heard Jesse James once killed a man with knitting needles . . . just for snoring." Given the circumstances, I laid off the jokes. After all, the 9/11 hijackers had overtaken four airplanes with only box cutters.

Somehow, at JFK, at O'Hare, and at DTW, Rachel managed to get the needles, and herself, through security without a hitch. I did not have the same experience. I was pulled aside for a search—"randomly selected"—at every single airport.

> Day after day, he told himself, "I am an American.
> I speak American English. I read American poetry.
> I was born in Detroit, a city as American as it gets.
> I vote. I work. I pay taxes, too many taxes.
> I own a car. I make mortgage payments. I am not hungry.
> I worry less than the rest of the world. I could stand
> to lose five pounds. I eat several types of cuisine
> on a regular basis. I flush toilets. I let the faucet drip.
> I have central air-conditioning. I will never starve
> to death or experience famine. I will never die of malaria.
> I can say whatever the fuck I please."

The above is an excerpt from a poem of mine titled "Usage." I make no apologies for being an American. I am fully aware of the fact that as an American I am privileged. Because I was born and raised in the United States, I inherited many of the benefits that come with membership in this most prestigious of clubs. But I'm also an Arab man, and as such I am regularly associated with the most negative of traits.

The Arab male is viewed to be essentially dangerous, uncivilized, barbaric, hostile to Americans and things American, incapable of reason, capable of understanding only through violence and brute force, religiously fundamentalist, having little to no regard for human life (especially the lives of innocents), misogynistic, oppressive (to women, to families, to communities, to non-Muslims, and to Muslims), anti-human, anti-Semitic, antimodern, politically militant, uneducated, backwards, militarily weak, illogical, overtly emotional, intolerant of difference and change (particularly if the "change" is viewed as "progress"), and stuck in the past. The most common figures that Arab men are associated with are the sheik, the terrorist, the religious radical. And to make matters worse, public enemy number one is an Arab guy named Osama.

When I lived in Detroit, the perception most people had of Arabs was bad. We were called sand niggers and camel jockeys all the time, and we were told to go back to where we came from, and we saw ourselves on the news, usually as hijackers or hostage-takers, and people worried about what we might do to them. Yet no matter how badly the media portrayed us then, the lives of every single Arab I knew flew in the face of those depictions. On a daily basis, and several times each day, I encountered Arabs who were not terrorists. My father was not a terrorist. My mother was not a terrorist. My aunts and uncles were not terrorists. Nor were my cousins or my friends. The next door neighbor who was Arab and owned a fruit market, he was not a terrorist. The Arab students at Fordson High School, they were not terrorists. The Arabs attending Henry Ford Community College, the University of Michigan, and Wayne State University, they weren't terrorists either. The cooks and waiters and waitresses at Al-Ameer and Cedarland and La Shish, not one of them turned out to be a terrorist. The Arab factory workers at Ford and Chrysler and GM, there were no terrorists among them. The Arabs I saw at weddings and funerals, they never blew up planes or buses or themselves. The dancers and singers and musicians at the Arab festivals at Hart Plaza, they were dancers and singers and musicians, not terrorists.

A lot of people tried hard to tell us otherwise—politicians, journalists, "experts" on the Middle East, and ordinary citizens—but they were all in competition with a formidable opponent: the everyday reality of living in one of the largest Arab communities outside the Arab world. If I had doubts about what it meant to be Arab, or wanted to know how Arabs thought or lived or felt, I turned to actual people, not to representations of them. My view was certainly limited, for Arabs in Detroit—and I certainly didn't know them all—obviously did not and could not stand in for every other Arab in America. They were, however, a far better example than I found in books or on TV or in the movies or in the news.

When I read about the trial of suspected terrorists in Detroit, or the breaking up of a suspected terrorist cell in Brooklyn, or a group of Arabs anywhere in America arrested for plotting a terrorist act or funding a terrorist organization, you would think my first reaction is suspicion, or apprehension. You would think that in hearing about Arabs suspected and interrogated and judged guilty even before a trial, I would conjure up the image of my father, or my uncles, or a neighbor, a friend or cousin, or even the face I see every day in the mirror, and feel indignation. I do, but not always.

When I see the faces of the accused or read their names or hear about them in the news, the first thought I sometimes now have is, "They just might be terrorists." I am not saying that I don't believe Arabs can never be terrorists. Of course they can. It's the immediate rush to judgment that worries me—to assume right away *that* possibility, of guilt by association. In the past, if the facts took me to that conclusion, then fine. But I never started out assuming the worst.

They seem different, the Arabs I now see on the news. I know I'm wrong in thinking this way. I tell myself to step back a moment, and when I do, after a while, I'm eventually able to reserve judgment and condemnation. Of course, none of this alters the fact that I went there to begin with.

> first, please god, let it be a mistake, the pilot's heart failed,
> the plane's engine died.
> then, please god, let it be a nightmare, wake me now.
> please god, after the second plane, don't let it be anyone
> who looks like my brothers.
> —Suheir Hammad, from "First Writing Since"

Unfortunately, the hijackers did look like her brothers—they looked like me.

All nineteen hijackers were Arab, the majority from Saudi Arabia, a few from the United Arab Emirates, one was Egyptian, and another Lebanese. They were also young. Except for Muhammed Atta, 33 years old, who crashed the first plane into the north face of the North Tower at a speed of roughly 500mph, every other hijacker was only in his twenties.

The image of the Arab terrorist was obviously not invented on this most infamous of days. The swarthy Arab, whether portrayed as a hijacker or a suicide bomber or one of many dark, *keffiyeh*-wearing, gun-toting, American-flag-burning types in a mob, was so engrained in our minds and for so long a part of the American imagination that even the most intelligent and aware of Arabs—poets, scholars, activists—immediately went to that image when it became clear that the crashing of two airliners into the World Trade Center was not an accident. It's hard not to go there. The Arab (especially the Arab Muslim) has preoccupied the Western imagination, as a menace, for nearly fourteen centuries. America came late to the game, but it caught up quickly, and the dissemination of the menacing Arab image is so vast and pervasive, I don't know why I am surprised that even Arabs fall back on the negative stereotypes and presumptions about themselves. What's worse: if we cannot help but fall into the trap, what chance do men and women who know close to nothing about "real" Arabs have in arriving at something like an uncorrupted image of us?

According to the 2000 U.S. census count, 70,000 Arabs live in New York City. That's more than double the number living in Dearborn during the same period. Yet, for me, Dearborn feels significantly more "Arab," and a reason for this must be the concentration of so many of them in a relatively small area. I think of my family's house: to the right lives an older Arab woman, and to the left, an Arab family, and in front of and behind the house, there are more Arabs. In fact, I would have to walk past several blocks of houses before arriving at one in which an Arab did not live. In New York City, I could go days without seeing an Arab. In Texas, where I live now, if not for a handful of friends and a few students at the university where I teach, I could go weeks, even months, without running into an Arab.

When I fly into Detroit, I take I-94 home. I head east. The twelve-ton, eighty-foot tall Uniroyal tire on the side of highway still brings a smile to my face. When I pass Telegraph Road, I think of the summers I worked at Jack Dunworth Memorial Pool, where Dearborn's families—Arab and otherwise—dropped off their kids for hours at a time. I continue down the Ford Freeway and pass the exit to the Southfield Freeway, which I took countless times to Fairlane Town Center, where I got into my fair share of trouble as a kid. Across from the shopping center, on Evergreen Road, is Henry Ford Community College (HFCC), where I taught for a semester and where, for the first time as a teacher, I had Arab students. My family's house, where my sister still lives, is on Dearborn's east side, not far from Hemlock Park, which for a while went by the nickname "Yemlock" because of the Yemeni boys and girls who played there. I go past the house and the park and I take Miller Road and keep driving until I reach Warren Avenue and I pull into the parking lot of Al-Ameer Restaurant.

Al-Ameer may not be the best Middle Eastern restaurant in town, but it is still my favorite. I used to eat there two or three times a week. Usually, I sat in a window booth. I liked to see people coming and going, and I was constantly running into friends or acquaintances. The waiters and waitresses knew me, and if not by name, then by face, or what I ate. For years, I ordered the same three items off the menu—a *shawarma* sandwich, a plate of hummus, and a cup of coffee. On one of my visits not long after I'd moved out of Detroit, a former student from HFCC who'd been working at Al-Ameer for some time waited on me. I recognized her immediately, and she me.

"Professor," she said. "You want a coffee, right?"

"Yes."

"And a *shawarma* and hummus."

I smiled and nodded. She turned to walk away, and I stopped her. "I'm sorry, I don't remember your name." She told me, and I greeted her again. "One other thing I don't remember . . ." I hesitated a moment but finally asked, "Did I give you a good grade?"

She thought about it a moment and then returned the smile I had given and walked away.

A short while later, I invited her to sit with me. I had shown up just before the lunch rush, the restaurant was mostly empty, and I was the only customer seated in her section, and so she agreed. We chatted for a while. She was still a student but had transferred to Wayne State University. She was also applying for admission to pharmacy school. She had a daughter, a little girl, about to enter grade school. She was a single mom. I learned more about her in five minutes than I had in an entire semester.

"What about you," she asked. "Where are you now?"

I began telling her about New York, but before I got very far a customer showed up, and he was seated in her section, and soon enough the restaurant started filling up. We talked a bit more, but only when she came by to refill my coffee—nothing more than chitchat.

In 2004, my father moved back to Lebanon after living in the States for nearly forty years. With him gone, I went back to Detroit less and less. And in what seemed like the blink of an eye, I found myself having been away sixteen years. I still go to Al-Ameer first thing when I visit, and the last time I went, I showed up at dinnertime. The place was packed. I waited close to fifteen minutes before being seated. I asked about my former student—she'd quit awhile back, and no one at the restaurant knew what had become of her. I imagined her in a hospital, or a pharmacy, wearing a white lab coat. As for the wait staff now, they were entirely new to me. A few of the cooks looked familiar, but I couldn't say for sure if I knew them or if they knew me.

I ordered the usual, and while waiting for my food to come, I took a good look around. At nearly every table in the restaurant was a man or a group of men who could have passed for the ones I saw on TV or read about in the papers, those accused of masterminding terrorist plots right under our noses. The thought ran through my mind again: *They just might be terrorists.* Something felt different this time—not for a second did I believe that thought. I realized, too, that any one of these men I was looking at could have stopped what he was doing and looked up and had exactly the same thought about me—*He just might be a terrorist*—and of course, he would be dead wrong. For all I knew—for all I know—any of us, any day, could be accused of something sinister. More than ever before, the monumental differences between actual persons and the representations we have of them had become clear to me. Just as meaningful, I also realized, was being *in* a community as opposed to looking at one from the outside. I'd known this my whole life—I relied on it to make my way through the world. I was ashamed for having forgotten. There, in Al-Ameer, I vowed to go back home as often as possible, if only not to forget.

I was living in Detroit during the first attempt to bring down the World Trade Center. On that day, February 26, 1993, I was scheduled for the lunch shift at the Soup Kitchen Saloon, a blues bar now long gone. I showed up to work just as news of the attack was being broadcast on TVs and radios across the country. I walked into the Soup Kitchen and one of the bartenders, a burly, middle-aged man who liked to joke about everything, stopped me and looked me dead in the eyes and shaking his head in disgust, he said only, "You people."

I am pretty sure he meant Arabs, but he could have also meant Muslims. It was also possible he assumed these to be one and the same.

If *you people* referred only to Arabs, the facts did not entirely accommodate the reference. Not all the men involved in the 1993 WTC bombing were Arab. Ramzi Yousef and Khaled Shaikh Mohammed, two of the central figures, were of Pakistani descent. If by *you people* the bartender meant to associate me with Muslims, he either knew close to nothing about Islam or he mistook me for the worst kind of Muslim. After all, I worked at a bar, I was dating one of the barmaids, and at the end of my shifts, around 3:00 a.m., I would pull up a seat at the counter—and he was usually the bartender who mixed the drink or poured the beer I ordered. Now and then— sometimes before the start of a shift but more often than not at the end of one—he would offer me a hit from a joint, and a bunch of times I took him up on his offer. I never brought a prayer rug to the saloon. I did not fast during Ramadan, and not once in the time I knew him had I ever invoked the name of God—not as a Muslim, or as any other kind of believer. Regardless of what he knew about me, on this day he saw me as an Arab *and* as a Muslim, and in his eyes, taken together these were a singular threat. It was also clear that he had arrived at this notion (Arab = Islam = terrorism) long before we ever met, for he expressed it immediately, less than a minute after hearing about the attack, which was before anyone had claimed responsibility and long before the suspects involved were identified.

He wasn't the only one presuming a link between terrorism and Arabs and Islam, nor was he alone in blurring the distinctions between them. Even supposedly educated persons routinely, and wrongly, used the terms and what they represented interchangeably. This became painfully clear two years later following the bombing of the Alfred P. Murrah Federal Building in Oklahoma City, not by Arabs or Muslims, but at the hands of "homegrown" terrorists Timothy McVeigh and Terry Nichols. Nearly every journalist and terrorism expert in America took it for granted that behind the worst act of domestic terrorism yet visited upon American soil were men from the Middle East who prayed to Allah. The fact that no Arabs or Muslims were involved did not deter many of these same people from continuing to make sweeping generalizations about the Middle East and Islam. Even after McVeigh and Nichols were arrested, Steven Emerson, a "leading authority" on terrorism whose documentary film *Jihad in America* aired on public television following the bombing, repeatedly made references to Oklahoma City as a "hotbed of Islamic fundamentalism."

A little over six years later, the sheer scale of the 9/11 attacks seemed to prefigure the extent to which Arabs and Muslims would pay for them. Within months, the United States announced it was going to war in Afghanistan. Soon after, it began making the case for going to war in Iraq. Even the most conservative estimates of the combined death tolls of these two conflicts are staggering. The destruction to the infrastructures of Iraq and Afghanistan, to the land and environment of each country, and to their futures and the future of their people, is equally devastating. Difficult to measure, but deeply felt, is the way the War on Terror—of which the wars in Afghanistan and Iraq are a part—affects the lives of Arabs and Muslims in America. One thing is clear: what happens in the War on Terror dramatically shapes the way Arabs and Muslims are perceived and treated.

As a result of U.S. foreign policy in the Middle East and in the Islamic world, Arabs and Muslims in the United States (many of whom are of course Americans) often find themselves having to apologize for crimes they did not commit or repeatedly having to prove loyalties (as Americans) that are never questioned with other Americans. The bartender saying "You people" was an example of this. The FBI visiting my father's house in Dearborn to inquire about my whereabouts was another. The consequences for others is sometimes much more dramatic—a person may find himself or herself imprisoned for suspicions of terrorism based simply on birthplace; more tragically, people find themselves or people they know victims of violence—the kind perpetrated by individuals and the kind perpetrated by states and their armies.

Over the last few years, a shift seems to have taken place in terms of this by-product of the War on Terror. Americans still worry about Arabs and Muslims, and Arabs and Muslims must still worry about how Americans view them and how their lives will be impacted by those views. But attention has switched over more so to Muslims—Muslims who aren't necessarily Arab. One reason for this may be that the war in Iraq is being nudged off center stage by the war in Afghanistan. The shift may also have something to do with the fact that since 9/11, two Muslim men, neither of whom was Arab, each attempted to blow up an airliner over U.S. soil. Richard Reid, the shoe-bomber, a British citizen and convert to Islam, failed to ignite explosives in his shoes on a flight on December 22, 2001. Eight years later, almost to the day, on December 25, a Nigerian man, Umar Farouk Abdulmutallab tried but failed to detonate an explosive on a Detroit-bound flight. Another individual, Jose Padilla, a Latino born in Brooklyn, who most news reports described as having tried to build and detonate a "dirty bomb," a crime for which he was never charged or convicted, was also Muslim, a convert. The most recent failed attempt to launch a terrorist attack in the United States was made by an American citizen born in Pakistan who tried to blow up an SUV in Times Square.

When I travel now, which is frequently and a lot more than I did in the first few years after the 9/11 attacks, I experience the shift that is taking place. Which is to say I am hardly searched any more, or bothered in any way, except for the usual—waiting in long lines and keeping up with changing regulations about what can and cannot be carried onto a plane. These, however, are inconveniences most everyone endures. Arabs are still profiled. Just ask them. But attention is moving away from Arabs—not entirely, but significantly—and toward Muslims. The turn parallels the shift in attention of U.S. foreign policy. Whereas the Reagan-era war on terror focused mainly on the Middle East threat, today's version focuses more on things Islamic. Attention is turning away from the Arab world—again, not entirely, but significantly—and toward Afghanistan, Pakistan, Indonesia, and even Africa.

For many Americans, Muslims are easier to spot than Arabs. Islam "marks" Muslims, at least the more traditional among them. The headscarf worn by women, the *hijab*, serves as a marker, as does the *abaya* sometimes worn by both men and women. These and other "signs"—entering a mosque, praying, reading a Quran, and so on—are read as "Islam," which is understood to be the polar opposite of everything American and Western or modern and civilized. "Islam" is a thing to be feared; it is the ultimate threat. Today, we are more likely to hear about a group of Muslims—rather than a group of Arabs—being asked to get off a plane. In most cases, the removal is prompted by the concerns of a passenger who was made to feel, in some way, uncomfortable by the Muslims on board. Features or traits as inherently nonthreatening as a headscarf or a beard have caused people to feel unsafe. In one case a Muslim family was removed from a flight after one of them commented, in English, about the safest place to sit on a plane. The Council on American-Islamic Relations noted in a complaint to the U.S. Department of Transportation, "We believe this disturbing incident would never have occurred had the Muslim passengers removed from the plane not been perceived by other travelers and airline personnel as members of the Islamic faith."

A recent ABC News story about opposition to the building of a mosque brought again to national attention the extent to which "Islam" is deemed threatening. The Islamic Center of Murfreesboro, which has had a center in the small Tennessee town since 1997, planned to build a larger facility. At a county commission meeting where more than 600 residents turned out to express their concerns about the new mosque, Allan Jackson, the pastor of

World Outreach Church, said, "We have a duty to investigate anyone under the banner of Islam." Of the Muslims living in Murfreesboro, one resident was quoted as saying, "They seem to be against everything I believe in, and so I don't want them necessarily in my neighborhood."

I have no doubt that I experience less discrimination now (especially on airplanes) in large part because there is little about my appearance or manner of dress that labels me a Muslim. I look Arab. That's undeniable. I have the dark hair and dark eyes, and the stereotypical Middle Eastern nose and bushy eyebrows. But more than Arab or Middle Eastern, the markers that the fearful and the reactionary and the ignorant and the bigoted among us are looking for are Islamic. An irony of all this is that for a very long time now, people from all walks of life have worked hard to explain and make clear the distinctions between things Arab and things Islamic—many people are finally making distinctions, but for all the wrong reasons.

A few hundred Arab Muslims gather, elbow to elbow. The atmosphere is that of a fair. There are signs in the prevailing languages, rows of newspaper boxes, magazine stands, smells of food in the air, smokers arguing politics around ashtray stands, garbled announcements made over loudspeakers, flashing lights and sirens, carousels, and every few minutes, on center stage, an airplane touching down or taking off.

The flight, which originated in Mecca, finally lands and the crowd erupts with cheers. Several of the Arabs and Muslims, young men, join hands and raise them high above their heads and dance in a circle. Later, as the arrivals they've been waiting for begin exiting customs, a chorus of trills fills the terminal.

We're in the Michael Berry terminal of the Detroit airport. I'm with my parents. We're standing next to a young woman with braided blond hair. She is wearing a *Star Wars* T-shirt and dark blue jeans. If her hair were just a few shades darker, she'd look like Brooke Shields in the famous Calvin Klein ads. My mother turns to her and asks, "Who are you here for?"

"My boyfriend," she says smiling.

"Ah. Was he on the Hajj?"

"The . . . ?

"The Hajj."

"I don't think so," she says with a degree of uncertainty and tugs at her hair. "He's on American Airlines."

"Oh, I thought . . ."

But before my mother has a chance to explain or change the subject, the woman looks away, taken by the scene the Muslims are making, which is boisterous, carefree, and jubilant, as if they are celebrating a marriage, not the arrival of a flight. A minute or two later, she turns back around.

"Can I ask you something?"

My mother nods her head.

"These people coming off the plane," she says, and once more she gives the crowd a long hard look and takes a deep breath. "Are they all like famous movie stars or something?"

In 1982, a young woman mistakes a mass of Muslims and Arabs for celebrities. This is one of the most vivid memories I have of Detroit in the pre-9/11 world—that of airports and air travel, of the way that some people saw Arabs and Muslims. How much has changed? Today, I simply cannot imagine a few hundred Arabs and Muslims descending on a major U.S. airport without incident. We couldn't even if we wanted. Not you, or me. Not like that. For one, we're no longer permitted to greet arrivals at the gate. More important, we live in an age of "heightened security," encouraged to be vigilant against possible acts of terrorism and to report suspicious activity and suspicious individuals. When I travel by airplane, I present myself accordingly. Before leaving for the airport, I shave so as not to resemble too much the physical profile of a hijacker. At the airport, I never request last-minute changes to my itinerary so as not to send the wrong message. At security, I smile and make pleasant chitchat but I don't overdo it. I keep my small talk to "Hello" or "Good morning" or "Have a nice day." I don't want to give anyone any excuse to single me out. I wear shoes without laces so I can pass quickly through security, and I never wear my favorite T-shirt, which has on its front the stylized McDonald's "M," and just beneath the Golden Arches the fast-food giant's name is spelled out in Arabic. Years ago, my fellow passengers might have found the graphic amusing. Now, it would probably alarm them, so I leave it at home. My goal is to reach my destination on time. The last thing I want to do is encourage security personnel to have an extended conversation with me about who I am or what I am, or what I am not.

I liked going to the airport. I met people there—grandparents, aunts and uncles, cousins—for the very first time. My family got dressed up to meet airport arrivals. Sometimes, we drove to the airport early to eat dinner there. The airport was fun. When I was a boy, I thought of the terminal as a kind of playground. I played games with other children—races up and down the escalators, hide-and-seek in the visitor waiting areas, and when no one was paying attention we rode the baggage carousels. Even as an adult, for a few short years at least, I liked going to the airport. So much so, now and then I would receive phone calls from friends who were stuck in the terminal during a layover, and I would drive out to meet them for a drink at the airport bar.

Not anymore. That chapter of American life is over. Gone with it, I suspect, is the innocence of the young woman who asked my mother about the men and women returning from the Hajj. She expressed not fear but something like exhilaration, even wonder, at being surrounded by so many Arabs and Muslims. She wasn't threatened. She didn't immediately go to the worst possible conclusions. She didn't think terrorists or hijackers or villains. She thought movie stars.

And Then You Add the Arab Thing

LAWRENCE JOSEPH

On Wednesday, October 1, 2008, at 12:28 p.m., an e-mail with the subject "An Ozymandias Moment" popped up in my Inbox. It read: "I was driving down John R this morning as the wrecking ball was being taken to your dad's old building. It's gone now."

It was sent by a friend in Detroit, a law professor at Wayne State University Law School, who is originally from New York City. He moved to Detroit to teach at Wayne in 2003 and lives in one of the Grosse Pointes. Before he began teaching, I told him that if he drove to work on I-94, west to the John R exit, then south on John R to Palmer, then west on Palmer to Woodward, then, from Woodward, over to the law school, he would notice an abandoned building on John R just south of the freeway. "It has billboards on top of it," I said. "That was my uncle's and my father's store."

The first time that my friend drove by it, he called me from his cell phone and left a voice mail message. "I just drove by the store," he said. "*That* was your dad's store? I can't believe it! I can't believe *that* was your dad's store!"

So, by the afternoon of October 1, 2008, the abandoned building at the corner of John R and Hendrie had been demolished, its old walls and its ceiling, and what was left inside it, reduced to piles of debris. I forwarded my friend's e-mail to my brothers and my sister, and to my uncle's two eldest sons, who then forwarded it to their four sisters and younger brother.

Almost three years earlier (on October 20, 2005, to be exact), Bill McGraw, who wrote the popular column "Bill McGraw's Journal" for the *Detroit Free Press*, wrote a feature about my poetry and a poetry reading that I was giving that evening at Marygrove College. In his column, "Well-Versed in Detroit Images: Poet Remains Obsessed with Hometown as His Life Moves On," I

254

am quoted as saying that I'm "'sort of the poet of grocers,'" because, as McGraw explained, my "father and grandfathers owned grocery stores in Detroit." "From 1935 to 1972," he went on, my father and uncle owned "the small market at John R and Hendrie, near the Detroit Institute of Arts," which, he added, "still stands, boarded up and covered with graffiti."

I understood McGraw's description of the store as "the small market on the corner of John R and Hendrie" to be emphatic—it was "*the* small market." McGraw—who, for a remarkable online *Free Press* Web site, had driven down and taken photographs on every street within Detroit's city limits—told me during my phone conversation with him for the feature that he knew that abandoned building, that he'd actually gone into it. "Everybody who's ever gotten off at that exit—it has to be hundreds of thousands of people over the past fifty years, because of its proximity to the museum, to Wayne State, to the library, to the medical center—has seen that building," he said. "Millions of people since 1935 may have seen that store."

Two weeks after the store on John R was demolished, Bill McGraw wrote a column for the *Free Press* titled "Arab American Writer Lawrence Joseph Keeps Memories of Old Store Alive." "The long-abandoned building at 5770 John R looked like thousands of other abandoned buildings in Detroit," he said. "Graffiti and weeds gradually covered its broken façade. The front door remained locked, but the side door was open, so anyone could go in and do whatever they wanted. Yet," McGraw continued, "this building was different than thousands of other decaying, anonymous buildings in the city. This building has a recorded history. All buildings were important, busy places, but few of them leave any trace of the love, commerce, production, brutality, and other human activity that transpired within their walls." But 5770 John R was different, McGraw said, because it served as a source for poems and prose of mine. Over the years, according to McGraw, I had "chronicled the smells of salt pork and the brown light and the Silver Satin wine of Joseph's Market." The store,

at the corner of Hendrie, was on a busy street one block south of the Ford Freeway and a few blocks north of the Detroit Institute of Arts. Before the freeways, it sat in the midst of Detroit's main African-American community. Joseph's family was Catholic and of Lebanese and Syrian ancestry, and its members were part of a long tradition of Mideastern store owners in Detroit. . . . The neighborhood became poorer as the years went on, and the market became caught up in the violence that began wracking Detroit. In the early 1960s, a young thief slashed his uncle's throat. . . . A junkie shot his father, Joseph Joseph, February 2, 1970. . . . On the first night of the 1967 riot,

Joseph's Market, 1956. Courtesy of Lawrence Joseph.

looters ransacked the store. Lawrence Joseph wrote about his father driving away after inspecting the damage. . . . Lawrence Joseph, sixty, grew up in Royal Oak, attended the University of Detroit High School and University of Michigan for undergraduate studies and law school. He lives in New York with his wife, Nancy Van Goethem, an artist who grew up in Detroit. He teaches law at St. John's University. Joseph left Detroit in 1981 but visits periodically, and said that he is amazed at how the city keeps disappearing, how "suddenly whole blocks are gone." Joseph's Market is gone. The city demolished it October 1.

The store, I'm quoted in McGraw's article as saying, "metaphorically stands for all the small markets, the racial and class negotiations that went on, and then you add the Arab thing. It represents Detroit."

My father, Joseph Alexander Joseph, was born in Detroit in 1918, and died in Detroit in 1997. My father's father, my grandfather Alexander George Joseph, was born in 1890 in the village of Chartoun, in the Chouf Mountains of the Lebanon district of what was then Ottoman Syria. His family name, Nahed, was changed to Joseph (his father's first name, in Arabic, was Yousef) by a U.S. immigration official on Ellis Island. My Grandfather Joseph died in Detroit in 1952. My father's mother, my grandmother Martha Ann Joseph (her maiden name was Martha Ann Kaleb) was born in the Hadeth district of Beirut in 1890. She died in Detroit in 1969. My Grandfather and Grandmother Joseph married in Lebanon and then emigrated to Detroit in 1911 or 1912. There appear not to have been any overt political reasons for their emigration (which was before the outbreak of World War I and the disintegration of the Ottoman Empire). My grandparents were part of the massive wave of immigration to the United States during the 1890s and early 1900s, up until World War I. One of my Grandfather Joseph's brothers, and one of his sisters, emigrated at the same time that he did. My Grandfather and Grandmother Joseph were—as my father was and as I am—baptized Catholic in the Maronite rite. My grandfather, his brother, and his brother-in-law operated grocery stores in Detroit.

My father's brother Thomas was born in Detroit in 1916. My uncle and my father were educated in Roman Catholic schools in Detroit through high school. In 1935, six years into the Great Depression, my Grandpa Joseph borrowed money and bought a store in Detroit on the corner of John R and Hendrie, in a neighborhood of tenements populated mostly by blacks who in the late 1920s had managed to move two miles north from Detroit's Black Bottom. After my father graduated from high school, my grandparents moved from the west side of Detroit to Pleasant Ridge, a small suburb a mile and a half north of Eight Mile, Detroit's northern boundary. My uncle and father both served in the armed forces during World War II. In 1944, my uncle Tom married my mother's younger sister Ida. In 1945, my father and mother married, having met through my uncle and aunt. My brother Robert was born in Detroit in 1946, and I was born in Detroit in 1948. We lived with Grandpa and Grandma Joseph in their home in Pleasant Ridge. The house was a half-block east of Woodward Avenue. In the late 1940s, my grandfather became increasingly ill from diabetes and heart disease. My father and uncle took over running the store, which, by then, was a small "supermarket" in a postwar neighborhood of working and middle-class blacks. In 1950, my parents bought a new home in Royal Oak, two miles north of the house in Pleasant Ridge, a block east of Woodward, near Twelve Mile Road, which we moved into in the fall of 1951. In January 1952, Grandpa Joseph died. My sister Barbara was born that June and my brother Mark was born two years later, in 1954. In late 1952, Uncle Tom and Aunt Ida moved from the east side of Detroit into the house in Pleasant Ridge, living with my Grandma Joseph.

In the spring of 2001 I was asked by *Tin House* magazine to contribute something for a forthcoming issue on music. I gave "The Music Is" (a prose piece) to the *Tin House* editor in a café on the upper east side of Manhattan near its New York City office late on the afternoon of September 10, 2001.

Tin House's "Music Issue" came out in January 2002. "The Music Is" includes a photograph that my father took of the store on John R in 1956. In "The Music Is" (*Tin House* added the subtitle "The Deep Roots of Detroit R&B"; the piece was later included in *Best Music Writing 2003*, edited by Matt Groening and Paul Bresnick), I quote from the liner notes written by Saeeda Lateef for Yusef Lateef's album *Detroit: Latitude 42 30—Longitude 83* (in which she mentions "'Woodward Avenue . . . Big Parades . . . The library, the museum . . . the Toddle House—BEST pecan waffles'"). Then, I write: "When I was ten years old, I used to go to that Toddle House on Woodward and Palmer. My father and my uncle owned a store on John R, a one-way street that ran downtown, one block east of Woodward. If, from the Toddle House, you walked one block east on Palmer to John R, then one block up, there, on the southwest corner of John R and Hendrie, was Joseph's Market." I then mention the 1956 photograph of the store. "Above the store," I write, is "a billboard, 'CHEVROLET,' with a two-tone silver and white 1956 Chevrolet, 'filled with spirit and splendor!'" On the wall of the store facing Hendrie is "'JOSEPH'S MARKET. MON. TUE. WED. THUR. 9 TO 9. FRI. SAT. 9 TO 11' 'YOUR NEIGHBORHOOD GROCER SINCE 1935 FREE PARKING AROUND THE CORNER.'" Near the door is: "'5770 JOHN R' 'BEER. WINE.' 'DETROIT PACKAGE LIQUOR DEALER.' 'BAR B. Q. TO TAKE OUT. RIBS. CHICKEN. PEPSI COLA.'" Later in "The Music Is," I quote from Lars Bjorn's and Jim Gallert's classic book *Before Motown: A History of Jazz in Detroit, 1920–60*: "'The latter half of the 1940s saw the development of the "Street of Music" in two blocks of John R, between Forest and Canfield,'" noting that this was "nine to ten blocks south of Hendrie." When I note that Motown founder Berry Gordy Jr., in his autobiography *To Be Loved*, tells how, in 1953, he opened the 3-D Record Mart in the Gordy's family building on Farnsworth and St. Antoine, I add, parenthetically, that Gordy's store was located "eight or so blocks from Joseph's Market."

In the summer of 1981, my wife Nancy and I moved to New York City from Detroit. We have lived since then in downtown Manhattan—in Battery Park City since 1994, and, before that, on the other side of lower Manhattan, on Water Street near Dover, next to the Brooklyn Bridge. In May 1997, a prose book of mine, *Lawyerland*, was published. A book of documentary fiction and nonfiction (generically a novel), *Lawyerland* is composed of eight pieces. Common to each piece is the fact that only lawyers speak (including a first-person character, who, biographically, approximates me) and that every conversation takes place south of Canal Street in downtown Manhattan. The final piece in *Lawyerland*, "MacKnight Was Murdered"—unlike the earlier pieces in the book—is spoken mostly in the first person. MacKnight was a classmate of the "I" of the piece, at the University of Detroit High School in Detroit in the 1960s. MacKnight was murdered in Detroit when he was 23 years old. The conversation takes place at the Bridge Café, on Water Street and Dover, between the "I" of the piece and a lawyer friend of his who practices law in Los Angeles and who is in New York City on business. In it, I say to my lawyer friend:

> My uncle and dad owned a small bodega-type liquor and grocery store on what was then the most violent strip in the city—there's a store on the corner of One Twenty-fifth and Madison that looks just like it . . . May of seventy-one . . . my uncle and father's store—which, by that time, was in real bad shape. It had been burned in sixty-seven in the riots. My father had gotten shot in a robbery by a heroin addict when I was a senior in college. My father, since nineteen-sixty, had worked—in addition to four nights a week at the store—a full-time job as a meat cutter with A&P. My uncle sold the store a few months later, in early seventy-two. I remember my mother's letter. I was in Strasbourg—in a café across from the Cathedral. My uncle sold it for almost nothing. He was how old, my uncle, when he sold the store? Fifty-six. My father was fifty-four. My uncle went to work for Dodge truck, on the assembly line.

My mother, Clara Barbara Joseph (her maiden name was Clara Barbara Francis) was born in Detroit in 1919. She died in Detroit in 1994. My mother's father, my grandfather Louis George Francis, was born in Damascus, Syria, in 1890, and died in Detroit in 1964. He came to the United States in 1911 or 1912, settling first in southern Illinois, opening small confectionary and grocery stores. He helped two of his sisters to emigrate and join him. My mother's mother, my Grandmother Mary Francis (her maiden name was Mary Sfeir) was born in 1896 in Ajaltoun, Lebanon, and died in Detroit in 1992. My Grandma Francis emigrated to the United States from Lebanon with an older brother in 1911 or 1912, and met and married my grandfather Francis in Rock Island, Illinois, in 1915. Grandpa Francis was baptized Melkite Catholic, Grandma Francis, Maronite Catholic.

After they married, my grandparents moved to Detroit, where my grandfather opened the first of a number of grocery stores. They had six children, five daughters and a son. The Francis children attended Roman Catholic elementary and high schools on Detroit's east side. After high school, my mother's younger brother, John, entered a Roman Catholic seminary to become a diocesan priest. He left a year before ordination and then attended the University of Detroit School of Law. In the early 1950s, he and Michael Berry founded the first law firm in Detroit with partners predominantly of

Arab descent. Uncle John was the only one of either of my parents' families to attend college or professional school. My mother's sisters and my uncle John each married Maronite or Melkite Catholics of Lebanese or Syrian descent. My uncles and aunts have had a total of twenty-three children—my first cousins. Because my father's only brother, Uncle Tom, married my mother's younger sister, my Aunt Ida, I have, among my first cousins, seven "double first cousins," who, with me and my brothers and sister, share the same paternal and maternal grandparents.

On September 8, 2008, I received, along with my brothers, an e-mail from my sister Barbara: "Aunt Lila called me last night to tell me that the building on Baldwin and Lafayette, Uncle Chuck's business as well as Grandpa's store and the flat, burned to the ground. She wanted to tell me and for me to tell you. She is stunned and saddened. She cried while reminiscing."

My Aunt Lila, my mother's younger sister by four years and my god-mother, was 85 years old at the time of my sister's e-mail. She has been married for almost fifty years to Charles Abud, who, since the early 1960s, used the building on Baldwin and East Lafayette for his small business. Grandpa Francis bought the building in the early 1930s, during the Depression. The ground floor was a small grocery store, the second floor a flat where he and my grandma and their six children lived until the early 1940s.

The building on the corner of Baldwin and Lafayette on Detroit's near east side, like tens of thousands of others in Detroit, was set on fire by arsonists. "So," my brother Bob said after the store on John R was demolished three weeks later, "in a period of less than a month, the old store on the corner of Baldwin and Lafayette—gone. . . . The old store on the corner of John R and Hendrie—gone."

On April 3, 2002, Chris Hedges wrote about me in his "Public Lives" column in the *New York Times*. For the column, "Love Conquers Evil: Poetry Is about the Timetable," Hedges interviewed me in our apartment.

"Lawrence Joseph, fifty-four," Hedges wrote, "is an olive-skinned Arab-American poet" whose poems "struggle with the endemic violence in American culture, the dislocation of exile, the lives of common men and women . . . the curses of urban life—racism, murder, poverty, sickness, loneliness, work, and suffering. Yet,

> at his core he believes that evil is only finally challenged, if not vanquished, by love. "I want to capture the mysterious circumstances of being alive in America today," he said. All these themes loom larger now for a man who lives a block from where the World Trade Center stood. He has spent two decades wandering about this tip of the city. His novel . . . *Lawyerland* is set in lower

Manhattan. These few blocks have long been his canvas. These motifs color his work. But his palette changed instantly and irrevocably last September . . . Mr. Joseph lives in a modest high-rise apartment with his wife, Nancy Van Goethem, overlooking New York Harbor. He is a collector of stories. Legal folders bulge with newspaper and magazine clippings, photocopied poems and essays. Many are underlined. Books lie in disordered stacks, making it hard to maneuver around the two-bedroom apartment. He calls his collecting, which he says informs his poetry, "nonacademic scholarship." He is of Lebanese and Syrian descent and grew up in Detroit. He was nineteen during the city's 1967 riot, which left sections of . . . Detroit a gutted shell. His father, a grocery store owner, was shot and wounded in 1970 in a botched hold-up. He said he had felt the sting of racism as a Catholic Arab-American, and some of his poetry speaks of slights from a society that brands a particular race or class responsible for violence. "There are things said about Arabs in America that would be considered inappropriate if said about any other ethnic group," he said. . . . In the days after the attack, he pored through works . . . which examined force and violence. He tried to make sense of it, not through the mind-set of the hijackers, whom he said he could not understand, but the suffering endured by innocents. His reaction to the September attacks was also intensely personal. He left his wife to teach at St. John's shortly before the first plane hit. It was more than twenty-four hours before he saw her again, and he hiked up more than thirty flights of stairs to find her. And those twenty-four hours, he said, were a lifetime, as they were for thousands of others who were cut off from family. Yet amid the despair, the vast concentric circles of hate, he said, radiating out over the city, were swiftly countered with equally powerful concentric circles of love. "When you love someone, one of the deepest, perhaps the deepest, desire is in a moment like this to be in the physical presence of the beloved," he said. "This is an essential human truth."

In late January 2008, I participated on a panel at the Association of Writers & Writing Programs' annual conference, held that year in New York City. The panel, "Arab American Writings about War," included Hayan Charara, Philip Metres, Elmaz Abinader, Fady Joudah, and Sinan Antoon.

The first to speak, I read from prepared text. I said: "Those of us here this morning are here as writers—all of us are writers of poetry—who write in the American language. We're here, too, as Arabs. Each of us is identified with a culture, with a people, who speak the Arabic language. Each of us has complicated personal biographies of family, class, religion, and politics. Each of us, as poets—given our individual biographical realities—moves through our writing from these given biographies into the larger structures of America's social realities, its histories of the rights of individuals against the state, its histories of labor and finance corporatist capital, its histories of race and of war, and, for the poet, its histories of poetry and of the American language that we live and write in.

"After World War II," I continued, "peace in the United States was a se-
quence of limited military or political wars. As I speak, war in America is no
longer limited. During the past eight years, the entire world has seen an
America transmogrified into a state of permanent war, wars directed toward
Arabs and non-Arab Muslims, murderous and racist. In a state of permanent
war, all poetry is, in effect, war poetry. Poets with Arab identities are, in this
state of permanent war, often patronized. Adonis and Mahmoud Dar-
wish—we are told by those few non-Arab critics in the United States even
willing to review them—happily do not write just about being Arab: They
also, we are told, write about love. The implication, of course, is that a poet
with an Arab identity also has—who would have guessed?—an inner sensibil-
ity, an inner imaginative life, an inner life rooted, as every great poet's inner
life is rooted, in human love.

"Each Arab American," I went on, "inherits her or his own family history
of immigration. When my grandparents emigrated from Lebanon and Syria
to Detroit almost a hundred years ago—my parents were born in Detroit
ninety years ago (my grandparents were born in Asia—look at a map: Lebanon and Syria are located in southwest Asia)—the number of émigrés from
the Arabic-speaking provinces of the Ottoman Empire was, because of immigration laws then, miniscule relative to immigration from Europe. Immigration laws enacted in the 1920s froze those small numbers until 1965,
when a Democratic Congress and president brought into law an immigration act worldwide in scope. Many in this room today—tens of millions of
Americans today—would not be here except for that 1965 legislative change
in law that allowed for equal immigration to the United States from every
part of the world."

I then quoted from Edmund White's 1988 introduction to Jean Genet's
Prisoner of Love. "For an Arab American poet," I said, "a part of American
history that each of us inherits includes Edmund White's following chronol-
ogy: '*1948–54*: Palestinian exodus from Israel of 1,900,000 . . . *1956*: Suez
War: Great Britain, France, and Israel against Egypt . . . *1967*: June War:
Israel destroys the Arab League and occupies a territory several times
greater than its original state. Some 700,000 Palestinians are put to flight . . .
1970–71: Jordanian civil war—Palestinian camps destroyed in Aman, then
in Jerash and Aljoun . . . *1973*: In October, a new Israeli-Arab war, which
leads to an oil embargo . . . *1975–1976*: Beginnings of Lebanese civil
war . . . *1982*: Invasion of Lebanon by Israeli army. September 16 to 18,
massacre in the Palestinian camps of Sabra and Shatila.'

"And since then? Since then," I added, "we've experienced the so-called
1991 Gulf War, the ongoing systematic killing of Palestinians in Gaza and in

the West Bank, five years of a war without provocation unleashed by the United States against Iraq, the summer 2006 invasion of Lebanon by Israel . . . "And, yes," I said, "just yesterday, in Gaza . . . Did you see that? Just yesterday, in Gaza . . ."

In late September 2009, I visited Detroit. Two weeks before, *Granta* magazine published a *Lawyerland*-type prose piece of mine on Chicago. "What Is Chicago" is set in the city's North Michigan Avenue area in early March 2009, shortly after Barack Obama's inauguration. Both of its characters are from Detroit. The "I" of the piece (as in *Lawyerland*) biographically approximates me. The other character, "Harrison," is a friend of mine and a classmate from the University of Detroit High School, who has lived and worked as a labor union lawyer in Chicago since the early 1970s.

In "What Is Chicago," I ask Harrison if he's recently been back to Detroit. "During Christmas," he answers. The dialogue continues:

"We visited my sister and her family," Harrison said. "They live in Birmingham, near Woodward and Maple. It's incredible. I got up early on a Sunday morning and drove for two, three hours, by myself. Down Woodward, over on Six Mile, down Livernois to Puritan, Puritan back to Woodward. Highland Park—the original Ford plant. Down John R. Mack Avenue. Fucking incredible. Entire sections of streets no longer there—real wasteland, your real unreal city. One-third of the city that we were born in is no longer physically there. When I was a boy, I remember my father talking about Harry Truman beginning his nineteen forty-eight presidential campaign on Labor Day in Cadillac Square in downtown Detroit—two weeks before I was born. Nineteen forty-eight to two-thousand eight. Sixty years. General Motors, Chrysler, Ford, the UAW—sixty years ago and now. I spoke with a UAW lawyer I know—his read is that Chrysler, GM, Ford if necessary, will come out of this after some form of nationalized bankruptcy, the Treasury of the United States of America the creditor of last resort. This, he says, at least preserves collective bargaining. There still will be a union. It's fucking depressing, is what it is."

Harrison looked at his watch again. "Why don't we get going? Let's walk over to the lake. It's already getting dark—before it gets too cold. You know," he said, as we were putting on our coats, "Chicago's at least three times the size of Detroit. But a third of Chicago is the same as Detroit. The bad news keeps coming. Everybody knows somebody who's lost a job and looking for a job, and can't find one."

We walked out onto St. Clair. Harrison put on his gloves. "It's gotten cold," he said. "Look at the clouds—it could snow. You know," he said, "it all comes down to labor, management and banks. Your labor markets, your commercial markets, your capital markets, are radically—I mean radically—changing. I've never seen anything like it—no one has. You got how many millions of people laid-off, stressed out, no chance of getting a real job, people with children, aging parents, mortgage payments they can't make, credit card debt they can't pay. It's not like working people—people who work for wages—were doing that well before the banks' proverbial shit hit the fan back in September. They carry out, under false pretenses, their war in Iraq, putting two trillion dollars into their pockets, the cost of lives lost and ruined be damned. They cut the highest-end income taxes and cut corporate taxes, and capital gains taxes, putting several trillion more into their pockets. They unconditionally hand another two to three trillion to the largest banks. Criminal—there is no other word for it. Fucking criminal."

When I was in Detroit, I stayed with my younger brother Mark, who lives in the house in Royal Oak that we grew up in. I drove by where the store on John R was—nothing there, nothing across the street all the way to Woodward, nothing on either side of John R down to Palmer except weeds. I spoke to several Arab Detroiters, as I always do when I go back to Detroit—professors and lawyer friends, cousins. One friend said that she had become obsessed with the notion of her own personal "changing Arabness." She asked me how my being Arab American, being an Arab Detroiter, had changed. I was taken a bit back by the question.

"Two things come immediately to mind," I said after a long pause. "First, there are the numbers, which are into the hundreds of thousands now, and the diversity, and the different communities, the different communal consciousnesses. Detroit Arabness is on the street, it's throughout the metro area's culture, it's in the area's and the state's politics, it's a crucial dimension of its politics and its economy. The second thing . . ."

I paused again. "The second thing," I said, "is how much Detroit—by which I mean not only the city, but the metro area, which extends now to Ann Arbor, to Flint, to Port Huron—how much Detroit has changed and is changing. How America has changed and America is changing. As Detroit changes, so does Arab Detroit," I added, laughing. "As America changes, so do Arab Americans. Arab Detroiters are an integral part of Detroit's history now. Arab Americans are an integral part of American history now. And there's a third thing. In my lifetime, Arab American experience has become increasingly racialized and increasingly violent.

"You know, it's strange," I said after another long pause. "What changes, what doesn't change. My Grandfather Joseph, my father's father, died when I was almost 4. We lived with him and my grandmother—six of us, my grandma and grandpa, my mother and dad, my older brother, and me. I was the baby. My first memories are of my grandpa. He was dying from what, today, they describe as 'complications from diabetes.' Before he died they amputated both his legs. He died at the same age that I am now. I think of

Joe Joseph, early 1950s, Detroit. Courtesy of Lawrence Joseph.

him a lot—I think of him every day. He read and wrote Arabic, he read ex-
tensively, he was an educated man. He spoke English well, and, I was told,
taught himself how to read it. He and his brother—who, to us, was our
uncle Charlie—my grandfather and my great uncle Charlie, and my grandmother and my great aunt Angele, they used to speak Arabic among themselves, as my grandmother and grandfather, of course, did between themselves. My mother and dad—neither could speak nor understand much
Arabic. They were Arabs but they were Detroiters from birth. I remember—
remember more as a feeling, of something that I perceived—listening to my

grandparents speaking Arabic, understanding what they were saying, my first language, really. My grandfather would speak to me alone—I remember it. He knew that I knew that he was going to die. He knew that he would have to leave this world. He did not want to leave this world. His love for me—I carry it in me, it's in me always. It will always be in me. He was Arab, my grandpa. I mention him in my poem 'Sand Nigger,' 'in the house in Detroit,' my Arab grandpa who gives me 'my first coin secretly, secretly holding my face in his hands, kissing me and promising me the whole world.' "

Part 5

*Protective Shield
and Glass Ceiling*

Domestic Foreign Policy

*Arab Detroit as a Special Place in
the War on Terror*

WILLIAM YOUMANS

In post-9/11 America, Arab Detroit emerged as a special place, a location deemed of particular political and cultural significance in relation to the Bush administration's War on Terror. National and international media, federal government agencies, civil liberties advocates, and terrorism "experts" discovered the Arab Americans of Detroit, or at least came to see them in a new, exaggerated light. Nationally, Arab Americans were no longer "invisible" (Jamal and Naber 2008), but their sudden visibility came with "special scrutiny" (Cainkar 2002, 22). Arab Americans became a suspect class. This was also true for Arab Detroit (hereafter AD), despite the community's longtime presence and growth. All the new attention elevated the platform of AD politics, raising the representational and reputational stakes for community representatives, government officials, and outside activists. All took an interest in AD's heightened profile and competed over how to interpret the place and its people. This competition, which is marked by rivalries, shifting alliances, and strange complementarities, at least partially accounts for the story of AD's enigmatic progress during the War on Terror.

Howell and Jamal (2008, 47) have noted that local and external observers tend to see AD paradoxically as typical of Arab America as a whole, yet unique. This chapter proposes that the notion of AD as a special place in the fight against anti-American militancy is fictive, that it came out of purely symbolic interpretations of the place, rather than material realities or actual connections to the attacks of September 11. Key stakeholders propagated this notion of AD as unique. Yet there was no tangible connection between AD and the global network of Al Qaeda–allied terrorists who were painted as the primary targets of the war. Arab Detroit came to signify larger concerns related to the War on Terror: namely, the threat of sleeper cells, or attacks from within, but also the promise of civilizational coexistence. Both possibilities ultimately proved hyperbolic. Public discourse about the threat from within and the role of the state in preventing attacks was primed by right-wing pundits, think tanks, and government officials. These internal threats never materialized in AD. For many, including both liberal multiculturalists and Bush administration conservatives, AD showed how cultural coexistence could happen. Local business leaders tried for years to depict AD as a gateway to the Arab world (see Part 2, "Aftermath Chronicles," in this volume).

As of 2010, it is not clear that any of these "special place" rationales have borne much fruit. Aside from minor contributions to government public relations campaigns abroad and recruitment to government agencies and contractors, AD has been of little use to the American government in the global War on Terror. It did not diminish anti-Americanism, despite Detroit's prominence in American public diplomacy campaigns broadcast to the Arab world and in international media. By the same token, despite multiple investigations, arrests, and controversies, the major sleeper cells and imminent terrorist conspiracies envisioned by the doomsayers have not materialized. Some locals were found guilty of fund-raising for Hizballah, which is on the State Department's list of terrorist groups, but Hizballah was not responsible for the 2001 strikes on the World Trade Center and the Pentagon.

What is so interesting about the contestation over AD is that public adversaries on all sides, from overzealous law enforcement officials and right-wing pundits to local governments and Arab American institutions and representatives, all advanced the AD-as-a-special-place myth. Although I believe it is a special place, it is not special for reasons pertaining to the War on Terror, a nebulous term for a series of American government policies and practices that included two foreign invasions (or three, including Pakistan), targeted assassinations, secret prisons, torture, military tribunals, the closing down of Islamic aid organizations, and immigration restrictions, as well as political co-optation of foreign leaders, public diplomacy, and humanitarian aid. In other words, the actual policies and practices of the War on Terror, although sometimes tested in AD and often impacting it, did not truly require or involve AD any more than they did other locales. Arab Detroit was one community among many on the receiving end of these measures domestically. However, Detroit received disproportionate attention. As we have seen in previous essays, this attention brought as much of the good as it did the bad. Foundations started paying attention, national media brought wider publicity, and Arab American political clout at the local and state levels seemed to increase. As a special place, the community earned more official recognition, and with that, material resources and influence. Arab American organizations and figures competed over these resources, and right-wing activists sought to cut them off.

Although seeing AD as special is a fairly broad concept that contains a range of incongruent positions, I am interested in how divergent parties contended for resources and prestige, all based on the assumption that analyzing, politicking over, and mobilizing for or against AD was worthwhile and useful within the context of the War on Terror. Given that politically opposed parties shared an interest in depicting AD as something special, I think the term "frenemy" is quite appropriate. This portmanteau of "friend" and "enemy" will be used in this chapter to refer to partners who are rivals, or, put another way, to enemies who share mutual commitments. The term "frenemy" describes well the relations among AD's leaders, between them and federal and local governments, and even, on occasion, between Arab American leaders and the right-wing pundits who clamor for harsher policies against Arab and Muslim communities in the United States. What makes these various actors enemies is their competition to attain mutually exclusive goals. They are friends in the sense that, for any of them to be relevant at all, they must agree that AD has a special relationship to the War on Terror.

The Stakeholders

Building on Howell and Jamal's observation that "the special relationship between Arab Detroit, the media, and law enforcement agencies intensified significantly" (2008, 47), this analysis hones in on three categories of actors: Arab American leaders, government agencies and officials, and right-wing activists/pundits.

The first category includes Arab American institutions, media, and activists in Detroit. The central actors include organizations and media, such as the Arab Community Center for Economic and Social Services (ACCESS), the American Arab Chamber of Commerce, the *Arab American News*, the Michigan and Detroit chapters of the American-Arab Anti-Discrimination Committee (ADC), the Arab American Political Action Committee (AAPAC), the American Muslim Council (AMC), and other groups affiliated with the Congress of Arab American Organizations (CAAO). Religious centers, such as the Islamic Center of America, are also included. The individuals who lead these organizations are central to the story of competition.

The second category involves governmental actors and agencies. This is a broad category. It refers to city, county, and state governments, as well as federal agencies, such as the FBI, Immigration and Customs Enforcement

(ICE), the Departments of State and Commerce, and the U.S. Attorney General's office. At the local level, this essay looks mostly at police departments and mayors' offices (other chapters in this volume look more closely at FBI, ICE, and Commerce and State involvements; see, for example, Muslims as Moving Targets). Different levels of government have different interests and constituencies, a fact that sometimes leads to conflict. The possibility of community cooperation amid conflict was, I will argue, an important factor in making Arab Detroit a noteworthy place.

The final group includes pundits and bloggers who propagate the image of "Dearbornistan," or treat AD as a central threat in the War on Terror. This sphere of activity centers on the efforts of one leading right-wing observer of AD: Debbie Schlussel. Her blogging, articles, and op-eds inform other right-wing activists, who mobilize against government-community relations when they seem too cozy. This group has called for greater scrutiny of Arab and Muslim Americans by government officials, and officials they consider pro-Arab are frequent targets of their protests. Consistently, Schlussel and her allies have sought to expose the "true nature" of Detroit's Arab Americans as potential terrorists.

After the Attacks: The Media Take Notice

Media attention to Arab Detroit after the September 11 attacks was immediate. One of the first national stories that focused on AD was a *Newsweek* Web exclusive that ran the day of the 2001 attacks. In "The Blame Game," Keith Naughton cited Arab American representatives such as Osama Siblani, Hassan Jaber, and Yahya Basha. This established a media script that featured Arab American leaders as the first voices to speak from the community. In Naughton's piece, Siblani, publisher of the *Arab American News*, described several hostile phone calls he had received, one of which was a death threat. He compared the backlash with the violence that followed the 1995 Oklahoma City bombing, which many initially thought was the work of Middle Eastern terrorists. Naughton also cited Hassan Jaber, then associate director of ACCESS, an organization that helped calm the community and prepared measures in case of widespread backlash. According to Jaber, ACCESS helped with other preventive steps, such as removing children from school early. Local police were deployed to protect Arab businesses and community centers, and this development became another institution-level news bit. Naughton quoted Dr. Yahya Basha, then-president of the American Muslim Council, who said, "I hope our community is protected."

The day after the September 11 attacks, the *New York Times*, the primary agenda-setting source for much of the U.S. news media, ran a page 12 story that highlighted Arab Americans in Detroit, among other places. The article noted that in Dearborn, "one of nearly every three residents is Arab-American" (Bradsher 2001). This likely explained why Dearborn became a popular location for Arab American man-on-the-street quotes in news reports. However, much of the initial ink went to Arab American leaders. Even when news stories featured the "average person" quotes, these were often found via Arab American institutions. For example, the *Times* article quoted Sam Meheidli, who was interviewed as he "distributed flyers endorsing Abed Hammoud, an Arab-American candidate in the Dearborn mayoral primary." The *Newsweek* piece mentioned that Hammoud's campaign celebration was canceled for security reasons. The following day, September 13, the *Times* ran another story with the subtitle "Shock and Anger among Arab-Americans." The dateline was "DEARBORN, Mich." Every person quoted in the article was in fact from Dearborn, but they were found "in the waiting room of an Arab community center." The earliest coverage established AD's institutional leaders as gatekeepers of the community's sentiments for national media. It also elevated the status of local leaders, such as Siblani, as well as Imam Hassan Qazwini of the Islamic Center of America, Imad Hamad of the ADC, Ismael Ahmed of ACCESS, and Nasser Beydoun of the American Arab Chamber of Commerce. It was not long before local observers began to complain privately that some spokespeople were taking the spotlight, steering journalists away from alternative sources and views, and using press coverage to promote the interests of their own organizations. The spike in media interest and the free publicity it entailed quickly became a zone of contestation, producing frenemies in predictable fashion.

Media coverage was a cause of concern for local residents and officials in other ways as well. Imad Hamad referred to the prominence of Dearborn in national media discourses about terrorism as "the Dearborn Syndrome" (Niemiec 2002). The subtext of the coverage was that the area was somehow important to understanding the homeland security challenge, as well as how Arab Americans in general felt about the 9/11 attacks. Thacher (2005) found that many local residents felt media stories often suggested that Dearborn was a possible location of terrorists or their sympathizers, calling into question the community's patriotism. Many businesses, public figures, and organizations sought to answer these accusations by flying American flags, holding demonstrations against the 9/11 attacks, denouncing them frequently and publicly, as if to assuage the fears held by non-Arabs.

It is important to recognize that Arab American leaders, community organizations, local media, religious groups, and civil rights organizations preexisted the 9/11 attacks. The prominence of civil society in AD is vital to understanding why the Arab community advanced during the War on Terror years.

The presence of media-savvy gatekeepers and sociopolitical infrastructure suggests a level of political maturation and complexity. Civil society institutions mobilized to buffer the community from outsiders, attracting resources in the process and setting the community's public agenda. Although young and underdeveloped compared with those of other American immigrant groups, these preexisting structures are thought to have softened harsher enforcement measures seen elsewhere (Thacher 2005; Howell and Jamal 2008; Bakalian and Bozorgmehr 2009). This fabric of already well-incorporated organizations also helped advance the notion of AD as a special place. I offer this argument while also acknowledging that the institutions and leaders of AD were very often overpowered, not always benevolent, and may have squandered as many opportunities as they exploited effectively.

Dearborn, it must also be understood, suffered many of the shortcomings, and gained from the strengths, of being an ethnic enclave in the United States. Wherever there is a high concentration of relatively unassimilated ethnic group members, they develop separate institutions that can mediate connections with the larger society. Although powerful within the enclave, these institutions and their leaders are often weaker and less confident in the face of society's dominant institutions. This makes them dependent on outside legitimation and recognition, which bolsters their positions within the enclave. Given that leadership positions within ethnic enclaves are usually informal, not based on popular elections or clear lines of legal authority over enclave residents, there is steady competition for local influence and control over links to mainstream institutions and allies. As I will show, this process is important to the story of AD's advancement during the War on Terror.

Given the richness of its organizational life, AD is indeed unique compared with other Arab American communities. However, it is not clear that AD was as crucial to the country's War on Terror mission as the different actors presumed. Those who were heavily invested in its importance to the War on Terror advocated for its relevance, either as a site for potential terrorists or as a bridge between cultures. One of the key venues in which AD's relevance was asserted was that of cooperation with governmental agencies at city, state, and federal levels.

The Government and Community Leaders

Reflecting the American federalist system, different levels of government came into conflict during the War on Terror. Federal agencies focused on investigation and enforcement, and local police functioned to protect the community (Thacher 2005). The FBI doubled the size of its Michigan office and increased its presence in the community; local and county governments served different purposes. From the Arab community's perspective, the work and reputations of these different arms of government varied greatly. For example, the director of the American Arab Chamber of Commerce observed that the local police department actively sought the Arab community's trust, whereas the FBI did not (Richman 2004/2005).

If local police were to undertake War on Terror activities, such as surveillance, it would threaten community trust, which is essential to general policing, requiring a public willing to report crimes and give witness statements. If Arab residents feared being interrogated for links to Al Qaeda every time they saw the police, they would make police work very difficult. The Arab community had enough fear of the local police historically, which was something local police had been trying to address since the 1990s, when community-police relations were at a low point in Dearborn. City officials responded to this tension by hiring more Arab Americans as police officers, coordinating more directly with Arab community leaders, and by opening, in 1996, a community policing substation in east Dearborn (Thacher 2005). By the time of the 2001 attacks, relations were much improved, though not perfect. Similarly, county officials actively tried to prevent anti-Arab retaliations after high-profile events. For example, after the American invasion of Iraq, the Wayne County sheriff sent officers to guard mosques. This could account for why anti-Arab hate crimes in greater Detroit actually decreased in the wake of September 11, 2001, according to Wayne County Commissioner Robert Ficano (Howell and Jamal 2008). The landmark Detroit Arab American Study reported that 33 percent of Detroit Arab Americans said they were shown solidarity or support during the 2001 anti-Arab backlash, compared with 15 percent who reported being subject to attacks, hateful remarks, or discrimination (Detroit Arab American Study Team 2009). These trends were in stark contrast to other cities and national data.

On the other hand, mistrust of the FBI was growing nationally owing to its controversial policies and antics. Alarming FBI actions around the country included its 2003 mosque counting project. Federal agents recorded the number of mosques in their areas as groundwork for future investigative work (Isikoff 2003). Before the 2004 U.S. presidential election, the FBI accelerated its interviews of Muslims based on vague, generalized increases in the color-coded threat level. The FBI also secretly investigated mosques' radiation levels (Kaplan 2005). In early 2009, evidence mounted that the FBI had been sending spies into mosques around the country (see Howell, "Muslims as Moving Targets," this volume).

The revelation of mosque infiltrations threatened one of the FBI's regular activities with community leaders, a program called BRIDGES, or Building Respect in Diverse Groups to Enhance Sensitivity. The program's bimonthly

meetings between federal officials and community activists and lawyers began shortly after the 2001 attacks, when the FBI was interviewing thousands
of Arab immigrants and foreign nationals. The largest number of those interviewed per capita lived in greater Detroit (Thacher 2005). These measures
frightened the community and caused many to worry about the ends of these
investigations. BRIDGES was based on the idea of partnership and cooperation to facilitate the work of the FBI and several other federal agencies, without needlessly scaring the community. For Imad Hamad of ADC, a co-chair
of BRIDGES, the story that the FBI had informants in mosques was "very
sensitive because it touches the core of the trust that we've been working hard
on over the years. It's a very serious, sticky situation—there's no doubt about
it" (Schlussel 2009b). If this reflected the enemy portion of frenemy, federal
officials made sure to be friend-like as well, offering Hamad commendations
for his work, consulting with ADC on its initiatives, letting ADC arrange important meetings with visiting federal authorities, and regularly buying a table at ADC's annual fund-raising banquet.

Another example of "friendly" behavior on the part of federal authorities
came much later in the decade, when collaboration with Arab American
leaders was required to combat hate crimes. Prosecution and prevention of
hate crimes was seen as one way to improve government-community relations. Shortly after the 2009 shooting at Fort Hood in Texas by an Arab
American psychiatrist in the military, federal agents called Hamad to find
out if there was any backlash. The government had set up an Incident Community Coordination Team, in which federal law enforcement agencies and
community leaders would be in contact in the aftermath of highly publicized incidents. Other formalized avenues of consultation include organs
such as the FBI's Multicultural Advisory Boards, which have been set up
nationally to maintain the FBI's relations with community organizations
and civil rights groups. However, the bulk of federal mobilization in AD has
been focused on Arabs and Arab Americans as potential terrorists.

One of the challenges local authorities faced was that the ill will generated by the federal government often bled over into community-police relations. They did not always understand why this was the case. After the government began its interview of 5,000 Arabs nationally in November 2001,
local police in Detroit assisted its efforts, despite local police refusal elsewhere, most notably in Portland, Oregon. The Dearborn police, responding
to community concerns, did reject the federal government's request that they
carry out the actual interviews, a decision that came from the Dearborn
mayor's office. Rather, they let federal officers take the lead, told interviewees
what was taking place, tried to calm them, and monitored the federal agents'

conduct and questions (Thacher 2005). Overall, community-police relations were rated as model by observers, including Human Rights Watch (2002). The police solicited complaints about the interview process, but received none. Local police later supported community leaders who urged Jeff Collins, the U.S. Attorney for eastern Michigan, to alter the Justice Department's plans for interviews in his district. For example, the federal government changed the wording of letters sent before the interviews to calm the recipients and to give them time to retain a lawyer. In this sense, local government balanced the federal government's concerns against those of community leaders.

Part of the federal government's special engagement with AD was based in its utility as a lab for policy testing. Some domestic War on Terror policies were first tried out in Detroit, then replicated nationwide. For example, the BRIDGES program became a model for community relations work in other metropolitan areas. Also, the National Security Entry-Exit Registration System (NSEERS) debuted in Detroit. It required nonimmigrants from mostly Arab and Muslim countries to register at ports of entry and local immigration offices; their fingerprints were taken, they were photographed, and they were subjected to lengthy questioning. The government also called on more than 80,000 people in the United States on temporary visas to register. Many were further investigated, and nearly 3,000 were detained. In this experimentation, the working relations with Arab American organizations helped federal authorities tailor and pursue policies elsewhere, although the community's growing opposition to these extra measures limited their role. The American-Arab Anti-Discrimination Committee called regularly for the end of NSEERS.

The federal government has also held up AD as a potential resource in soft power aspects of the War on Terror. The Bush administration's Assistant Secretary of State for Educational and Cultural Affairs, Patricia S. Harrison, spoke in Dearborn in 2003 to show appreciation for the city's efforts in public diplomacy work—basically, communications between the U.S. government and foreign publics (Harrison 2003). Dearborn was a stopping place for international visitors, or Arab opinion leaders brought over by the State Department. Later that year, President Bush stopped in Dearborn to speak to Iraqi Americans, telling them, "You are living proof the Iraqi people love freedom and living proof the Iraqi people can flourish in democracy" (Nelson 2010). Arab Detroit was being displayed as a model of American ideals. Similarly, the government recruited heavily for its military and intelligence arms, putting special value on speakers of Arabic. The federal government's conception of AD as a special place meant it offered utility in the

War on Terror. Community organizers and local Arab American media welcomed—in a frenemy sort of way—federal agencies' sponsorship of banquet tables and ad space, which provided resources but also was virtually impossible to turn down, given the extent of working relations and the animosity such refusals might generate. It should be noted that this tactical embrace had its critics in AD. Many felt that official representatives of the military, intelligence agencies, and law enforcement should not be welcome at community events.

The Dearbornistan Crowd

As governmental agencies treated Arab Detroit as a "special place" in the pursuit of homeland security initiatives, community leaders made obvious gains in political influence. Standing in the wings, a coterie of right-wing bloggers and activists warned that AD was a terrorist hotbed that should not be coddled by government officials. Referring to Dearborn as "Dearbornistan," they constantly sought to demonstrate the imminent threat posed by the area's Muslim Arab population. They frequently characterized specific Arab American organizations and leaders as terrorist sympathizers driven by anti-American and anti-Israeli agendas. These agendas, they argued, were something the government needed to scrutinize more closely and act against more harshly. They saw community-government relations as proof of corruption and a failure of the state to do its job.

One of the leading personalities within this group is Debbie Schlussel, a Michigan-based attorney and blogger whose Web site, www.debbieschlussel .com, is read by thousands of supporters and critics. Schlussel has little regard for groups like BRIDGES, dismissing them as politically correct pandering to Islamofascists and as evidence of the detrimental influence of the extremist AD leadership. She has called such outreach by the government "a joke," saying "Muslims don't respect people who kowtow to them. I think they respect those whom they fear" (Schlussel 2010). This view has motivated Schlussel to attend and heavily criticize Arab community events, which she routinely characterizes as hate-filled and terror-promoting.

In a lengthy report ("What I Saw in Dearbornistan") for *Front Page* magazine, a right-wing online publication, Schlussel begins with the provocation, "I did the work Michigan's FBI Special Agent in Charge Daniel Roberts and his agents should be doing" (2006b). She then suggested that the agency and "Islamo-gladhander" Agent Roberts were not taking on the organized Arab American community, which she thinks is a façade for terrorists. Schlussel attended an event at the Bint Jebail Cultural Center, a Dearborn banquet facility where community gatherings, from panels and political events to weddings, frequently take place. She described the center as "a hangout for thousands of Hezbollah supporters on our shores" that hosts events marked by "anti-American and anti-Christian hate, not just anti-Semitism." Schlussel's anger, however, was fixated on public officials who attend functions at the club. She was outraged that one-time U.S. Attorney Stephen Murphy III, who became a Bush nominee to the U.S. Court of Appeals, was often a guest there. At one event, he had the audacity to suggest the U.S. government had "issues of common interest and concern" with Detroit's Arab Americans. Schlussel was also livid about the security being provided for "Hezbollah supporters" by Dearborn police.

The event Schlussel covered was intended to mourn members of the Bazzi family killed in Israel's 2006 bombing and invasion of Lebanon. "But this was no memorial service," she wrote. "It was a Nazi-style hate-fest" (Schlussel 2006b). The only difference between this event and the many others, she noted, was the absence of "bloated, pandering federal officials." Yet she felt the need to dwell on that exception: the government officials. Schlussel's attacks are a veritable Who's Who of AD politics, both community leaders and the government officials who interface with them. Although she was glad to tar Arab American and Muslim leaders, she aimed most vigorously at what she perceived to be their influence over American officials. She saw these close relations as compromising the Bush administration's ability to prosecute cases arising from the War on Terror, as if terrorists would be given a free hand simply because government officials had been invited to dinner events and made the center of cheesy community award presentations. At the Bazzi memorial, which she called a "very religious Islamic event," she was forced to sit in the back with "many bitter-looking, *hijab*-encrusted women in black." At the event were local imams Hassan Qazwini, of the Islamic Center of America, Mohammed Ali Elahi, of the Islamic House of Wisdom, and Husham Al-Hussainy, of the Karbalaa Islamic Institute. Schlussel's dirt on them was largely based on alleged ties to Iran and Hizballah. Imam Al-Hussainy, she noted, held a poster of his hero, Ayatollah Khomeini, at a Dearborn rally in memory of Yasser Arafat. She noted with contempt that "both Qazwini and Al-Hussainy were hugged by President Bush in media photo ops when he came to town upon Iraq's liberation." Even if the Imams served some positive publicity in American war efforts, they were not to be trusted or hugged by politicians like Bush, who were less vigorous in fighting the War on Terror than Schlussel felt was necessary.

Other speakers with access to the government included Dr. Ali Ajami, the Lebanese Consul General in Detroit. Schlussel described his speech as "a fire-and-brimstone anti-Semitic tirade that would make Father Coughlin blush" (2006b). She said he was a Hizballah supporter who was installed by the group, according to "sources." Schlussel protested that he was often "feted by Department of Homeland Security officials." She also attacked Nasser Beydoun, then-chairman of the American Arab Chamber of Commerce and an organizer of the U.S.-Arab Economic Conference, for being there and cheering the speeches. Schlussel made sure to point out that the economic conference he helped organize was attended by President George H. W. Bush and State Department public diplomacy head Karen Hughes, whom Schlussel called a panderer in her blog posts. She reported with outrage that Michigan Republican Party Chairman Saul Anuzis, who was "so desperate to get the minuscule Muslim vote," floated Beydoun as a possible U.S. Senate candidate. Her outrage was aimed not only at Arab access to government leaders, but at their presence in the media as well. She referred to Imam Mohammed Ali Elahi as an "Islamic David Duke," who, "incredibly," had a regular column in the *Detroit News*. Extending her list of co-conspirators, she said this was due to the *News*'s "editorial page editor Nolan Finley." She concluded the piece by asking why Arabs have access and are able to speak publicly: "Why are these extremists—Nasser Beydoun, Mohammed Ali Elahi, Husham Al-Hussainy, etc., etc., *ad absurdum*—commanding the respect and attention of U.S. officials? Why do these supporters of Hezbollah terrorism against Americans and Jews support genocide in the light of day?"

In another blog post during Israel's 2006 attack on Lebanon, Schlussel took aim at other community leaders whose influence she opposed. She described a protest at Dearborn City Hall as a "pro-Hezbollah rally" (2006a). It was sponsored by the "extremist" CAAO. She reported that Osama Siblani, editor and publisher of the *Arab American News*, openly supported Hizballah and other terrorist groups. She wrote that Siblani is "notable because of his close friendship with U.S. Attorney Stephen Murphy III." Schlussel found this alarming because Murphy was "the Justice Department's chief official in the heart of Islamic America." She was equally disturbed to discover that Murphy and Siblani met on a monthly basis and have openly discussed "their lunch dates and joked around about Hezbollah, saying it is just a charitable organization and not a terrorist group."

Also in this post (2006a), Schlussel criticized the Dearborn police for being present at the protest. She observed that one of the officers was Daniel Saab. Officer Saab was, in Schlussel's words, "hailed and glorified" in mainstream media outlets such as *USA Today*, CNN, and the *New York Times* as a "superhero Muslim Arab community police officer who is a moderate." She claimed that his "superhero" status was all a charade because of allegations that he harassed a Michigan politician in 2005. However, he remained on the Dearborn police force because "hey, he's a Muslim Arab. And anything goes in Dearbornistan." Saab was eventually fired in 2007 after being accused of job-related misconduct. He faced federal charges of tampering with witnesses and evidence and of submitting a false police report. Saab was acquitted in 2008, but Schlussel continued to level allegations against him in subsequent posts (such as Schlussel 2009a). None of the accusations against Saab were terror-related; nonetheless, Schlussel presented them as evidence of Dearborn's unique Muslim-world corruption.

Another of Schlussel's targets is Imad Hamad, whom she calls a "'former' PFLP[1] terrorist." She has worked against his influence with government officials. Hamad, the Midwest regional director of ADC, was to be given an Exceptional Service Award by the FBI for his work with BRIDGES in 2003. The award was revoked after Schlussel published a column in the *New York Post* bringing to light the FBI's own inconclusive investigations of Hamad (see Howell and Jamal, "Backlash, Part 2," this volume). She argued that Hamad's political views and his alleged ties to terrorism made him undeserving of positive recognition. Although Schlussel lacked hard evidence and a coherent story about Hamad—for instance, she called him an "Islamic" terrorist while saying he was a member of a Communist group—she was able to politicize his work with the FBI. According to Schlussel, Detroit FBI Special Agent in Charge Willie Hulon and Detroit U.S. Attorney Jeffrey Collins were to blame for overlooking Hamad's record. One of Schlussel's consistent themes is that association with Hamad should be embarrassing for government officials. She has also attacked Brian Moskowitz, the Michigan/Ohio Special Agent in Charge of ICE, for his relationship with Hamad (2006a, 2006b).

Schlussel's characterization of Dearborn as a town run by "Hezbos" has spread throughout much of the right-wing punditry. She sees the city as a place marked by a high level of Arab and Muslim influence and believes that taking over the United States is the aim of immigrants from the Middle East and their offspring. Her message is alarmist and xenophobic: "Dearbornistan is ground zero and a scary omen for America's future." Many have picked up on this message. Conservative radio host Michael Reagan used the term "Dearbornistan" in a 2010 trip to Genoa Township, Michigan. Following Schlussel, the California-based pundit said that many people in Detroit are connected to terrorist organizations or are actual terrorists. Reagan admitted he lacked proof, but said he was sure of his claim (Behnan 2010). "You probably have to go in there with guards," Reagan said. Another pundit, Michelle Malkin, picked up the term "Dearbornistan" as well, using it as a framework for making sense of other stories about Arab Americans from Detroit. In a 2006 blog post, "The Dearbornistan duo" (2006), she wrote about two young men who were charged with supporting terrorism after they bought thousands of TracFone cell phones. Although the charges were dropped when it became clear it was a money-making scheme—phones sold at big-box retail stores in the Midwest could be sold for higher prices down south—Malkin, like many others, assumed the activity was terrorism-related because of the engrained Dearbornistan framework. While Malkin and others followed the government's cue by labeling this incident as a case of suspected terrorism, they also criticized the government for failing to successfully prosecute the accused men despite a dearth of evidence. This logic reduces everything about Dearborn to terrorism.

One interesting element of Schlussel's writings is the surprising detail and insider information she is able to employ. Although the ideological agenda is overt, her access to insider intelligence betrays her own network of sources in both the FBI and other federal offices as well as within the Arab American and Muslim communities. There is reason to believe that both government agents and competing community leaders, frenemies par excellence, fed Schlussel information in their own efforts to shift agendas or diminish their competitors' standing. This is a complex interaction, to be sure, one animated by rivalries and political jousting. As an outsider with a national audience and the ability to break exclusive stories, such as Officer Saab's termination, Schlussel can affect actual events on the ground, even if her tone is frequently that of the powerless reformer seeking to shake up Dearbornistan's entrenched political machine. While her characterizations overstate Arab American influence, they bolster the idea that AD is a special place in the War on Terror. Right-wing pundits like Schlussel, with their agenda, connections, and proclaimed expertise, have a vested interest in portraying AD as a central locale in the War on Terror. Ironically, by depicting relations between the government and the Arab community as meaningful and important—even if they are corrupt and counter-productive in her eyes—Schlussel empowers Detroit's Arab and Muslim leaders by exaggerating the influence they have. The perception of power can be power itself. Thus, Schlussel turned even relatively trivial symbolic acts, such as the FBI award for Hamad, into national scandals. This politicization of Arab American influence is yet another means by which AD was promoted as a place important to the War on Terror. As political adversaries sparred, AD's visibility increased.

Arab Detroit as a Domestic Foreign Population

Building on the findings of the Detroit Arab American Study—a survey of 1,000 Arab Americans in Detroit—Shryock and Lin (2009) have recently argued that, since 2001, Arab Detroit has been the recipient of greater mainstream institutional, educational, and political resources and legitimation. However, as the study shows, AD is still seen by non-Arabs and Arab Americans alike as an essentially foreign population. In this sense, it is helpful to understand Arab American advancement as a paradox. Although substantial, the advancement is also limited by a tendency to subject the citizens of AD to a *domestic foreign policy*. Although the city's Arab and Muslim leaders are mostly U.S. citizens, the federal government interacts with them as if they were foreign emissaries or colonial administrators, not local partners and co-patriots.

The term "domestic foreign policy" can be read in two ways. The first brings out a certain analogy: AD is treated as a semi-autonomous Arab republic, with federal emissaries meeting recognized native authorities, who serve as gatekeepers, interpreters, and administrators of the locals. In short, they collaborate with the overarching power to facilitate governance and also to validate their own positions—a sort of indirect rule. In this analogy, the FBI office in Detroit is an embassy. Coincidentally, just as the U.S. Embassy in Iraq vastly expanded, so did the FBI headquarters in Detroit. Both facilities serve as key functional nodes in the War on Terror. Like the Iraqi population and the "Arab street" in general, the AD street was one to be policed and surveilled. At the same time, the denizens of AD had hearts and minds to win over, with the help of native interlocutors, and shows of good relations between them and the government. Hence, the CIA sponsors a fun-filled booth at the International Arab Festival and designs attractive recruitment ads touting Arab American patriotism. Government officials such as CIA head Leon Panetta make high-profile visits to AD and pose for photo-ops with local civic and religious leaders.

It all has the feel of public diplomacy efforts to build trust, to make the "occupation" run smoothly. Just as Iraqi police and soldiers are being trained to govern their own people as part of the master plan to hand back power to Iraqis, Department of Homeland Security Secretary Janet Napolitano has asked the Homeland Security Advisory Council to study and devise recommendations on how homeland security can be changed from a centralized federal agency, like the FBI, to one based on localized models of community-based law enforcement (Carey 2010). Clark Ervin, director of the homeland security program at the Aspen Institute, Homeland Security's first inspector general, and a member of the council tasked with the study, claimed explicitly that this shift in approaches was learned from the experience in Iraq: "The military discovered in Iraq that reaching out to a community and involving local leaders brought much better results than working without them" (Carey 2010).

Second, "domestic foreign policy" also captures the transnational character of AD, which is intrinsically connected to U.S. foreign policy in the Arab world. McAlister (2001) puts Lebanese immigration since the 1970s in the context of the Lebanese civil war, a proxy war between regional and international powers, including the United States. Palestinian immigration flows directly from U.S.-supported Israeli policies. Iraq's refugees stem from nearly two decades of American invasions and sanctions there, as well as from Saddam Hussein's despotic reign. Many Yemenis came to the country as a result of the civil war—also a proxy war between USSR-backed Egypt and U.S.-supported Saudi Arabia—and subsequent nondevelopment. These are the largest national groups in AD, incidentally. Thus AD, and many Arab Americans, are an extension or an effect of American foreign policy.

Conclusion

This domestic foreign policy conceptualization should not be seen as completely discounting Arab American agency in Detroit, in which case it would be little more than a mirror image of the Dearbornistan coterie's tendency to exaggerate the extent and efficacy of Arab American political influence. Community organizations and leaders have managed not only to benefit and empower themselves, but also to improve the community overall, even if some members gained more than others. Older immigrant groups (e.g., Lebanese Americans) likely gained more, as did established institutions (e.g., ACCESS and the Islamic Center of America). It is possible that competition in the community helped increase overall gains somewhat and helped boost Arab Detroit's standing in the region and nationally. It is also likely that better coordination among the institutions would have meant greater political gains. In AD, organizations and community representatives built strategic coalitions with those in power, something many of them surely felt they had no choice but to do. This decision actually modified some policy outcomes, even if it did little to mitigate the War on Terror's chilling effects and the stripping away of civil liberties.

The story of AD in the Terror Decade is not a story of pure community empowerment. It is a story of frenemies. All the stakeholders colluded in the symbolic magnification of AD's significance, though from different standpoints and for different ends. They all treated it as a special place, a transnational place of crucial import in the War on Terror. It became a place that was simultaneously local and global, a threat and a resource, agreeable (flag-waving) and disagreeable (challenging foreign policy). These contradictory images fed into the construction of AD as exceptional. As a unique ideological resource, it could be used to decrease anti-American militancy overseas and to build bridges to the Arab world. Perhaps, by watching it closely, federal agencies could prevent more terrorist attacks. There is not much evidence that Arab Detroit was essential to any of these projects, but many considered it as such and mobilized on these premises. And this had the strange consequence of advancing this enclave community.

Note

1. The Popular Front for the Liberation of Palestine is a Marxist group and a member of the Palestine Liberation Organization.

REFERENCES

Bakalian, Anny, and Medhi Bozorgmehr. 2009. *Backlash 9/11: Middle Eastern and Muslim Americans Respond.* Berkeley: University of California Press.

Behnan, Christopher. 2010. "Pundit's Take on 'Dearbornistan' Angers Muslims." *Daily Press & Argus,* April 25, http://www.livingstondaily.com/article/20100425/ NEWS01/4250320/Pundit-s-take-on-Dearbornistan-angers-Muslims.

Bradsher, Keith. 2001. "After the Attacks: Voices." *New York Times,* September 13, A19.

Cainkar, Louise. 2002. "No Longer Invisible: Arab and Muslim Exclusion after September 11." *Middle East Report* 224 (Autumn): 22–29, http://www.jstor.org/stable/ 1559419.

Carey, Nick. 2010. "Special Report: U.S. Shifts Gears to Tackle Homespun Terrorism." Reuters, April 16, http://www.reuters.com/article/idUSTRE63F2HZ20100416.

Detroit Arab American Study Team. 2009. *Citizenship and Crisis: Arab Detroit after 9/11.* New York: Russell Sage Foundation.

Goodstein, Laurie. 2001. "A Day of Terror: The Ties." *New York Times,* September 12, A12.

Gozubenli, Murat, and Halil Akbas. 2007. "Adaptation of Community Policing in Arab and Muslim Communities in Response to Terrorism." In *Understanding Terrorism: Analysis of Sociological and Psychological Aspects,* ed. Suleyman Ozeren, Ismail Dincer Gunes, and Diab M. Al-Badayneh. Fairfax, Va.: IOS Press, NATO Science for Peace and Security Programme.

Harrison, Patricia S. 2003. "Michigan and the World." Keynote address, Coalition of American Leadership Abroad Conference, Dearborn, Mich., May 6. America.gov, http://www.america.gov/st/washfile-english/2003/May/20030509170941namremv lisv0.7209436.html.

Howell, Sally, and Amaney Jamal. 2008. "Detroit Exceptionalism and the Limits of Political Incorporation." In *Being and Belonging: Muslims in the United States since 9/11,* ed. Katherine Pratt Ewing. New York: Russell Sage Foundation.

Human Rights Watch. 2002. *We Are Not the Enemy: Hate Crimes against Arabs, Muslims, and Those Perceived to Be Arab or Muslim after September 11.* Washington, D.C.: Human Rights Watch.

Isikoff, Michael. 2003. "Investigators: The FBI Says, Count the Mosques." *Newsweek,* February 3, http://www.newsweek.com/2003/02/02/investigators-the-fbi-says -count-the-mosques.html.

Jamal, Amaney, and Nadine Naber. 2008. *Race and Arab Americans before and after 9/11: From Invisible Citizens to Visible Subjects.* Syracuse, N.Y.: Syracuse University Press.

Kaplan, David. 2005. "Nuclear Monitoring of Muslims Done without Search Warrants." *U.S. News & World Report,* December 22, http://www.usnews.com/usnews/news/articles/nest/051222nest.htm.

Malkin, Michelle. 2006. "The Dearbornistan Duo." michellemalkin.com, August 10, http://michellemalkin.com/2006/08/10/the-dearbornistan-duo/.

McAlister, Melani. 2001. *Epic Encounters: Culture, Media, and U.S. Interests in the Middle East, 1945–2000.* Berkeley: University of California Press.

Naughton, Keith. 2001. "The Blame Game." http://www.newsweek.com/2001/09/10/the-blame-game.html.

Nelson, Robert. 2010. *The New Holy Wars: Economic Religion vs. Environmental Religion in Contemporary America.* University Park: Pennsylvania State University Press.

Niemiec, Dennis. 2002. "Dearborn to Adopt Anti-Terror Program." *Detroit Free Press,* January 14, B-1.

Richman, Daniel. 2004/2005. "The Right Fight." *Boston Review,* December–January, http://www.bostonreview.net/BR29.6/richman.phpb.

Schlussel, Debbie. 2006a. "Honoring Hezbollah: Feds' Friends' Moment of Silence 'For the Martyrs' in Dearbornistan, Yesterday." DebbieSchlussel.com, July 28, http://www.debbieschlussel.com/2204/honoring-hezbollah-feds-friends-moment-of-silence-for-the-martyrs-in-dearbornistan-yesterday/.

———. 2006b. "What I Saw in Dearbornistan." Frontpagemag.com, July 28, http://97.74.65.51/readArticle.aspx?ARTID=3348.

———. 2009a. "Hezbollahstan, USA: Dearbornistan Cop Laundered Bribes from Hezbollah Financier? Cheated on Taxes/Was City's Terrorism Cop; Dearbornistan Cop Takes Muslim Bribes to Fix Tix." DebbieSchlussel.com., March 13, http://www.debbieschlussel.com/4936/hezbollahstan-usa-dearbornistan-cop-laundered-bribes-from-hezbollah-financier-cheated-on-taxeswas-citys-terrorism-cop-dearbornistan-cop-takes-muslim-bribes-to-fix-tix/.

———. 2009b. "What'choo Talkin' 'bout Willis? Told Ya So—FBI Still Meeting with CAIR; FBI's Arena Fete's CAIR Dude w/Long Rap Sheet." DebbieSchlussel.com, April 30, http://www.debbieschlussel.com/5130/whatchoo-talkin-bout-willis-told-ya-so-fbi-still-meeting-with-cair-fbis-arena-fetes-cair-dude-wlong-rap-sheet/.

———. 2010. "Reuters Quotes Schlussel on Obama's, Cops' Islamic 'Outreach' & Homegrown Terrorists." DebbieSchlussel.com, April 21, http://www.debbieschlussel.com/20809/reuters-quotes-schlussel-on-obamas-law-enforcements-islamic-outreach/.

Shryock, Andrew, and Ann Lin. 2009. "The Limits of Citizenship." In *Citizenship and Crisis: Arab Detroit after 9/11,* by the Detroit Arab American Study Team, 265–286. New York: Russell Sage Foundation.

Thacher, David. 2005. "The Local Role in Homeland Security." *Law & Society Review* 39(3): 635–676.

The Arab American National Museum

Sanctioning Arabness
for a Post-9/11 America

RACHEL YEZBICK

If you go through our exhibits, you realize that this is the
story of the Italian American, the Mexican American, and I
say the Arab American story is really the American story. It is
the story of people who come to this country for better lives
for themselves and for their families. And that's what the Arab
American story is. I believe that if we are able to convey that
message, then we succeed. . . . The message is to show the
public how much Arab Americans have been part of American
society, basically.
—Anan Ameri, Founding Director, Arab American National
Museum, 2008 interview

Plans for erecting the Arab American National Museum (AANM) were
well under way before September 11, 2001. The AANM, a department of
the Arab Community Center for Economic and Social Services (ACCESS),
was formerly the Cultural Arts Program operating out of ACCESS's main
administration building. Established in 1987, the program grew rapidly in
the 1990s (Howell 2000), and a museum was but one of several ambitious
projects in motion. Then, the 9/11 attacks occurred, and the need for a new
museum, and pressure to build it, greatly increased.

Before the Terror Decade, many Arab Americans had successfully migrated from America's margins into mainstream society. Arab Detroit's image was that of "an immigrant success story," "the capital of Arab America"
(Shryock 2002, 917). However, only hours after the 9/11 attacks, the community's profile changed. It was now a domestic front in the War on Terror,

287

and it was the responsibility of local Arab American leaders to defend the reputation and civil liberties of their community. The official spokespersons of Arab Detroit—prominent individuals who are part of a larger social network of activists, politicians, businesspeople, lawyers, and cultural educators who lobby on behalf of Arab Americans—attempted to manage and mediate the increased national attention Arab Detroit received after 9/11. They sought to influence how non-Arab American citizens viewed the Arab American community. Numerous times during my own research in Detroit, I was told by community spokespersons that September 11 had brought people "like yourself" to town to speak with Arab American representatives. Arab Detroit's spokespersons are accustomed to directing and responding to the interests of "outside" inquirers. As Shryock notes, they have created a "rich accumulation of images, objects, and historical narratives" that

> functions as an elaborate buffer zone in which outsiders—journalists, certainly, but also academics, government officials, and business interests—can be told what they "need to know" about Arab Americans and, at the same time, be kept from straying into parts of the Arab immigrant community believed, by many Arabs in Detroit, to be "old country," exceedingly Other, and a potential embarrassment when exposed to the uncomprehending eye of the American mainstream. (2002, 918)

The Arab American National Museum, since it opened its doors in May 2005, has played an integral part in this facilitation process.

Although the museum's content mostly emphasizes migration stories and the professional and domestic aspects of Arab and Arab American lives in the United States, for the purpose of this paper, I deliberately focus on how the museum's cultural artifacts, content, exhibits, and tours are political.[1] In other words, I focus on how the politics of 9/11 functions at the museum. I contend that the museum's exhibits—both its included and excluded artifacts—have been directly influenced by the events of 9/11 and the politics of fear. I argue that the politics of 9/11 operates in ways that are, for the most part, inadvertent and only semi-apparent to AANM employees. Nonetheless, this politics of fear seeps into the museum's tours, workshops, material objects, and displays.

In an interview I conducted with a board member of the AANM, he explicitly stated that the co-founders of the museum were not going to let 9/11 define the museum or the community. Making the War on Terror a prominent focus in the museum's layout would, according to the board member, undercut the diversity of the Arab American population. It would diminish the long history of Arab immigration to the United States and Arab American contributions to American society. More important, the board member

The Arab American National Museum. Photograph by Cedric Tai.

stated that such a focus would perpetuate anti-Arab and anti-Muslim essentialisms by relegating Arabs and Muslims to an overtly political time and place in American history.

Although the museum's exhibits do avoid dwelling on the events of 9/11, exhibit content nonetheless conforms to a post-9/11 politics of fear by reinforcing hegemonic understandings of what it means to be a patriotic, ethnic American citizen. Those at the AANM with whom I spoke believe that their representations of Arab American identities are in many ways counterhegemonic because they challenge negative portrayals of Arabs by telling positive stories of everyday Arab Americans. I would argue, however, that the museum's narration of Arab American identities is consistent with the tone and temper of the dominant society's values of culture, citizenship, and nationality. The AANM attempts to gain national acceptance for Arab Americans by repetitively displaying and promoting the social worth and legitimacy of Arabs as members of American society. These rituals of inclusion perpetuate Arab Detroit's own subjection to dominant ideologies of citizenship, clearly demonstrating the terms on which ethnic citizens are allowed to claim part of America's collective historical consciousness (Ong 2003).

In order to gain inclusion in the national community, the Arab American National Museum employs two principal methods: it represents a larger material culture and history that is symbolically shared by Arab Americans and other U.S. citizens; and it uses multicultural rhetoric and values to buttress the perceived social worth of Arab Americans. I argue that the museum focuses on the rich immigration history of Arab Americans in order to sanction discussions of their belonging in the United States. By emphasizing early waves of Arab immigration, the museum draws attention to Arab Detroit's mainstream and integrated ethnic residents. In other words, immigration history is used to reroot the Arab American in American soil, in America's past, and, finally, in America's present, giving depth to Arab American existence in the United States. The Arab American National Museum sanctions discussions of Arab American civil and cultural inclusion in the United States by using multicultural rhetoric, by personalizing the Arab American experience, by highlighting Arab American historical integration, and by emphasizing Arab American military sacrifice on behalf of the United States (a decision that, I will argue, was directly influenced by the demands of the War on Terror).[2] Museum personnel also attempt to solidify local Arab identities by linking them to a unified, national, pan-ethnic Arab American identity, one that encompasses the incredible diversity of America's Arab populations. These representational devices contest negative portrayals of Arabs by invoking institutionally sanctioned forms of ethnic identification in America.

Image portraying Arab Americans in the military, Arab American National Museum. Photograph by Cedric Tai.

The AANM is thus a public space in which Arab Americans are presented and present themselves as active citizens and carriers of U.S. national memory. Although ordinary residents of Arab Detroit and immigrants from across the Arab world are represented in the museum, those who created and curate the exhibits are mostly affluent U.S.-born Arabs and immigrants who have access to local prestige and influence, along with the non-Arab professionals they employed to design and build the AANM's permanent exhibits. Those who represent Arab Americans at the AANM possess a particular form of symbolic capital, which they display on behalf of average Arab Detroit residents. Because it is the only museum of its kind in the United States, the AANM is ideally equipped to influence popular representations of Arab American identity.

Dominant discourses and commemorative practices surrounding 9/11 have shaped the types of narratives possible at the museum, limiting the ways in which the AANM can portray Arabness and develop creative challenges to essentialist understandings of Arabs and Muslims. Here I ask: how do AANM personnel manage the symbols and residual meanings that surround popular memory of September 11? How do museum employees negotiate the museum's images, as a specifically ethnic museum? And if practices of inclusion are a necessary facet of full cultural and legal citizenship in the United States, then what are the costs of minority inclusion in the national community?

As they develop representations of Arab identity that are appropriate to the American public sphere, AANM personnel negotiate and actively manage the discursive practices of the state and of popular society. Forms of remembrance used at the AANM should therefore be understood as ongoing constructions and pedagogical techniques. I will give special attention to how these pedagogical techniques are established, how they operate, and how they affect the individuals who employ and experience them (Scott 1991, 777; Klein 2000). I do not, however, want to address only the internalization of popular knowledge and state-endorsed discourse at the museum; I also want to examine moments of contestation, uncertainty, and ambiguity, where gaps in official AANM discourse open up, for instance, in Cultural Competency Workshops. Which historical materials are included and excluded from the museum, the types of discussions held there, the persons, cultural performances, and group interactions on display—all of these things constitute specific forms of remembrance for museum visitors, who must interpret state discourse in relation to their own experiences (Goodman and Mizrachi 2008). The events of 9/11 influence how meaning and memory are expressed at the museum, often in abrupt moments of rupture in which snippets of violent narrative are introduced, then left unexplained and unarticulated. These ruptures create space for alternative modes of memory creation. Meaning making at the museum should not be thought of as single in purpose, but rather as multilayered, as a process from which museum visitors can extract a diverse range of interpretations and conclusions.

Cultural Competency and Narrating the Socially Dispossessed

AANM Educator: Where do Arab Americans come from? How many Arab countries do you think exist?

Participant 1: Eleven.

Participant 2: Fourteen.

Participant 3: Seventeen?

AANM Educator: More than that.

Participant 4: Twenty.

AANM Educator: More than that. Plus two. Twenty-two. There are twenty-two Arab countries. . . . Arabs come from the Arab world. . . . Can you name some of the Arab countries?

Participant 5: Iraq.

AANM Educator: Yes, very good.

Participant 6: Algeria.

AANM Educator: Yes, Algeria, Northern Africa. Good.

Participant 7: Afghanistan?

AANM Educator: Afghanistan is not Arab, but it is constantly confused for Arab because they have a high Muslim population. Also, we will talk about using the term "Middle East." Often when we use the term "Middle East," a lot of non-Arab countries get put into Arab countries.

Participant 8: Is Pakistan?

AANM Educator: Pakistan is not Arab either. It is Muslim, but it is constantly being confused for being Arab. And you know why Afghanistan and Pakistan and some other countries such as Iran get confused with as being Arab? Because there is this constant idea in the media that all Arabs are Muslims and that all Muslims are Arab and actually that is not the case. The biggest Muslim population is in a non-Arab country called Indonesia. Arab Muslims make up about 20 percent of Muslims worldwide. So this is a big misconception. . . . So what makes them Arab?

Participant 9: Religion?

As I sat in on the AANM's many Cultural Competency Workshops, I could not help but think of myself as located in the middle of a buffer zone, what James Clifford calls a "contact zone," designed for mediated dialogue (Harrison 2005, 32). Indeed, AANM workshops function as just that: as dialogic spaces non-Arabs can enter to inquire about socially sensitive issues pertaining to Arab and Muslim Americans, such as "the role of women, dress code, marriage, gender, and family relationships" (AANM 2008a). The dialogue above shows how a seemingly innocent question about Arab geography can speak to larger ideas and practices of the state, media, and society. That several participants continually conflated Islam and Arabness, despite the educator's attempts to clarify religious and ethnic distinctions, indicates the degree to which museum employees must correct visitors' (mis)understandings of Arab Americans. The dialogue also shows how the politics of 9/11—the conflation of race and religion and the demonization of Arabs and Muslims in the media—affects the types of discussions and narratives possible in Arab Detroit. Within this workshop session, questions about Muslim practices increased the amount of time spent on Islam as a topic, rendering other discussion items unimportant and not worth talking about. The discussion concisely depicts the ongoing struggle in which Arab Americans, in this instance a museum employee, try in vain to separate themselves from the images of radical Muslims that circulate in the media.

Pervasive depictions of Arabs and Muslims in popular media, film, and on the Internet serve as an easily accessible "electronic archive of and for national sentiment" (White 2004, 294). They allow citizens to identify emotionally with the imagined community of the nation (Anderson 1983). The AANM workshops provide educational tools for ameliorating pervasive negative depictions of Arabs and Muslims in popular media and film by supplying cultural, ethnic, and geographical facts about the Arab world and the Arab American community. The workshop is a pedagogical technique. The museum employee attempts to create an educational atmosphere in which non-Arab participants can engage in cultural and religious discussions before touring the museum. The goal is to encourage visitors to embrace new understandings of Arab Americans that the museum, within the museum space, designates as real and authentic.

In other words, the museum partakes in what James Clifford calls "culture collecting," a process in which artifacts, history, and culture are fashioned according to moral and political criteria that determine what is socially valued (Clifford 1988, 221). According to Clifford, how the museum authenticates the culture it collects is a political process. Although this process is imbued with meaning, most museum employees and visitors do not experience their time at the museum as politically charged; rather, they interpret the museum's content in diverse and disparate ways. This is due in part to the museum's successful use of socially sanctioned commemorative practices. As Clifford suggests, these practices are embedded in claims to authenticity and truth: "Like any successful discursive arrangement, the art-culture authenticity system articulates considerable domains of truth and scientific progress as well as areas of blindness and controversy" (Clifford 1988, 235). And although the museum's content and workshops attempt to authenticate a self-determined, socially integrated Arab American identity, the types of discussions occurring at the museum generate their own discursive pluralism, and visitors extrapolate contested meaning from the museum's exhibits and workshops.

Workshop discussions pertaining to the *hijab* illustrate this plurality of meaning. During a section of the workshop entitled "Arab American Women," one visitor asked which Arab countries make women cover up fully, her curiosity piqued by a story she saw on the news in which a female reporter could not enter a store because she was not covered properly. Another participant related the experience of an acquaintance: "She says she covers up because her husband is the only person who is supposed to see her hair" (AANM Cultural Competency Workshop field notes, May 18, 2008). In response to this curiosity, AANM educators gave varying answers. One educator stated that some women find it liberating to wear the *hijab* in their day-to-day lives. Another added that as Arab women assimilate, they tend to start working outside the home and become more professional. Both educators emphasized this second reply, stressing that there is a natural assimilation process immigrants undergo as they become accustomed to American society.

At a later point in the conversation, one man said that he sees a lot of Arab American men just standing on the streets talking. "What are they talking about?" he asked. An educator answered this suspicious question with the following reply: "They are most likely talking about politics as there has been strife and conflict in Lebanon in the past few weeks" (AANM Cultural Competency Workshop field notes, May 18, 2008). When the conversation shifted to Arab American family values, one woman expressed nostalgia for the kind of communal values cherished in Arab American society. She added that traditional family values used to be appreciated in the United States in the 1960s and 1970s. This remark stimulated a wave of comments and bodily gestures of agreement on the inevitable assimilation and dissipation of family values and kinship networks in the Arab American community. There seemed to be mild anxiety about this future change as well as acceptance that it would inevitably come to pass.

What this brief synopsis captures is the diversity of visitor inquiries and concerns, which reflect attitudes ranging from curiosity and suspicion to nostalgia for romanticized American values that are assumed to be deteriorating. The visitors' questions also show how individual dispositions and personal priorities interact with the information being conveyed in the workshops. The sanctioned discourse of multiculturalism allows participants to abstract numerous forms of meaning from the discussion. AANM educators rooted the discussion in themes of acceptance while reinforcing notions of assimilation and progress. In short, they emphasized the importance of appreciating ethnic difference in America, but they reassured their audience that Arab immigrants assimilate and become "American."

These pedagogical techniques might appear incongruous, but they are born from the same American value: freedom of choice. The first interpretation encourages participants to embrace multicultural values in order to accept the fact that many Muslim women choose to wear the *hijab*. The same value, freedom of choice, underscores the possibility that even women who cover will eventually assimilate into professional, mainstream society. By foregrounding values most Americans accept, these pedagogical practices maximize the likelihood that visitors will come to empathize with Arab Americans.

Although these workshops started in 1987, long before the 9/11 attacks, today they are likely to address topics such as Islam vs. Arabs, Islam vs. terrorism, and the Patriot Act. Workshop participants are increasingly curious about topics related to 9/11. The AANM *Cultural Competency Workshop* brochure (2008a) seems to impart its own sense of urgency around the growing need to understand and tolerate diversity within local communities: "Diversity presents a *challenge* to all of us, and cultural competency is becoming a *necessity* for living and working in a multicultural society" (emphasis added). This diversity "challenge" establishes an overall somber tone, employing multicultural ideology to reinforce interethnic tolerance.

The cultural education workshops justify the overall mission of the museum: "The AANM documents, preserves, celebrates, and educates the public on the history, life, culture, and contributions of Arab Americans. We serve as a resource to enhance the knowledge and understanding about Arab Americans and their presence in the United States" (AANM 2008b). The museum's practices are not limited, however, to the creation of a dialogic space in which socially disparate groups can learn about each other. As Julia Harrison argues, meaning making within museums is a nuanced, complex process, and it cannot be reduced to a single purpose (2005, 32). Cultural Competency Workshops should be thought of as one aspect of a much larger set of museum agendas that explicitly addresses relations of power, namely, between the nation and its Arab citizens.

When federal surveillance in Arab Detroit is taken into account and popular anti-Arab sentiment is noted, public representation of any kind is not a task to be taken lightly. In such circumstances, carving out a space in which Arab Americans can belong to the national community becomes crucial; it humanizes Arabs and normalizes their everyday lives; it roots them in American culture—as American citizens and as important members of American society. At stake are claims to citizenship, cultural and legal, and the humanization of a repeatedly demonized ethnic American population. To reclaim "good citizen" standing, however, Arab Americans must pay steep sociopolitical costs.

Museum Layout, Artifacts, and Attempts to "Authorize the 'Real' "

"All right, everybody. We are going to gather our things and head upstairs for a tour of the museum!"

Ascending the stairs, we step into a traditional Arab courtyard with mosaic tile and a large dome that opens to the upstairs portion of the exhibit. The first floor features the contributions of Arab civilization to various scholarly and cultural domains, such as art, science, math, language, and religion. The artifacts are encased behind glass panels that outline the walls of the courtyard.

On the second floor, workshop participants enter "The Arab American Story," a section of the museum that focuses on themes of arrival, adaptation, and incorporation. These processes are displayed in three separate exhibit spaces: "Coming to America," "Living in America," and "Making an Impact." As the AANM educator leads us toward the first exhibit, "Coming to America," workshop participants come face-to-face with portraits of early twentieth-century Arab immigrants in period costume. In front of the portraits sit storage trunks and suitcases stuffed with personal belongings, the shared material culture that links Arab immigrants to each other and to a mainstream American society shaped by its own history of immigration. The displays in this section of the AANM emphasize the diversity of immigrants from the Arab world, from the sixteenth century to the present day, concentrating on the lives and stories of individual Arabs as they travel to, settle in, and become part of the United States.

This mix of images and narratives is clearly meant to counter negative depictions of Arabs in mainstream media by reinforcing what conventional media typically deny this subpopulation: the claim to an American history, to a historical consciousness shaped by longtime residence in U.S. society. By looking at scores of old photographs and family heirlooms, the kind that fill attics and basements or rest proudly on mantles across America, visitors come to know a rich, but rarely told story of Arab immigration to the United States. Here, exhibit content is used to naturalize Arabs by linking them to the sanctioned discourse of American immigration. The displays foster affective ties to the Arab American story by inviting us into the intimate space of ancestry, prized material possessions, and the idiosyncrasies of personal memory: for instance, audio recordings of Arab American narrators enhance and personalize the visitor's experience of immigrant testimony.

The final portion of the "Coming to America" exhibit stands in stark contrast to the rest of the display, creating an abrupt rupture in the exhibit's pedagogical technique. For the first time, politically charged memories of the 9/11 attacks and their aftermath are brought into the immigration narrative. In a brightly lit yellow room, a letter from the U.S. Department of Justice is mounted on the wall, graced with the signatures of U.S. Attorney Jeffrey Collins and Assistant U.S. Attorney Robert Caves. The letter was

The Arab American National Museum's Arab-style courtyard, as seen from the second floor. Photograph by Cedric Tai.

An immigrant's suitcase and belongings, featured in the "Coming to America" exhibit. Photograph by Cedric Tai.

sent to roughly 2,000 Arabs in greater Detroit asking them to speak with government officials on the assumption that they might be able to provide useful information pertaining to the events of 9/11:

> As you know, law enforcement officers and federal agents have been acquiring information that may be helpful in determining the persons responsible for the September 11th attacks on the World Trade Center and Pentagon. . . . I am asking that you assist us in this important investigation. Your name was brought to our attention because, among other things, you came to Michigan on a visa from a country where there are groups that support, advocate, or finance international terrorism. **We have no reason to believe that you are, in any way, associated with terrorist activities.** Nevertheless, you may know something that could be helpful in our efforts. . . . During this interview, you will be asked questions that could reasonably assist in the efforts to learn about those who support, commit, or associate with persons who commit terrorism. (U.S. Department of Justice; emphasis in original)

Many who received this letter were detained, interrogated, and eventually deported in the U.S. government's initial efforts to boost homeland security. This letter is the only artifact in the museum that directly addresses the events of 9/11 and the vindictive backlash that ensued against Arab and

Muslim Americans. As someone who has studied this larger political context, I am very interested in this artifact, and I am especially curious to see how the educator will describe it and what my fellow workshop participants might make of it. For me, if for no one else in our group, this single display is the representational pivot on which the AANM, as a political project, turns.

The letter from the U.S. Department of Justice is supposed to accomplish several goals at once. By focusing on the government's extrajudicial detention and deportation of Arabs and Muslims, the AANM allocates space for an alternative understanding of the events of 9/11, one that establishes a public claim to marginalization as a key aspect of the Arab American experience (Das and Das 2007, 76). The inclusion of this letter in the "Coming to America" exhibit allows museum employees to unsettle normative, mainstream understandings of the events of 9/11 through an implicit critique of the state, reclaiming moral legitimacy for Arab Americans by challenging exclusive narratives of U.S. innocence and victimization post-9/11. Here, AANM employees can highlight the experiences of Arab Americans who were wronged by the U.S. government because of their imagined ties to a culture of terrorism. For many museum visitors, this may be the first time they have heard of specific U.S. government actions carried out against Arabs and Muslims in greater Detroit. The museum's use of the U.S. Department of Justice letter has the potential to localize, recontextualize, and pluralize visitors' understandings of 9/11 and terrorism.

However, the AANM educator's discussion of this topic is limited. Her narration of the 9/11 backlash against Arab and Muslim Americans is rushed and lacking in detail, if not misleading. The educator tells us that some individuals who received this letter were deported because they did not have valid visas or green cards. She does not mention, however, the scope and violence of this process, which occurred across the United States as government officials confronted Arabs and Muslims in their homes and workplaces, brought them in for questioning, held them without charge for indeterminate lengths of time without due legal process and often without revealing their whereabouts to their families, or deported them. Also unspoken is the continual targeted surveillance of Arab and Muslim Americans, the monitoring of their e-mails, financial transactions, phone calls, intellectual interests, travel, and bodies.

Gerald Conaty's thoughts on the challenge of promoting change at museums are relevant here. Conaty argues that allocating space for alternative forms of memorialization at museums "requires a critique of 'normative values,' " which is "problematic for potential corporate sponsors of museum exhibitions" (Harrison 2005, 39). The AANM is no exception to this rule. In the

9/11/2001

The Arab American community suffered two-fold as a result of the tragic events of September 11th. As with all Americans, they suffered the horror and grief. However, Arab Americans were unfairly held responsible, yet not a single Arab American was found guilty of any connection to September 11th.

U.S. Department of Justice

United States Attorney
Eastern District of Michigan

211 W. Fort Street	AUSA Robert Cares
Suite 2000	Telephone (313)226-9736
Detroit, Michigan 48226	Facsimile (313)226-2372

November 26, 2001

Dearborn, MI 48126

Dear

As you know, law enforcement officers and federal agents have been acquiring information that may be helpful in determining the persons responsible for the September 11th attacks on the World Trade Center and the Pentagon. Furthermore, they are pursuing all leads that may assist in preventing any further attacks. I am asking that you assist us in this important investigation.

Your name was brought to our attention because, among other things, you came to Michigan on a visa from a country where there are groups that support, advocate, or finance international terrorism. **We have no reason to believe that you are, in any way, associated with terrorist activities.** Nevertheless, you may know something that could be helpful in our efforts. In fact, it is quite possible that you have information that may seem irrelevant to you but which may help us piece together this puzzle.

Please contact my office to set up an interview at a location, date, and time that is convenient for you. During this interview, you will be asked questions that could reasonably assist in the efforts to learn about those who support, commit, or associate with persons who commit terrorism.

While this interview is voluntary, it is crucial that the investigation be broad based and thorough, and the interview is important to achieve that goal. We need to hear from you as soon as possible - **by December 4.** Please call my office at (313) 226-9665 between 9:00 a.m. and 5:00 p.m. any day, including Saturday and Sunday. We will work with you to accommodate your schedule.

Yours truly,

JEFFREY COLLINS
United States Attorney

ROBERT P. CARES
Assistant United States Attorney

Approximately, 2,000 Arab and Muslim men were held as "Special Interest Detainees," though virtually none were charged. A government investigation subsequently ruled that these detainees had been denied their basic legal rights.

While the government placed stricter legal controls on many aspects of immigration following September 11th, special programs were adopted for persons from Arab and Muslim countries. People from these countries were subject to a new system of registration, and many people were deported for minor visa violations or petty offenses which previously would have been overlooked.

Coming to America became increasingly difficult for Arabs and Muslims, as security checks took much longer and many were denied visas for undisclosed reasons. These new checks and regulations resulted in a substantial decrease in the numbers of Arabs and Muslims coming as visitors and students. It is likely that a similar decrease will be seen in the number of Arab and Muslim immigrants.

U.S. Department of Justice letter sent to 2,000 Arab Detroit residents in the days after 9/11. Photograph by Rachel Yezbick.

days that followed 9/11, donations to Arab American organizations in greater Detroit were surprisingly high. Much of the AANM's funding comes from private, corporate, and government donors who poured approximately $5 million in financial support into ACCESS programs in the first year of the Terror Decade alone (Shryock 2002, 921). The U.S. State Department and the U.S. Department of Housing and Urban Development are in fact two of the largest financial contributors to the museum (2005–2007 AANM Report). Additionally, in 2008 the U.S. Congress donated a line item of $2.7 million to the museum. Most visitors to the AANM would be surprised to learn that the U.S. government is now a major funder of the museum.

Complex funding networks shape the nature of appropriate content in any ethnic museum. They also determine who can serve as a museum's principal agents or subjects of change. At the AANM, what Harrison calls the "burden of change" (2005, 39) is effectively shifted to the museum's visitors, and the degree to which the museum is willing to discuss controversial topics, including the marginalization of Arab Americans, is limited.

This reluctance to engage directly with controversial issues cannot be fully explained by the AANM's heavy reliance on funding provided by mainstream institutions, including the U.S. government. To address outright state violence against Arabs and Muslims post-9/11 would be problematic not only for certain donors, but also for many of the museum's non-Arab visitors. To criticize U.S. state policy and have this judgment be well received by visitors, as opposed to being admonished as unpatriotic, the critique must not question the authority of powerful, mainstream ideologies: namely, the American dream, American civil liberties, American multiculturalism, and immigration to America in search of freedom and opportunity. These ideals, which are celebrated in the "Coming to America" exhibit, take moral precedence over state acts of violence. The U.S. government's failure to uphold American ideals can be treated as an issue separate from the ultimate value of a constitutional system protecting equality and justice. Government actions that threaten this system are presented as exceptions, as flawed administrative policy, while the museum's content and tours are championed as examples of free speech. By submerging the 9/11 backlash within a higher ethical system that is unquestionably American, exhibit designers at the AANM obviously wanted to create a situation in which visitors would be able to empathize with Arabs and Muslims as fellow Americans. The intended lesson of "Coming to America" is that freedom and the American dream are things Arabs and Muslims believe in, too, even when they suffer at the hands of their own government.

But is this the lesson visitors are actually learning today? The educator leading our tour seems reluctant to dwell on the letter from the U.S. Department of Justice. Placed starkly at the end of the "Coming to America" exhibit, it feels out of place in this otherwise positive, politically correct tour. What makes the letter so dissonant is the fact that, for most museum visitors, U.S. government actions taken against Arab and Muslim Americans lack the status of an "event" in popular history (Fogelson 1989). With the exception of a few reports conducted by National Public Radio and a thin stratum of progressive and left-leaning media, U.S. media coverage of the War on Terror consistently mimicked the discourse produced by official government sources. Mass media rarely reported on the errors that filled the often-outrageous allegations made against Arab and Muslim Americans—as exemplified in the nonskeptical coverage of "Operation Green Quest" and the "operational combat sleeper cell" in Detroit (Howell and Shryock 2003, 450). Consumers of mainstream media instead received sound bites of domestic, wartime rhetoric that either vilified Arab and Muslim Americans or implied that suspicion of these populations was perhaps unfair, but otherwise understandable, even prudent.

Seen in this light, the Department of Justice letter, and our educator's minimalist explication of it, are attempts to disclose what has been relegated to the historically noneventful in U.S. history, to challenge popular narratives of 9/11, and to expose what popular media conceal or help us forget: the U.S. government's widespread and systematic discrimination against a sector of its own population (Fogelson 1989, 143). It is too much weight for a single artifact to carry, and our museum educator's spare account of the letter's content, and what it meant for millions of Arab and Muslim Americans, virtually assures that the letter's critical impact will be slight.

After this brief political interlude, we are led next to the "Living in America" exhibit. This display focuses on the life and culture of Arab Americans in the United States, and we find ourselves transported suddenly into the domestic sphere of a contemporary Arab American home. Typically, when museums exhibit domestic scenes of previous decades and centuries, it is because visitors have trouble imagining what life was like in earlier times. That the interior of a *present-day* Arab American home is on display at the AANM speaks to the imagined foreignness of Arabs, an ethnic group so often portrayed as anti-American that showing scenes from their private lives, thereby suggesting that they, too, have homes and families, can be interpreted as politically corrective. Here, the AANM uses the affective, normalizing power of the domestic sphere to influence how we will see and interpret the museum's exhibits. Moving immediately from a display that depicts state violence against Arab American citizens into the warmth of the domestic sphere—specifically, into a space most people associate with love, food, leisure, informality, and acceptance—museum educators can moderate

From the "Living in America" exhibit, this image depicts an Arab American family at home. The image is a still shot from a short documentary that focuses on ordinary Arab Americans. Photograph by Cedric Tai.

and personalize the "distant, imagined events" depicted only moments prior (White 2004, 294).

Although ample meaning can be extracted from these exhibits and their placement, I would rather look at how the political operates at this juncture in the museum tour. There are two probable interpretations of the sharp transition between "Coming to America" and "Living in America." In one reading, visitors could draw unpleasant parallels between the forced deportation of individuals from their homes and the soothing depiction of the Arab American household they enter, realizing that the former threatens the latter. In the "Living in America" exhibit, our group walks through a "front door" into the living room of an Arab American household, then through the intimate spaces of the kitchen, and even into a daughter's bedroom, where no stranger visiting any real Arab home would ever expect to venture. A second, equally possible interpretation of this display is to conclude that this Arab home space is not related to the earlier imagery of homeland security, that each belongs to a completely separate narrative. The domestic comforts displayed in the "Living in America" exhibit might simply remind visitors of the amenities of their own life, allowing them to temporarily reinsert themselves, and Arab Americans,

"Citizenship," a display featured in the "Living in America" exhibit. Photograph by Cedric Tai.

into a familiar culture of comfort. Here, pedagogical practices at the museum are not singular in purpose; nor are they fully predictable or precisely mediated. In fact, the museum educator does not comment on the transition between "Coming to America" and "Living in America."

"Living in America" emphasizes the many contributions Arab Americans have made to American society, stressing culinary innovations (from the ice cream cone to Dannon yogurt to hummus) and Arabic dance and music, as well as other cultural traditions. A lighthearted documentary film featuring numerous interviews with ordinary Arab Americans from around the United States allows us, once again, to enjoy a broad sample of individual Arab American stories. The exhibit also stresses the importance many Arab immigrants place on obtaining U.S. citizenship. An entire display within this exhibit is devoted to relating personal stories about the trials, tribulations, and triumphs of obtaining U.S. citizenship. Simply entitled "Citizenship," this display challenges mainstream assumptions that Arab Americans are exceedingly foreign and ambivalent about their allegiance to the state.

It is the emphasis on service in the U.S. military, however, that is the exhibit's most distinctive tool for reclaiming moral and cultural citizenship for Arab Americans. To accentuate military service is to remind the public that Arab Americans, too, are willing to give the ultimate gift of patriotic sacrifice: the offering up of the self in times of war to protect the state from its foreign and domestic enemies. For a population that is often portrayed as the state's internal enemy, participating in the ethics of military sacrifice reinforces nationalist sentiment and unifies disparate Arab and Muslim American groups through a common appeal to patriotism. Joseba Zulaika points to the roots of this logic in Western thought: "It is no accident that we find the enigmatic 'dying for another' turned into the maximum expression of love and freedom, the triumph of life, at the center of Western thought from Plato to Heidegger. Nowhere is the gift of death as massive, universal, and unconditional as in war" (2003, 90–91).

The AANM, in its attempts to validate a demonized population, figuratively situates the Arab American as one whose ethics necessitate the ultimate sacrifice. By reaffirming the loyalty of one of the nation's most morally ambiguous ethnic populations through metaphors of sacrifice, the museum symbolically unites and binds the nation, and particularly Arab and Muslim Americans, by linking them to a higher ethic of American morality and to the values of freedom, equality, and justice. Here, morality and American values are hardened into societal "truths" as Arab Americans' devotion to country is displayed in their willingness to die for it.

Much of the AANM is constructed around this notion of a greater ethic and higher truth. Zulaika refers to this transcendent morality as the "service of truth," in which individuals who have been exposed to excessive forms of violence ultimately embrace self-sacrifice as a personal calling (2003, 90). Showcasing Arab American military service at the AANM is an attempt to challenge negative portrayals of Arabs and Muslims in popular media and film. However, if it succeeds, it does so by pandering to larger, hegemonic ideas of what it means to be a full citizen of the United States post-9/11, a period in which one's willingness to die for the nation—and to fight against enemies commonly assumed to be Arab and Muslim—became emblematic of patriotism and loyalty to the state. It reinforces the notion that to be a patriotic ethnic group within the United States, members of the group must publicly display their willingness to be sacrificed on behalf of the nation. The military display at the museum thus speaks to the ongoing crisis of a nation that is at war with an Arab country (Iraq) and with a nation populated by Muslims (Afghanistan).

Yet in this act of patriotic display and sacrifice, the museum bears excessive witness to the crimes of modern history—in this case the events of

Arab Americans in the military, from the "Living in America" exhibit. Photograph by Cedric Tai.

9/11—by playing into a 9/11 politics of fear that has demonized Arab and Muslim identities. Conspicuous references to the ethics of sacrifice at the AANM allude to, and have the potential to reinforce, popular perceptions of Arab and Muslim Americans as morally ambiguous, and associations of this kind indirectly augment the imagined connection between Arabness and terrorism. Sacrificial metaphors attempt to reclaim moral standing by figuratively uniting sacrifice with the attainment of mainstream status and national belonging. By binding sacrifice to admission into the American mainstream, the museum reaffirms the violence inherent in America's social system of multicultural acceptance. The AANM reconfigures sacrifice as a symbolic motif of Arab and Muslim American belonging, in turn placing Arabs and Muslims definitively on the margins of mainstream society.

The idea of sacrifice operates at three levels in the museum. First, controversial Arab immigrants are omitted from the realm of public display; in this group are all those who, because their beliefs, cultural practices, or appearance might seem un-American to mainstream viewers, must be sacrificed for the greater representational good of the Arab American community. Second, details pertaining to state discrimination against and harassment of Arab and Muslim American populations post-9/11 must be omitted, especially if they could be interpreted as extreme or critical of key American values. Third,

Arab Americans themselves, in the form of military figures, are offered as proof of the community's willingness to sacrifice on behalf of the state. Although the latter gesture is overtly enacted at the museum in order to restore the good citizenship standing of Arab American populations, the first two gestures of sacrifice are implicit and work almost invisibly, as if in the folds of a lexicon unable to express them. To address what is omitted in these sacrificial forms would be to commit a form of excessive witnessing. As the director of the museum told me, we should not let "September 11 define our community" (interview with AANM director, July 31, 2008). However, the concessions the museum makes to avoid politicizing itself manage only to obscure what everyone knows already: the AANM is necessary because Arab Americans do not possess full cultural citizenship and because, in the post-9/11 era, they have seen an erosion of their civil rights.

Not ironically, it is with these militaristic depictions of Arab Americans that the AANM shifts its focus to the positive role Arab Americans have played in American culture and society. In its final exhibit space, "Making an Impact," the museum roots Arab Americans firmly in America's past and present. Here, the stories and artifacts tell visitors how Arab Americans and their organizations have contributed to the American way of life, in fields such as music and entertainment, sports, literature, education, medicine, science, law, and politics. As our tour group exits the "Living in America" exhibit, we gaze up at a large wall covered with portraits of famous Arab Americans. The exhibit uses celebrity and the personal accomplishments of hundreds of Arab Americans to prove that the American dream can be attained by members of this community. As its final message, the AANM assures us that success and civic involvement are the best tools for reclaiming cultural citizenship.

In a brochure made available to us in the "Making an Impact" exhibit, famous radio personality Casey Kasem offers the following observation:

> "Ask not what your country can do for you, ask what you can do for your country"—a famous quote by an Irish-American president, John F. Kennedy, that inspired an entire generation. These words were first written by, among others, the Arab American author of *The Prophet,* Kahlil Gibran. And that sentiment, so beautifully expressed by Gibran more than 70 years ago, has inspired Americans of all heritages. We Arab Americans are proud of our heritage and proud to be Americans. It's this pride that keeps us all asking, "What can we do for our country?"—the good old U.S.A. (Casey Kasem, *Arab Americans: Making a Difference* brochure)

Notice how Kasem emphasizes the importance of cultural diversity in the United States by noting a beloved former president's ethnic heritage. He

This collage, depicting famous Arab Americans, is the front display of the "Making an Impact" exhibit. Photograph by Rachel Yezbick.

then shows how Kennedy's famous words were actually written by an Arab American author, highlighting Arab American contributions to the nation. These words, Kasem adds, have "inspired Americans of all heritages." The lessons are obvious: there is tremendous value in American multicultural- ism; Arab Americans, like other ethnic Americans, are patriotic citizens; and every citizen can and should contribute to the well-being of the United States of America. Although the quote serves well as a sound bite for senti- mental patriotism, it speaks more specifically to a belief in the U.S. Consti- tution and in the nation's values and morals that has special significance to this state-targeted ethnic community: to be a patriotic Arab American citi- zen is to hear and respond affirmatively to the call of sacrificial citizenship.

Conclusion

Rachel: Did you ever feel like the museum or the organization had to cooper- ate with the government or with the FBI?

Bashir: We cooperated with the FBI?

Rachel: Well no, cooperate is a bad word . . . um . . . but worked with government agencies in terms of giving them cultural knowledge, where "we" want "you" to know about these things about our culture . . . through workshops.

Bashir: No, no, I wouldn't call it cooperation; no, I wouldn't call it that, I mean, or cooperated or partnership. No. *We target law enforcement agencies through cultural education because we think that it is important for them to learn about our culture. That is very different than cooperating because they want information about the Arab community, or partnership because they want us to work with them against certain people.* That's . . . I really hope you will be very, very careful about using this.

Rachel: Oh. Yes, I know. I will. I'm very sorry. I know someone else had used that.

Bashir: Maybe someone else . . .

Rachel: Yes, right.

Bashir: For us it's about *providing education about the community to law enforcement agencies because we think it's important in the way they will see the community.*

Rachel: Right, and I will be very careful about using that term. My mistake. All right . . . I think that may be it . . . is there anything else you would like to add?

Bashir: No . . . just make sure you don't use this word "cooperation."

My stumbling misuse of terms in this interview with Bashir (a pseudonym), one of the AANM's board members, highlights more than conversational tension; it highlights, among other things, the confidence with which prominent community leaders and institutions navigate the overt federal presence in Arab Detroit so as to safeguard their community from unnecessary government policies and prosecutions. My inquiry into this tactical relationship between the federal government and Arab Detroit had left me puzzled, and slightly paranoid about government wire-tapping. My heightened sensitivity to my surroundings was directly related to Bashir's cautionary admonition. Both were grounded in conditions particular to Arab and Muslim Americans post-9/11, a period in which the political struggle for safety, cultural inclusion, and national recognition became part of everyday life.

The awkward tension between Bashir and me reflects larger tales of government brutality and the institutional confines within which the Arab American National Museum functions. It points to patterns of state intervention and surveillance and the difficulties of combating deeply entrenched notions of Arab Americans as Other and anti-American. These negative connotations of Arab American identity pervade the thoughts, interactions, and private behaviors of community spokespersons who consider themselves responsible for the communal well-being of Arab Detroit. Of equal importance, this tense dialogue illustrates a unique relationship between an ethnic museum and the government. Not only does the museum receive millions of dollars in funding from federal agencies, but also the AANM is being paid to educate and sensitize federal agencies, such as the FBI and the CIA, about "fundamental" Arab cultural characteristics. Museum employees serve as guides to the local Arab community for non-Arab American visitors, and in addition, they serve as cultural experts and guides for the federal government.

Providing cultural sensitivity training for federal agents protects local interests. It is believed that such training will help reduce ill-founded or ill-advised federal policies that fail to distinguish "fiction from facts" about Arab and Muslim people. Cultural sensitivity training is thus seen as a strategy for reorienting the efforts of federal agencies so that these organizations can fulfill their intended purposes of protecting the country and its citizens, including the residents of Arab Detroit, from "wrongdoers" who seek to do America harm (field interview, May 8, 2008). Cultural sensitivity training also brings needed income to the AANM and several other Arab American institutions that educate government workers, agencies, and the public about Arab culture. As a service provided to state and society, cultural sensitivity training reinforces the notion that Arab Detroit is a place of cultural worth for war-related endeavors. Today, the AANM and many other Arab American institutions are inadvertently assessing their community's value according to what has become, in the Terror Decade, their most respected (and unfortunate) function in the national community: to serve as ambassadors to and for a perceived culture of terror.

To assert its right to represent "Arab culture" to the national community and federal government, the AANM uses multicultural rhetoric. Multicultural ideology enables museum employees to conduct public discussions of Arab American civil and cultural inclusion in the United States by insuring that these discussions are carried out in politically correct language. By expressing their cultural worth in terms of multicultural value, the residents of Arab Detroit can be included in the national community on the basis of their distinction and difference. Arab Americans are "accepted" on "their terms," with much of their cultural difference included, as long as the boundaries between "them" and "us" remain clear. These boundaries of distinction often mask the countless ways in which "minorities" resemble and are already genuinely integrated into the "mainstream" of American society. In Arab Detroit, these boundaries reinforce the notion that the real value of Arab American identity lies in its imagined connection to the community's essential Arabness, and therefore to its propaganda role in the War on Terror. The numerous social, political, and economic contributions Arab Americans have made to Detroit and the state of Michigan are not what brings visitors, or the FBI, to the AANM, despite the museum's best efforts to promote these contributions.

By engaging actively in the politics of ethnic representation, Arab Americans may or may not succeed in grafting themselves onto the national body politic. Many people believe multiculturalism will save Arab and Muslim Americans from their perceived moral ambiguity. I would argue, however, that multicultural rhetoric further entrenches Arab and Muslim identities in the politics of difference and sameness. As an institution whose special mission is to represent a community marked, in popular media and government policy, as a potential threat to national security, the AANM gives shape and nuance to the space of contradiction surrounding issues of being and belonging for Arabs and Muslims in America.

The discourse of Arab American cultural citizenship at the Arab American National Museum is producing a wealth of contradictions and unintended consequences. It instills pride, yet it reinforces damaging notions about Arab Detroit. It extols patriotism, yet it reinforces models of Arab American difference based on an imagined connection between Arabness and terrorism. It refuses to let 9/11 define the community, yet it panders to a 9/11 politics of fear. It argues vigorously for inclusion, yet it masks the injustices committed against Arab and Muslim American populations by the state post-9/11. It speaks for an invisible community, yet it mutes the voices of Arab immigrants whose practices and beliefs may appear un-American. It binds sacrifice to mainstream acceptance, urging Arab Americans to take up excessive demands for citizenship. Finally, it advocates equality, yet it frames the worth of Arab and Muslim Americans against a hegemonic backdrop that determines who is and is not a valued U.S. citizen. As a museum that attempts to gain full acceptance for Arabs in mainstream American society, these contradictory aspects of the AANM's exhibits, workshops, and tours have the potential to reinforce negative perceptions of a community that simply wants to be seen and recognized as American.

Notes

1. For a virtual tour, visit the official AANM Web site at http://www.arabamericanmuseum.org/.

2. Since 9/11, rhetoric surrounding the War on Terror has drawn implicit and explicit parallels between Arab and Muslim Americans and the 9/11 terrorists. The AANM military

exhibit challenges this association by displaying Arab American military involvement as evidence of the ethnic group's loyalty to the state. This exhibit is overstated in a manner that speaks directly to the popular belief that Arab culture and Islam are anti-American.

REFERENCES

Anderson, Benedict. 1983. *Imagined Communities: Reflections on the Origin and Spread of Nationalism*. London: Verso.

Arab American National Museum. http://www.arabamericanmuseum.org/.

———. 2005–2007. *Report*. Detroit: AANM, http://www.arabamericanmuseum.org/siteMap.asp.

———. 2008a. *Cultural Competency Workshop*. Brochure. Detroit: AANM.

———. 2008b. *General Information and Membership*. Brochure. Detroit: AANM.

Clifford, James. 1988. *The Predicament of Culture: Twentieth-Century Ethnography, Literature, and Art*. Cambridge, Mass.: Harvard University Press.

Das, Veena, and Ranendra K. Das. 2007. "How the Body Speaks: Illness and the Lifeworld among the Urban Poor." In *Subjectivity*, ed. Joao Biehl, Byron Good, and Arthur Kleinman. Berkeley: University of California Press.

Fogelson, Raymond D. 1989. "The Ethnohistory of Events and Nonevents." *Ethnohistory* 36(2): 133–147.

Goodman, C. Yehuda, and Nissim Mizrachi. 2008. "The Holocaust Does Not Belong to European Jews Alone: The Differential Use of Memory Techniques in Israeli High Schools." *American Ethnologist* 35(1): 95–114.

Harrison, Julia. 2005. "What Matters: Seeing the Museum Differently." *Museum Anthropology* 28(2): 31–42.

Herzfeld, Michael. 2004. *The Body Impolitic: Artisans and Artifice in the Global Hierarchy of Value*. Chicago: University of Chicago Press.

Howell, Sally. 2000. "Cultural Interventions: Arab American Aesthetics between the Transnational and the Ethnic." *Diaspora* 9(1): 59–82.

Howell, Sally, and Amaney Jamal. 2008. "Detroit Exceptionalism and the Limits of Political Incorporation." In *Being and Belonging: Muslims in the United States since 9/11*, ed. Katherine Pratt Ewing. New York: Russell Sage Foundation.

Howell, Sally, and Andrew Shryock. 2003. "Cracking Down on Diaspora: Arab Detroit and America's 'War on Terror.' " *Anthropological Quarterly* 76(3): 443–462.

Kasem, Casey. 2005. *Arab Americans: Making a Difference*. Brochure. Detroit: AANM.

Klein, Kerwin Lee. 2000. "On the Emergence of Memory in Historical Discourse." In "Grounds for Remembering," special issue, *Representations* 69: 127–150.

Ong, Aihwa. 2003. *Buddha Is Hiding: Refugees, Citizenship, the New America*. Berkeley: University of California Press.

Scott, Joan W. 1991. "The Evidence of Experience." *Critical Inquiry* 17(4): 773–797.

———. 2007. *The Politics of the Veil*. Princeton, N.J.: Princeton University Press.

Shryock, Andrew. 2002. "New Images of Arab Detroit: Seeing Otherness and Identity through the Lens of September 11." *American Anthropologist* 104(3): 917–938.

314   *Rachel Yezbick*

Sturken, Marita. 2007. *Tourists of History: Memory, Kitsch, and Consumerism from Oklahoma City to Ground Zero.* Durham, N.C.: Duke University Press.

White, M. Geoffrey. 2004. "National Subjects: September 11 and Pearl Harbor." *American Ethnologist* 31(3): 293–310.

Zulaika, Joseba. 2003. "Excessive Witnessing: The Ethical as Temptation." In *Witness and Memory: The Discourse of Trauma,* ed. Ana Douglass and Thomas A. Volger. New York: Routledge.

Toward Electability

Public Office and the Arab Vote

ABDULKADER H. SINNO AND EREN TATARI

Both Arab and Muslim Americans have a visible social presence in Michigan and the greater Detroit area, but they are considerably underrepresented at all levels of elected office, including in electoral districts where they are concentrated. In this chapter, we quantify and attempt to explain patterns of political representation in elected office among Arabs and Muslims of the greater Detroit area. To do so, we evaluate the different factors that we suspect may influence the persistent underrepresentation of Muslim and Arab Americans in elected office by collecting election data and by interviewing politicians, party activists, community leaders, and other key players in metropolitan Detroit.

We decided to simultaneously explore the representation of Arab, Chaldean, and Muslim Americans because there is substantial demographic overlap among these populations in greater Detroit—42 percent of Arab Americans identify as Muslims (Howell and Jamal 2008) and almost half of Detroit's Muslims have Middle Eastern ancestry (Shryock 2004). And members of all three groups have been targets of ethnic profiling and voters' fears after 9/11. We even find opponents of a non-Muslim Chaldean American candidate trying to frame him as Muslim to achieve electoral gains. The dynamics affecting these groups' representation are therefore generally similar. Differences do exist, however, and they are instructive (e.g., how the electorate and opponents react to a candidate's obviously Muslim name). We therefore discuss the representation of all three groups simultaneously unless there is a reason to think that belonging to one minority but not another affects the ability of a candidate to successfully run for office.

We find that Arab and Muslim cultures in metro Detroit have no effect on the supply of Arab and Muslim American candidates and that the communities

315

are well organized and fairly well integrated.[1] And there is no obvious discrimination against Arab and Muslim candidates within the political parties at the state and local level, at least not within the Democratic Party, which has attracted most Arab and Muslim voters and activists since 9/11.

Instead, three factors, two of which come together in a potent combination, explain Arab and Muslim American underrepresentation in elected office. The first is the effective representation of Arab and Muslim American interests by elected officials who are not from these communities. These enduring alliances between community leaders and elected officials who are not from the community limit the potential for Arab and Muslim American candidates to get elected by depriving them of community support. In addition, and more important, we found that the combination of single-district city elections, Muslim and Arab demographic minority status, and hostile attitudes by non-Arab and non-Muslim voters make it challenging for candidates from these communities to get elected. We also find mixed support for the hypothesis that divisions within Arab and Muslim communities hinder the electability of officials from within their ranks.

The State of Arab and Muslim American Representation

Table 1 summarizes the representation of Arab and Muslim Americans in elected office in metropolitan Detroit and the legislature of the state of Michigan.[2] As of November 2009, there were nine elected Arab Americans and seven Muslim Americans (including four of the Arab Americans) in nine city governments, three county governments, and the Michigan House and Senate.[3]

Most elected Arab Americans serve in city governments. Dearborn Heights, whose population is at least 8.8 percent Arab American according to the 2000 U.S. census, but possibly twice as many today, has one Arab American elected official, Thomas Berry, in the council. His is one of ten elected city government positions (mayor, city clerk, treasurer, and seven city councilors). Berry is a Shi'a Muslim Arab from a politically active family who ran successfully for his second term in the November 2009 elections.

Three of Dearborn's (at least 33.4 percent Arab American) seven current councilors, and nine elected officials, are of Arab origin. Two of the three, Robert Abraham and George Darany, are heavily assimilated third-generation Americans who are not active in Arab American organizations and do not attend predominantly Arab American churches.[4] The third, Suzanne Sareini, was both the first Muslim and the first Arab elected to office in Dearborn, and the first Muslim and Arab woman elected to office in the state of Michigan in

Table 1. Arab Populations and Number of Elected Arab and Muslim Americans

	Arab American Population (percent)[a]	Elected Positions Available[b]	Arab Americans Elected (2009 elections)	Muslim Americans Elected (2009 elections)
City of Dearborn Heights	5,127 (8.8%)	10 (7)	1 councilor (T. Berry)	1 councilor (T. Berry)
City of Dearborn	29,181 (33.4%)	9 (7)	3 councilors (R. Abraham, G. Darany, and S. Sareini)	1 councilor (S. Sareini)
City of Hamtramck	2,160 (9.4%)	7 (6)	—	3 councilors (S. Ahmed, K. Miah, and M. Hassan)
City of Detroit	8,287 (0.9%)	11 (9)	—	—
City of Highland Park	687 (4.1%)	8 (5)	—	—
City of Sterling Heights	4,598 (3.7%)	9 (7)	—	—
City of Warren	3,470 (2.5%)	12 (9)	—	—
City of Livonia	1,953 (1.9%)	10 (7)	—	—
City of Wayne	— (~0%)	7 (6)	1 mayor (A. Al-Haidous)	1 mayor (A. Al-Haidous)
Oakland County	27,500 (2.3%)	31[c]	1 sheriff (M. Bouchard)	—
Macomb County	17,300 (2.2%)	57[d]	1 treasurer (T. Wahby)	—
Wayne County	55,650 (2.7%)	21[e]	—	—
State of Michigan	138,269 (1.2%)	110 representatives, 38 senators	2 representatives (J. Amash, R. Tlaib)	1 representative (R. Tlaib)

[a]Figures are from the 2000 U.S. Census. They represent the greater of the sum of Arabic and Assyrian speakers (first language) and those who declare being of Arab ancestry. Odds are that these proportions are both outdated and that they underestimate the numbers of those of Arabic and Chaldean ancestry. Of course, the U.S. census does not ask respondents about their religious affiliation. Some data on the Arab American population can be found in G. Patricia de la Cruz and Angela Brittingham, "The Arab Population: 2000," Census 2000 Brief, December 2003, http://www.census.gov/prod/2003pubs/c2kbr-23.pdf.

[b]Number of city councilors is provided in parentheses.

[c]Oakland County elected officials: County Executive, Prosecuting Attorney, Clerk/Registrar of Deeds, Sheriff, Treasurer, Water Resources Commissioners, County Commissioners (25). In addition, there are 65 elected and appointed judges.

[d]Macomb County elected officials: County Executive, Sheriff, Clerk/Registrar of Deeds, Treasurer, Public Works Commissioner, County Commission (26), Charter Commission (26). In addition, there are 12 Circuit Court and 2 Probate Court judges.

[e]Wayne County elected officials: County Executive, Prosecuting Attorney, Sheriff, County Clerk, County Treasurer, Register of Deeds, County Board of Commissioners (15). In addition, there are 61 judges in the Third Circuit Court and 8 judges in the Probate Court.

Source: Compiled by authors.

1990. In the August 2009 primaries, eight of the twenty-five candidates were of Arab descent (Darany, Abraham, David Bazzy, Sareini, Ali Sayed, Khalil Dakhlallah, Rabih Hammoud, and Hussein Sobh), out of whom five (Darany, Abraham, Bazzy, Sareini, and Sayed) made it to the final fourteen. However, only the three incumbent Arab Americans were reelected in the November 3, 2009 election.[5]

The city of Hamtramck (at least 9.4 percent Arab American and perhaps 50 percent mostly non-Arab Muslim minorities, such as Bengali) currently has no Arab Americans but three non-Arab Muslims serving on its six-seat council. Complaints about discrimination against minorities in the 1999 elections led the Justice Department to send staff to monitor the 2003 elections. Shahab Ahmed, a Bengali immigrant, became the first minority candidate elected to the Hamramck city government in 2003, to be followed by Abdul Al-Ghazali, a Yemeni immigrant. Al-Ghazali came in second in the mayoral primary for the 2009 elections, losing by only 123 votes to the incumbent Mayor Karen Majewski. Four of the twelve city council candidates who made the 2009 primaries were Muslims—three of Bengali origin (Kazi Miah, Mohammed Hassan, and Anam Ahmed Miah), and one from Bosnia (Arif Huskic). Miah and Hassan were elected on November 3 to join Ahmed, whose seat was not up for election in 2009.

Close to 1 percent of Detroit's population is Arab American, and there are currently no Arabs or Muslims in the city's government. Adam Shakoor has served as deputy mayor of Detroit and was the first Muslim African American judge in the state of Michigan. Out of 169 candidates running in Detroit's city council primaries in 2009, there were four Muslims—Abdullah El-Amin, T. Pharaoh Mohammad, Mohamed Okdie, and Raphael B. Johnson (a member of the Nation of Islam). The last two made it to the list of eighteen who ran for the nine council seats, but neither was elected. Okdie is of Arab heritage and is the vice chair of the Thirteenth Congressional District's Democratic Party. El-Amin, who is the assistant imam of the Muslim Center of Detroit and co-owner of a funeral home for Muslims, and Johnson are both African American Muslims.

Both Highland Park and Sterling Heights are close to 4 percent Arab or Muslim American, but neither has Arab Americans in elected office. Ameenah Omar, sister-in-law of Malcolm X and a member of the Nation of Islam, served as city councilwoman in Highland Park from 1995 to January 2009, when she resigned because of health problems. None of Warren's (whose population is at least 2.5 percent Arab American) twelve city council seats are currently held by Arab Americans. Richard Sulaka, an Arab American Christian of Lebanese descent, served as Warren city councilman for eight years

(1991–1999) and as city clerk for eight years (1999–2007). He unsuccessfully ran for mayor in 2007. None of Livonia's Arab Americans (comprising 2 percent of the population) have been elected to its city government.

The city of Wayne has few Arab Americans, but Abdul Al-Haidous, a Lebanese-born Shi'a Muslim, was elected mayor on November 26, 2001, soon after the attacks of 9/11, with 54 percent of the vote and has been re-elected four times since. He previously served as a Wayne city councilor between 1993 and 2001.

In Wayne County (2.7 percent Arab American), Arab and Muslim Americans are much better represented in appointed positions than in elected office. None of the county's twenty-one elected officials and sixty-nine elected judges is Arab American. However, there are high-ranking Arab and Muslim Americans in Robert Ficano's County Executive cabinet. Three of the seven appointed cabinet members are Arab Americans. Azzam Elder is deputy CEO, Nader Fakhouri serves as an assistant CEO, and Turkia Awada Mullin is both an assistant CEO and chief development officer for Wayne County.

Oakland County, which is at least 2.3 percent Arab American, has an elected Arab American sheriff but no other Arab or Muslim Americans among its twenty-five commissioners and other elected officers. Sheriff Michael Bouchard (in office since 1999) is a politically active Arab American of Christian background who also served in the Michigan State House of Representatives (1990–1991) and in the Michigan State Senate (1991–1999). His bid to become the Republican candidate for governor of Michigan in the 2010 elections was unsuccessful.

Macomb County, 2.2 percent Arab American, has one Arab American among its fifty-seven elected officials and fourteen judges. Ted Wahby was elected as treasurer of Macomb County in 1995 and has been serving in this position since then. Before that, he served as a councilman (1981–1983) and as mayor (1983–1995) in the city of St. Clair Shores.

At the state level, at least 1.2 percent of Michigan's population was Arab American in 2000. Currently, two Arab Americans serve in Michigan's House of Representatives out of 110 members—Rashida Tlaib and Justin Amash. Tlaib is a Muslim woman of Palestinian origin, and Amash is a Christian Arab. Tlaib is the first Muslim woman to serve in the Michigan state legislature, and only the second in the United States (after Jamilah Nasheed, an African American Democrat who got elected to the Missouri House of Representatives in November 2006). She represents the twelfth district, which is predominantly Hispanic (40 percent), 25 percent African American, 30 percent white and only 2 percent Arab American. Amash represents the seventy-second district, city of Kentwood and the townships of Caledonia, Cascade, and Gaines, all of which have very small Arab American populations. James H. Karoub (1961–1963 and 1965–1968) was the first known Arab American and Muslim Michigan State Representative, after serving as the police and fire commissioner in Highland Park from 1959 to 1964. Michael Bouchard served from 1990 to 1991. No Arab Americans currently serve in the elected thirty-eight-member Michigan State Senate, though Michael Bouchard served previously (1991–1999). Hansen Clarke, who is of Bangladeshi Muslim and African American heritage, also served as a state representative (1990–2002) and senator (2002–2009) from a district in Detroit before being elected to the U.S. House of Representatives in 2010.

In addition, there are several elected and appointed judges of Arab American origin or Muslim faith in Michigan.[6] Some are highly active in the Arab American community (e.g., David Allen), and a few are practicing Muslims (e.g., David Turfe and Charlene Mekled-Elder). Their appointment by the governor is generally viewed as a major accomplishment for Arab Americans because the process is elaborate and requires the acquiescence or support of a number of officials.

Table 2 lists all the Arab and Muslim candidates who ran for city government or whose seats were not contested in greater Detroit during the 2009 elections. The twenty candidates include twelve Arabs (eleven Lebanese and one Yemeni), three of whom are Christian and nine Muslim. The seventeen Muslims include eight of Lebanese descent, four Bengalis, three African Americans, one Yemeni and one Bosnian.

Of the twenty candidates, eight were elected or continued to serve in office. Five of the twelve Arabs, two of the three Christian Arabs, and six of the seventeen Muslims were elected. Only four out of the thirteen with Arab- or Muslim-sounding names were elected as opposed to four out of seven candidates with Anglicized names. Four of twelve U.S.-born candidates succeeded as opposed to four out of eight who were born out of the country.

Methodology

We conducted semistructured interviews with nineteen Arab, Chaldean, and Muslim Americans in metropolitan Detroit and in Lansing, Michigan's capital. We interviewed leaders of Arab and Muslim civic, business, religious, and advocacy organizations; Arab and Muslim elected officials and unsuccessful candidates; and Arab and Muslim appointees and party officials. We identified the Arab and Muslim elected and appointed officials through lists maintained by the Arab American Institute and media searches and verified this information during interviews. Out of nineteen interviewees, there were sixteen Arab, one Chaldean, and two African Americans. Thirteen of the in-

Table 2. Arab and Muslim American Candidates for City Government in the 2009 Elections in Greater Detroit (including positions that were not contested)

Candidate	Office	Ethnicity	Religion	Born in United States?	Elected?
Robert Abraham	Dearborn City Council	Lebanese	Christian	Yes	Yes
George Darany	Dearborn City Council	Syrian/ Lebanese	Christian	Yes	Yes
David Bazzy	Dearborn City Council	Lebanese	Christian	Yes	No
Suzanne Sareini	Dearborn City Council	Lebanese	Muslim	Yes	Yes
Khalil Dakhlallah	Dearborn City Council	Lebanese	Muslim	Yes	No
Rabih Hammoud	Dearborn City Council	Lebanese	Muslim	Yes	No
Ali Sayed	Dearborn City Council	Lebanese	Muslim	Yes	No
Hussein Sobh	Dearborn City Council	Lebanese	Muslim	No	No
Thomas Berry	Dearborn Heights City Council	Lebanese	Muslim	Yes	Yes
Kazi Miah	Hamtramck City Council	Bengali	Muslim	No	Yes
Mohammad Hassan	Hamtramck City Council	Bengali	Muslim	No	Yes
Anam Ahmed Miah	Hamtramck City Council	Bengali	Muslim	No	No
Arif Huskic	Hamtramck City Council	Bosnian	Muslim	No	No
Shahab Ahmed	Hamtramck City Council	Bengali	Muslim	No	Yes (not contested)
Abdul Al-Ghazali	Hamtramck Mayor	Yemeni	Muslim	No	No
Abdullah El-Amin	Detroit City Council	African American	Muslim	Yes	No
T. Pharoh Mohammad	Detroit City Council	African American	Muslim	Yes	No
Mohamed Okdie	Detroit City Council	Lebanese	Muslim	Yes	No
Raphael B. Johnson	Detroit City Council	African American	Muslim[a]	Yes	No
Abdul Al-Haidous	City of Wayne Mayor	Lebanese	Muslim	No	Yes

[a]Raphael B. Johnson is associated with the Nation of Islam.
Source: Compiled by authors.

terviewees were Muslims—six Sunni and seven Shi'a. The remaining six interviewees were Christian. We obtained demographic data from the 2000 U.S. census and compared it with estimates from the Arab American Institute and the Immigration Policy Center.

Explaining Patterns of Arab American and Muslim American Representation

We test nine hypotheses to explain patterns of Arab American and Muslim American representation in greater Detroit by considering relevant quantitative and qualitative evidence.

Arab and Muslim Culture in the Area Discourages Civic and Political Participation

Yvonne Haddad (2001) has argued that most Arab and Muslim Americans had little interest in political participation before community organizations emerged in the 1980s for Arabs and the 1990s for Muslims. A few of our interviewees agreed that residual resistance to participation in the American electoral process continued until recently and that as recently as ten years ago a few local religious leaders argued that participation was in fact *haram* (prohibited in Islamic law). Yet other religious leaders were active themselves in politics and encouraged the political participation of their congregants (Howell 2009). Any resistance to political engagement has petered out since then, and the overwhelming majority of religious and community leaders fully support Muslim engagement and candidates today. Every community leader we interviewed was either actively engaged in politics or supportive of political participation. No interviewee thought that there is meaningful resistance to political participation in Arab and Muslim American communities today.

The vibrant civic and political culture of the Arab community in greater Detroit is reflected in the number and level of activity of its organizations. Politically active Arab American organizations include the Arab American Political Action Committee (AAPAC) and the Yemeni American Political Action Committee (YAPAC). Others, like the American-Arab Anti-Discrimination Committee (ADC), the Council on American-Islamic Relations (CAIR), the Arab Community Center for Economic and Social Services (ACCESS), and the American Arab Chamber of Commerce, do not work directly on increasing Arab American political representation but are very active in empowering the Arab American community in general and have strong connections with elected and appointed politicians.

And many Arab Americans in the area participate in these organizations' activities. Howell and Jamal (2008) mention that 39 percent of respondents in the 2003 Detroit Arab American Study reported being involved in an Arab ethnic association such as ADC, the Yemeni Benevolent Association, or the Chaldean Federation. The Detroit Arab American Study (DAAS) (Baker et al. 2004, 32) finds that:

> A large majority of Arabs and Chaldeans believe that their local organizations are effective. Over 70 percent say that their business and professional organizations, civil liberties and anti-discrimination groups, and local Arab media are very or somewhat effective. Arab and Chaldean social service agencies top this list, with 40 percent saying that they are very effective, and another 45 percent saying they are somewhat effective.

The political engagement of Arab and Muslim Americans in the Detroit area is part of a nationwide trend. Ayers and Hofstetter (2008) analyzed the nationwide 2004 Muslim Americans in the Public Square (MAPS) survey of Muslim American attitudes, for example, and found that American Muslims have a very high rate of political participation compared with other Americans. They also report that political resources and awareness, particularly post-9/11 anxiety, were all positively related to participation. Gimpel, Cho, and Wu (2007) examined Arab American voter registration in the months following September 11, 2001, and also found that "9/11 has acted as an accelerant to Arab American political incorporation." And Jen'nan Read (2007) dispels gender-centered notions of cultural inhibition in her analysis of the MAPS datasets. She argues that Arab Muslim women and men both have high levels of political engagement, with men slightly more involved than women because of their greater participation in religious activities and higher levels of religiosity. She also finds that subjective dimensions of religiosity have no effect on political engagement.

Still, there appear to be issues. Ramzi Dalloo, president of the Democratic Chaldean Caucus, told us that Chaldeans are politically inactive in spite of their socioeconomic success in America because they have been conditioned to be passive as a persecuted group in their country of emigration, Iraq. Still, Dalloo, and the few active Chaldeans in the caucus, do lobby the federal government to help fellow Chaldeans and other Christians in Iraq (see Hanoosh, "Fighting Our Own Battles," this volume).

Arab and Muslim Americans Are So Poorly
Organized That They Cannot Effectively Support
Candidates from the Community

Again, the high density of Arab and Muslim American organizations implies that this is not the case. Of these organizations, AAPAC is the most influential in shaping the Arab vote in the area. It endorses candidates through campaigning, mailers, volunteering, and fund-raising. It also conducts large voter registration drives. Many Arabs vote the AAPAC list on Election Day. Although AAPAC's endorsement process is cumbersome, many candidates seek it in the hope of getting the Arab American vote. AAPAC has managed to become influential in spite of divisions within the Arab American community. Government officials at all levels and community leaders use AAPAC as an interlocutor for the Arab American community. AAPAC leaders feel that the organization's ability to muster support among Arab Americans in the area and to be recognized by others as representing Arab American preferences has helped the Arab American community to be seen as an active and influential minority group in electoral politics, and has led candidates to take the Arab vote, and Arab issues, more seriously.[7] Several candidates we interviewed confirmed the importance of AAPAC's and YAPAC's endorsement.[8]

In addition to ad hoc civic and political organizations, the Arab American community in metropolitan Detroit benefits from the high concentration of mosques and churches. As Jamal (2005) argues, the mosque "takes on the multifaceted role of mobilization vehicle and school of civic participation" and promotes group consciousness among Arab and black Muslims. Ethnic churches have played a similar role historically. The DAAS survey (Baker et al. 2004) finds that 93 percent of Christians say churches are very effective or somewhat effective in meeting community needs and that 84 percent of Muslims agree that mosques meet the same standard. And Judge David Turfe explained how mosques encourage political engagement: "The churches [and mosques], in all the functions that they have, in *'ashura* [a Shi'a commemoration] programs, Ramadan programs, they have tables to register people to vote and even imams are telling people to get out and vote."[9] Arab and Muslim Americans in metro Detroit have a high organizational density, the kind that galvanizes mobilization and interest in political involvement. Although these organizations and their leaders do not always agree on whom to endorse, this does not necessarily explain underrepresentation in elected office. In fact, competition may increase the supply of candidates and their effectiveness.

*Few Arab and Muslim Americans Are Willing or Able
to Compete for Elected Office Because They Suffer
from Poor Integration (Low Familiarity with and
Ability to Function in American Political Institutions)*

This hypothesis is not particularly convincing either. Arabs, Chaldeans, and Muslims do as well as, or better than, other Americans on metrics of socioeconomic integration. In contrast to African American Muslims, the immigrant segment among Arab American Muslims has higher levels of educational attainment and income than the general public.[10] Arab Americans of all religious backgrounds are even more ahead of the American public in education and income, according to data compiled by the Arab American Institute (AAI) based on a survey by the U.S. Census Bureau: "Arab Americans with at least a high school diploma number 85 percent. More than four out of ten Americans of Arab descent have a bachelor's degree or higher, compared to 24% of Americans at large. Seventeen percent of Arab Americans have a post-graduate degree, which is nearly twice the American average (9%)."[11]

Numbers seem comparable in metropolitan Detroit. Data from the DAAS (Baker et al. 2004) suggest that U.S.-born Arabs tend to be wealthier and more educated than the Detroit public, whereas immigrant Arabs tend to be, as one would expect from a population in transition, both less wealthy and less educated. The DAAS researchers also find that Arabs and Chaldeans in Detroit ranked quite high in 2003 on several measures of political integration: 79 percent were U.S. citizens, 80 percent spoke English well or very well, 86 percent said they feel at home in the United States, and 91 percent said they are proud to be American. The study also finds rates of political expression that are comparable with the Detroit public among Arab and Chaldeans who were born in the United States, but less involvement among immigrants, as one would expect.

Arab Americans in Dearborn have also considerably improved their registration rates from 8,800 registered voters out of 60,000 in 1998 to some 17,000 out of 54,000 today, according to AAPAC sources. However, evidence is mixed about turnout rates. AAPAC officers told us that very rarely do more than 30 percent of those registered vote, with the exception of the 2008 election when some two-thirds of Arab American registered voters exercised their right and overwhelmingly supported Barack Obama, in spite of the Obama campaign's slight of removing a Muslim woman wearing a scarf from camera range in a campaign rally in Detroit.[12] But the DAAS survey (Baker et al. 2004, 33) finds that 51 percent of Arab and Chaldean Americans in the region voted in the 2000 election, which is exactly the percentage for the national voting age population for this election.

In addition, Muslim and Arab Americans have been galvanized to become more active after the transgressions on civil rights and liberties that followed the attacks of 9/11. As Bakalian and Bozorgmehr (2009) argue, Muslim American community leaders felt the necessity to participate in American society and political life after 9/11. Many Muslim American organizations started teaching their members and communities the basics of political engagement. And the 9/11 attacks have provided unexpected opportunities for Arab and Muslim American community leaders in terms of political empowerment because they are taken much more seriously by U.S. officials, law enforcement, and other community actors. This combination of internal motivation and external validation produced substantial mobilization among Muslim and Arab Americans around common interests.

Just as important, political candidates in Michigan recognize the importance of Arab and Muslim voters, particularly in tight races, and Arab and Muslim community leaders know this. They now realize their clout in local, state, and national elections, including the 2000 presidential election when Michigan was closely contested (Bakalian and Bozorgmehr 2009, 241–242). This feedback loop is likely to continue to motivate Michigan's Arabs and Muslims to mobilize effectively.

Yet, some of the Chaldean and Arab Americans we interviewed felt that their communities are less integrated than they should be. ADC's Imad Hamad believes that the biggest hurdle facing Arab American candidates is the community's inability to raise enough funds to support them.[13] He believes that there are not enough affluent Arab Americans who are willing to run for office or to financially support those who do and that fund-raising by Arab American organizations is still inadequate. Osama Siblani, publisher of the *Arab American News* and current president of AAPAC, argues that many Arab Americans are isolated and continue to cling to habits and attitudes from their countries of origin. Newcomers, he argues, suffer from poor fluency in English, do not have citizenship, and are too focused on bare survival to be involved politically.[14] And Ramzi Dalloo said that younger Chaldeans who enjoy comfortable lives because of their parents' hard work have little incentive to pay attention to politics.[15]

So what explains the divergence between the quantitative evidence and some of our knowledgeable interviewees' perceptions? It could be that our interviewees, who are motivated community activists, have high expectations that their communities have yet to meet and were expressing their views about why members of their communities have not met the threshold of their own aspirations instead of comparing them with other communities. Another possibility is that the complex Chaldean, Arab, and Muslim communities are polarized between those who can be galvanized to act (wealthy, U.S. born, educated) and those who are not empowered to act even if motivated to do so (poor, foreign born and uneducated). As Cho, Gimpel, and Wu (2006) tell us:

> Arab American participation patterns suggest that the effects of socioeconomic status are mediated by socialization experiences and policy threat. If

the political learning process includes the apprehension of worrisome government policy actions, it may provide the motivation for participation from those who have the ability to participate, but heretofore have chosen not to do so.

In other words, those who don't think that members of their community are politically active enough probably interact with the segments of these very diverse communities that are indeed less active than they would hope for these or other reasons. Such diversity exists within many communities and does not explain underrepresentation in elected office.

And the best evidence that Muslim and Arab Americans are not particularly poorly integrated on the whole is that, in spite of their underrepresentation in elected office, they are fairly well represented in appointed positions that require involved contacts and sophistication in interacting with government institutions. The answer to Arab and Muslim underrepresentation in elected office is to be found elsewhere.

The Fragmentation of the Middle Eastern and
Muslim Community along Ethnic, Religious, and
Sectarian Lines Makes It Difficult for an Arab
or Muslim American Candidate to Receive
Support from It

Evidence is mixed for this hypothesis. There is no doubt that Arab and Muslim Americans are quite diverse and that members of each group have subidentities that sometimes become political fault lines that hinder cooperation and generate conflict. Among immigrants from Arab countries, potential differences exist between Arabs and non-Arabs such as Chaldeans and Kurds, countries of origin,[16] Christians and Muslims, Christians of different denominations, Sunni and Shi'a Arab Muslims, those who are secular and religious within each religious tradition, regionalism and tribalism within countries of origins, and families (Haddad 2009).[17] Among Muslim Americans, potentially politicized differences include those between Sunnis and Shi'a, different ethnicities and regions of origin, immigrant versus African American identity, and degrees of religiosity. But every immigrant, ethnic, and religious population has many such potential fault lines and whether they are used politically depends in large part on leaders' choices, outside pressures, and organizational development.

These differences could also become salient in one context and irrelevant in another. For example, meetings among Muslim activists and leaders regarding priorities often produce a substantial divide between African Americans,

who are more interested in inner-city development and reintegration programs, and "immigrant" Muslims, who have a greater interest in foreign
policy matters. But these differences were meaningless when Keith Ellison,
an African American Muslim, was campaigning for a congressional seat in
2006. American Muslims of Middle Eastern and South Asian origins provided a third of Ellison's campaign budget, helping him become the first
Muslim congressman (Sinno 2009). This cross-ethnic support exists in Detroit as well. For example, Judge Adam Shakoor, who is an African American Muslim, told us that he receives very strong support from Muslims of
South Asian, East Asian, and Arab ancestries.

We encountered some aspects of politicized differences.[18] Chaldeans
seemed sensitive about their heritage and still harbored feelings of victimization at the hands of Arabs, and were therefore reluctant to be grouped
with Arab Americans. Dawud Walid, Executive Director of CAIR-Michigan,
an African American convert, emphasized the need to distinguish the African American Muslim community from the rest of the American Muslims
of Michigan because they have been established much longer and were
active in political life long before immigrant Muslims. He illustrated his
point by saying that African American Muslims settled the question of
whether political participation is *haram* well before immigrant Muslims did.
He adds:

> There is some overlap, but there really are different issues. Palestine, for in-
> stance . . . all Muslims sympathize with Palestine, but non-Arab Muslims do
> not feel that Palestine is the number one issue or "the" issue that we as Mus-
> lims unite on, and everything else is secondary. This is the mentality of a lot
> of people, Arab Americans, in Dearborn. They do not care about Darfur, or
> what is going on in Kashmir, Muslims in the Democratic Republic of Congo
> or Burma. They only care about what is going on in Palestine or somewhere
> else in that region. So there is some tension or hostility in the Muslim com-
> munity.[19]

Walid also suggested that there are tensions among Arab and Muslim community leaders, some of whom resent that CAIR attracted more religious
Arab Muslims. In a similar vein, Abed Hammoud mentioned that prominent leaders of the community were against AAPAC and worked to undermine it.

Other interviewees suggested that intragroup fragmentation is an issue,
though not necessarily a cause of underrepresentation. Most said that the
Arab American community acts in cohesion but when probed further, mentioned that the religious, sectarian, and ethnic divisions are a serious problem.

Some (e.g., Imad Hamad) said that the divisions are no more problematic than in other communities but are exaggerated because of the intense focus on Arabs and Muslims.[20] James Allen, a former chairman of the Arab American Chamber of Commerce who comes from a politically active family, went further, arguing that the Arab American community is more united than many other minorities. He illustrated his point by referring to the Palestine issue and the march in Dearborn to protest the Israeli bombings of Lebanon, issues on which Muslim and Christian Arabs in the area act together. In addition, several interviewees mentioned ongoing cooperation among different community organizations, such as ADC and AAPAC.

Johnson (1991) once argued that "it is highly likely that the large congregational splits typifying Christian groups in America will become the rule for Islam in America, with each group politically lobbying for its own concerns." And Suleiman (2006) reports that many have argued that Arab American political participation is poor because of a lack of national group solidarity, weak communal solidarity, and an overemphasis on family, religious sect, and individualism. There are some signs of this, but a more powerful countertrend to Muslim fragmentation has surfaced—the development of a Muslim American macro-ethnicity (Sinno 2009). What is at work here is a process of generational change. As Khan (2000) argues, identity issues that prevent American Muslims (particularly immigrants) from collaborating across sectarian lines are less of a problem for U.S.-born Muslims because they did not grow up being affected by the identity politics of their countries of origin.

Arab and Muslim Organizations Are Not Motivated
to Support Candidates from Their Communities
Because They Feel Well Represented by Elected
Officials Who Are Not Arab or Muslim

Arab and Muslim community leaders today feel that it is less urgent or necessary to support officials from within their ranks because some elected officials who are not of Arab background assist the Arab American community and address its concerns. Osama Siblani, for example, said that Dearborn's Mayor John (Jack) O'Reilly supports the community and that the city's Arabs therefore do not necessarily need an Arab American mayor "with the name Ali or Muhammad." He would rather have a non-Arab in office who is sympathetic to the Arab community than a poorly qualified Arab official.[21] Mayor O'Reilly has strategically appointed an Arab American, Joe Beydoun, to serve as the Mayor's Citizens' Liaison. Likewise, Imad Hamad from ADC said that his organization would not support candidates just because they happen to be Arab, unless they are well qualified.[22] Ismael Ahmed and others explained that Wayne County Executive Robert Ficano, who is of Italian descent, has had very good relations with the Arab community for more than twenty years.[23] He has appointed three Arab Americans to his Wayne County cabinet (Azzam Elder, deputy CEO; Nader Fakhouri, assistant CEO; and Turkia Awada Mullin, assistant CEO and chief development officer of Economic Development Growth Engine). Dawud Walid confirmed that as the director of CAIR, he meets with local politicians when issues of concern come up, but not necessarily with Arab or Muslim ones.

James Allen explained the representation of the community in Wayne County government:

> Wayne County has a tradition of being very influenced by the high population of Arab Americans and that goes back to the 1950s when Michael Berry was the head of the Democratic congressional district here. . . . It was Mike Berry who blazed the trail for Arab Americans to enter to all of these offices. He made it easy for the mainstream to look at us as part of the mainstream. He also appointed a lot of people to positions who helped people, brought them into civil service.[24]

Another supportive elected official is Governor Jennifer Granholm. She appointed Lebanese American James Stokes, former deputy director of the Governor's Office for Southeast Michigan, as the state director of Appointments, and Arab and Muslim American Ismael Ahmed, a co-chair of the state's Democratic Party and a co-founder of ACCESS, as director of Human Services, overseeing the department with the second-largest budget in state government.

There even seems to be an implicit pact between Arab American organizations and non-Arab politicians—the politicians effectively advocate on behalf of the community in return for support—which inevitably weakens the prospects of Arab American candidates. The *Arab American News* and AAPAC endorse non-Arab candidates who have a proven or promised commitment to the issues of interest to the Arab American community, which shifts attention from Arab and Muslim American candidates or even discourages them from running in the first place.

Government funding for the Arab Community Center for Economic and Social Services and the establishment of the program Building Respect in Diverse Groups to Enhance Sensitivity (BRIDGES) are two examples of the benefits to the community that such a pact produces. With its $18 million annual budget, ACCESS is the most powerful Arab American organization in the area because it benefits from substantial funding, most of it from the state of Michigan and other government sources. ACCESS focuses mostly on economic and social development, immigrant support, and outreach for Arab and Muslim Americans in the area.[25] ACCESS also provides active support to organizations that engage in lobbying and organizing voter registration drives. The Arab American and Chaldean Council plays a similar role for its own constituency.

Following 9/11, BRIDGES was established as a forum to facilitate sustained dialogue between government agencies and the community. The forum attempts to smooth tensions and address grievances, particularly over legal and law enforcement practices that transgress the civil rights and liberties of Muslim and Arab Americans and create resentment (see Howell, "Muslims as Moving Targets," this volume).

Community Leaders View Elected Officials as Rivals
and Therefore Discourage Community Support for
Such Candidates

Cooperation between community leaders and elected officials who are not from the community, however, does not seem to reflect a rivalry among Arab and Muslim organization leaders, candidates, and elected officials from these communities. Candidates and elected officials we interviewed mentioned that Arab and Muslim community leaders actively support them. Osama Siblani of AAPAC told us that he is mentoring promising Arab youths to become successful politicians. Suzanne Sareini said she has helped out young Arab hopefuls and taught them all she knew about the art of politics and getting elected. Ali Sayed, a young Muslim American candidate of Lebanese heritage who ran unsuccessfully for the Dearborn council in 2009, said he received "full backing" from Arab American leaders and that he consults with Rashida Tlaib, David Turfe, and Abdul Al-Haidous, a relative, who give him advice.[26] And different organizational leaders and Arab and Muslim elected officials mentioned that they consult with each other. Arab and Muslim organizations also facilitate communication among community-oriented candidates and elected officials by inviting them to the same activities and events. Also, most Arab and Muslim American candidates reported strong support from the community and its organizations.

But there were some exceptions, even if they belong to the past. Suzanne Sareini, who was elected to the Dearborn city council in 1990 on her second attempt, said that community organizations did not support her when she first ran in the 1980s, mostly because she was a woman.[27] Abed Hammoud stated that the Arab American leadership is made up of what he called "the old establishment." He explained that he worked hard to build up AAPAC in spite of attempts by established community organizations to undermine him during the early years.[28]

Arab and Muslim Americans Suffer from Hurdles and Discrimination within the Democratic and Republican Parties

Barreto and Bozonelos (2009) argue that both major parties have done little to no outreach to Muslim Americans, and have instead regularly alienated Muslims. Thus, more religious Muslims might choose "none of the above" with respect to partisanship in America. That is quite correct on the national level, where Arab and Muslim Americans are diffuse and small minorities that are marginalized by core constituencies of both parties—pro-Israel liberals within the Democratic Party and evangelicals and conservatives in the Republican Party. The situation is a little different in metro Detroit, with its high concentration of Arabs and Muslims. The chokepoint of Arab and Muslim representation is not at the level of the parties, at least not the Democratic Party.

Some party officials may still be affected by a strong tradition of racism or hostility toward non-whites (see below), but such attitudes are definitely on the decline. The current president pro tem of the Dearborn council is Nancy Hubbard, daughter of the late Orville Hubbard, a Dearborn mayor who ran segregationist campaigns and nurtured a culture of ethnic hatred. Even though she attended a recent Arab Student Union event at the University of Michigan–Dearborn, her disconnect with the community was apparent because of her lack of knowledge about the issues of concern to Arab Americans. She referred to the community as "Arabic people," drawing laughter from the audience. The president of the Arab Student Union, Rashid Beydoun, mentioned that many non-Arab candidates decline the organization's invitations to attend their events.

Some of our interviewees have voiced their desire to see the two parties doing more to recruit talented Arab Americans. And Ramzi Dalloo lamented that, even though Chaldeans are very supportive of the Republican Party because many in the community have small businesses and a strong anti-abortion stance, the party still does not recruit from among them or co-opt them into its institutions.

And yet, almost all interviewees said that the parties encourage and support Arab American candidates at the local and state level. As early as 2000, there were twenty-eight Arab American delegates to the National Democratic Convention and four to the National Republican Convention (Nimer 2004). And Arab Americans are well represented within Democratic institutions. According to AAI figures, there are fifty precinct delegates in the

Michigan Democratic Party.[29] They are primarily concentrated in the Fourteenth and Fifteenth Congressional Districts, with high percentages of Arab American residents. More important, the Michigan Democratic Party has high-ranking Arab American officials, including one of its three vice chairs (Ismael Ahmed) and several members of the Central and Executive committees.[30] The Democratic Party also has an Arab caucus, but the Republican Party does not. Most activists we interviewed report that the Democratic Party reaches out to them more than the Republican Party does.[31]

Arab and Muslim Americans are not particularly penalized by not being well represented in the Republican Party because Wayne County is overwhelmingly Democratic (69 percent voted Democratic in the 2000 and 2004 presidential elections and 74 percent in the 2008 presidential elections). Voters in Macomb and Oakland counties are more evenly split. And Arab and Muslim Americans today strongly lean to the Democrats anyway. According to 2008 Zogby polls, more than twice as many Arab Americans identify as Democrat than as Republican.[32] And three surveys of Muslim Americans from 2007 and 2008 found 48 to 63 percent identifying as Democrat as opposed to just 7 to 11 percent identifying as Republican (Barreto and Bozonelos 2009). Also, campaigns for city government are not partisan in greater Detroit.

And the best evidence that the chokepoint of Arab and Muslim representation is not at the party level, at least not among Democrats and for local government, is that the number of candidates from these groups is substantial. The problem is that not enough of them get elected.

The two remaining hypotheses, in combination, provide a much more powerful explanation of Arab and Muslim underrepresentation in elected office.

The Electoral System Disadvantages Minority
Candidates, including Arab and Muslim Americans

On the one hand, the electoral system for local government in Michigan disadvantages minority candidates, particularly Arab and Muslim Americans, who are subject to bias from others. Local elections in the cities of Dearborn Heights, Dearborn, Hamtramck, Detroit, Highland Park, Sterling Heights, Warren, Livonia, and Wayne are held every four years, with the entire city comprising a single district (at-large elections). Each city holds primary elections two to three months prior to the November general elections. Although Arab Americans in Dearborn number between 30 and 40 percent of the population, the number of registered Arab Americans who turn out to vote is not enough to elect Arab American candidates without support from non-Arab voters. Ethnic hostility (see below) therefore makes it difficult for Arab candidates to get elected. Dividing the cities into multiple single-member districts would have made it relatively easier for Arab and Muslim Americans to get elected from districts where their communities are heavily concentrated.

On the other hand, Arab American voters can effectively keep a non-Arab candidate they boycott from getting elected. They are key swing voters in local elections, at least in Dearborn. As Suzanne Sareini told us, she needs the Arab vote on top of a substantial portion of the white vote to get elected. And Robert Abraham and George Darany, who are of Arab ancestry but have weak ties to the communities, appeal to Arab Americans around election time because of the same calculus. Osama Siblani also confirmed that a successful candidate in Dearborn must appeal to the Arab community.[33]

Unlike city elections, elections in the three counties with considerable Arab American populations (Wayne, Macomb, and Oakland) are held within districts.[34] Based on our argument, we would expect to find higher proportions of Arabs and Muslims elected to county government than to city government, but this is not the case. There are no Arab American elected officials in Wayne County, one out of fifty-seven in Macomb County, and another one out of thirty-one in Oakland County (see Table 1). This paltry level of representation does not necessarily weaken our argument because, as many of our interviewees indicated, Arab and Muslim politicians appear to have little interest in county government. Ismael Ahmed also explained that those who run for a county commission seat normally do so as part of a long-term political career and that most Arab and Muslim candidates do not engage in such patient and sophisticated planning.[35]

Bias by Non-Arab/Muslim Voters Reduces the Chance of an Arab or Muslim Candidate to Get Elected

Without bias, demographic distribution and electoral systems would not affect the odds of a minority candidate's getting elected if we assume that the supply of candidates from this minority is comparable with the supply from other groups. For Arab and Muslim American candidates, these factors combine to undermine their election prospects. And most of the exceptions confirm the rule.

Most of the candidates and elected officials we interviewed cited voter prejudice as a challenge. The only exceptions are Justin Amash, a first-term Michigan House Representative who is a third-generation American of Christian Arab heritage, and Abdul Al-Haidous, mayor of the city of Wayne. Amash is a young politician. He regularly attends an Arab American church, but is difficult to identify as an Arab from his looks, behavior, or speech. He is elected from a district that does not have many Arab Americans, and he is not vocal and active on Arab American issues.

Abdul Al-Haidous is the mayor of the city of Wayne, a well-off city with hardly any Arab Americans. Higher income and education are normally negatively correlated with ethnic and religious bias. Al-Haidous was very active and widely recognized in the wider community prior to election, including as a Wayne city councilor between 1993 and 2001. He was elected mayor soon after 9/11 with a strong majority. He is open about his identity, but it rarely comes up as a political issue because too few Arab or Muslim Americans live in the city of Wayne to raise issues or make claims. He is also not involved with Arab and Muslim organizations—most Muslim and Arab American activists we talked to haven't heard of Mayor Al-Haidous and were surprised to learn that there is an Arab Muslim mayor in the region. Mayor Al-Haidous explains why ethnicity and religion did not affect his electoral prospects by referring to his long history of serving the community on committees and the city council before running for mayor. Once the people of the small township (population of 19,050 in 2000) became used to him and trusted him over his many years of service, his identity mattered little.

Three factors interact to increase bias against Arab and Muslim American candidates: the effect of 9/11 and ongoing conflicts in the Muslim world, a legacy of ethnic hostility, and the use of smear campaigns by opponents of Arab and Muslim candidates to undermine them. The effect of ongoing conflicts and media coverage, particularly religious and conservative media, on attitudes toward Arab and Muslim Americans has been well documented (e.g., Nisbet, Ostman, and Shanahan 2009). Data from the DAAS suggests that they affect attitudes toward Arabs and Muslims in the Detroit area in similar ways (Jamal 2009).

Dearborn politicians have traditionally resorted to crude ethnic attacks and to elevating ethnic fears. One prominent example is Orville Hubbard, who served as the mayor of Dearborn for thirty-six years (1942–1978). He was known as an outspoken segregationist who consistently used the campaign slogan "Keep Dearborn Clean," which was widely understood to mean keeping it white. Although Hubbard's distaste was mostly focused on blacks, he disparaged within his influential circle many minorities, including Arabs (Good 1989). His successor, Michael Guido (Dearborn mayor, 1986–2006), used a similar approach toward minorities until late in his political career.

This tradition of leveraging and aggravating ethnic and religious hostility for electoral purposes continues today. Most Arab and Muslim American candidates have faced harsh smear campaigns directed at their ethnic and religious background. Following the election of Ahmed and Al-Ghazali to Hamtramck's city council in 2003, for example, an online media campaign claimed that the city council has been "hijacked by Muslims." Such charges continued when in April 2004, with a unanimous vote by the city council, Hamtramck amended the city noise ordinance to allow the broadcast of the Islamic call to prayer from mosques. Many of the online attacks were directed by aggressively anti-Muslim activists who do not live in Hamtramck, such as David Horowitz, Robert Spencer, and Debbie Schlussel, who focuses much of her energy on lamenting the growth of the Muslim population in the area and attacking its leaders and institutions by using innuendo and other dubious methods.[36]

Opponents of Rashida Tlaib told voters "if you cannot pronounce her name, you should not vote for her."[37] David Turfe unsuccessfully ran for a seat on the Dearborn Heights council twice, in November 2001 and 2005 after serving for one year as an appointed councilor. Supporters of his opponents called voters and said, "How would you like it if you had a Muslim on your city council?"[38] Turfe, however, was elected to serve as the Twentieth District Court Judge on November 2006. James Allen provided other examples of smear campaigns against Arab and Chaldean American candidates, including Richard Sulaka, the Chaldean city clerk who ran in 2007 against the then city council president James R. Fouts for the post of mayor of Warren:

> Jim Fouts employed a Lebanese American political consultant who very publicly said that his job was to make Richard Sulaka the first cousin of Osama Bin Laden and Saddam Hussein. It was a whisper campaign waged against Richard, who is a very good man. And in the end, Fouts won out because he was able to convince people that Richard was not going to be a mayor for all of Warren but just for its Arab population. [In the] Dearborn Heights city council race in 2001, a couple of Arab American candidates, David Turfe and Jumana Judeh, both lost in very close races. Whether the [opposing] candidates themselves were involved in the whisper campaigns or not, there was little doubt in my mind after that race that those people's elections were affected by their ethnic background. . . . A lot of people are turned off by that, quite frankly, and it is difficult to get people to stand up and run because they know that smear is going to happen.[39]

With few exceptions, those who are spared the attacks tend to be highly assimilated Christian Arab Americans who are not recognized by voters, and probably not by opponents, as being Arab. Those who seem Arab even if they are not (e.g., the Chaldean Richard Sulaka) or have a Muslim-sounding name even if they are not Muslim could be just as vulnerable as Muslim candidates because of political expediency. Conversely, it helps an Arab or a Muslim candidate not to be easily recognizable as such.

All three Arab American councilors in Dearborn, for example, have names that do not appear Arab or Muslim (Robert Abraham, George Darany, and Suzanne Sareini). Abraham and Darany are third-generation Arab American Christians who are not active in Arab American organizations and do not attend predominantly Arab American churches. The only Muslim to be elected to Dearborn's council as of today is Sareini, who owns a bar, is U.S.-born, is extremely outgoing, and does not convey in her demeanor that she is of Lebanese Arab and Shi'a Muslim background. Several people we spoke to told us they thought she was of Italian ancestry or Christian Arab, even though Sareini does not try to hide her ethnic and religious background, is proud of it, and actively helps the Arab American community. To our surprise, even a Muslim staffer at the Dearborn council did not know that Darany and Abraham were Arab Americans and that Sareini was Muslim. As Ismael Ahmed told us based on his long experience to explain the success of the three Arab Americans in Dearborn, "there is still too much division between whites and Arabs . . . the more they blend, the more likely they would get elected."

Muslims, whether Arabs or not, are considerably less well represented in elected office than Christian Arabs with English-sounding names. Four of the nine Arabs who serve in the elected bodies we are considering are Muslim, but only two have easily distinguishable Muslim names (Abdul Al-Haidous and Rashida Tlaib). Three additional Muslims, Bengali Americans, serve in Hamtramck where a high concentration of Muslims in the electorate has made such a shift in electoral fortunes possible—perhaps half of Hamtramck's population is Muslim today (mostly Bengalis, Bosnians, Albanians, and African Americans), and the small township and surrounding neighborhoods are home to ten mosques.

The Arab and Muslim penalty does not afflict highly assimilated Christian Arabs like George Darany, Robert Abraham, and Justin Amash—they do not need to address Arab or Muslim issues, they are accepted more easily by the non-Arab majority, they are not subject to attacks based on their ethnicity or religion, and they do not necessarily work on issues of concern to the Arab American community once elected. From an electoral perspective, they are white.[40] Even if Arab and Muslim candidates' perception of the attacks they faced are exaggerated, wide acceptance within these communities that their candidates face smear campaigns deters Arab and Muslim Americans who are considering becoming politicians from doing so.

Many therefore attempt instead to serve their communities through appointed positions or social activism.[41] Some even see a common thread linking all the smear campaigns and ascribe them to interest groups who are trying to undermine Arab and Muslim Americans because of Zionist, evangelical, or ultra-conservative beliefs.[42]

Multiple minority identities can mitigate the penalty for being a Muslim. One case in point is Adam Shakoor, a 62-year-old African American attorney who once was the deputy mayor of Detroit and chief judge. Judge Shakoor believes that Muslims are underrepresented because qualified Muslims avoid politics.[43] He also faults Muslim candidates for not appealing to voters from other communities. He does not believe that voters in Detroit would discriminate against a capable Muslim candidate.

Shakoor is widely known to be Muslim. He became a Muslim in college and participates in the activities of W. D. Muhammad's mainstream Sunni institutions. In the late 1970s, he successfully brought a case against the city of Detroit to allow the Islamic call to prayer in the city and another against the Michigan correctional system to provide *halal* food, Muslim chaplains, and Friday prayer facilities to Muslim inmates. He has good relations with Muslims from all ethnicities and is active in Muslim causes. This would be an electorally fatal personal history in most districts, but Detroit is about 82 percent black, and being black mitigates being Muslim within this population. Indeed, Judge Shakoor mentioned a long list of African American churches that supported him in his election campaigns.

The Future of Arab and Muslim Representation in Metro Detroit

To sum up, we find that three factors, two of which come together in a potent combination, jointly explain Arab and Muslim American underrepresentation in elected office. The first is the effective representation of Arab and Muslim American interests by elected officials who are not from these communities. In addition, and more important, we found that the combination of single-district city elections, Muslim and Arab demographic minority status, and hostile and wary attitudes by non-Arab and non-Muslim voters make it very difficult for candidates from these communities to get elected. It is also possible that divisions within Arab and Muslim communities hinder the electability of officials from within their ranks.

Most of our interviewees were very optimistic about the future of Arab American representation. Imad Hamad, Abdul Al-Haidous, and Osama Siblani, for example, were confident that the Arab American community will have a much greater presence and impact on politics in the near future. A minority was not sure that the transition to more representation is coming soon. Based on our findings, we believe that several processes will be at work simultaneously in coming years to shape the future of Arab and Muslim representation.

.: hm... .

Continuing Christian Arab Assimilation Will Lead to Increased Representation from This Population

We expect rates of representation of Christian Arabs to increase over time as continuing assimilation makes them indistinguishable from non-Arab whites for electoral purposes. Ajrouch and Jamal (2007) find that Christian Arabs are more likely than Muslim Arabs to identify as white and this trend is likely to continue. There will likely be more elected officials like Councilors Abraham and Darany and Sheriff Bouchard, or even former Senator Spencer Abraham, with hardly any links to Arab American communities, organizations, or causes, and some like Representative Amash with ties to their Arab American ancestry that are mostly limited to their Arab American church and family.

The Development of a Muslim Macro-ethnicity Will Improve the Ability of Muslims of All Ethnicities to Be Elected

A Muslim American identity that makes ethnic, sectarian, and other subidentities less important will probably continue to develop. Although some secular Arab Muslims may choose to assimilate into "white" culture and others may identify more as Arabs than Muslims, the majority will probably develop a greater sense of community with other Muslims because of the integrative role of mosques, Islamic schools, and outside pressures on Muslims. This may create a greater sense of difference between Muslim and Christian Arabs. The Muslim American community may gain in clout, influence, and representation over time as it expands demographically, develops its organizations further, and a new generation of American Muslims asserts itself and replaces older leaders for whom subidentities are important.

One example of the younger group of political activists is 34-year-old Representative Rashida Tlaib, a second-generation Palestinian American who is open and proud about being Muslim but refuses to be identified as Sunni or Shi'a. She worked with ACCESS for several years as a community activist. She received extensive support for her campaign across the board from Arab (particularly from those sharing her Palestinian heritage) and Muslim communities of many ethnicities. Her district is mostly Latino and black—only 2 percent are Arab (primarily Yemeni), but she won the Democratic primaries against seven Latino and African American opponents with 44 percent of the vote and the general election with 90 percent of the vote. In addition to serving her district, she advocates for Arab and Muslim American issues such as having an Arab American heritage day in Lansing, the state capital.

Another example is Ali Sayed, an ambitious 28-year-old third-generation American Muslim of Lebanese heritage who ran unsuccessfully for the Dearborn city council in 2009. He is very active in the community and established a nonprofit organization to bring youths of all backgrounds together to lessen tensions and promote positive values. Many in the community predict a promising future for him. He is very open about his Muslim identity, but sees no reason to identify with a sect: "I know who I am but it's not productive to society or Islam to be recognized as Shi'a or Sunni . . . we are all Muslims, we are all practicing, and there is only one God who will judge." In addition to his broader mission to serve his city in general, he wants to help the integration of Arab and Muslim communities and reduce intercommunal tensions, to act as liaison between people and government to facilitate their interaction, and to provide positive representation for Muslims that improves how they are perceived.

Almost all other younger candidates and elected officials we interviewed, from both Sunni and Shi'a backgrounds, also self-identify as religious and refuse to adopt a sectarian identity. Judge David Turfe (45 years old) said, "We are all Muslims . . . we will all die someday and, *inshallah* [God willing], will go to heaven with our deeds, not our designations."[44] This contrasts with older elected officials such as Suzanne Sareini and Abdul al-Haidous (in their sixties) who self-identify as moderately religious and as Shi'a Muslims. The broad trend toward the gradual consolidation of an overarching, more politically meaningful Muslim American identity that supplants subidentities seems to be reflected in this generational attitudinal change.

The Worsening Economic Situation
in the Metropolitan Detroit Area Will Delay
the Easing of Ethnic and Religious Bias

In general, younger, wealthier, and more educated Americans are more accepting of Muslim candidates. One could therefore expect better prospects for Muslim and Arab American candidates over time as generational change takes place and more people become educated and better off. Michigan and metro Detroit's economic troubles will probably delay this transformation, as would a continuation of geopolitical conflicts between the United States and Muslim-majority nation-states.

The Increase in the Muslim and Arab Populations in
the Area May Lead to a Dramatic Increase in
Representation Unless Current Elites Change
Electoral Rules

Osama Siblani explains that AAPAC considers citywide elections to currently disadvantage the Arab American community, but hopes that the reverse will become true in five or six years when Arab Americans may form a majority within city limits.[45] He may very well be right, but if a study by Trebbi, Aghion, and Alesina (2008) of the history of electoral rule changes in American cities is any indication, the ruling establishment may very well change from a "winner-take-all" citywide electoral rule to a single-member district rule in order to limit Arab representation as the community approaches becoming a majority. This was the consistent strategy used by white politicians in southern cities and elsewhere after the Voting Rights Act of 1965 to maintain their influence. Of course, these are different times, and responsible officials who already have a good relationship with Arab and Muslim Americans may shun such an approach in Hamtramck, Dearborn, and other districts where demographics may tilt in favor of Arab and Muslim Americans.

The Retirement of Non-Arab Elected Officials
Supported by Arab and Muslim Organizations
Would Provide an Opening for Candidates from
These Communities

The arrangement between Arab and Muslim community organizations and elected officials who are not from the community will logically have to be reevaluated whenever a supportive elected official retires, loses, or moves on to other pursuits. If qualified Arab or Muslim candidates happen to be running for any of these offices, they may very well be able to enjoy their endorsement and the resources and support they channel. The more the supply of qualified candidates increases, the more likely this is to happen.

Of course, unpredictable events may dramatically affect prospects of the two minorities' representation, such as a new war in the Middle East, a terrorist attack, a stable peace in the Middle East, an economic recession or depression, the influence of political or cultural change from outside of Michigan, and so forth. If nothing of the kind happens, however, we expect Arab and Muslim representation to gradually improve in the metro Detroit area because of the interplay of the five factors discussed above.

Notes

Funding for this study was provided by a grant from the Carnegie Corporation of New York.

1. We sometimes use the term "community" to refer to Arab Americans and Muslim Americans for convenience, but recognize that it is at best a metaphor because of internal divisions within each group and because of the ease of exit from them. As our discussion shows, for example, some Arab American politicians have become socially and politically "white" and some politicians who had a Muslim parent grew up, and self-identify, as Christians.

2. For a history of Arab American representation in Michigan, see Ahmed (2006).

3. The percentages of Arab Americans are from the 2000 U.S. census and are minimum estimates because it takes initiative for a respondent to figure out that she can write "Arab" or the name of her Arab country of ancestry under Other Race in the census form. Also, many Arabs consider themselves, and are legally considered, white and may therefore just check the legally appropriate box in the U.S. census form or American Community Survey questionnaire. See also Schopmeyer, "Arab Detroit after 9/11," this volume.

4. Abraham's father is Muslim, but he was raised as and identifies as Catholic, like his mother.

5. Incidentally, Hussein Berry was elected to the Dearborn Public School Board of Education in 2009.

6. They are: David Allen, Judge, Third Circuit Court, Wayne County; Annette Berry, Circuit Court Judge, Wayne County; Dianne Dickow D'Agostini, Oakland County District Judge, Forty-eighth District; Joseph J. Farah, Circuit Judge, Genesee County; Linda Saoud Hallmark, Probate Judge, Oakland County; Karen Khalil, Judge, Seventeenth District Court; Charlene Mekled-Elder, Judge, Third Circuit Court; James J. Rashid, Wayne County Circuit Court Judge; Henry William Saad, Judge, Michigan Court of Appeals; Sam Salamey, Magistrate Judge, Dearborn District Court; George Steeh, U.S. District Court Judge, Eastern District of Michigan; David Turfe, District Court Judge, Twentieth District; Tracy A. Yokich, Circuit Court Judge, Macomb County.

7. Interview with Osama Siblani, publisher of the *Arab American News* and a founding member of AAPAC, Dearborn, Michigan, October 12, 2009.

8. For example, David Bazzy, a Dearborn council candidate, told us that he was eagerly waiting the endorsement of YAPAC (interview with David Bazzy, Dearborn, Michigan, October 15, 2009).

9. Interview with David Turfe, Dearborn Heights, Michigan, October 16, 2009.

10. The MAPS surveys find Muslim Americans to be better off than other Americans in education and income, and the Pew Research Center's survey (2007, "Muslim Americans: Middle Class and Mostly Mainstream," 18) found them to "mirror the U.S. public in education and income."

11. AAI, "Arab Americans," http://www.aaiusa.org/arab-americans/22/demographics. Data is culled from the U.S. Census Bureau, Census 2000 Summary File 4, but we couldn't access the raw data.

12. The Obama campaign later apologized for its staffers' behavior. Incidentally, the McCain campaign also alienated Michigan Muslims by removing Ali Jawad from a campaign position after a smear campaign by an Islamophobic campaign against him. See "Arab Americans Seek Apology from McCain Campaign," *Arab American News*, May 5, 2008, http://www.arabamericannews.com/news/index.php?mod=article&cat=Community &article=1006.

13. Interview with Imad Hamad, Dearborn, Michigan, October 12, 2009.

14. Interview with Osama Siblani.

15. Interview with Ramzi Dalloo, Troy, Michigan October 11, 2009.
16. According to the 2010 U.S. census, the four major Arab American groups in metropolitan Detroit are Lebanese/Syrian (59.7 percent), Palestinian/Jordanian (7.6 percent), Yemeni (2.7 percent), and Iraqi (13.3 percent).
17. One Arab American candidate claimed that opponents were trying to put a wedge between him and a rival family from his ancestral village to undermine his electoral chances.
18. Historically, Dearborn mayors Orville Hubbard and Michael Guido would manipulate and encourage divisions within the Arab American community, many of them personal, to get some support from it in spite of their hostility toward Arab Americans.
19. Interview with Dawud Walid, Southfield, Michigan, October 14, 2009.
20. Interview with Imad Hamad.
21. Interview with Osama Siblani.
22. Interview with Imad Hamad.
23. Interview with Ismael Ahmed, Dearborn, Michigan, October 12, 2009. His predecessor, Edward McNamara, was on equally friendly terms with Arab Americans.
24. Interview with James Allen, Detroit, Michigan, October 15, 2009.
25. Some community leaders were very critical of ACCESS's leadership, describing it as a monopoly that doesn't consult with those it is supposed to serve and that keeps other service organizations from developing (interview with Abed Hammoud, Dearborn, Michigan, October 14, 2009).
26. Interview with Ali Sayed, Dearborn, Michigan, October 16, 2009.
27. Interview with Suzanne Sareini, Dearborn, Michigan, October 12, 2009. Some claim that she did not receive community support because she was too close to Mayor Guido, who was hostile to Arabs at the time.
28. Interview with Abed Hammoud.
29. One in the Third District, 3 in the Fifth District, 1 in the Eighth District, 3 in the Ninth District, 5 in the Eleventh District, 1 in the Twelfth District, 3 in the Thirteenth District, 20 in the Fourteenth District, and 13 in the Fifteenth District (http://www.aaiusa.org/arab-americans/3923). The Republican Party does not have such positions.
30. *Democratic Party*: Ismael Ahmed, Third Vice Chair, Michigan Democratic Party; Jumana Judeh, Member, Democratic State Central Committee; Masoud al-Awamleh, Officer at Large, Michigan Democratic Party; Taleb Salhab, Officer at Large, Michigan Democratic Party; Mohamed Okdie, Vice Chair, Thirteenth Congressional District Democratic Party; Abed Hammoud, Treasurer, Dearborn Democratic Club; Mark Hanna, Chair, Oakland County Democratic Party; Ahmad Chebbani, Executive Board, Thirteenth District Democratic Party, Member, State Democratic Party; Fay Beydoun, Officer at Large, Michigan Democratic Party; Florence Nasser, Executive Board Member, Genesee County Democratic Party; Kenwah Dabaja, Regional Director for Michigan Young Democrats (Thirteenth, Fourteenth, and Fifteenth districts). *Republican Party*: Nicola Hawatmeh, Youth Chairman, Macomb County Republican Party and Vice President, Tri-City Republican Club; Abe Munfakh, Chairman, Eleventh Congressional District Republican Party; Abdul M. Mackie, Chairman, Dearborn Republican Club; Paul Sophiea, Vice Chair, Coalitions and Outreach Committee, Michigan Republican Party; Ken Harb, Secretary, Livonia Republican Club.
31. Historically this was true as well. The Democrats were encouraged to consider Arab Americans a supportive constituency as far back as the early 1950s; the Republicans organized the Arab American Republican Club to reverse this trend in the early 1960s (interview with Chuck Alawan, Dearborn, Michigan, June 16, 2010).
32. "Barack Obama Holds Lead among Arab American Vote: Historic Shift toward Democratic Party Continues," Zogby International, September 18, 2008, http://www

.zogby.com/news/ReadNews.cfm?ID=1553. See also "Zogby/AAI Poll: Arab American Voters to Decide on 2008 Presidential Candidates by Stance on Iraq War," Zogby International, June 28, 2007, http://www.zogby.com/news/ReadNews.cfm?ID=1330.

33. Interview with Osama Siblani.

34. Wayne County is divided into fifteen districts, Oakland County into twenty-five, and Macomb County into twenty-six. Commissioners are elected every two years in even-year elections. Wayne and Oakland counties elect one commissioner from each district, whereas Macomb County elects two, one to the County Commission and one to the Charter Commission.

35. Follow-up phone interview with Ismael Ahmed, April 23, 2010.

36. See, inter alia, http://americaslaststand.blogspot.com/2007/08/hamtramck-michigan. html and http://www.jihadwatch.org/2004/04/michigan-its-christian-bells-vs-muslim-prayer -calls.html.

37. Interview with Rashida Tlaib, Detroit, Michigan, October 16, 2009. Also confirmed in other interviews.

38. Interview with David Turfe. For wild threats from the blogosphere, see, inter alia, http://www.debbieschlussel.com/2611/islamerica-hezbollah-judge-elected-in-michigan/.

39. Interview with James Allen.

40. This is consistent with national studies and polls conducted between 1999 and 2007 by Gallup, Fox News, the *Los Angeles Times*, Rasmussen, and Pew that find that between 31 and 61 percent of their respondents claim that they would not vote for a Muslim candidate for president. Those rates are generally two to five times the rates for Catholics or Jews, slightly worse than the proportion of those who wouldn't vote for a Mormon, but a little better than the proportion of those who wouldn't vote for an "atheist" (Sinno 2009).

41. Inter alia, interview with James Allen.

42. Interview with Ismael Ahmed. See Haddad (1991) on this issue on the national level.

43. Interview with Adam Shakoor, Detroit, Michigan, October 13, 2009.

44. Incidentally, he made a similar statement about followers of all religions and expressed considerable respect for those who do not follow a religion as well.

45. Some estimate that two-thirds of Dearborn's under-18 population is Arab today.

REFERENCES

Ahmed, Ismael. 2006. "Michigan Arab Americans: A Case Study of Electoral and Non-Electoral Empowerment." In *American Arabs and Political Participation*, ed. Philippa Strum. Washington, D.C.: Woodrow Wilson International Center for Scholars.

Ajrouch, Kristine, and Amaney Jamal. 2007. "Assimilating to a White Identity: The Case of Arab Americans." *International Migration Review* 41(4): 860–879.

Ayers, John W., and C. Richard Hofstetter. 2008. "American Muslim Political Participation Following 9/11: Religious Belief, Political Resources, Social Structures, and Political Awareness." *Politics and Religion* 1: 3–26.

Bakalian, Anny, and Mehdi Borzorgmehr. 2009. *Backlash 9/11: Middle Eastern and Muslim Americans Respond*. Berkeley: University of California Press.

Baker, Wayne, Sally Howell, Amaney Jamal, Ann Chih Lin, Andrew Shryock, Ron Stockton, and Mark Tessler. 2004. *Preliminary Findings from the Detroit Arab American Study*. Detroit: Detroit Arab American Study.

Barreto, Matt A., and Dino Bozonelos. 2009. "Democrat, Republican, or None of the Above? The Role of Religiosity in Muslim American Party Identification." *Politics and Religion* 2(1): 1–31.

Cho, Wendy K. Tam, James G. Gimpel, and Tony Wu. 2006. "Clarifying the Role of SES in Political Participation: Policy Threat and Arab American Mobilization." *The Journal of Politics* 68(4): 977–991.

Gimpel, James G.., Wendy K. Tam Cho, and Tony Wu. 2007. "Spatial Dimensions of Arab American Voter Mobilization after September 11." *Political Geography* 26: 330–351.

Good, David L. 1989. *Orvie: The Dictator of Dearborn*. Wayne, Mich.: Wayne State University Press.

Haddad, Yvonne. 1991. "American Foreign Policy in the Middle East and Its Impact on the Identity of Arab Muslims in the United States." In *The Muslims of America*, ed. Y. Y. Haddad. Oxford: Oxford University Press.

———. 2001. "Muslims in U.S. Politics: Recognized and Integrated, or Seduced and Abandoned?" *SAIS Review* 21(2) (Summer–Fall): 91–102.

Howell, Sally. 2009. "Inventing the American Mosque: Early Muslims and Their Institutions in Detroit, 1910–1980." PhD diss., Rackham Graduate School, University of Michigan.

Howell, Sally, and Amaney Jamal. 2008. "Detroit Exceptionalism and the Limits of Political Incorporation." In *Being and Belonging: Muslims in the United States since 9/11*, ed. K. P. Ewing. New York: Russell Sage Foundation.

Jamal, Amaney. 2005. "The Political Participation and Engagement of Muslim Americans: Mosque Involvement and Group Consciousness." *American Politics Research* 33(4): 521–544.

———. 2009. "The Racialization of Muslim Americans." In *Muslims in Western Politics*, ed. A. H. Sinno. Bloomington: Indiana University Press.

Johnson, Steve A. 1991. "Political Activity of Muslims in America." In *The Muslims of America*, ed. Y. Y. Haddad. Oxford: Oxford University Press.

Khan, Mohommed A. Muqtedar. 2000. "Muslims and Identity Politics in America." In *Muslims on the Americanization Path?* ed. Y. Y. Haddad and J. L. Esposito. Oxford: Oxford University Press.

Nimer, Mohammed. 2004. "Muslims in the American Body Politic." In *Muslims' Place in the American Public Square: Hope, Fears, and Aspirations*, ed. Z. H. Bukhari, S. S. Nyang, M. Ahmad, and J. L. Esposito. New York: Rowman and Littlefield.

Nisbet, Erik C., Ronald Ostman, and James Shanahan. 2009. "Public Opinion toward Muslim Americans: Civil Liberties and the Role of Religiosity, Ideology, and Media Use." In *Muslims in Western Politics*, ed. A. H. Sinno. Bloomington: Indiana University Press.

Read, Jen'nan G. 2007. "More of a Bridge than a Gap: Gender Differences in Arab-American Political Engagement." *Social Science Quarterly* 88: 1072–1091.

Shryock, Andrew. 2004. "Finding Islam in Detroit: The Multiple Histories, Identities, and Locations of a City and Its Muslims." Working paper, France-Stanford Center, Stanford University, http://stanford.edu/dept/france-stanford/Conferences/Islam/Shryock.pdf.

Sinno, Abdulkader. 2009. "Muslim Representation in American Politics." In *Muslims in Western Politics*, ed. A. H. Sinno. Bloomington: Indiana University Press.

Suleiman, Michael W. 2006. "A History of Arab-American Political Participation." In *American Arabs and Political Participation*, ed. P. Strum. Washington, D.C.: Woodrow Wilson International Center for Scholars.

Trebbi, Francesco, Philippe Aghion, and Alberto Alesina. 2008. "Electoral Rules and Minority Representation in U.S. Cities." *The Quarterly Journal of Economics* 123(1): 325–357.

Arabs Behaving Badly

The Limits of Containment in a Post-9/11 World

NABEEL ABRAHAM

> That knowledge is true which comes from searching into
> doubt and beliefs, and from the depth of the searching.
> —Hung Tzu-ch'eng

On the morning of September 13, 2001, a community college professor entered his classroom, where he noticed a crude drawing on the blackboard that he took as an offensive reference to the terrorist attacks two days earlier. He turned to the students in the classroom and demanded to know what was implied by the drawing and who drew it.

When no one responded, the professor singled out a young Arab student sitting in the back of the room and asked if he was behind the drawing. The student, whom I shall call Kaid, denied any involvement. Unconvinced, the professor demanded that Kaid come up to the blackboard and erase the drawing. Kaid refused, taking umbrage at the implication behind the request. Words were exchanged, which quickly spiraled, turning heated. Now irate, the professor demanded that Kaid leave his classroom. Kaid complied, but as he was passing the professor on his way out the door, the professor allegedly placed a hand on the scruff of Kaid's neck hastening his departure. In the process, Kaid dropped his books, which the professor, in a dramatic gesture of disgust, tossed outside the door of the classroom prior to slamming it shut. Kaid filed suit against the professor, which was ultimately settled out of court from the standpoint of the college. Kaid pressed a separate case against the professor. A striking aspect of this incident is that *both* actors were technically Arab in the broad sense of that term, a topic to which I will return.

347

I recount this story by way of underscoring the thesis of this essay. The attacks of September 11 set in motion a delicate interplay between two protagonists—ostensibly one Arab and one American—that continues to be played out in Arab Detroit in the shadow of 9/11. But just as often, *both* protagonists are Arab American. Suffice it to say, everyday encounters between average Americans—Arab and non-Arab, Arab and Arab—take place in classrooms, hallways, workplaces, and neighborhoods that could in a moment's flash erupt on the front pages and on television screens across the world.

To prevent quotidian encounters from reaching "epic proportions," an ad hoc network of Arab community organizations and local institutions—schools, municipalities, law enforcement agencies—quickly arose to contain and stamp out brush fires like the classroom encounter before they spread out of control. For the sake of convenience, I shall henceforth refer to this amorphous network as the "Containment System."

Given the size and visibility of Arab Detroit, a system to monitor and contain conflicts and passions linked ideologically to the terror decade had to emerge and assume containment duty. Simply put, Arab Detroit has too many Arabs and too many daily encounters within itself and with the wider community for there not to have arisen a Containment System. The stakes are too high, given the reach of mass media pundits and ambitious federal prosecutors and politicians, as well as an array of political and religious organizations who, for one reason or another, are eager to fan the flames of anti-Arab, anti-Muslim suspicion and hatred.

This is the story of the Containment System viewed from the ground up, from the lived reality of people—Arabs and non-Arabs—caught up in various circumstances to which the Containment System has successfully reacted or, as the case may be, *over*reacted. But mostly this is a story about the limitations of the Containment System; how it lacks the means and even the language to detect and comprehend many of the daily problems of life involving two protagonists living in close proximity. In the age of the War on Terror such failings can have long-term consequences.

Post-9/11 Containment: The System at Work

It took several years after 9/11 for the outspoken, ethnically assertive and politically militant Arab American college students—the Kaids of Arab Detroit—to gradually curb their anger, mellow their public utterances, shave their beards, and shed their Army surplus fatigues. In the meantime, a widening coalition of Arab and Islamic community organizations accelerated their drive to make Arab Detroit acceptable (and thereby safe) to the wider society. The community organizations took up containment duties often in tandem with local school districts, municipal governments, local news media, and state government. Slightly behind the scenes stood a powerful phalanx of federal agencies of the national security state tasked with counterterrorism duties.[1]

The best example thus far, in my opinion, of how well the Containment System can function occurred on the eve of the sixth anniversary of the 9/11 attacks. On the evening of September 8, 2007, callers notified police that a man "dressed in dark clothing and wearing black face paint" was carrying a firearm in Hemlock Park in east Dearborn, Michigan, the heart of Arab Detroit. The suspect turned out to be Houssein Zorkot, a 26-year-old Lebanese American resident of Dearborn and a one-time medical student.

A search of his vehicle produced an AK-47, a receipt for the rifle and ammunition, two pairs of cloth gloves, a military combat belt with a canteen and two knives, boots with socks, a gunlock and keys, a list of metropolitan Detroit shooting ranges, numerous photographs of Zorkot standing in front of a billboard depicting "various Muslim extremists," a briefcase containing a laptop, and a cell phone. Police also found "a Lebanese flag" and a VCR cassette of *The Neverending Story*, among other sundry items (Delaney 2007).

The arrest of an Arab male armed with an assault rifle and other paraphernalia on the eve of a 9/11 anniversary could have become a national media sensation. Instead it hardly caused a whimper outside metro Detroit.[2] The incident was contained by Dearborn authorities, who wisely withheld announcing the arrest for three days, until after Zorkot's arraignment, to "avoid stirring up fears of another terrorist attack" (Delaney 2008b).

Zorkot eventually pled guilty to "charges of possessing a weapon in a vehicle, possessing a weapon with unlawful intent and felony firearm" (Delaney 2008a). He was sentenced to two years probation. In this case the Containment System stretched from the municipality to the county prosecutor's office (and no doubt had the tacit assent of federal authorities). In heavily Arab American Wayne County, it was unremarkable that the prosecutor in Zorkot's case, Suzy Taweel, possessed an Arab surname, indicating the role Arab Americans, especially professionals, play in the workings of the Containment System.

The Containment System in Overdrive

Schools are another natural zone of containment. Public schools have a long tradition of political indoctrination and social control of young people. Nearly a decade of post-9/11 containment indicates the system may be working too efficiently. With each passing semester since 9/11, fewer and fewer Arab American students in my Dearborn college classes seem willing to share their political views about U.S. foreign policy and its impact on the Middle East. This is all the more remarkable since many of them hail from countries that have become battlefields in the War on Terror—Iraq, Yemen, Palestine, Lebanon. By 2010, I would encounter a classroom full of Arab American students who would hotly debate whether eyebrow plucking and other cosmetic alterations were in keeping with Islamic precepts, but would turn eerily silent when I brought up U.S. wars in Iraq and Afghanistan, drone attacks in Yemen, Israeli aggression against Lebanon and Gaza—issues that should have been of utmost concern to them both as Arabs and as Americans.

Upon reflection, it occurred to me that perhaps they had been sufficiently indoctrinated by the Containment System operating in the schools, by community organizations, and by their families to keep their opinions about such matters to themselves.[3] Experience acquired from public school would have sufficed to convince them that expressing themselves critically on U.S. foreign policy issues could bring the Containment System down on their heads. What follows are several recent examples of the system at work in Dearborn schools.

Censoring the Unmentionable

In January 2009, in the aftermath of Israel's massive attack on Gaza, Dearborn student Deanna Suleiman published an essay in the Edsel Ford High School newspaper, *The Bolt*. She opened with a rhetorical question: "How do we solve the problem of Gaza? With tanks, bombs, and guns?" After twice assuring readers that she does "not support Hamas in any way," Suleiman pointed out a salient feature of the conflict routinely sidestepped by the major news media:

> First, the United States pushes for democracy upon Palestine and it is all good until the people they least wanted to win, do: Hamas. Then they completely strip democracy away from them because the choices the Palestinians made did not benefit themselves or Israel. How is that supposed to make the Palestinian people feel? They no longer have control over anything in their lives, even the person running their country.

Suleiman noted that most of the weaponry deployed against Gaza's hapless civilians was made in the United States, adding: "If Hamas was as lethal as everyone made them seem, then I would not blame Israel in the least. But comparing the weapons that Hamas is using to the weapons that Israel is using is like comparing fireworks to an atomic bomb."[4]

She ended her seven-paragraph editorial poignantly enough: "This is no way to handle Hamas—no matter how dangerous. Israel has no excuse for killing so many civilians, and the United States has no excuse for allowing it."[5]

Suleiman's essay also ran in the school paper's online version, which made its debut at the same time. Complaints reached the school principal, Hassane Jaafar, who ordered the essay withdrawn. Jaafar, the school's first Lebanese American principal, justified his action by claiming the essay was "not highlighted clearly as an editorial." Instead of rectifying this alleged shortcoming (by his own admission, the essay was properly identified as an opinion piece inside the paper), however, he ordered the entire online issue pulled, only to put it back up on the Web—*minus* Suleiman's essay. When asked about this by a local Arab American reporter, Jaafar was evasive: "My position is—we move on" (AlHajal 2009).

Jaafar's containment task was complicated by the fact that the high school is in the midst of major demographic changes. The school's largely first- and second-generation Yemeni and Iraqi students are rapidly accounting for half of the school's student body, with all the attendant complications.[6]

About the same time that Deanna Suleiman's editorial on Gaza was being censored at Edsel Ford High (EFHS), a display case at Edsel's sister high school—Fordson High—was facing similar censorship pressures. When members of the school's National Honor Society (NHS) put up a showcase display of pictures about the massacre of civilians in Gaza at the hands of U.S.-backed Israeli aggression, the school administration sought to have the display removed. A compromise was worked out allowing the display to remain in place until the date of an after-school fund-raiser that the NHS students had planned and organized.[7] Like his colleague at EFHS, Fordson's principal is a Lebanese American immigrant. (He retired at the end of the 2009–2010 school year.) Fordson, on the other hand, underwent the demographic changes Edsel is currently experiencing several decades ago and is now about 95 percent Arab. This fact renders the school the object of greater scrutiny by the public, placing the Containment System in an even heightened state of alert.

In response to public pressure spearheaded by Osama Siblani, publisher of the local *Arab American News*, the Dearborn City Council issued a carefully worded resolution "mourning those lives lost on both sides of the conflict" and condemning "the attacks on civilians, the massive loss of life, and the destruction of property" without mentioning Israel's documented war crimes. Containment through channeling community anger appears to be the order of the day.[8]

"You Can't Bring Us Down"

Another incident demonstrates the workings of the Containment System and, crucially, how it isn't interested in creative student expression, let alone entertaining students' First Amendment rights.[9]

When classes resumed at Dearborn's EFHS after the Christmas holiday break in early January 2010, a group of male Arab students arrived wearing identical sweatshirts (hoodies) sporting an oversized "11" (a reference to their graduating class of 2011). Each numeral had what appeared to be four sets of "windows," giving the impression of two towers. The high school mascot, the thunderbird, was depicted airborne to the right of the "towers." Beneath the towers ran the slogan: "You can't bring us down."

A straight surface reading would lead an observer to concur with Jennifer Browne, president of the EFHS Parent Teacher Student Association, who observed, "The students were simply trying to promote their class." In fact, the boys indicated that all they wanted to do was show support for their school. Hiab Mussa, one of the high school juniors who wore the hoodie, said, "We just wanted to show our support [for our class]" (Pardo 2010). Indicating a greater political maturity than their critics, another hoodie wearer told a local television news reporter, "The design was made out of frustration over some media portrayals of Arab Americans in the wake of the Christmas Day terror attack."[10]

The mere fact that "Arabs" and "twin towers" might share the same mental category sent some into apoplexy. This minor story was picked up by the national press, and anti-Arab and anti-Muslim sites twisted the story into a sinister display of anti-American hatred. (Similar opposition has erupted around plans to build a mosque near Ground Zero in New York City, as well as plans to build mosques in Tennessee and elsewhere in the country.)

Instead of defending the students' First Amendment rights and challenging critics on the merits of the issues, the school administration played into the hands of angry critics like senior Donovan Golich, who opined that the Arab students should be suspended. A teachable moment quickly folded into rearguard containment. Thus, in statements to the media, Dearborn Public Schools spokesman David Mustonen decried the sweatshirts as "offensive" and in "poor taste" (Pardo 2010).

Principal Jaafar confiscated the hoodies and prevailed on the students to publicly apologize, although for what exactly was never clear, as indicated by

The Edsel Ford High School Hoodie, courtesy of Nabeel Abraham.

the apologies themselves. Wadhah Almadhagi, one of the students who helped design the sweatshirts, stated publicly: "I was foolish to do it and I'm very sorry . . . I can promise that as long as I'm in Edsel Ford I'll do my best to ensure something like this, as foolish and naive as this, will never happen again."[11]

The school's Containment System also extended to the Arab community as the school superintendent, Brian Whiston, and Principal Jaafar "addressed a predominantly Arab American crowd during the twenty-minute meeting" in the Southend, home to a majority of Dearborn's Yemeni population. The exercise in containment appears to have led to the aforementioned student apologies, and, not surprisingly, no details about the meeting were forthcoming.[12]

"Oh Say Can You See?"

American schools traditionally are inhospitable to political expression by students. Dearborn's public schools are no different.[13] As we have seen, the Containment System in Dearborn schools has effectively shut down political expression even in Dearborn's predominantly Arab high schools, which would normally be expected to hold countervailing political views from mainstream society on questions of U.S. wars in the Middle East. In the Terror

Decade, allowable political expression by high school students appears to be increasingly limited to formal expressions of patriotism.[14]

It should not come as a surprise, then, that some Arab students attempt to express their criticism of U.S. foreign policy in ways that are both furtive and difficult to detect by the Containment System. Furthermore, because these expressions also come off as hostile and shorn of context, they are easily misconstrued by observers as acts of disloyalty.

In the immediate aftermath of Israel's aggression against Gaza in January 2009, a number of Arab American students booed the singer of the national anthem at a basketball game at Dearborn High. The young high school singer, an award-winning soprano, mistakenly thought they were booing her performance. Given the recentness of Israeli atrocities in Gaza, which enjoyed overwhelming U.S. support, it was fairly obvious that students used the occasion to express visceral opposition to what they correctly saw as official U.S. complicity in Israel's war crimes.[15]

Containment off the Playing Field

Containment isn't limited to top-down actions. Many of the players and bystanders involved in skirmishes between Arabs and non-Arabs have little interest in challenging the workings of the Containment System and, in fact, internalize its measures. People tend to default to the system's rapid responses with little, if any, consideration for the collateral damage generated by the incidents. An incident between Dearborn High School (DHS), Dearborn's "whitest" high school, and Fordson High (FHS), Dearborn's most "Arab" school, illustrates this. The football rivalry between the two schools goes back to a time when both schools were predominantly white.

In the fall 2007 season, the two teams met on DHS's home turf. As the DHS marching band filed past the stands, an Arab male wearing pink-tinted glasses and matching wig charged into the DHS formation. He smashed into several band members before landing atop a female clarinet player, breaking her instrument in the process.

Word of the incident quickly spread to DHS students and parents. I heard about it because my daughter was attending DHS at the time. My first thought was that the incident might foment anti-Arab sentiment. Surprisingly, it didn't, so far as I could tell. The story never made it into the local paper or onto the agenda of the school board meetings. It disappeared, at least in polite conversation.[16]

It just so happened that, during the fall semester, a large number of Fordson High "dual enrollment" students were taking my college anthropology course, among them three football players, including the star quarterback.

In our first meeting after the incident, I asked the class if they had heard about it. Several students starting laughing, saying they had witnessed it and knew the assailant, whom they described as "deranged." They found the slapstick antics of the assailant humorous. When I wondered aloud if they knew that he had knocked down a girl and broke her instrument, some said that their school principal was "taking care of it." They wrote it off as a simple prank, all in good fun. I asked if they had considered how this incident might reflect on Fordson High. Moreover, I asked, since FHS is the Arab school, how might the prank reflect on Arab Americans generally in the minds of west Dearborn (code for "white" Dearborn)?

The students turned silent. Had they spoken their minds, some of them might have responded with a shrug of the shoulders, seconded by "What's the big deal? Dearborn's whites hate Arabs. If they can't take a joke, so what?" But they didn't have to be honest. The Containment System had provided a ready-made, all-purpose answer: Their school principal was on the case; the perpetrator has been suspended; and the school was going to replace the broken instrument. Everyone was moving on. Or so they were led to believe.[17]

The victim and her mother pressed charges against the alleged assailant, but the case was dismissed for lack of witnesses who could positively identify him. The school district has quietly adopted new policies. Visiting fans are physically isolated at DHS football games. The DHS marching band no longer visits Fordson when DHS is playing its rival. Yet, much as the Containment System would like to pretend the issue is dead and buried, bitter feelings continue to linger two years later. According to the victim, Arab American students attending *her* school—DHS—sided with the assailant on purely ethnic solidarity grounds, even telling her, "You deserve what happened to you" for having pressed charges. The incident remains a topic of backroom conversation among DHS marching band players and their parents.[18]

Workplace Tensions: The Limits of Containment

The Containment System in public schools notably lacks the ability to respond to matters involving social etiquette and cultural transgressions by Arab American staff. A subtle but potent area of etiquette transgression is found in the tendency of Arab American employees to converse with one another in Arabic in the presence of non-Arabic speakers.

Workplace tensions related to this issue appear to have reached a boiling point in Dearborn Public Schools during the Terror Decade. Growing numbers of Arabic-speaking employees and students in the public schools meant that Arabic was increasingly heard in the hallways, locker rooms, classrooms, and offices of Dearborn schools. The rise of Arabic bilingual programs designed to help transition immigrant students into the English curriculum opened the path to new staffing positions that were quickly filled by Arab Americans, many themselves first-generation immigrants.

Already by the late 1990s one researcher had documented a litany of complaints by non-Arab staff over Arab co-workers self-segregating during lunch and related staff and student demands for acknowledgment of Islam in the school, recognition of Muslim holidays, and allowing Muslim students to leave school to attend Friday communal prayers. In addition, school staff resented acceptance of "religious" customs surrounding *hijab*-wearing females, such as a ban on handshaking between males and females, special allowances for classroom seating, and allowances for their refusal to look at nudes in art history classes, among others.[19]

These developments and the attendant resentment appear to have moved the school district to act. The district commissioned an outside organization to conduct a review "to determine those areas where the schools were experiencing successes" as well as "to identify opportunities for improvement." The review, limited to the district's three high schools, would examine each school's internal operations pertaining to "personnel; operational procedures; human relationships; and school climate and culture" (MLI 2008, i).[20]

The MLI report found a number of "deficiencies" common to American high schools—poor proficiencies in math and in core subjects, poorly performing teachers, poor student discipline, and the like. The report further noted that too many resources had been diverted from general education programs to ESL (English as a Second Language) and bilingual programs.

The report also hit a nerve in the local Arab American community when it pointed out:

> While unintended, the use of languages other than English *contributes to an atmosphere of distrust and suspicion* on the part of English only speaking adults in the school. Such actions appear to separate the staff and the community and significantly diminishes the potential for high performing [school] work teams to be created and exist over time. (MLI 2008, 5; emphasis added)

The MLI report singled out Fordson High for a special recommendation pertaining to use of Arabic language in the building, recommending that the school:

> Prohibit the use of any language other than English within the school. (Except as required when dealing with parents or students who are not proficient in the English Language)[.] *This should include commencement addresses.* To do

otherwise reinforces a perception by some that Fordson is an Arab school in America rather than an American school with Arab students. (MLI 2008, 17; emphasis added)[21]

The highly sensitive issue of Arab staffers speaking Arabic around non-Arabic speakers quickly morphed into rumors that the district intended to ban spoken Arabic from the schools, first and foremost at Fordson. One Arab community leader turned the matter into a First Amendment issue, saying, "That's in the first amendment. You should be able to speak the language you know." The local *Arab American News* found solace in a statement by one of the school board trustees who declared: "You can't create a rule that's impossible to enforce."[22]

The reaction of Arab American leaders and their allies in Dearborn to the recommendation banning nonessential use of Arabic reflected their obliviousness to a common American etiquette rule: Americans consider it rude for people to converse in another language when in the presence of those who do not speak that language. It seems likely the school district attempted to address the issue in a roundabout way by commissioning an outside party to examine the internal operations of Dearborn's three high schools. Instead of recognizing the problem, Arab American containment organizations reacted with alarm at what they perceived to be a threat to the community as a whole. The net effect was lingering resentment by both the Arabic-speaking and non-Arabic-speaking staffers, along with suspicions on the part of the wider Arab community of an anti-Arab animus toward it.

Being essentially reactive in nature—putting out brush fires instead of proactively culling brush to prevent fires—neither side has the requisite tools with which to tackle matters of social etiquette and cultural misunderstandings. On occasion, acculturated Arab Americans are called on to fill the gap left by the reactive Containment System. In the terror decade the personal is often political.

Below the Radar: Social Indiscretions in the Workplace

Use of Arabic in the presence of non-Arabic speakers was only one manifestation of many workplace frictions arising from what can only be described as exclusionary social practices by some Arab staffers (teachers, paraprofessionals, maintenance workers, administrators). Case in point: A white female former employee—Peggy—recalls an incident when she worked as a paraprofessional (henceforth "parapro") at a predominantly Arab east Dearborn elementary school in 2003–2004.

Sitting around a lunch table with Peggy were two Arab parapros and an Arab female bilingual teacher. Speaking in halting English, one of the two Arab parapros shared her frustrations in getting her son married.

Parapro One: Any girl who my son will marry is going to have to be Muslim, Lebanese, and from our village.
Parapro Two nods in agreement.

Parapro One: If he brings home an American girl, I would be opposed to it completely!
Turning to Peggy, Parapro One said with an apologetic smile, "No offense."

At which point, the Arab bilingual teacher jumps up: "What do you mean, 'No offense'? That's offensive!"

"That's how it has to be," retorted Parapro One. "If my son marries an American woman, he's dead to us."

Such encounters occur countless times as members of two communities interact in ways that are bound to sow doubt and negativity until the side giving offense sufficiently acculturates and exercises greater care in its public discourse or alters its attitudes. (It is worth pointing out that the Arab bilingual teacher who spoke up is married to a non-Arab.)

This is the sort of offense that the surface Containment System is not designed to detect, let alone handle. There is no polite way for the system to tell newcomers to the workforce that words like "no offense" cannot remove the sting of what are essentially cultural or religious exclusionary preferences even if they are couched as personal or cultural preferences. If they sound exclusionary and culturally chauvinist, even racist, they will be read as such by the wider society. As will become increasingly evident, the formal Containment System seems equally helpless to manage such interpersonal interactions both inside and outside the classroom. Yet, it is precisely at these loci that general attitudes are formed and reinforced. The personal is political.

School Daze

"Arab kids at Stout Middle School will sit quietly for only three types of teachers: Arab male, Arab female, and younger white female. Weak white males need not apply." This is the conclusion of a former Dearborn teacher and parent. Delving further, I discovered that even Arab teachers are not spared the disruptive classroom antics that Arab American students have come to be known for in the school district. Arab teachers are helpless if they cannot display sufficient toughness and authority or, lacking that, act as a surrogate of the student's family at school (through kinship or personal connections). An approach one Arab American female teacher uses is to force the offending student to consider how his behavior reflects on his family upbringing. Attractive younger female teachers will succeed in controlling classroom behavior if they can deploy their attractiveness in such a way as to get male students to compete for her approval.

Disruptive behavior was cited as a problem in the MLI study in all three Dearborn high schools. The report couched the problem in general terms—the need "to improve student discipline in [each] building," a vague statement that appears to pass over the quotidian challenges faced by teachers in the classroom (MLI 2008, 3). Although it would be unfair to place the widespread problem of classroom disruptions only at the feet of the growing Arab American student population, Arab Americans have earned a districtwide reputation for obstreperousness, even as some of the best and brightest graduating from the district are also Arab Americans.

Curiously, the MLI study team never tied student academic performance to classroom disruptions, which (based on informal reports from students and teachers) appears to be the *crucial* hindrance impeding classroom instruction. Here is the take of high school senior L.W. in 2010:

> Another huge problem at our school is the fact that some teachers don't follow the rules [against] disruptive conduct. I would sometimes have a class where the teacher would spend a majority of the hour yelling at another student to stop disrupting class. The next day I would come back to class and the same thing would happen again . . . [t]here is a student being yelled at for being obnoxious everyday.[23]

L.W., an honor student, also cited the use of foul language, "either joking or meant to be hurtful, all around the halls" of her school. Teachers appear to have given up, as "it is unusual to see a teacher actually do something about these kids. Sometimes they don't even do anything in class about it!"

To what extent academic performance has suffered as a result of unruly classroom behavior in Dearborn schools is anyone's guess, since the MLI report never looked into the question. However, there is no doubt that scholastic performance is far from adequate in many areas, as the MLI team discovered. More than half of all Dearborn Public Schools students, the team found, "have not shown proficiency in mathematics," and "additional core subject areas also have been found to show remarkable student deficiencies." Moreover, "many students did not take the Michigan Merit Exam seriously and in some cases did not make a serious effort to be successful on the test." Student proficiencies at the predominantly Arab high school, Fordson, stood at the bottom. "Fordson High School," the report concluded, "is an under-performing school" (MLI 2008, 2–3, 15).[24]

To proffer a connection between substandard academic performance and classroom disciplinary problems is to suggest that parents also have a role to play. In the specific case of the district's Arab American pupils one has to inquire as to why parents who often genuinely express concern about their children's educational progress appear unable (or unwilling) to impart self-discipline to their children so essential for academic success. To raise the question, at least within the highly charged atmosphere of the Terror Decade, is to risk the charge of racism, as well as possibly open the door to placing the failure of the schools only on the shoulders of Dearborn's growing Arab community. It's a conundrum for the Containment System.

The disciplinary problem is not going away. Evidence of the existence of a breakdown of parental control in some Arab American families comes from the students themselves. In a short essay that a Lebanese American high school student wrote for my anthropology class in 2009, Ali (not his real name) recalls a parent/teacher conference at Woodworth Middle School that he attended with his father, "who knows a little English," because his English-speaking mother was unable to attend. Ali recalls:

> I was translating something in[to] Arabic for him, by accident I translated [that] the teacher said I was a bad kid and I gave him trouble, when the teacher really said I was good. So when I said that, I could see [Father's] face turn into [a] frown and he got mad at me and the whole time I didn't know why in tell [*sic*] we got home, he told my mother and she asked me about it and I told her I think you need to put me back in Arabic school.

Later Ali shared an admission that bears directly on the challenges district teachers face:

> This is one of my funny stories, when it was my last year at Woodworth Middle School; I was in an honors algebra class. I had a big old woman with short hair that looked and acted mean. Therefore, my friend and I could not stand it no more, so one day we gave her a hard time and we just started acting up. Therefore, she told us stop messing around you camel jockeys and sit in your seats. I honestly thought camel jockeys meant Arabs that are good in sports because of the word jockey. When school ended, I went home and told my mother and she was in shock because she knew what it meant and that it was a racist remark. Therefore, she went to school the next day and told the principle [*sic*], there was already other parents there about the problem. At the end, the big scary woman was fired for her racist remark.

Here is the perspective of a U.S.-born Yemeni male (whom I shall call "Nasser"), now a college student, recalling his early days at Salina Intermediate and Stout Middle schools:

> Looking back, school made me become more Arabic than Americanized. I was thrown into bilingual classes with bilingual teachers. From the first through the sixth grades I was stuck in bilingual classes. Most of us were born in America and were illiterate in the Arabic language. I remember my teacher giving out instructions in Arabic and I didn't understand what the hell the teacher was saying. The foreign kids in class from Yemen, Palestine and Lebanon would talk about how America is evil and the Americans are all going to burn in hell.
>
> Eventually my parents enrolled my older brother and me in Islamic school at the Dix Mosque. There I would learn how to pray and memorize the Koran. After pounding the words of the holy book into my head, I was able to memorize about a dozen chapters (*suras*). When my friends and I would be playing basketball or football and hear the prayer call (*ethan*), we would drop the ball and go and pray. As the years went on it was harder to just drop the ball and go pray; we eventually ignored the prayer call and continued playing.
>
> Eventually mainstream America would catch up to me. Since Salina school was overpopulated, we were being shipped out to Stout Middle School. There I saw white boys and girls. There were boys and girls holding hands and even making out. The white girls would have on mini-skirts and tight clothes. To my friends and me, we were in heaven. I was also confused about myself and where I stood. That was the first time I felt like an unwanted foreigner. I heard the words "Sand Nigger" and "Camel Jockey" for the first time and I reacted. Some of the white students would tell us to go back to Saudi Arabia, even though none of us were Saudi—we got the picture.
>
> There was a lot of good and bad that came out of this. First of all most of the students that came from Salina were separated by country. The Lebanese, Yemenis, and Palestinians would have their own cliques in Salina. But when we arrived at Stout, we merged as one. We stood our ground and kicked ass. We were considered crazy because, when they fight, it would be one-on-one, but our style of fighting was different. If one of the Arabic students would be fighting a white student, we would all jump in and join the fight. Eventually the white students got the idea and began to form their own clique. So when a fight broke out, there were about fifty students going at it. Sometimes they had to call the Dearborn Police to come in and help break up the fights. I think for both the white and Arabic students, this was the first encounter with racism. What both sides heard or were taught growing up came into play when the two worlds collided.

Ali and Nasser represent the feelings and experiences of many Arab American youth. They find themselves caught between the world at home and the novel experiences of school. Authority figures in each world demand obedience and loyalty to a different set of norms, values, and beliefs. There is little latitude for personal discovery and self-expression. One common reaction is youthful rebellion through boisterous behavior at school coupled with tacit obedience at home, areas that usually fall below the radar of the formal Containment System.

The Personal Is Political: Stories from the Hood

Jennifer's Story

Jennifer, a white student, tells of being bullied by Arab kids after moving to the heavily Arab Dearborn neighborhood of River Oaks. It was the late 1990s, when she was about 10 years old. Now a college student, Jennifer reflects back on this time in her life:

> One day when I was about 12 or 13 years old a group of Arabic kids my age chased me from the school bus to my house. They started calling me "whitey" and kept asking me if I worshiped Satan. This taunting continued for a number of years and only grew worse. I tried convincing myself that it would stop once these boys grew up and stopped acting so childish.
>
> When I got my first car at the age of sixteen, the car got egged and paintballed at least once a week. These "gangs" of boys grew a bit larger as they grew older. Our house became subject to graffiti and even more eggs. Our house was not the only one in the neighborhood to be defiled. My best friend (one of the other white families in the community) only lived half-a-block down from me. Her house would get it just as bad as mine.
>
> Now that the taunting has stopped, I look back at the whole situation and look for the cause of it. I know a few of my Arabic neighbors moved from mainly white and Mexican neighborhoods. If they had endured some kind of racism there, they could just be taking out their pent up aggression out on the "minority" (non-Arab) in their new community.

Jennifer may be excused for her charitable attempt to comprehend the torment meted out to her and her fellow white neighbor. She was after all a student in a Middle East anthropology course when she wrote her reflections in the aftermath of 9/11. She, however, was aiming in the right direction in my opinion. Might her attitude have been different had her experiences occurred after 9/11? It's difficult to say.

Arab Americans, like other minorities, sense the wider society's antipathy and suspicion of them and they want to lash out in return. They form "gangs," whether actual or merely informal clusters of like-minded neighborhood kids. They attempt to lay claim to something in their confused lives, where they are constantly conflicted and pulled by countervailing pressures of an ethnic family and culture, a homogenizing, sexualizing consumer culture that is at once seductive and out of reach, and a society that is generally dismissive of youth, especially working-class youth (cf. Giroux 2009; Naber 2008; Cainkar 2009).

Jake and Elaine's Story

Jake grew up in predominantly white west Dearborn, never having knowingly encountered an Arab until he entered middle school in the early 1990s. By the time he reached his late twenties, Jake's negative experiences with Arabs outweighed the positive. By his own admission, he is still haunted by dark suspicions of Dearborn's Arabs at the tail end of the Terror Decade.

I first heard about Jake from a colleague who is related to Jake's wife, Elaine. Like Jake, Elaine grew up on the west side of town, even though her mother and grandparents grew up on the east side, in and around the house her great-grandfather had built. Today that neighborhood is nearly all Arab. The couple married and settled into Elaine's east-side ancestral home.

The hook that snagged my interest was a bizarre story of an Arab woman in traditional dress who was pilfering vegetables from Jake and Elaine's backyard garden. The story sounded eerily similar to one I had briefly commented on twenty years earlier. Unlike Jake and Elaine's story, however, this one had appeared in print as a letter to the editor in one of Detroit's major dailies. The letter, written in response to a favorable cover story on Arab Detroit in the Sunday supplement of the *Detroit News*, went as follows:

> Too bad the Arab issue (April 6, 1986) was so one-sided, playing for sympathy from all who read it. However, it's hard to give sympathy when you see the Arabs take over. It's difficult to sit on your porch and watch women and children urinate in the street, on sidewalks and against trees. It is equally difficult to understand them when they take flowers off your porch, vegetables from gardens and fruit from your own trees and be told by them that it is their right to take if they wish to.
>
> You should devote an issue to the Arab who takes everything—free lunch, clothes, food, ADC welfare and, of course opens a business and pays no taxes. (Cited in Abraham 1994, 189–190)

Back in 1986, the claims of the letter writer (who withheld his/her name) seemed utterly preposterous to me, especially in light of the openly anti-Arab campaign run the previous year by a candidate in the Dearborn mayoral race. The candidate, who eventually won the race and served as mayor until his untimely death in 2006, galvanized support using campaign literature under the provocative heading "Let's Talk about City Parks and the Arab Problem" (Abraham 1994, 189ff.). Jake's story coming as it did twenty-five years later lent credence to the seemingly fanciful charges in the letter to the editor and the implications latent in the campaign literature.

Signs of pilfering in Jake and Elaine's garden began appearing gradually, first one thing, then another. The backyard gate leading to the alley behind the garage was found mysteriously open one day. The gate was found open on another occasion, and then another. This caused alarm as Jake and Elaine let their dogs out in the backyard and now had to be careful to make sure the gate was closed.

They returned home one day to find their entire stand of mint gone. Next the tomatoes started disappearing. Soon afterward, all the parsley was gone. The Arab kids next door told Jake and Elaine that an Arab woman was helping herself to the plums from the old tree in the backyard. One day in 2007, Jake and Elaine caught sight of the mystery woman leaving their backyard and confronted her. She wasn't very old, most likely in her thirties, but she was wearing a headcover and a long robe. They tried to question her, but all they got back was a heavily accented "No speak English." On another occasion, the little Syrian kids next door tried to stop her, but she managed to get away on a scooter.

Jake and Elaine conferred with neighbors on the block and discovered that the woman they had confronted was helping herself to their backyard fruits and vegetables as well. One day, Elaine spied the mystery woman and followed her down the alley, but another neighbor, an Arab man, interceded, dismissing Elaine's concerns with "It's only mint." After she explained that the woman had also taken their tomatoes and parsley, the man turned silent. Elaine called the police, but they were of no help.

Jake's contact with Arabs began with the bussing of kids to his Dearborn middle school. Before then, he had no idea any Arabs lived in North America, let alone Dearborn. At Bryant Junior High, he started getting pushed around by Arab boys. Typical of the harassment: an Arab boy would slam him up against the lockers. The bullies always seemed to have at least one buddy standing by.

He developed the impression that Arabs tend to push around people who are or appear weak. This conclusion also was reinforced at Dearborn High School, where the bullying continued, even though DHS, like Bryant Junior High, is mostly white. And that may be precisely why the Arabs students are driven to act up. The bullying occurred mostly in the hallways or after school, when authority figures weren't around. "If they had a chance to get at you, they would on the football field or the basketball court," Jake says in the somber tones of a person recollecting a bad experience.[25]

Although Jake has all the appearances of a classic "geek," he participated in a number of competitive sports—diving, cross country, and track. He also was a pole vaulter. He recalls working out one day in the high school gym, his poles leaning in a corner, when two Arab boys began chasing him around the gym using his poles like lances. Although he did not know them, they seemed to know him. Jake graduated from DHS with "an extreme hatred of Arabs."

His hatred gradually dissipated in college as he encountered Arab international students in his classes with whom he had positive experiences. September 11, however, ignited his suspicions of Arabs as potential terrorists. His suspicion developed into a persistent fear, which he can't seem to dispel. His suspicions have been heightened by what he sees and hears going on around him. "Dearborn," he concludes, "is a place where someone could hide, or they could form cells."

I asked Jake whether he could cite any evidence to substantiate his fears. He pointed to "raids" on some Arab businesses in the 13000 block of Michigan Avenue, the major thoroughfare running through the old east and west Dearborn business districts. (This appears to be a reference to the federal raid on the famed La Shish Restaurant, whose flagship restaurant was located at 12918 Michigan Avenue. The clampdown centered on tax evasion, but prosecutors charged the Lebanese owner, now a fugitive, with giving material support to Hizballah, a U.S. government–designated terrorist organization.)

Arabs, in Jake's mind, seemed to be mixed up in an assortment of shady and nefarious operations: home foreclosure scams, cigarette smuggling, driver's license forgeries. "Two doors down," Jake notes, "the Arab guy appears to be dealing drugs." Anything specific? Just lots of comings and goings at odd hours, along with lots of surveillance cameras around the house. And the guy always seems to park his van in the alley in such a way as to annoy Jake.

I wondered if the Arab habit of sitting and socializing on front porches and in garages also annoyed him. Jake's answer surprised me: "It's a good thing," he said. I asked him to explain. "They are out in the open," not "creeping around" like the alleged drug dealer down the street.

Jake and Elaine seemed to have observations about many of their neighbors, who are all Arab. The lady across the street uses a broom-squeegee on the sidewalk in front of her house. Her kids remove litter from her yard and toss it in the neighbor's yard. She uses a leaf blower to do the same. Her neighbors throw garbage on her property in apparent retaliation. Squeegee

Lady also prevents neighborhood children, her own included, from playing on the sidewalk in front of her house. They are encouraged to play on the neighbor's sidewalk.

According to Elaine and Jake, Squeegee Lady always keeps one of the family cars parked in front of her house, even if they have to jockey cars from one parking place to another to keep a car there. Meanwhile, the driveway goes unused, following what appears to be an unspoken rule of many Arabs on the street who avoid parking cars in their driveways.[26]

Jake's take on street noise and Arabs? "Way too many watts," a reference to the heart-stopping bass sounds emanating from the audio systems of cars driven by young males—sounds familiar to urban America. Jake and Elaine are emphatic about their version of street etiquette: have as minimal a footprint—in sound and space—as possible.

The use of car horns to announce the arrival of one's ride violates their sense of decorum, as does the practice of drivers who are in the habit of leaning on their horn to express impatience with their tarrying passengers.

The same drivers will claim an unspoken right to stop in the middle of the street, effectively blocking traffic, while waiting for their passengers. Dearborn's residential streets, especially in the Arab east side of town, are crowded and narrow with cars parked on both sides. The unfortunate driver coming down a street must often exercise patience while a waiting car blocks the path.[27] To ask that the waiting car make way by moving into an open parking space or even onto an driveway is to invite a confrontation.

Beginnings and Endings

Confrontation is what the Containment System is designed to preempt. Yet, in those unpatrolled zones, the post-9/11 Containment System is nowhere to be found. Individuals and families are at the mercy of their wits and/or their fists. Like so much in contemporary America, citizens are on their own in the neighborhood, on the streets, in the shopping malls. Most lack adroit social skills for conflict avoidance and resolution, short of calling the police and reliance on an overburdened judicial system. And although neighborhood conflicts are superficially personal and individual, they, like so much else in life, can become the foundation for deep-seated hostility toward ethnic and racial groups. At the very least, they project an undesirable image to the wider society. In the terror decade, social animosity and crime can spell retribution.[28]

The Containment System seeks to disarm the suspicions Americans like Jake feel toward Arabs and Muslims in the Terror Decade. These suspicions had been simmering long before 9/11, but they took on a renewed life after that watershed moment. The suspicions, moreover, need not be based on any empirical evidence, as in the case of the rumor that Arab workers at a popular Middle East restaurant cheered as the 9/11 planes crashed into the Twin Towers. The e-mail rumor spread within metro Detroit's Jewish community and led to the closing of an upscale Arab-owned restaurant (Langlois 2005).

From the standpoint of community organizations, the Containment System is also intended to foster goodwill with the agencies of the national security state, which seems to view everyone with suspicion. This powerful apparatus has not figured at all in this essay, but it lurked behind the scenes just the same. If the Containment System's task in the grander scheme of things is to reduce the negative profile of the Arabs and Muslims as a suspect community before the mainstream, the task of the national security apparatus is to patrol the periphery—activists, Islamic charities, edge mosques, and the like—sending the unmistakable message that loyalty in the form of muted political criticism and obedience to the rules of the War on Terror are expected. This clampdown has generated a growing body of literature, which serves as a powerful reminder of the awesome power of the national security state and its far-reaching tentacles.[29]

An often-overlooked aspect of the Containment System (and to some extent the national security apparatus as well) is how dependent it is on the services and compliance of Arab Americans. By it's very localized nature, the Containment System couldn't function very effectively without the contribution of Arabs and Arab Americans. This observation is apparent in the behavior of school administrators and other professionals acting on an institutional level.

This tendency was also evident on an individual level in the college classroom confrontation with which this essay began. The professor in that drama was himself technically an Arab American in that his grandparents emigrated from Lebanon several generations ago. Being highly assimilated, he never spoke of himself as an Arab American, choosing instead to self-identify as "an American before all else." Although a person's motives are necessarily difficult to parse, the clash between the professor and the Arab student mirrors a wider unease between assimilated Arab Americans and Arab immigrants and their offspring. This situation is not unique to Arab Americans. It has a long pedigree in U.S. immigrant/ethnic history—assimilated ethnics are often appalled or annoyed by the behaviors and habits of their newcomer brethren. The same quirks, manners, and habits that annoy mainstream Americans often embarrass and alarm assimilated Arabs.

It is not surprising, then, that assimilated Arab Americans would be eager to contain the behavior of their "uninitiated" fellow ethnics, even if it leads to overreacting, as in the censorship of student speech in the Dearborn high schools and the ritualistic displays of patriotism at many community functions. Returning to the classroom incident, it was never clear what the "offensive" blackboard drawing depicted or what its intended meaning was. The professor thought he discerned disrespect to the image of the American flag turned upside down. To others, including the alleged culprit, the graphic depicted a nation in distress. To others still, the graphic amounted to a scribble, mere gibberish. Behind the incident on that fateful day in that portentous week, lay long-simmering tensions between the two protagonists— one nominally "Arab," the other nominally "American." The drama of 9/11 had apparently triggered something latent within each man. The professor clearly overreacted as other Americans had. Unlike other incidents, however, this clash centered on two *Arab* Americans standing at extreme opposites of the sociopolitical spectrum.

To live in a town with so many immigrants with whom one shares an ethnic affiliation is to be constantly reminded of the distance separating Arabs and Muslims not only from the wider mainstream, but also from one another. Long before 9/11 and the Terror Decade, the gap between assimilated and immigrant, and between highly assimilated and assimilating Arab Americans was a regular topic of discussion within and among families. It was mostly private. And in many respects it remains private today, in part because the Containment System has precluded opening the door to public discussion of Arab American cultural habits and idiosyncrasies, rendering instead the preference to project a uniform image of loyalty and political correctness. Unless the discussion can be couched in patriotic terms, there is no way of airing differences over child rearing, personal hygiene, dress, doing business, public comportment and displays of affection between the sexes, noise levels in public spaces, and so forth with members of one's ethnic community. Paradoxically, the Containment System is placing a lid on public criticism of the very issues behind many of the tensions within the Arab community and between its members and the wider society. In so doing, it is reinforcing the conclusion in the mainstream in the Terror Decade that what used to pass for different and odd ethnic behavior is turned into something much more ominous and threatening. In short, Arab "badness" gets assimilated into "proof" of something. What exactly? Answer: "terrorism and anti-Americanism."

Even if the post-9/11 Containment System consciously tried to reach into these zones, it decidedly lacks the means to serve as a mediating agency.

This limitation is evident in the schools, where the Containment System appears paralyzed before a raft of behavioral problems occurring in the classrooms and hallways of a school district known for its large Arab American population. In contrast, the Containment System *is* effective in quashing political speech and in enforcing an unspoken ban on American Arabs and Muslims claiming any affinity with the 9/11 tragedy, however remote. A system that is quick to decry racism and bigotry appears unable to engage the community in critical self-examination in matters related to cultural transgressions and social etiquette. The first shortcoming—political censorship—leaves Arab American students feeling alienated in school, and the second further alienates society from Arab Americans. Teachable moments are passed over in favor of political posturing.[30]

To be sure, some of the blame for the unedifying behavior of Arab youth—boisterous classroom behavior, bullying of whites inside and outside school, boorishness during national rituals—can be laid at the feet of weakening parental control inside many Arab families, their embrace of consumerism, with its superficial and ostentatious display of material wealth, coupled with the concomitant devaluation of education and individual self-cultivation by some. By the same token, there can be no denying that the quashing of free expression (historically a problem in America's public schools) contributes significantly to the alienation of Arab American youth in the schools. If Arab youth see the school as a place that does not respect them or the world they and their families come from, they will react with suspicion and detachment, never developing alternative forms of thought and expression that would enable them to contribute meaningfully to society.[31]

The one area in which the Containment System performed remarkably well was in managing the fallout from the arrest of Houssein Zorkot on the eve of the sixth anniversary of the 9/11 tragedy. Fortunately, the incident lent itself to quick resolution—Zorkot was not a terrorist seeking to harm Americans; he was a confused Lebanese American frustrated over Israel's massive violence against his native Lebanon the previous year. Even so, the incident raised the specter of a serious containment challenge. To their credit, Dearborn civic leaders deftly prevented a minor incident from being exploited by a cynical mass media to fan anti-Arab hatreds, dragging their city into the mix.

In this vein, consideration has to be given to the wider events over which Arab and Muslim Americans have no control, but from which they cannot easily extricate themselves however much they may want to. The War on Terror will soon enter its tenth year. And, although the Obama administration dropped the name, there is no indication the War on Terror, also known as the Long War, is going to subside anytime soon. On the contrary, the administration has intensified the war in Afghanistan while also expanding it to Pakistan, Yemen, and Somalia, among other places.

The expansion of the war has brought with it a predicted rise in terrorism both around the world and in the United States, much to the dismay of the current administration and its predecessor, who both like to pretend there is no connection between U.S. actions—increased civilian casualties, torture, drone attacks, targeted assassination—and a rise in terrorism. The relationship, however, is well documented.[32]

That being the case, the question naturally arises: whither the Containment System and with it the fate of Arab and Muslim Americans? The fact that it has been able to survive intact the first terror decade seems to bode well for the long haul. It endured several dramatic tests—the 2009 shootings at the Fort Hood (Texas) Army base, the 2010 attempted bombings in Times Square (New York)—remarkably well. But both incidents occurred far from Arab Detroit. The 2009 Christmas Day attempted bombing of an airplane landing at Detroit Metro Airport hit closer to the comfort zone of Arab Detroit, even though the alleged bomber was a Nigerian Muslim and an organization in far-off Yemen claimed responsibility. In response, a group of Arabs and Muslims organized a demonstration in front of a Detroit courthouse where the alleged bomber was being arraigned. The estimated 150 demonstrators rallied around the slogan "Not in the Name of Islam." Many Muslims were also prompted to distance themselves individually and publicly, as this quote attests: " 'He's ruining our reputation,' said Moad Taleb, a Yemeni Muslim living in Dearborn, referring to the 23-year-old Nigerian" (Meyer 2010).[33]

The real test for the Containment System will be when a long-feared catastrophic event occurs, igniting pent-up resentments and dark fears in the mainstream. Faced with cascading events, the center may not hold and instead may give way to hostile forces seeking a scapegoat. In that event, even constitutional guarantees may not suffice to protect Arab and Muslim Americans. Already, the terror decade has witnessed serious erosion of civil liberties. The process is far from over.[34]

How much pressure the Containment System can withstand is anyone's guess. One shudders to contemplate the various scenarios that an erratic War on Terror may yet unleash. Yet the irony remains that the decade that began with Arabs as the target of much American hatred and suspicion is coming to a close with Arabs seemingly coming into favor in limited, albeit important ways—an Arab American from Dearborn was recently crowned Miss USA, another Dearborn woman was picked to be on a national reality TV show. Arab American literature, poetry, and comedy appear to be reaching ever-wider audiences; in September 2010, an Arab American, Khaled Mattawa, was awarded a major American literary prize. If this is indeed the beginnings of a new trend, to what extent does it owe its existence to the Containment System as opposed to, say, a shift in the fortunes of the War on Terror, which appears to have zeroed in on Muslims, instead of Arabs, as the principal enemy? Only time will tell.

Notes

Epigraph source: *A Chinese Garden of Serenity: Epigrams from the Ming Dynasty*, trans. Chao Tze-chiang (Mount Vernon, N.Y.: The Peter Pauper Press, 1959). I gratefully acknowledge input from the following readers: Lisa Abraham, Sameer Abraham, Amira Kassem, Ernest G. Nassar, and Rachel Rumberger. A special debt of gratitude is owed to Andrew Shryock and Sally Howell for their critical contribution in the shaping of this essay. Of course, any faults or errors are solely mine.

1. The entire edifice stood against a backdrop of arrests and prosecutions of "terrorists" and "terrorist sympathizers," mass roundups of immigrants, closing of Muslim charities, widespread use of informers, surveillance, and the like, which, by design or not, struck fear into the hearts of many. For a comprehensive discussion of these developments, see Howell and Shryock (2003); OMB Watch (2006); Pew Research (2009); Center on Law and Security (2010); Salisbury (2010).

2. Not surprisingly, the story continues to circulate on sites specializing in beating the drums about a jihadist terrorist threat to America—Fox News, Michelle Malkin, Robert Spencer, and Debbie Schlussel. A Google News search failed to turn up any coverage by the mainstream national news media, save for a story on foxnews.com, dated March 27, 2008, http://www.foxnews.com/story/0,2933,342248,00.html.

3. Most of my current students would have been 8 or 9 years old in 2001, and thus may have been insulated by their parents from the worst excesses of the post-9/11 crackdown—the arrests of Arab airport workers at nearby Detroit Metro Airport and related arrests in Arab Detroit and across the nation that continued for several years with noticeable frequency. But the fear these and related state measures generated throughout Arab Detroit—"The police can come and arrest me and accuse me of being a terrorist . . . and people would not blink an eye"—would have surely been felt by Arab American children growing up in this period (quote of Osama Siblani cited in Fracassa 2002). For a comprehensive discussion of the manifold fallout of 9/11 on Arab Detroit, consult the references in note 1.

4. For a comprehensive review of misrepresentations of Israel's assault against Gaza (December 2008–January 2009) by U.S. officials and the news media, see Chomsky (2009); for the grim record of war crimes and atrocities committed mostly by the Israeli side, see the United Nations' Goldstone Report (2009) and Finkelstein (2010).

5. The editorial is unavailable at the school newspaper Web site, but a facsimile can be found at http://www.myfoxdetroit.com/generic/news/student_gaza_conflict _editorial.

6. The high school, one of Dearborn's three, has been experiencing growing pains since the 1990s as first Yemeni and then Iraqi immigrants, and to a lesser extent African Americans, have altered the demographic and social makeup of the once all-white school. Many of these developments and tensions as they pertain to the Yemeni population are discussed in Sarroub (2005).

7. The fund-raiser was a major success, raising more than $60,000 for medical supplies and other emergency medical relief. The funds were channeled through the International Medical Corps (IMC), an organization with a long history of working in medical disaster relief. IMC was founded and led by a physician who grew up in the Southend area of Dearborn and attended Fordson High. Even so, the fund-raiser was highly political, with poetry, speeches, and a video narrative exposing many of the atrocities inflicted on the 1.5 million people of Gaza. The political tone was indicative of how the entire Dearborn Arab community felt but generally refrained from expressing openly. The allegations of atrocities committed by Israel and much more were subsequently documented by a United Nations investigation known as the Goldstone Report (United Nations 2009), dilated on extensively by Finkelstein (2010).

8. Siblani's original resolution was reworked and reintroduced by the two Arab American members of City Council, one of whom—George Darany—self-identified publicly as an Arab American for the first time in his career. "Darany also said he regretted that Dearborn wasn't the first city in America to pass such a resolution, as Cambridge, Mass., passed one on Jan. 12," two weeks before the Dearborn resolution (Meyer 2009). The councilman, no doubt, had correctly sensed the simmering anger of the local Arab community. The Dearborn City Council resolution can be found at http://www.ci.dearborn .mi.us/cityclerk/archivedminutes.shtml.

9. In late 2009, a group of Fordson High students went to the state capital to protest proposed budget cuts for education. Even though they pooled their own money to rent the buses and for many this was their first act of public protest, the school threatened the students with suspension for skipping school (personal communication from Rachel Rumberger).

10. "Christmas Day terror attack" is an overblown reference to the failed Nigerian underwear bomber on a flight to Detroit Metro Airport on Christmas Day 2009. See http://www.clickondetroit.com/news/22146212/index.html.

11. Mlive.com citing WDIV TV News and other news sources.

12. WZZM 13 Online, http://wzzm13.com/news/news_story.aspx?storyid=117250.

13. In the run-up to the 2003 invasion of Iraq, Dearborn High student Bretton Barber was prohibited by his school from wearing a T-shirt emblazoned with the likeness of then President George W. Bush accompanied by the caption "International Terrorist." A vice principal told Barber that his shirt was "promoting terrorism"(Kaffer 2003a). He sued the school board with the help of the Michigan American Civil Liberties Union and won (Kaffer 2003b). The federal court decision appears to have had no lasting restraint on the impulse of school authorities to censor inconvenient political speech. Compare how the school handles real problems of classroom disruption discussed below.

14. Since 9/11, Arab American community organizations that host school officials and students invariably open their events with an Arab high school student singing the national anthem. At one event I attended, the color guard and ROTC from a suburban school district ceremoniously marched into a community banquet hall leading the assembly in a rendition of the national anthem.

15. This same high school singer encountered backstage criticism by a group of male Arab American athletes at another athletic event when she presented herself as the designated singer of the national anthem. On overwhelming U.S. complicity in Israeli war crimes, see Chomsky (2009) and Finkelstein (2010).

16. In June 2010, a scuffle broke out on the grounds of Dearborn High, where graduating seniors were meeting for an unofficial road rally. A fight ensued when some uninvited Fordson High students, all Arab Americans, arrived. Although a white female student was injured in an altercation, it's not entirely clear that she was without fault. She, among others, are rumored to have hurled insults at the Fordson students, pointedly telling

them, "Go back to where you came from!" a line with a long pedigree in American history. Alcohol and drugs may have played a role. The entire incident has been shrouded in obscurity.

17. The facts of the story were significantly different. The assailant was on long-term suspension at the time of the incident. Fordson High's principal *never* contacted the victim's family nor replaced her instrument. Instead, the superintendent's office told the victim's mother (a district employee) to "pick out an instrument" at a local music store and send the bill to the district. "It all happened fairly quickly," the victim's mother stated. She also wondered, "Why is the school district paying for the instrument and not the assailant?" Her question went unanswered. (Personal communication from Annette Klauke, May 4, 2010.)

18. Personal communication from Madison Klauke, May 4, 2010.

19. Sarroub (2005), especially chapter 5. Referring to the situation at Edsel Ford High, Sarroub found: "Most teachers were disturbed by the Yemeni students' imposed gender segregation and the self-segregation of the Yemeni community. As one teacher put it, 'They just don't buy into being an American' " (2005, 108).

20. My pagination for the Michigan Leadership Institute report.

21. Much has been made of Fordson's large Arab student population and its Lebanese principal by anti-Arab, anti-Islam blogger Debbie Schlussel, http://www.debbieschlussel .com/. Her archives, at least on the topic of Fordson High, appear to have been reedited and shifted around on the Web site, making it difficult to return to previous postings even with hard copies in hand. A taste of her approach can be deduced from her references to Fordson High as "Hezbollah High" and the city of Dearborn as "Dearbornistan."

Guilt by name association seems emblematic, as Schlussel makes a point of linking Fordson High's then principal Imad Fadlallah to the late Sheikh Mohammed Hussein Fadlallah, alleged spiritual leader of the Hizballah movement in Lebanon. In this regard, Schlussel fails to mention that on March 8, 1985, Sheikh Fadlallah was the *target* of a massive car bombing that killed eighty people and wounded 256, the worst single terrorist act that year, reports Noam Chomsky (1991). " 'About 250 girls and women in flowing black chadors, pouring out of Friday prayers at the Imam Rida Mosque, took the brunt of the blast,' " Chomsky reports citing a news story by Nora Boustany that appeared three years later in the *Washington Post*. "The attack," Chomsky continues, "was arranged by the CIA and its Saudi clients with the assistance of Lebanese intelligence and a British specialist, specifically authorized by CIA director William Casey, according to Bob Woodward's account in his book on Casey and the CIA" (cited in Chomsky 1991, 11).

22. ADC director Imad Hamad quoted in Davis (2009); School Board Trustee Aimee Blackburn cited in Baydoun and AlHajal (2009).

23. Student paper, "Student Code of Conduct," L.W., March 3, 2010. (L.W. wishes to remain anonymous.)

24. Of course, Dearborn Public Schools are not alone in declining test scores, disciplinary problems, student apathy, and alienation. School districts in metro Detroit, especially those with burgeoning immigrant populations, face similar challenges.

25. Growing up in the 1960s, I witnessed similar bullying of whites at Wilson Junior High in Detroit. Back then the bullies were Mexicans, who typically picked on white boys who appeared, as Jake noted, "weak"—nerds or loners, lacking a significant support group.

26. The parking of cars on many of Dearborn's narrow streets—designed in the era of the Model T when homeowners owned one small car—has an etiquette of its own. Parking in front of a neighbor's house is frowned on, especially if there is room in front of your own house.

27. When Dearborn first went to no street parking on "Public Service Days" in 2008, police discovered many of the parked cars on the predominantly Arab east side of town belonged to informal "car dealers."

28. As I write these lines, the local Dearborn newspaper carried three stories involving Arabs and the law. One involved a fight in which a young man was stabbed to death and three others were wounded, all apparently by the same man, A. T. Yono, as the victims and their alleged assailant returned together in a limo bus from a birthday party (page 1). In the second story, a homeless man, Mohamed Saleh, 30, was arrested for allegedly starting fires inside a popular Italian restaurant in Dearborn's Southend neighborhood (page 2). In the third story, the Saad family filed suit against the Dearborn Heights police claiming harassment and retaliation against a family member sought in a stalking complaint (page 1). Although the news stories scrupulously avoided mentioning the ethnic identity of the individuals involved, their names said it all (*Dearborn Press & Guide*, July 18, 2010).

29. See the many references cited previously, but especially Stephan Salisbury's tour de force, *Mohamed's Ghosts* (2010). In a similar vein, see Dave Eggers's *Zeitoun* (2009) for an in-depth story of how one Arab American entrepreneur's life was turned upside down by the national security state in the wake of Hurricane Katrina.

30. A leading Arab American civil rights organization spends a good deal of its political capital congratulating politicians, issuing condolences on the death of local dignitaries, and even wishing influential personalities a happy birthday. Among other actions, it issued a request to local e-mail recipients to vote for an Arab American sweet shop in a "Best Cakes Contest" sponsored by a metro Detroit television station.

31. In this regard, it is worth comparing Ralph Nader's experiences growing up in a Lebanese immigrant household, and the lessons he drew, to what we see taking place several generations later (*The Seventeen Traditions*, 2007).

32. Known as the "the Iraq Effect," the U.S. invasion "generated a stunning sevenfold increase in the yearly rate of fatal jihadist attacks," a major study found. The Iraq war "has some disquieting implications for American security in the future," the study concluded (Bergen and Cruickshank 2007). In a similar vein, the U.S. practice of torture inadvertently served to recruit foreign suicide bombers to Iraq, according to Major Matthew Alexander, a former U.S. military interrogator, who has recently published a book about his Iraq experience, *How to Break a Terrorist* (Cockburn 2009). Also see in this vein Pape and Feldman (2010).

33. Many in Arab Detroit appear to have further hedged their bets by working in one capacity or another with various branches of the U.S. military, the FBI, the CIA, and other agencies of the national security state. Arab Americans tend to conceal these arrangements from each other even as government organizations recruit publicly (Associated Press 2009).

34. The ever-growing literature on the erosion of civil liberties in the terror decade is too large to survey here. In addition to these now standard works (Cole and Dempsey 2002; Cole 2003, 2009; Hagopian 2004; Cole and Lobel 2007; Bakalian and Bozorgmehr 2009; Hafetz 2011), it is important to take note of developments under the Obama administration in this area. There are currently no attempts to prosecute Bush administration officials for torture and illegal wire taps. Presidential powers continue to widen over state secrets and targeted assassinations of U.S. citizens abroad. The current administration also favors preventive detention, military tribunals, and indefinite detention of detainees, even in cases of acquittal (Greenberg 2010; Greenwald 2010; Hentoff 2010; Savage and Risen 2010). None of this bodes well for any U.S. citizen, let alone Arab and Muslim Americans.

REFERENCES

Abraham, Nabeel. 1994. "Anti-Arab Racism and Violence in the United States." In *The Development of Arab-American Identity*, ed. Ernest McCarus, 155–214. Ann Arbor: University of Michigan Press.

AlHajal, Khalil. 2009. "Censorship at High School in Dearborn." *The Arab American News*, February 28–March 6.

Associated Press. 2009. "CIA Commercials Seek to Recruit Arab Americans." *Dearborn Press & Guide*, November 25.

Bakalian, Any, and Mehdi Bozorgmehr. 2009. *Backlash 9/11: Middle Eastern and Muslim Americans Respond*. Berkeley: University of California Press.

Baydoun, Tarek M., and Khalil AlHajal. 2009. "District Denies Arabic Will Be Banned at Fordson." *Dearborn Press & Guide*, January 17–23.

Bergen, Peter, and Paul Cruickshank. 2007. "The Iraq Effect: The Iraq War and Its Impact on the War on Terrorism." *Mother Jones* (March/April).

Cainkar, Louise A. 2009. *Homeland Insecurity: The Arab American and Muslim American Experience after 9/11*. New York: Russell Sage Foundation.

Center on Law and Security. 2010. *Terrorist Trial Report Card: September 11, 2001–September 11, 2009*. New York: New York University School of Law.

Chomsky, Noam. 1991. "International Terrorism: Image and Reality." December. http://chomsky.info/articles/199112–02.htm.

———. 2009. "'Eliminate All the Brutes': Gaza 2009." January 19, rev. June 6, http://www.chomsky.info/articles/20090119.htm.

Cockburn, Patrick. 2009. "Torture? It Probably Killed More Americans than 9/11." *The Independent* (London), April 26.

Cole, David. 2003. *Enemy Aliens*. New York: The New Press.

———. 2009. *The Torture Memos: Rationalizing the Unthinkable*. New York: The New Press.

Cole, David, and James X. Dempsey. 2002. *Terrorism and the Constitution*. New York: The New Press.

Cole, David, and Jules Lobel. 2007. *Less Safe, Less Free*. New York: The New Press.

Davis, Jason Carmel. 2009. "DPS Independent Report: Limit Use of Arabic at High Schools." *Dearborn Press & Guide*, January 18.

Delaney, Sean. 2007. "Documents Reveal New Details in Zorkot Case." *Dearborn Press & Guide*, September 20.

———. 2008a. "Conference Between Zorkot, Judge Could Determine If Case Goes to Trial." *Dearborn Press & Guide*, June 29.

———. 2008b. "Hemlock Park Gunman Gets 2 Years Probation." *Dearborn Press & Guide*, August 17.

Eggers, Dave. 2009. *Zeitoun*. San Francisco: McSweeney's Books.

Finkelstein, Norman. 2010. *This Time We Went Too Far: Truth & Consequences of the Gaza Invasion*. New York: OR Books.

Fracassa, Hawke. 2002. "Metro Arabs Question Charges." *Detroit News*, August 29.

Giroux, Henry A. 2009. *Youth in a Suspect Society*. New York: Palgrave Macmillan.

Greenberg, Karen J. 2010. "Obama's 'Remainees': Will Not One But Two Guantanamos Define the American Future?" *TomDispatch.com*, April 19, http://www .tomdispatch.com/blog/175234/tomgram:_karen_greenberg,_the_two-guantanamo _solution/.

Greenwald, Glenn. 2010. "The Criminal NSA Eavesdropping Program." *Salon.com*, April 1, http://www.salon.com/news/opinion/glenn_greenwald/2010/04/01/nsa.

Hafetz, Jonathan. 2011. *Habeas Corpus after 9/11*. New York: New York University Press.

Hagopian, Elaine C. 2004. *Civil Rights in Peril: The Targeting of Arabs and Muslims*. Chicago and Ann Arbor, Mich.: Haymarket/Pluto Press.

Hentoff, Nat. 2010. "George W. Obama." *The Village Voice*, January 13.

Howell, Sally, and Andrew Shryock. 2003. "Cracking Down on Diaspora: Arab Detroit and America's War on Terror." *Anthropological Quarterly* 76(3): 443–462.

Jun, Catherine. 2009. "Yemenis, Muslims Fear Backlash." *Detroit News*, December 30.

Kaffer, Nancy. 2003a. "Boy Sent Home for Wearing Shirt." *Dearborn Press & Guide*, February 27.

———. 2003b. "Decision Made in T-Shirt Case." *Dearborn Press & Guide*, October 5.

Langlois, Janet L. 2005. "'Celebrating Arabs': Tracing Legend and Rumor Labyrinths in Post-9/11 Detroit." *Journal of American Folklore* 118(468): 219–236.

Meyer, Nick. 2009. "Dearborn City Council Passes Gaza Resolution." *Arab American News*, January 24–30.

———. 2010. "Muslims March to Express Shared Moral Values." *Arab American News*, January 16–22.

Michigan Leadership Institute (MLI). 2008. *Dearborn Public Schools: High School Operation Review Team—Final Report*. December, fordsonhigh.info/MLI_Dbn_ High_Schools_Rpt.pdf.

Naber, Nadine. 2008. "'Look, Mohammed, the Terrorist Is Coming!'" In *Race and Arab Americans before and after 9/11*, ed. Amaney Jamal and Nadine Naber. Syracuse, N.Y.: Syracuse University Press.

Nader, Ralph. 2007. *The Seventeen Traditions*. New York: HarperCollins.

OMB Watch. 2006. *Muslim Charities and the War on Terror*. Washington, D.C.: OMB Watch.

Pape, Robert A., and James K. Feldman. 2010. *Cutting the Fuse: The Explosion of Global Suicide Terrorism and How to Stop It*. Chicago: University of Chicago Press.

Pardo, Steve. 2010. "Dearborn Students' Sweatshirts Stir Outrage." *Dearborn Press & Guide*, January 26.

Pew Research Center. 2009. *Views of Religious Similarities and Differences: Muslims Widely Seen as Facing Discrimination*. Results from the 2009 Annual Religion and Public Life Survey. Washington, D.C.: Pew Research Center.

Salisbury, Stephan. 2010. *Mohamed's Ghosts: An American Story of Love and Fear in the Homeland*. New York: Nation Books.

Sarroub, Loukia K. 2005. *All American Yemeni Girls: Being Muslim in a Public School*. Philadelphia: University of Pennsylvania Press.

Savage, Charlie, and James Risen. 2010. "Federal Judge Finds N.S.A. Wiretaps Were Illegal." *New York Times*, March 31.

United Nations Goldstone Report. 2009. *U.N. Fact Finding Mission on the Conflict in Gaza*. September 29, http://www2.ohchr.org/english/bodies/hrcouncil/special session/9/FactFindingMission.htm.

Woodward, Bob. 1987. *Veil: The Secret Wars of the CIA, 1981–1987*. New York: Simon & Schuster.

Part 6

Hard Lessons

The New Order and
Its Forgotten Histories

ANDREW SHRYOCK, NABEEL ABRAHAM,
AND SALLY HOWELL

Repetition teaches the genius and the jackass alike.
—Traditional Arab saying

In the practical use of our intellect, forgetting is as important
as remembering.
—William James

All profound changes in consciousness, by their very
nature, bring with them characteristic amnesias. Out
of these oblivions, in specific historical circumstances, spring
narratives.
—Benedict Anderson

The determined reader who arrives at this chapter after a close study of
the first sixteen will have learned a great deal from the recurrent themes and
arguments of this book. Readers who took shortcuts along the way will
have missed crucial bits of instruction, but this is perhaps appropriate. After
sampling these essays and examining our own memory banks, we have concluded that some forms of repetition do not teach anyone. Instead, they
erase what we already know. They make it hard to remember things, even
very similar things, that have happened before. Traumatic events often have
this slate-clearing effect. The 9/11 attacks, we will argue in this parting reflection, made people forget (all over again) essential aspects of their collective history. This amnesia took hold not because 9/11 was a singular historical event—it was certainly that—but because it was part of a long series

of traumatic events, of crises and disasters that have shaped Arab and Muslim identity in the United States.

We have all heard that "9/11 changed America," but the 9/11 backlash, as it unfolded in Arab Detroit, followed well-worn paths. Indeed, the ghastly list of post-9/11 beatings and killings provided in Hayan Charara's memoir, "Going Places," is marked by the obvious fact that none of them occurred in greater Detroit. Despite hundreds of thousands of easy targets, there were no such killings in Detroit. Community leaders, Arab and non-Arab, already knew how to deal with anti-Arab violence. They knew the community would be a target; they even knew who would be pulling the trigger, and this foresight gave them exceptional ability to maneuver.[1] With this flexibility, however, came the need to jettison older historical and cultural investments that would draw negative attention to Arab Detroit.

The History of Forgetting

Arab Detroit was a "target of opportunity" long before 9/11. The changes the city experienced during the last decade are pervasive, and some were traumatic, but few were unprecedented. In the 1990s, the Arab/Muslim and Chaldean populations of Michigan experienced steady increases in political incorporation, even as the United States waged war against Iraq, imposed brutal sanctions on that country, and occasionally lobbed rockets at Al Qaeda targets in Afghanistan, Pakistan, Sudan and Yemen (Gordon 2010). Institutions and events now taken as evidence of Arab American cultural acceptance—for instance, the Arab American National Museum and the Dearborn Arab International Festival—have their origins in the mid-1990s, when Arab American organizations reaped the benefits of increased public and private sector funding. The latter came in the wake of the 1993 Oslo Accords, when Israel and the Palestine Liberation Organization worked out a tentative peace agreement and Arabs living in the United States were brought into the larger geopolitical control mechanism known as "the peace process." Throughout the 1990s, America's generalized antipathy toward its own Arab/Muslim citizens gave way to Ramadan breakfasts in the White House and brazen attempts by U.S. presidential candidates to woo Michigan's Arab vote. George W. Bush, while running for president in 1999, told Arab Americans he would end profiling of their community if elected.[2]

Americans have short memories. So do Arab Americans. Younger scholars and activists often tell us that Detroit's Arabs were "invisible" before 9/11. They seem unaware that during the first Gulf War (1990–1991), young Arab American activists and scholars made similar pronouncements about their former invisibility. Traveling further into the past, we find that

Arabs stepped out of obscurity during the Lebanese civil war (1975–1990), the Iran hostage crisis (1979–1981), the Israeli invasions of Lebanon (1978, 1982), the Arab oil embargo (1973), the Yom Kippur war (1973), the Six Day War (1967), the Suez War (1956), and the first Arab-Israeli war (1948). Only a handful of archival scholars and lay historians know that, going back to the late nineteenth century, both the *Detroit Free Press* and the *Detroit News* have provided continuous coverage of the communities we now call Arab and Muslim. These communities were once called Syrian, Turk, Lebanese, Mohammedan, and Eastern; only after World War II did they evolve into Arab Americans and Muslims. Simply put, there has not been a time during the last century that Detroit was unaware of its Middle Eastern communities. Governors attended their fund-raising banquets in the 1950s, mayors attended their mosque openings in the 1930s; their political meetings and community protests were dutifully reported by the local press in the 1920s, and the opening of the first purpose-built mosque in the United States, which occurred in Highland Park in 1921, received several columns— plus photographs of turban-wearing, flag-waving immigrants—in the big Detroit papers (Howell 2009).

The Trauma Cycle

Why does this ample historical record so consistently fall into obscurity? There are several reasons. First, new immigrants tend to know little, and to care less, about the early Arab presence in Detroit. In a real sense, each new wave of Arab immigration washes over the popular memory of older communities. Recent arrivals tend to start from scratch, historically, picking up useful details from family members who came before; the memoir, the anecdote, and the life history often substitute for more generalized accounts of the past. Second, there have been few institutions committed to preserving and retelling the history of Arab Detroit as a whole. Official archives are new and rare,[3] and even grand ventures like the Arab American National Museum offer only the most schematic depictions of Detroit's rich Arab past. Although several histories of the national Arab American experience have been written, the oldest dating to the 1920s (Hitti 1924; Naff 1985; Khater 2001; Orfalea 2006; Gualtieri 2009), no similarly inclusive history of Arab Detroit has yet been produced. As a rule, scholars at work in America's largest Arab urban concentration tend to write about its ethnonational and sectarian subcommunities; their work tends to gravitate toward the present, with quick, formulaic renderings of the pre-1967 communities; it poses geopolitical conflict and immigrant incorporation as its overarching context; it tends to be collaborative, appearing in edited volumes like this one; and, to close the circle, it often announces its own importance by noting a new visibility, an awakening, or a drastic change.[4] It is as if Detroit's Arab/Muslim communities are continually reborn, their present rendered fascinating and vital, their past rendered dim and insignificant, in every new attempt to declare their presence to a larger society that already knew they were there.

This recurrent pattern of forgetting can be interpreted in multiple ways. It is typical of young, energetic, entrepreneurial immigrant populations concerned more with the present and the future than with a past that does not fully belong to them. It is shaped, too, by the endless industrial collapse that has caused hundreds of thousands of people to leave Detroit, emptying neighborhoods and altering the landscapes in which popular memory can accumulate. For the city's Arabs and Chaldeans, however, patterns of recurrent forgetting are also (and principally) the result of political crisis, of the collective panic triggered by the sudden shining of an intense spotlight. For more than sixty years, U.S. policy in the Middle East has been committed to the propping up of dictatorial regimes and strong support for Israel. Resistance to these policies in the Arab and Muslim world has been steady, and both the popular media and the intellectual elites in the United States have consistently portrayed Arabs and Muslims as cultural enemies of the United States, Israel, and the West.[5] That millions of American citizens are Arab and Muslim means, quite simply, that they too are cast as aliens and potential enemies. Their Americanness is questioned whenever people defined as Arab or Muslim respond violently to U.S. foreign policies. Italian, German, and Japanese Americans have all experienced this trial by fire, but most Americans have no intimate understanding of what it is like to have the rug of national identity pulled from beneath their feet. Arab and Muslim Americans do know. They had already experienced the sensation dozens of times before the 9/11 attacks. In each case, their immediate response has been to repair a damaged sense of American identity, and this task has been shared with members of the larger society who, in times of crisis, manifest an equally strong desire to find, and to protect, the Arabs and Muslims who are "safe," who are vulnerable and "on our side." Their existence, and our willingness to embrace, defend, and support them, sends many Americans a reassuring message. It says that we are good, just as our ability to find and destroy "bad Arabs" says that we are capable and strong.

The "target of opportunity" scenario is built into this search for good and bad Arabs, good and bad Muslims. Likewise, the weight of the encounter determines its outcome: the larger society's need for "good Arabs," and its ways of distinguishing good from bad, immediately overwhelm the representational autonomy of the Arab/Muslim community. As Rachel Yezbick shows in her analysis of the Arab American National Museum, attempts to prove one's Americanness require a simultaneous silencing and stigmatization of any belief, image, or behavior that an imagined mainstream audience would find strange or threatening. In describing what he calls "the Containment System," Nabeel Abraham demonstrates how crisply this system cuts off any expression of genuinely oppositional Arab/Muslim politics among youth in Dearborn. The urgency with which these "amputations" occur can, once political conditions return to normal, seem embarrassing to people on all sides of the process. But the tactical evasion of stigmatized difference never seems wrong during times of national crisis—when the basic protections of citizenship are at stake—and they come with built-in defense mechanisms. As we saw in "Cracking Down on Diaspora," ties to foreign regimes and identities defined as enemy/alien are reconfigured during times of crisis, ties to domestic institutions and identities are intensified, and a wide array of awards are distributed to Arab and Muslim Americans who assist in these realignments. Because it is undertaken in a context of fear and because it literally cuts people off from public identification with key aspects of their own past, and with their own ancestral places, this mainstreaming process culminates in forgetting. The identities that remain after the crisis cycle is complete usually conform nicely to the prevailing models of national belonging; thus, after the 1967 war, Arabs became a white ethnic group, like Italians and Jews; after the first Gulf War, they became part of the Clinton administration's multicultural America; after the 9/11 attacks, Arabs are remaking themselves as "engaged citizens," evidence that America is (for some observers) a pluralist democracy or (for others) a country struggling with its own racist and imperialist demons. Arabs today are either multicultural poster children, testament to America's commitment to diversity, or they are America's newest "people of color," discriminated against, despised, and in need of social justice. Either role, paradoxically, offers Arabs and Muslims a secure place in U.S. society.

Old Patterns in the New Order

Many readers will find this analysis grim, but we would suggest that the process described above, minus the forge-like intensity of geopolitical crises, is one familiar to most of the immigrant populations that have come to the United States since the 1965 immigration reforms. These groups, like earlier waves of immigrants, have been enlisted in the endless work of turning themselves into Americans, and turning America into a country more accepting of their difference. Like Koreans, Mexicans, South Asians, Jamaicans, and other new immigrant communities, Arab Americans can build on the legacies of the Civil Rights Movement, led by African Americans. They can draw lessons from the continuous history of ethnic and racial self-help—the terrain on which newcomers and minority populations have built their own houses of worship, schools, financial institutions, business districts, and leisure worlds—that has made the United States an attractive destination for immigrants. In fact, we would argue that Arab Detroit can function as a "target of opportunity" only because it has become, over the last century, a strong, viable, and highly visible ethnic community. This relentless process of immigrant incorporation is exactly what cycles of trauma cause Arabs and other Americans to forget.[6]

A final glance back at the essays in this volume reveals several trends that have carried Arab Detroit through the terror decade, and will continue to make it an important community, even when the federal government, the big foundations, and the national media yet again lose interest in it. We would like to reduce these trends to a simple list, for the sake of argument, and we offer the list in a spirit of optimism. It is appropriate to end on an optimistic note, we think, if only because so much in the collective life of Arab Detroit seems to be working well, even (and especially) under heavy political pressure. The unique capacity of Detroit's Arab and Chaldean communities to remain highly adaptable, to withstand stigma and suspicion, and to keep a firm grip on their own Americanization is rooted in the following patterns.

Bigness

As Kim Schopmeyer has shown decisively, the Arab community is large, it has been large for decades, and it is getting larger. In a participatory democracy, and a market economy, where size brings political and commercial success, Arab Detroit can use numbers to its advantage. Indeed, one of the great ironies of Arab Detroit's recent history is the constant exaggeration of the community's size, often by a factor of three. As Abdulkader Sinno and Eren Tatari suggest, this distorted notion of how big Arab Detroit actually is has simultaneously boosted the influence of the community, securing it political appointments and attention, even as it has kept Arabs from accurately assessing their ability to win popular elections. As William Youmans smartly observes, almost everyone with a stake in Arab Detroit, pro or con, thinks it is more important to the War on Terror than, in fact, it is. One could add that multiple interest groups have a stake in pretending that Arab Detroit is much bigger than it has ever been.

Age

The memoirs provided by Mujan Seif, Khadigah Alasry, Hayan Charara, and Lawrence Joseph are a microcosm of more than a century in the life of

Arab migration to Detroit. Joseph knew personally some of the earliest Lebanese and Syrian residents of the city. Alasry represents one of the newest communities. Among Yemenis, the majority of U.S.-born citizens are not yet adults. Yet Sally Howell's chapter on Muslims in Detroit tells us that most of Dearborn's Yemeni newcomers worship in a mosque that is now more than 70 years old and was established by Lebanese immigrants whose descendants, for the most part, no longer speak Arabic but still identify strongly as Arab Americans. The alliances drawn across these age gaps, like relations across generations in a family, enable newcomers to adapt quickly, and in culturally protected space, to life in Detroit. The Arab community's most effective religious and civil institutions are run by U.S.-born Arabs and by immigrants who came to the United States long ago; the steady arrival of new immigrants ensures that these institutions will remain vital and that their Americanized leadership will remain influential.

Diversity

A by-product of bigness and age, the diversity of Arab Detroit protects it politically and empowers it economically. The northern suburbs are filled with Republican Iraqi Chaldeans; Dearborn is filled with Lebanese Muslim Democrats. Iraqi Shi'a aligned with Iraqi Chaldeans in support of the U.S. invasion of Iraq. Other Arabs tended to oppose it. Yemenis fill working-class niches. Lebanese buy up gas stations. Iraqis control the liquor trade. Palestinians enter the professions. Islamophobes must contend with an Arab community that is majority Christian, and with Christian Arabs, like the Antiochians studied by Matthew Stiffler, who are resolute Arabists and strong advocates for Palestinian statehood. This wide variation means Arabs and Muslims can form ties to multiple political interest groups in the larger society, pursuing agendas that fellow Arabs might oppose. Alasry, representing thousands of Yemenis, can build ties to local African American Muslims. The Chaldeans described by Yasmeen Hanoosh, by contrast, playing on the widespread belief that Arab Muslim societies are unfree and unsafe, can build transnational networks that bring tens of thousands of Chaldean refugees to greater Detroit.

Institutionalism

The Arab and Muslim communities of Detroit are incredibly well organized. When federal authorities or visiting journalists say, "Take me to your leader," the list of options will be long and impressive. The annual budgets of Arab Detroit's premier service agencies, the Arab Community Center for Economic and Social Services (ACCESS) and the Arab American and Chaldean Council (ACC), are now more than $15 million *each*, and their funding comes almost entirely from government and foundation sources in the United States. The religious communities, which must reach into their own pockets for funding, are as amply endowed and as well connected. As Youmans showed us, this ethnoreligious infrastructure attracts external investment, and its influence is a shock to anti-Arab, anti-Muslim activists who, in other American cities—most conspicuously, New York[7]—find it much easier to box out Arab political candidates, shut down Arabic-oriented schools, and prevent the opening of new mosques.

Americanism

Not to be confused with Americanization, which Arabs and Muslims in Detroit see as the gradual adjustment all immigrants make to life in the United States, Americanism is the belief in key American ideals: freedom, self-expression, opportunity, upward mobility, and "liberty and justice for all—period." Commitment to these beliefs is widespread among Arab and Muslim Americans, even when they realize that these ideals are not as freely available to them as to other U.S. citizens. Memoirists like Charara assert their Americanness without apology, knowing they disturb commonplace notions of what an American is like. Members of the newest immigrant communities seem the most attracted to popular American notions of freedom and opportunity, as witnessed in Howell's interviews with Yemeni mosque leaders, whose love for their country is palpable. It was also evident in the massive displays of patriotism under duress, the compulsive flag-waving and flag-wearing that marked the Arab neighborhoods of greater Detroit during the first years of the terror decade. Many observers interpreted these displays as defensive and inauthentic, but it is also possible to see them as a protest, as a defiant assertion of an Americanness genuinely felt by Arabs and Muslims but suddenly denied to them.

Transnationalism

As long as the United States is at war with Arab and Muslim countries and political movements, Arab Detroit will have exaggerated significance. It will be a locus of valuable contacts and suspect ties. Because Arab Detroit is diverse, large, old, institutionalized, and ideologically American, its transnational character is as likely to be an asset, or to be reconfigured as an asset, as it is to be a cost. Kristine Ajrouch shows how transnationalism can be experienced as a blend of opportunity and vulnerability whose exact proportions are determined by changes in U.S. policy. Her piece also shows the resilience of American identification in the face of vulnerability, as Ajrouch confidently engages with Lebanon and the Lebanese as an American who assumes the values and social capital she acquired growing up in Detroit can actually improve the political culture of Lebanon, even if U.S. foreign policy periodically allows large sectors of that country to be destroyed by Israel. Likewise, Hanoosh shows how successful Chaldeans have become at facilitating the movement of Iraqis out of Iraq, solidifying their influence as a transnational community by anchoring Chaldeans firmly in the affluent northern suburbs of Detroit. Even the Yemenis, Palestinians, and Lebanese whose transnational networks are now being cut off have found ways to reproduce them locally, channeling monies and political energies into local projects—mosques, charities, schools, and village clubs—that are imagined transnationally.

Arabism

Finally, the diverse Middle Eastern communities of Detroit are empowered, and continually threatened, by their hegemonic identification as Arabs. The Detroit Arab American Study (DAAS) found that more than 70 percent of the people it surveyed identified as Arab American; even among Iraqi Christians, who are overwhelmingly Chaldean, 45 percent identified as Arab (DAAS Team 2009). This shared ethnoracial and linguistic attachment, a product of postcolonial nation-building in the Arab world, is the fertile medium in which cross-community alliances are forged, pulling people toward an imagined unity that, in everyday life, is seldom attainable. The meanings of Arabism vary greatly across the community, but the concept gives Iraqis, Palestinians, Lebanese, and Yemenis a sense of co-responsibility, and it can even enhance the solidarity of communities that reject it, like the Chaldeans and Maronites, both of whom organize in opposition to, and in imitation of, trends adopted in the larger Arab Muslim communities. It is hardly coincidence that the Chaldeans described by Hanoosh have their own version of ACCESS (the ACC), the *Arab American News* (the *Chaldean Detroit Times*), the Arab American National Museum (the Chaldean Community Cultural Center at the Shenandoah Country Club), and so on. Whether one supports, opposes, or intermittently embraces it, Arabism is powerful fuel for collective action.

Each of these trends has an elaborate history. Most have their equivalents in other notable ethnoracial enclaves in the United States, past and present. What is most peculiar about Arab Detroit is the extent to which these trends have merged over time, reinforcing and intensifying each other. Equally fascinating is the fact that none of these trends was disturbed by the War on Terror. Instead, it solidified all of them, supercharging the qualities that have made Arab Detroit adaptable in former times of crisis. Some observers would argue that the terror decade has strengthened Muslim identities and institutions in greater Detroit at the expense of Christian and secular Arab ones,[8] but we see little evidence to support this assertion. Essays by Stiffler and Hanoosh clearly indicate that Detroit's Chaldean and Arab Christian communities flourished during the terror decade, growing larger and better organized in response to many of the same pressures that fueled growth in the Muslim sector. In the United States, very few people can meaningfully distinguish Arabs (who are mostly Christian in the United States) from Muslims (who are mostly non-Arab in the United States and globally). As a result, each population is implicated in the policies and political events associated with the other. Detroit is unique for the extent to which it has become a "big tent" in which diverse immigrants from the Arab world can live comfortably in a community defined loosely as Arab American, each subgroup backing global and domestic agendas that others might oppose. As long as the overarching Arab American constituency is successful and respected—Sinno and Tatari's essay on political participation suggests that this status is secure for now—a complex array of Christian, Muslim, and avowedly secular groups will be able to organize and create alternative interest groups within this pan-ethnic identity space.

The best proof of this convivial arrangement is Schopmeyer's finding that Detroit now attracts more Arab world immigrants (Christian *and* Muslim) than New York, Los Angeles, or Chicago. This pattern holds despite the fact that Detroit is economically moribund, that it is not considered a dynamic, immigrant-friendly "global city," and that the domestic War on Terror is headquartered there. Immigrants from the Arab world choose Detroit because they know it has a large community of Arabic-speakers, or Muslims, or Chaldeans. Yet in making this choice they take part in a deeper history, one located in the spaces between trauma and incorporation, where remembering and forgetting have merged to create new forms of community. The latter have tremendous staying power, and knowing their history is essential work. If this volume promotes a new awareness of Arab Detroit's past and the vitality of its present, we are confident that it will be a resource to the city's Arabs and Chaldeans in the years to come, as they contend with U.S. foreign policies that time and again bring political crisis, like an unwelcome guest, to their front door.

Notes

1. The early work of the American-Arab Anti-Discrimination Committee and the familiar patterns of anti-Arab racism that prevailed in greater Detroit into the 1990s have been carefully mapped out by Nabeel Abraham (1994). The Containment System Abraham describes in "Arabs Behaving Badly" (this volume) is a practical solution to the persistent

problem of anti-Arab discrimination, a problem that now affects the non-Arab leadership of cities like Dearborn as seriously as it affects the new Arab immigrant families who settle there.

2. Accounts of the political efflorescence of Arab Detroit in the 1990s, as seen from the perspective of Arab Community Center for Economic and Social Services, arguably the organization that benefited most directly during the period, are available in essays by Howell (2000) and Ahmed (2006).

3. To date, the only public archive dedicated to the preservation and study of Arab and Muslim historical materials from greater Detroit is the Arab Americans, Chaldeans, and Muslims in Michigan Collection at the Bentley Historical Library, at the University of Michigan (www.bentley.umich.edu/research/guides/arab_americans/). This collection was established in 2002.

4. For an instructive sampling of these tendencies, compare edited volumes by Aswad (1974), Abraham and Abraham (1983), and Abraham and Shryock (2000) with trends present in this volume. Edited volumes that set Arab Americans in national or diasporic contexts—Kadi (1994), McCarus (1994), Suleiman (1999), Jamal and Naber (2008)—share many of the same characteristics. Syrian-Lebanese Christians, who made up the vast majority of early Arabic-speaking immigrants to the United States, often receive fuller treatment when the volume stresses ethnic/American over immigrant/transnational themes. A delightful blend of these patterns is Benson and Kayal's (2002) volume on Arabs in New York, which features new Muslim immigrants, but gives pride of place to the city's old Syrian communities, Christian and Jewish. Oddly, Arab Detroit and Arab New York appear in the literature as inverted images of each other: the former is top-heavy with new immigrants (despite its nineteenth-century Syrian-Lebanese roots); the latter is bottom-heavy with Syrian historical capital (despite possessing one of the most diverse Arab immigrant populations in the world).

5. This judgment can take variably nuanced forms. A 2004 study commissioned by Secretary of Defense Donald Rumsfeld, for instance, concluded that "Muslims do not 'hate our freedoms,' but rather, they hate our policies," namely, "American direct intervention in the Muslim world" (Department of Defense 2004). This insight had very little impact on policy making.

6. The ability of new immigrants in the United States to build on political gains made by African Americans is explored in Foner and Alba (2010). The Civil Rights Movement, which confronted the legacy of slavery, has been taken almost seamlessly into immigrant activism as both model and inspiration. In contrast, Foner and Alba argue that in Europe, where pluralist politics is shaped by the legacy of the Holocaust, new immigrants, especially those from Muslim countries, are not seen (and do not see themselves) as natural beneficiaries of campaigns to foster greater tolerance and social inclusion. One might argue, though Foner and Alba do not, that Arabs and Muslims in the United States are caught between these two models of immigrant management.

7. The controversy surrounding the so-called Ground Zero mosque is only the most recent example from New York City, where anti-Arab and anti-Muslim politics is a local tradition. For a detailed look at how this politics works, see Paley's (2010) account of the campaign that activists in New York ran against the opening of an Arabic-focused public magnet school. It is hard to imagine similar events unfolding in Michigan. Just how differently Arabs and Muslims are treated by the educational establishment in Detroit and its suburbs is on vivid display in a recent essay by Howell (2010).

8. This claim is made across the identity spectrum, by Muslim and Christian activists, lay people, and scholars. We discuss it here, in fact, because a reviewer of this manuscript wondered if Muslim identities in Detroit are more influential now than Arab ones. It is true that more funding is being directed by research foundations toward the study of

Muslims; it is also true that media and governmental attention are often focused on Islam and Muslims, not on Arabs per se. In Detroit, however, it is the secular human service organizations (like ACCESS and ACC) and business groups (like the Arab American Chamber of Commerce) that have capitalized most effectively on the larger society's interest in Muslims. Their secular credentials and strong institutional networks are crucial to their success in dealing with the Ford Foundation, the U.S. Department of Commerce, the FBI, the Carnegie Foundation, General Motors, and Comerica Bank. Meanwhile, pan-Muslim organizations, like the Council on American-Islamic Relations, receive very little support from mainstream funders, private or public. The same is true of local mosques and Islamic charities.

REFERENCES

Abraham, Nabeel. 1994. "Anti-Arab Racism and Violence in the United States." In *The Development of Arab American Identity*, ed. Ernest McCarus. Ann Arbor: University of Michigan Press.

Abraham, Nabeel, and Andrew Shryock, eds. 2000. *Arab Detroit: From Margin to Mainstream*. Detroit: Wayne State University Press.

Abraham, Sameer, and Nabeel Abraham, eds. 1983. *Arabs in the New World: Studies on Arab-American Communities*. Detroit: Wayne State University Center for Urban Studies.

Ahmed, Ismael. 2006. "Michigan Arab Americans: A Case Study of Electoral and Non-electoral Empowerment." In *American Arabs and Political Participation*, ed. Philippa Strum. Washington, D.C.: Woodrow Wilson International Center for Scholars.

Aswad, Barbara, ed. 1974. *Arabic Speaking Communities in American Cities*. New York: Center for Migration Studies.

Benson, Kathleen, and Philip Kayal, eds. 2002. *A Community of Many Worlds: Arab Americans in New York City*. Syracuse, N.Y.: Syracuse University Press.

Department of Defense. 2004. *Report of the Defense Science Board Task Force on Strategic Communication*. Washington, D.C.: Office of the Under Secretary of Defense for Acquisition, Technology, and Logistics, http://www.fas.org/irp/agency/dod/dsb/commun.pdf.

Detroit Arab American Study Team. 2009. *Citizenship and Crisis: Arab Detroit after 9/11*. New York: Russell Sage Foundation.

Foner, Nancy, and Richard Alba. 2010. "Immigration and the Legacies of the Past: The Impact of Slavery and the Holocaust on Contemporary Immigrants in the United States and Western Europe." *Comparative Studies in Society and History* 52(4): 798–819.

Gordon, Joy. 2010. *Invisible War: The United States and the Iraq Sanctions*. Cambridge, Mass.: Harvard University Press.

Gualtieri, Sarah. 2009. *Between Arab and White*. Berkeley: University of California Press.

Hitti, Philip. 1924. *The Syrians in America*. New York: George H. Doran Co.

Howell, Sally. 2000. "Cultural Interventions: Arab American Aesthetics between the Transnational and the Ethnic." *Diaspora* 9(1): 59–82.

————. 2009. "Inventing the American Mosque: Early Muslims and Their Institutions in Detroit, 1910–1980." PhD diss., Rackham Graduate School, University of Michigan.

————. 2010. "The Competition for Muslims: New Strategies for Urban Renewal in Detroit." In *Islamophobia/Islamophilia: Beyond the Politics of Enemy and Friend*, ed. Andrew Shryock. Bloomington: Indiana University Press.

Jamal, Amaney, and Nadine Naber, eds. 2007. *Race and Arab Americans before and after 9/11: From Invisible Citizens to Visible Subjects*. Syracuse, N.Y.: Syracuse University Press.

Kadi, Joanna, ed. 1994. *Food for Our Grandmothers: Writings by Arab American and Arab Canadian Feminists*. Boston: South End Press.

Khater, Fouad. 2001. *Inventing Home: Immigration, Gender, and the Middle Class in Lebanon, 1870–1920*. Berkeley: University of California Press.

McCarus, Ernest, ed. 1994. *The Development of Arab American Identity*. Ann Arbor: University of Michigan Press.

Naff, Alixa. 1985. *Becoming American: The Early Arab Immigrant Experience*. Carbondale: Southern Illinois University Press.

Orfalea, Gregory. 2006. *The Arab Americans: A History*. Northampton, Mass.: Olive Branch Press.

Paley, Naamah. 2010. "The Khalil Gibran International Academy: Diasporic Confrontations with an Emerging Islamophobia." In *Islamophobia/Islamophilia: Beyond the Politics of Enemy and Friend*, ed. Andrew Shryock. Bloomington: Indiana University Press.

Suleiman, Michael, ed. 1999. *Arabs in America: Building a New Future*. Philadelphia: Temple University Press.

Contributors

NABEEL ABRAHAM grew up in Detroit in the 1950s and 1960s. He has taught anthropology at Henry Ford Community College in Dearborn, Michigan, since 1985, where he also directs the Henry Ford II Honors Program. In 2000 he and Andrew Shryock received the Award of Merit from the Historical Society of Michigan for *Arab Detroit: From Margin to Mainstream*.

KRISTINE J. AJROUCH is Professor of Sociology at Eastern Michigan University and Adjunct Research Professor at the Institute for Social Research at the University of Michigan. She has published in *Sociological Perspectives, International Migration Review, Ethnic and Racial Studies, Aging & Society, Social Science & Medicine, Journal of Cross-Cultural Gerontology, Journal of Social Issues*, and *Ethnicity & Health*. She recently edited a special issue of *Research in Human Development*.

KHADIGAH ALASRY is a teacher at Bridge Academy in Hamtramck, Michigan, and youth director for the Muslim American Society in Detroit.

HAYAN CHARARA is the author of two poetry books, *The Alchemist's Diary* and *The Sadness of Others*, and editor of *Inclined to Speak: An Anthology of Contemporary Arab American Poetry*. He is the recipient of a National Endowment for the Arts literature fellowship, the Lucille Joy Prize for Poetry, and the New Voices Award Honor for *The Three Lucys*, a children's book.

YASMEEN HANOOSH is Assistant Professor of Arabic Studies in the Department of World Languages and Literatures at Portland State University.

She defended her dissertation, "The Politics of Minority: Chaldeans between Iraq and America," at the University of Michigan in 2008. Her essays on Iraqi Chaldeans have appeared in *Arab Voices in Diaspora* (Layla Al Maleh, ed.) and the *Journal of Associated Graduates in Near Eastern Studies*.

SALLY HOWELL is Assistant Professor of History in the Center for Arab American Studies and the Department of Social Sciences at the University of Michigan–Dearborn. Her published works include *Citizenship and Crisis: Arab Detroit after 9/11* and essays in *Diaspora, Food and Foodways, Visual Anthropology, Anthropological Quarterly*, the *International Journal of Middle East Studies*, and the *UCLA Journal of Islamic and Near Eastern Law*.

AMANEY JAMAL is Associate Professor of Politics at Princeton University, where she directs the Workshop on Arab Political Development. Her books include *Barriers to Democracy, Citizenship and Crisis: Arab Detroit after 9/11*, and *Race and Arab Americans before and after 9/11*.

LAWRENCE JOSEPH is Tinnelly Professor of Law at St. John's University School of Law. His most recent books of poems are *Into It* and *Codes, Precepts, Biases and Taboos: Poems 1973–1993*. He is the author of *Lawyerland* and *The Game Changed: Essays and Other Prose*. Born in Detroit in 1948, his grandparents, Lebanese and Syrian Catholics, were among the first Arab American émigrés to the city.

KIM SCHOPMEYER is Associate Dean of Social Science at Henry Ford Community College in Dearborn, Michigan. A sociologist who focuses on social inequality, racial and ethnic groups, and survey research, Schopmeyer has conducted numerous studies related to demographic and educational issues in greater Detroit.

MUJAN SEIF, a senior at Andover High School in Bloomfield Hills, Michigan, is a poet, varsity athlete, and honors student.

ANDREW SHRYOCK is Arthur F. Thurnau Professor of Anthropology at the University of Michigan. He has done ethnographic and historical research in Yemen, Jordan, and among Arab immigrant and ethnic populations in North America. His books include *Nationalism and the Genealogical Imagination: Oral History and Textual Authority in Tribal Jordan, Arab Detroit: From Margin to Mainstream, Citizenship and Crisis: Arab Detroit After 9/11*, and *Islamophobia/Islamophilia: Beyond the Politics of Enemy and Friend*.

ABDULKADER H. SINNO is Associate Professor of Political Science and Middle Eastern Studies at Indiana University, Bloomington, and he is a Carnegie Scholar. His books include *Organizations at War in Afghanistan and Beyond* and *Muslims in Western Politics*. He has also published articles in the *Journal of Conflict Resolution, Religion and Politics*, and in several edited volumes.

MATTHEW W. STIFFLER is a researcher at the Arab American National Museum in Dearborn, Michigan. He received his PhD in American Culture from the University of Michigan in 2010. His dissertation is titled "Authentic Arabs, Authentic Christians: Antiochian Orthodox and the Mobilization of Cultural Identity."

EREN TATARI is Assistant Professor of Political Science at Rollins College. Her research on ethnic and religious minorities in the United States and Western Europe has been published in the *Journal of Ethnic and Migration Studies* and the *European Journal of Economics and Political Studies*.

RACHEL YEZBICK received her MA in anthropology from Michigan State University. She has conducted ethnographic research in Dearborn and greater Detroit and is currently doing fieldwork in Detroit proper. Yezbick teaches anthropology at Henry Ford Community College in Dearborn, Michigan.

WILLIAM YOUMANS is a PhD candidate in Communication Studies at the University of Michigan. His writings have been published in the *UCLA Journal of Islamic and Near Eastern Law, Westminster Papers in Communication and Culture*, and the *Middle East Journal of Culture and Communication*.

Index

399